LANCELOT
AND GUINEVERE

ARTHURIAN CHARACTERS AND THEMES
Norris J. Lacy, *Series Editor*

LANCELOT AND GUINEVERE
A Casebook

EDITED WITH AN INTRODUCTION BY
LORI J. WALTERS

Routledge
New York and London

Published in 2002 by
Routledge
29 West 35th Street
New York, NY 10001

Published in Great Britain by
Routledge
11 New Fetter Lane
London EC4P 4EE

Routledge is an imprint of the Taylor & Francis Group.

Printed in the United States of America on acid-free paer.

10 9 8 7 6 5 4 3 2 1

Library of Congress Cataloging–in–Publication Data

Lancelot and Guinevere : a casebook / edited with an introduction by Lori J. Walters.
    p. cm.—(Arthurian characters and themes ; vol. 4)
  (Garland reference library of the humanities ; vol. 1513)
  Includes bibliograhical references.
  ISBN 0–8153–0653–9
    1. Arthurian romances—History and criticism. 2. Lancelot (Legendary character)—
Romances—History and criticism. I. Walters, Lori. II. Series. III. Series: Garland reference
library of the humanities ; vol. 1513.
PN686.L3L37 1996
809'.93352—dc20   96–2536
                                                                                          CIP

ISBN 0–415–93911–9

For My Parents

CONTENTS

PREFACE

This is Volume 4 of Arthurian Characters and Themes, a series of casebooks from Garland Publishing. The series includes volumes devoted to the best-known characters from Arthurian legend: Tristan and Isolde, Arthur, Lancelot and Guinevere, Merlin, Gawain, and Perceval. One is also devoted to Arthurian women in general, and one to the Grail. Others may be added.

Each volume offers an extended introductory survey and a bibliography and presents fifteen or more major essays on its subject. Several of the essays in each volume are newly commissioned for the series; the others are reprinted from their original sources. The previously published contributions date for the most part from the past fifteen years, although a few older, "classic" essays are included in several of the volumes, the criterion being the continuing importance of the study. All contributions are presented in English, and most volumes include essays that are translated here for the first time.

In most of the volumes, heaviest emphasis remains on the development of the legend and its characters during the Middle Ages, but appropriate attention has been given also to modern, even very recent, treatments. Similarly, the central focus is on literature, without excluding important discussions of visual, musical, and filmic arts. Thus, a number of the volumes, including the present one, are intently interdisciplinary in focus.

Scholarly studies of Arthurian material are proliferating rapidly, making it very difficult even for the professional to keep abreast of Arthurian scholarship. That is true for any subject or character, and doubly so in this volume, the focus of which is one of the most famous pairs of lovers in literary history. The literature devoted to Lancelot and Guinevere is vast, but it is also notable that each of them has a history apart from the other, and Lori Walters has given appropriate attention to each of them, as well as to their pairing in a passionate and impossible love affair.

Walters, like the editors of other volumes in the series, has provided a detailed introduction that presents the history of the couple, surveys the writers and texts that develop their legend, and offers an extensive bibliography, thereby documenting a good many important studies that could find no room in this volume.

The essays included here cover a broad range of subjects, periods, and authors. As we would expect, Chrétien de Troyes, who first presented the love of Lancelot and Guinevere, is the focus of several of them. Two others survey Guinevere's presentation across an extended period, and still others deal with the French *Lancelot-Grail* cycle, with Malory, and with the lovers' presentation in the visual arts of the Middle Ages. One discusses the German *Lanzelet*, and another treats the Middle Dutch *Lancelot-Compilatie*. The development of Lancelot and/or Guinevere in the modern period is represented by articles devoted to analyses of their treatment in modern drama, fiction, and art; and there are specific studies of Walker Percy's and Sharan Newman's contributions and of Bresson's film, *Lancelot du Lac*. The majority of the essays were previously published and are reprinted here, some of them in revised form. Several—those by Elspeth Kennedy, Bart Besamusca, Alison Stones, Muriel Whitaker, and E. Jane Burns—were written for this volume.

Such a book could not be produced without the generosity of museum officials and editors of presses and journals, who kindly gave permission for us to reproduce illustrations and articles. We are pleased to express our gratitude to all of them. Credits accompany essays and plates.

Norris J. Lacy

INTRODUCTION

Lori J. Walters

Lancelot and Guinevere are the subjects of one of the most enduring love stories in western culture.[1] Benefiting from their privileged position at the center of the Arthurian universe, the two characters exercised a powerful hold on the medieval public. Their love, an overwhelming passion that defies the most sacred moral and social constraints, is portrayed in three medieval "best sellers": Chrétien de Troyes's *Chevalier de la Charrete* ("Knight of the Cart," also known as *Lancelot,* composed around 1177), the anonymous Prose *Lancelot* (ca. 1215–35), and Sir Thomas Malory's *Morte Darthur* ("Death of Arthur," completed by the author 1469–70). References to the story spread quickly throughout Europe and penetrated well beyond its borders, as witness a thirteenth-century Hebrew tale of King Arthur's court. In eclipse from the Renaissance through the eighteenth century, the legend experienced a remarkable revival of interest in the Victorian era, when writers and artists including Alfred Lord Tennyson, William Morris, and Dante Gabriel Rossetti employed it to examine yet again the tensions between individual happiness and the common good. Its appeal for modern audiences remains especially strong in English-speaking countries.

The story of the love triangle involving Lancelot, Guinevere, and Arthur had first taken form in Chrétien's *Chevalier de la Charrete.* To traditions gleaned from chronicles, oral and written tales, and folklore, Chrétien added innovations of his own. The invention of the Lancelot-Guinevere-Arthur triangle was his response to the tales about Tristan, Iseut, and Mark that had fired popular imagination in the preceding quarter century.[2] Reacting to the theme of the illicit passion responsible for creating the breach between Tristan and his liege lord and uncle Mark, Chrétien incorporated a new story of adulterous love into the context of his own romance universe, in which conjugal harmony had been a favored topic. In *Erec et Enide* ("Erec and Enide," ca. 1170) and the *Chevalier au Lion* ("Lion Knight," also known as *Yvain*, composed more or less simultaneously with the *Charrete*[3]), Chrétien, by questioning the initial plot resolution of marriage, produced meditations on the competing demands of personal, romantic concerns and the larger preoccupations of the social order. His second extant romance, *Cligés* (ca. 1176), exploited the ambiguities of the model of adulterous and antisocial passion provided by the Tristan legend, but its depiction of Cligés and Fénice, lovers who commit adultery in spirit if not in fact, lacked the human interest and primitive force of its source. Although devoid of explicit references to the Tristan legend, the *Charrete* is Chrétien's most thorough reworking of the well-known story of adulterous love and death.[4] The ending of the *Charrete*, which leaves the reader with the image of the single night of transcendent lovemaking enjoyed by Lancelot and Guinevere, never comes to grips with the future of the beautiful but illicit relationship within traditional societal and religious boundaries, a subject taken up by later writers.

EARLY TRADITIONS

To a much greater extent than Tristan and Iseut, Lancelot and Guinevere are products of separate traditions with their own themes and development. Guinevere is associated with accounts of abduction and adultery; Lancelot, with a story type known as the Fair Unknown, in which a young man, brought up in ignorance of his name and origin, is called the "Fair Unknown" when he arrives at Arthur's court.[5] Lancelot's origins as a Fair Unknown figure were to have a lasting effect on his depiction in many works, medieval and modern, where he is the outsider, the foreigner, the "upstart" who wins Arthur's heart and Guinevere's body and soul.[6]

Chrétien was the first author to differentiate Lancelot from the Fair Unknown paradigm and stamp him in popular consciousness as the queen's lover. Guinevere, however, had enjoyed a long existence in the Welsh tradition as Arthur's wife before becoming known as Lancelot's partner. Unlike Arthur, a character who appears in chronicles (e.g., the tenth-century *Annales Cambriae*, the "Annals of Wales") as a local warlord first victorious in the battle of Badon who subsequently died at Camlann in a vain attempt to repel Saxon invaders, Guinevere's name does not figure in any early records.[7] Prior to the influence of Geoffrey of Monmouth's *Historia Regum Britanniae* ("History of the Kings of Britain," ca. 1136), Guinevere's reputation in Welsh literature was fairly positive, although it contained some contradictions that may be the result of later additions.[8]

An underlying plot that later came to be associated with Guinevere was a Celtic tale, the *aithed*, dealing with the abduction and rescue of a woman. The story of Guinevere and her abduction is ultimately based on a

Celtic narrative in which a fairy leaves her otherworldly mate to become the wife of a mortal only to be reclaimed later by her original partner. Cross and Nitze have reconstructed the Celtic tale that appears to underlie the accounts of Guinevere's abduction in various texts.[9] The *Vita Gildae* ("Life of Gildas"), a Latin saint's life written by the Welsh monk Caradoc of Llancarfan around 1140, contains an account of Guennevar's abduction by Melwas.[10]

Guinevere appears as Arthur's queen for the first time in extant literature in the Welsh *Culhwch and Olwen* (ca. 1100). Several parenthetical references represent her exclusively in terms of her position as Arthur's wife: Gwenhwyfar, the "gentle gold-torqued first lady of the island," is one of the few possessions with which Arthur would not want to part.[11] Although the other three Welsh texts in which Guinevere appears—*Peredur*, *Owein and Lunet*, and *Gereint and Enid*, the "three romances"—were written after Geoffrey's *Historia*, they reflect little of the negative portrayal of Guinevere, which would come to color the tradition. Even though the three romances probably date from the thirteenth century, no hint is given of the adulterous nature that already had come to characterize Guinevere in other contexts. Thus, in the four Welsh stories in which Guinevere appears, *Culhwch and Olwen* and the three romances, she is a conventional queen who has a harmonious relationship with her husband. Although the cause of Arthur's downfall, Guinevere has little or no guilt in the matter, since she was abducted against her will and did not betray her husband.[12]

Guinevere is portrayed as an adulteress in several twelfth- and early thirteenth-century narratives. In his need to explain the downfall of a ruler as eminent as Arthur, Geoffrey in his *Historia* had her engage in acts of adultery and commit high treason with Mordred. Negative views of Guinevere also characterize several works in the romance tradition. In her late twelfth-century lai *Lanval*, Marie de France has King Arthur's wife take revenge on the young knight Lanval, whom she proves unable to seduce. In the *Lai du Cor* ("Lay of the Horn"), composed by Robert Biket in the second half of the twelfth century, and in the early thirteenth-century anonymous tale known as the *Mantel mal taillé* ("Ill-Fitting Cloak") or the *Lai du Cort Mantel* ("Tale of the Short Cloak"), the unnamed queen fails in a test of sexual fidelity to her husband. Adultery is a common failing at Arthur's court: all other ladies save one (usually the protagonist's lady) also fail to pass the test.

A brief survey of the chronicle tradition will help clarify the extent to which Chrétien adumbrates the portrait of the adulterous Guinevere in his *Chevalier de la Charrete*. In Geoffrey's *Historia,* the beautiful Guinevere, born to a noble Roman family, is raised by Duke Cador of Cornwall. After Arthur designates Mordred and Guinevere as co-regents when he leaves for the Continent, Mordred usurps Arthur's throne and the pair fall in love, setting off a bloody conflict between the forces of the two men. When Guinevere hears that Mordred is losing the battle against Arthur, she flees to a nunnery. Her betrayal of Arthur functions as an essential element of the plot; Geoffrey wants to show that only deception and treachery could bring down the powerful warrior-king. It is possible that Geoffrey assigned this role to Guinevere under the influence of the triads (see n. 8) or the oral tradition that existed about Camlann.[13]

In his adaptation of the *Historia*, entitled the *Roman de Brut* ("Romance of Brutus," composed 1155), the Anglo-Norman writer Wace makes Guinevere into a more cultivated and refined queen while increasing her responsibility in Arthur's betrayal. He mentions her in three passages.[14] In ll. 1101–18, "Genoivre" is "large et bone parliere" ("generous and well-spoken," l. 1115); Arthur loves her deeply despite her inability to give him an heir. In ll. 2625–41, Arthur leaves his kingdom and wife, "Gahunmare," in the hands of Mordred, one of his nephews, an act of special significance because Arthur has no son. When Mordred, who has long desired the queen, confesses his love, Guinevere shamefacedly accepts his proposition. Wace fails to mention Guinevere by name in the third passage, in which he suggests her complicity in the matter. Because of the shame arising from her misdeed, she shuts herself up in a convent (ll. 4653–54).[15]

Layamon's adaptation of the *Brut* into English alliterative verse (ca. 1191), the first occurrence of the story of Arthur in the English vernacular, was intended to glorify Arthur as an English leader. Whereas Wace's reworking of Geoffrey's *Historia* moves in the direction of romance, Layamon's adaptation of Wace harks back to the chronicle tradition that had served as Wace's source. Layamon departs from Wace's courtly atmosphere in a scene in which Arthur dreams of cutting Guinevere to pieces as retribution for her suspected infidelity. There is no ambiguity in Guinevere's preference for Mordred over Arthur, nor is there any doubt that Arthur loves her dearly. Layamon does not repeat Wace's concern that Guinevere is barren. In Layamon's version, Guinevere appears at once more guilty and more imperious than in Wace's account.

As for Lancelot, the Welsh sources never mention him, nor do Geoffrey of Monmouth, Wace, or Layamon. The first time Lancelot's name[16] occurs is in Chrétien's *Erec et Enide*; the first time he appears as a full-fledged protagonist is in the same author's *Chevalier de la Charrete*. Elements common to several narratives suggest the existence of a Lancelot "biography," which may have descended from Welsh storytellers through Breton intermediaries. Chrétien's stroke of genius was to combine the abduction and the Fair Unknown motifs and to make the queen's rescuer her lover.

CHRÉTIEN DE TROYES

Chrétien's *Chevalier de la Charrete* gave the love story of Lancelot and Guinevere the form in which it became widespread. Although Lancelot and Guinevere had played minor roles in Chrétien's earlier romances, they had not yet been presented as lovers. In *Erec et Enide*, Lancelot is the third knight cited (after Gauvain and Erec) in a long list of knights of the Round Table.[17] Despite the mention of Lancelot's name, it is Erec who serves the queen (Guenièvre) by accompanying her on the Hunt of the White Stag. In *Cligés*, Lancelot plays a minor role, being defeated by the eponymous hero. The sole reference in the *Chevalier au Lion* is to Lancelot's efforts to liberate the queen and the others held prisoner in the Land of Gorre, a story recounted in full in the *Charrete*. Chrétien makes no mention of Lancelot in the *Conte du Graal* ("Story of the Grail," also known as *Perceval*, ca. 1181–90).

Although Guenièvre figures in all of Chrétien's romances, she is a secondary character in four of them. In *Erec et Enide*, the hero is Guenièvre's devoted but chaste companion. The queen is a nurturing figure, providing guidance and counsel to Erec and to his inexperienced partner, Enide. Guenièvre continues to play a minor role in *Cligés*, although her efforts are crucial in persuading the protagonist's future parents to admit their love for one another and marry. Having been abducted and held captive by Meleagant, Guenièvre is absent for much of the *Chevalier au Lion*. Referred to only as "the queen" in the *Conte du Graal*, Guenièvre's part in the narrative is little more than ceremonial. Only in the *Charrete* is she a genuinely central character. Since Chrétien's other romances give no hint of an illicit love between Lancelot and Guinevere, it may seem surprising that the *Charrete* posits such a love as an established fact.[18]

Owing to the extraordinary influence of Chrétien's original version of the love story of Lancelot and Guinevere, it will be useful to give a detailed account of it here:

An unnamed knight (Meleagant) leads Guenièvre away from court using a stratagem involving a group of Arthur's men held prisoner. When Keu's (Kay's) attempts to rescue her are to no avail, Gauvain sets out in his place and discovers another knight already embarked on Guenièvre's traces. This knight is Lancelot, who remains unnamed for about half of the story. Following him, Gauvain observes an unusual sight: Lancelot enters an infamous type of cart in order to obtain information about the queen's where-abouts. Lodged at a castle with Gauvain, Lancelot survives the test of the Dangerous Bed and observes Meleagant leading the queen to the kingdom of Gorre. Gauvain and Lancelot's paths diverge: whereas Lancelot follows the path to the Sword Bridge, Gauvain will enter Gorre through the less threatening but still dangerous Water Bridge.

On his way to Gorre, Lancelot has a series of adventures: First oblivi-ous to a knight guarding a ford because he is lost in thoughts of Guenièvre, he recovers his composure and defeats him; he resists the advances of an im-modest damsel; he falls in ecstasy before a comb containing strands of Guenièvre's hair; and he raises a slab in a cemetery that designates him as the liberator of the prisoners. After sustaining serious injuries in crossing the Sword Bridge, Lancelot arrives in Gorre. In the fight with Meleagant, the queen's handmaiden, after having learned Lancelot's name from the queen herself, uses it to direct the weakened combatant's attention to Guenièvre. The sight of his beloved immediately restores Lancelot's strength. Interceding on behalf of his son Meleagant, Bademagus delays the decisive combat for a year.

In the encounter of the lovers following the battle, Lancelot, perplexed by Guenièvre's coldness to him, leaves in search of Gauvain. After learning of a ru-mor that her lover has been killed, Guenièvre, in despair because of her harsh treat-ment of him, falls sick. Hearing a false report of the queen's death, Lancelot tries to commit suicide. Following their reconciliation, Lancelot and Guenièvre experi-ence a night of supreme joy. When Meleagant accuses Keu of adultery with the queen, Lancelot announces himself as Keu's defender against him, but again the decisive combat between Lancelot and Meleagant is deferred.

After Lancelot rescues Gauvain from his comical fiasco at the Water Bridge, Meleagant has Lancelot seized and placed in confinement. Winning his guardian, the seneschal's wife, to his cause, Lancelot participates in the tourney at Noauz, where he fights well or badly according to Guenièvre's desires. Meleagant has Lancelot immured in a tower when a second author, Godefroy de Leigny, takes up the completion of the narrative. Lancelot is victorious in the final encounter with his adversary.

Chrétien's *Charrete* establishes the two traits that would come to char-acterize Lancelot throughout history: he is an exemplary Arthurian knight and an exemplary lover. As the rescuer of Guenièvre and others held pris-oner in the land of Gorre by Meleagant, he is the savior of the kingdom in place of the ineffectual Arthur. Lancelot's functions assume messianic pro-portions: his liberation of the prisoners has parallels with Christ's harrow-ing of Hell. The finest exemplar of chivalric prowess, Lancelot is also

Guenièvre's devoted lover. His ardor attains heights of quasi-religious intensity with comic overtones: he adores a comb containing strands of Guenièvre's golden hair as if it were a holy relic and genuflects in front of her bed after spending the night with her. Guenièvre dominates Lancelot's consciousness. Oblivious to the presence of a knight guarding a ford because he is lost in thoughts of her, Lancelot regains his composure only at the last minute to go on to defend himself successfully. The mere sight of Guenièvre is enough to make Lancelot forgetful of his own life: when he catches an unexpected glimpse of Guenièvre from his vantage point in a tower, Gauvain has to restrain him from falling to his death. During the tournament at Noauz, Lancelot again risks death when he chooses to contemplate his beloved Guenièvre rather than face his opponent Meleagant. Lancelot's behavior is so extraordinary that two women interested in him both realize intuitively that he is indifferent to them because of his love for another woman. Lancelot's actions at the tournament at Noauz give testimony to the necessary connection between love and prowess: Lancelot's perfection as knight is made possible only because of his total and unquestioning devotion to his lady. Chrétien in fact multiplies the paradoxes in his portrayal of Lancelot: Lancelot becomes Arthur's most resourceful knight precisely *because* of his adulterous love for Arthur's wife.[19] In exposing the humorous as well as the serious sides of the lovers' situation, Chrétien promotes a romantic ideal while viewing that ideal with amused irony.

As Lancelot's imperious beloved, Guenièvre has been the subject of heated critical controversy: to some, she reveals the potential dangers of a man's unquestioning devotion to a woman; to others, contemporary feminist scholars in particular, her treatment in the romance and in modern critical studies is an example of the distrust that surrounds the actions of a strong woman. One particularly problematical incident occurs at the tourney at Noauz, where Lancelot fights well or badly according to Guenièvre's desires. Guenièvre's directive to Lancelot to fight badly exposes a potential conflict between the demands of the knight's beloved and society: since a knight's prowess is a function of his devotion to his lady, that devotion may entail his seeming to forgo social approval for her love. Critics have even maintained that the devoted servant of love becomes in effect love's fool.[20]

The queen's puzzling behavior in another episode has likewise sparked debate. In the encounter of the lovers following the initial battle between Meleagant and Lancelot in Gorre, Lancelot is perplexed by Guenièvre's coldness to him. After a long and painful period of misunderstanding, during which each gives in to despair upon hearing that the other is dead, the queen at last offers Lancelot an explanation of her initial displeasure with him—

either her rejection of him was a joke or she was displeased because he had hesitated for two steps before climbing into a cart reserved for the most hardened criminals.[21] Like much that concerns Lancelot and Guenièvre's relationship, the cart incarnates a paradox: whereas Lancelot puts his chivalric reputation in jeopardy by entering the cart because it is the only way to find Guenièvre, she is offended because he hesitates slightly before getting in.

Although revealing something of their natures, the *Charrete*'s main characters retain an aura of mystery over the course of the narrative. Matilda Bruckner points out that the problems of interpretation and judgment in the romance center on the figure of Lancelot and specifically on the process of discovery of Lancelot's name (*Shaping Romance*, 60–69). The reader is initially confronted with Guenièvre's unnamed champion, then learns of his enigmatic title as the "Knight of the Cart," and finally discovers his name near the textual midpoint from the mouth of Guenièvre herself. Guenièvre's actions pose similar problems of interpretation for Lancelot as well as for scribal "editors" of the romance. It had never occurred to Lancelot that Guenièvre would be angry because he had hesitated for two steps before entering the infamous cart.[22] Chrétien seems to have written ambiguity into his text from the very beginning, with the fundamental opacity of the two lovers' natures one of its most baffling elements.

Another unresolved issue in the romance is the status of the conclusion.[23] What is the nature of Lancelot and Guenièvre's relationship at the end of the romance? Are we to infer that their night of love is never repeated and that the lovers' longing is sublimated permanently into the religious sentiment that often characterizes Lancelot's feelings toward Guenièvre? Although the continuity of the couple's love is projected beyond the limits of the romance, the future of their relationship is left indeterminate.[24] In Chrétien's *Charrete*, the love does not have the tragic ending imagined by Geoffrey of Monmouth and Wace or acquired in later versions. With Lancelot, a character who is neither Arthur's nephew nor a product of incest, Chrétien lets his reader imagine an ending free of the sins of treason and incest that had led to the destruction of Arthur's realm in earlier accounts. At least in this romance, Chrétien allows for the possibility of an ennobling and socially beneficial illicit love.

LANCELOT-GRAAL (VULGATE CYCLE) AND LATER FRENCH WORKS

Both the beauty and the tragic consequences of Lancelot and Guinevere's adulterous affair are explored in the *Lancelot-Graal*, or Vulgate Cycle (ca. 1215–35), an early example of the cyclical compositions in prose that would become increasingly popular in Europe in the following three centuries. The lovers' adventures figure prominently in three of the five sections of this vast compendium of Arthurian literature. Begun in the middle romance of the cycle known as the Prose *Lancelot* [25] (which is as long as the other four parts combined), the story of Lancelot and Guinevere is continued in the two subsequent romances, the *Queste del Saint Graal* ("Quest of the Holy Grail") and the *Mort Artu* ("Death of Arthur").[26]

Lancelot and Guinevere's love is viewed differently in the Prose *Lancelot* than in the *Queste* and the *Mort Artu*. Whereas the Prose *Lancelot*, which includes an extended prose version of Chrétien's *Charrete*, is based largely on secular romance values, the author of the *Queste* interprets and condemns the couple's love from a traditional religious perspective. Developing the notion of a sexual sin that undermines the Arthurian universe, the author of the *Mort Artu* portrays its final destruction.

A refashioning of the prior romance tradition's accumulated lore about Lancelot and Guinevere, the Prose *Lancelot* is especially indebted to Chrétien's *Chevalier de la Charrete* and Ulrich von Zatzikhoven's *Lanzelet* (1194–1205). As in Chrétien's work, Lancelot is the queen's lover and champion; as in Ulrich's poem (discussed in detail later), the Lady of the Lake takes him away and raises him after the death of his father, Ban of Benoyc. Later joined by his cousins, Bohort (or Bors) and Lionel, Lancelot at the age of eighteen is taken to Arthur's court by his foster mother, who reveals that he is of royal parentage but fails to mention his name. Charmed by Genièvre (Guinevere) at their first meeting, Lancelot receives the sword of knighthood from her rather than from Arthur, a symbolic indication of the nature of his true allegiance.[27]

Still a knight without a name, Lancelot accomplishes a series of adventures, the most important at the castle of Dolorous Guard, at which he succeeds with help from his foster mother. In a cemetery on the grounds of the castle, he learns that his name is Lancelot by finding it inscribed on the slab of the tomb he will some day occupy. A seemingly never-ending series of victories wins him the title of "the best knight in the world" dedicated to defending the rights of the weak and oppressed. A while after he begins his adulterous affair with Genièvre, the luster of Lancelot's name and title begins to tarnish. He learns that because of his sins, he will be unable to accomplish the quest of the Holy Grail, and his son, Galaad (Galahad),[28] will do so in his place.

Attitudes toward the lovers evidence a marked shift in the cycle. Portraying love, even adulterous love, as the source of all good, the author of the Prose *Lancelot* sides with the lovers. The author has Genièvre take a more active role in the story and makes her into a more admirable figure than in the *Charrete*. It is Genièvre who asks that the inexperienced young knight be brought to her upon his arrival at court, and it is she who takes the initiative in clasping Lancelot's chin to facilitate their first kiss. Less capricious than Chrétien's queen, she has more substantial reasons for snubbing Lancelot than his failure to climb into the cart: she believes that he has committed adultery with Morgan the Fay, and that he failed to take his leave of her before his last departure from court. Convinced from the beginning of the sincerity of Lancelot's love, Genièvre grants her love without asking her lover to humiliate himself on her behalf. She is a positive force for good in Lancelot's development as a knight in the Prose *Lancelot*.

The last two works in the Vulgate Cycle cast the love of Lancelot and Genièvre in a negative light. In the *Queste del Saint Graal,* their relationship is reinterpreted in the context of otherworldly rather than secular chivalry; thus, a holy man explains that the Devil himself had aimed his arrow at Lancelot to make him fall hopelessly in love with Genièvre. Since the *Queste* emphasizes the father-son relationship of Lancelot and Galaad, it is logical for Genièvre to play a greatly reduced role in the narrative. In this work, which exalts virginity (and male virginity in particular) over every other human virtue, Lancelot comes to repent of his sin with Genièvre and do penance for it. As sign of his renewed favor, he is allowed to participate in the Grail liturgy but is denied the vision obtained by Perceval, Bohort, and Lancelot's virgin son, Galaad.

The *Mort Artu* has Lancelot and Genièvre relapsing into their affair, setting off the rivalry between Lancelot and Arthur that ends in the downfall of the Arthurian world.[29] Instead of fostering chivalry as in the previous works, love here leads to the destruction of great knights and a glorious kingdom. The increasing intensity of the lovers' passion makes them careless, triggering a concatenation of events that pits the lineages of Ban and Lot against one another. The former savior of the kingdom, Lancelot becomes the greatest threat to its harmony. The lovers' ultimate punishment is to be the involuntary cause of the fall of the Arthurian kingdom.

New aspects of the lovers are revealed in the play of passions that hold sway in the *Mort Artu*. Suspecting Lancelot of infidelity with the Dame d'Escalot, Genièvre descends to jealousy and pettiness. More multifaceted than her predecessors, Genièvre also has a generous side to her nature. In contrast to the tale recounted in the chronicles, Genièvre does not conspire with Mordred and become his consort in the *Mort Artu*. Her nobility is apparent in the final scene in the convent where she has taken refuge from the vengeance of Mordred's sons. When Lancelot offers to reestablish her as queen, she rises above her personal desires and suggests that they spend the rest of their time on earth in God's service to make up for their transgressions. The portrait of Lancelot is likewise nuanced. Unlike the complete turnaround of the *Queste*, Lancelot's renouncement of Genièvre represents a victory over himself in which his love for her becomes purified of all imperfection. Lancelot never goes so far as to express remorse for his betrayal of Arthur. Rather, the sublimation of his very human love for Genièvre leads him to the religious ascent of the final section of the *Mort Artu*.

In post-Chrétien verse romance, Lancelot often functions simply as member of a general array of Arthurian knights (e.g., in *Hunbaut*, ca. 1215; in Robert de Blois's *Beaudous*, ca. 1250; and in the only surviving Provençal Arthurian romance, *Jaufré*, ca. 1180–1225), while Guinevere retains her role as queen of the Arthurian court (e.g., in *Gliglois*, ca. 1225–30; and in *Jaufré*, where she is called Guilalmier). Whereas these works usually make no mention of the love of Lancelot and Guinevere, that love is treated, for good or for ill, in the prose cycles written from the thirteenth century to the end of the Middle Ages in the wake of the *Lancelot-Graal*. The author of the Post-Vulgate Cycle (or the Post-Vulgate *Roman du Graal*, composed between 1230 and 1240) centers his attention on Arthur and the Grail quest rather than on the adulterous love of Lancelot and Guinevere. Unlike its major source, the Vulgate, which balances the conflicting loyalties of worldly love and the Grail, the Post-Vulgate is unified in its condemnation of the love of Lancelot and Guinevere.

In the verse and prose traditions, Lancelot can fare either well or poorly. The *Perlesvaus*, a French prose romance from the early thirteenth century and predating the Vulgate *Queste del Saint Graal*,[30] views Lancelot's chivalry in a generally positive light. Although the work includes many constants of the tradition regarding Lancelot and Guinevere, it introduces several developments rarely found elsewhere. Typically, Lancelot's passion for Guinevere at once keeps him from other temptations while preventing him from achieving a vision of the Grail. Untypically, the *Perlesvaus* mentions Guinevere's death and places an unfamiliar emphasis on maternal affection: the queen dies of grief following the death of Loholt, the son she has had with Arthur.

Although Chrétien firmly established Lancelot as Guinevere's faithful lover and as a consummate knight, some later romances offer a divergent view. In one of the last Arthurian verse romances, the *Merveilles de Rigomer* ("Marvels of Rigomer," ca. 1250), his fidelity to the queen is compromised by an affair with another woman. His diminished knightly status is revealed in several other ways. First, he is captured and must be liberated by Gauvain. Second, he is shown in an unflattering light when he is reduced to the level of a scullion who grows fat on scraps and is subjected to various humiliations. And finally, whereas Lancelot's character and destiny had earlier been emphasized in the Vulgate by his descent from biblical figures, such as David, *Rigomer* makes no reference to genealogy.

In many late-medieval Arthurian works, Lancelot receives extended development in relation to a small number of other characters that typically includes Gauvain. The tendency to play Lancelot's adventures off those of Gauvain can be traced back as far as Chrétien's *Yvain* and *Charrete*, where Lancelot was clearly the better knight because his chivalry was motivated by love for Guinevere. The author of the Prose *Lancelot* continued to depict Lancelot's superiority over Gauvain based on Gauvain's inability to devote himself to one woman.[31]

A new and widespread phenomenon in the prose tradition of Arthurian romance is the development of the character of Lancelot in relation to Tristan, either in place of or in addition to his relation to Gauvain. In these cases, the characterization of Tristan is based on the Prose *Tristan*, a recasting of the famous legend of the star-crossed lovers in light of the Prose *Lancelot*. The Lancelot-Tristan pairing represents a logical progression in the tradition since the author of the Prose *Tristan* had gone to considerable pains to establish Tristan as Lancelot's equal in chivalric prowess and love. In particular, in the Prose *Tristan* Lancelot's love for Guinevere, illustrated in Chrétien's *Charrete* and the Prose *Lancelot*, had become the measuring stick for Tristan's knightly valor inspired by his love for Iseut. By the fourteenth century, comparisons, both direct and implied, between Lancelot and Tristan and between the Lancelot-Guinevere and Tristan-Iseut pairings had become standard fare in the prose romances, undoubtedly encouraged and perhaps even inspired by the presence in many of the same manuscripts of sections of both the Prose *Tristan* and the Prose *Lancelot*. In supplying a prehistory for the *Lancelot-Graal* and the Prose *Tristan* by telling the story of the fathers of Arthur, Erec, and Tristan, *Palamedes*[32] testifies to the blending of the legends dealing with the two sets of adulterous lovers as early as the thirteenth century.

Further permutations of these relationships take place in the later Middle Ages. In the fourteenth-century Prose *Yvain*, the initial section dealing with Yvain is followed by sections relating the adventures of Lancelot and his two most popular partners, Tristan and Gauvain. In his prose *Tristan* (1525–29) composed for King François I, Pierre Sala places the friendship between Lancelot and Tristan at the center of the narrative for the first time. Sala uses their friendship to turn the *Tristan*, on one level an exuberant tale of male bonding, into an implicit critique of the Arthurian chivalric code.

The late fourteenth-century prose romance the *Chevalier du Papegau* ("Knight of the Parrot") demonstrates that the major events of Lancelot and Guinevere's love story as recounted by Chrétien in the *Charrete* had not been forgotten two centuries after its composition. Known by the sobriquet of the "chevalier au papegau," Arthur, in this first French romance in which he becomes a true protagonist, engages in a series of adventures patterned on Lancelot's in the *Charrete*.[33] The work addresses the question first raised in the *Charrete* of just how much a knight should subordinate himself to his beloved's wishes. Although neither Chrétien nor Lancelot is alluded to by name in the narrative, the *Chevalier du Papegau* is a fitting tribute to the continued popularity and influence of both the author and his original character in France at the end of the Middle Ages.

MEDIEVAL GERMAN TRADITION

The representation of the characters of Lancelot and Guinevere is marked by several phases in the medieval German tradition. In the first and earliest phase, Ginover (Guinevere) is Arthur's devoted and faithful queen; Lanzelet or Lanzilot (Lancelot), when he does appear in the narrative, is not the queen's lover. In the second phase, Ginover's reputation is at the least questionable, although her purported lover is still not Lanzilot. In the third and final phase, Lanzilot and Ginover assume the love relationship for which they had become famous.

Apparently unaware of Chrétien's *Charrete*, the early German tradition does not paint the portrait of an adulterous queen. In *Erec* (1180–85), Hartmann von Aue's recasting of Chrétien's *Erec et Enide*, the author makes frequent mention of Ginover's goodness, nobility, and graciousness. Her relationship with the court and with her husband, Arthur, is warm. The king and queen are well suited to each other; Ginover is a devoted and faithful wife who is a type of mother to other members of the court. Wolfram von Eschenbach's *Parzival* (1200–10) continues Hartmann's representation of an ideal marriage; Lanzilot is only mentioned in passing as one of Arthur's knights, a role he also plays in Wirnt von Gravenberg's *Wigalois* (1210–15).

Ulrich von Zatzikhoven's *Lanzelet* (1194–1205) involves Lanzelet and Ginover, but the work differs from Chrétien's in important ways. Rather than rescuing the queen from her abductor, Valerin, Lanzelet prevents the abduction from taking place. Even though Lanzelet is among the rescue party accompanying Arthur, Malduc is her real rescuer. The most important difference is that Lanzelet is never Ginover's lover. It is thus unlikely that Ulrich knew Chrétien's romance; rather, both authors appear to have been familiar with a similar source or sources. The text supplies the information that

Ulrich's source was a "welschez buoch" ("Welsh book") in possession of Hugh de Morville, one of the hostages taken to ensure the fulfillment of the terms of the ransom of Richard Coeur de Lion, son of Eleanor of Aquitaine and Henri II Plantagenêt. Critics are in general agreement that the "Welsh book" is a lost Anglo-Norman source used independently by Ulrich and Chrétien.

Although Ginover is not shown committing adultery in the *Lanzelet*—what happens during her captivity is left unstated—Ulrich makes allusion to Ginover's prior reputation as an adulteress by showing her failing at the trial of the magic cloak (as do all other women at Arthur's court except Iblis). In *Der Mantel*, the German version of the *Mantel mal taillé*, King Arthur has trouble controlling his anger when he learns of Guinevere's infidelity and even goes on to warn her to behave with greater circumspection in the future.[34]

Besides incorporating elements from *Lanzelet*, Heinrich von dem Türlin's *Diu Crône* ("The Crown," 1215–20), a voluminous verse romance that brings together motifs drawn from an astonishing variety of sources, reveals a familiarity with French chastity-test narratives and Chrétien's *Charrete*. Near the beginning of the romance, all the members of Arthur's court except the king himself reveal prior indiscretions by spilling some of the contents of a drinking cup. Although a character named Lanzelet again plays a minor role as one of Arthur's knights, Heinrich transfers functions usually associated with Lancelot to other characters; for instance, it is Gawain rather than Lanzelet who rescues Ginover from an abductor, and a knight named Gasozein claims to have been her first lover. After having raped the queen, Gasozein reveals that his allegations of a prior intimate relationship with her had been an entire fabrication. Ginover's contested chastity contributes to the depiction of an Arthurian universe whose values are in flux. The implication of infidelity that is eventually cleared affirms Guinevere's integrity according to a courtly ethos. While her courtliness accentuates the boorishness of the male figures, she is caught in the passivity and submissiveness characteristic of the medieval German heroine.[35]

The first substantial allusion to the adulterous relationship of Lancelot and Guinevere appears in the *Prosa-Lancelot* ("Prose Lancelot," ca. 1250). Since the work is almost a word-for-word translation from the French prose romance,[36] Lancelot and Guinevere are near-copies of their French models. Ulrich Füertrer's *Prosaroman von Lanzelot* ("Prose Lancelot Romance," ca. 1467), his first literary work, amounts to a greatly simplified version of the German *Prosa-Lancelot*; his *Strophische Lanzelot* ("Strophic Lanzelot," begun before 1484 and completed perhaps in 1487) is a strophic reworking some 39,000 lines long of his own prior text. Füertrer blunts the complexities of the French and German prose cycles that had served as the basis for his texts by reducing them to a catalog of bizarre and repetitive adventures,[37] thus producing portraits of Lancelot and Guinevere that lack the complexity of their French prototypes.

MEDIEVAL BRITISH TRADITION

Lancelot and Guinevere came to enjoy a secure existence in English literature only after the English royal court had freed itself from French domination around the middle of the fourteenth century and again began to consider the vernacular as a fitting vehicle for literary expression. The depiction of Lancelot and Guinevere in fourteenth-century England is an outgrowth of their portrayal in Latin or vernacular chronicles (the pseudo-historical or heroic tradition that had produced Layamon's late twelfth-century adaptation of Wace's *Brut*), where the two are not lovers, or in the French Vulgate Cycle (the romance tradition), where they are. *Sir Gawain and the Green Knight* (last quarter of the fourteenth century), one of the greatest of all Arthurian romances, mentions neither Lancelot nor material traditionally associated with him. In her oft-seen role as queen of the Arthurian court, Gaynour (Guinevere) provides the motivation for the "beheading game" that structures the plot of the romance. The Green Knight (Bercilak de Hautdesert) explains that Morgan the Fay devised the contest in order to frighten the queen to death[38] and to test the mettle of the knights of the Round Table. Although the references to Gaynour and Morgan in *Sir Gawain* are few and far between, it is nonetheless striking that males are used instrumentally as tokens of exchange in a plot largely structured by females. In this romance whose underlying structure is governed more by same- than opposite-sex bonds, Guinevere's role is more important than it might at first appear.[39]

Guinevere is a prominent character in the Alliterative *Morte Arthure* ("Death of Arthur"), a narrative poem composed near the end of the fourteenth century that also fails to mention her love for Lancelot. Gaynour (Guinevere), whose depiction in this work is largely negative, follows her representation in the chronicle tradition, with notable exceptions. Since her relationship with her husband is excellent, it is unclear what attracts her to Modrede (Mordred). This is one of the few instances in which the queen has children; the children of Modrede's wife present in another version may have been transferred to her. When Modrede advises her to take them to Ireland with her when his imminent defeat becomes apparent, she flees to a convent, leaving her children to Arthur's wrath. Lancelot plays a minor role in the work. Never the queen's lover, he is a relatively unimportant (only seven allusions) war-loving knight who is killed in Arthur's final battle with Modrede at Cornwall.[40] Arthur's downfall is more the result of his ambition and pride than of Gaynour and Modrede's lechery and treason. The story of Arthur as quintessential world conqueror, the Alliterative *Morte Arthure* forms a bridge between the romance and chronicle traditions.

It is in the Stanzaic *Le Morte Arthur*, a verse romance composed probably in the late fourteenth century, that Launcelot plays his first prominent role in English prior to Malory. Taking special pains to have him gain the reader's sympathy, the author sets up Arthur and Gawayne as foils to Launcelot's glory. Launcelot rather than the king has the qualities necessary to be an effective leader. The author shifts the responsibility for the civil wars that destroy the kingdom from the adultery to the accidental slaying of Gawayne's brothers.[41] If Launcelot is less subject to his capricious lady than in the *Chevalier de la Charrete*, he is also a less assertive lover, and thus less guilty than his French predecessors. Although a causal factor in the dissolution of Arthur's realm, Gaynour, who is absent during much of the central action of the work, is often shown to be a victim of circumstances. The reader believes in Launcelot's sincere repentance at the work's conclusion; even his deliverance into paradise by the heavenly hosts appears justified by his portrayal in the poem as a victim of lies and slanders rather than as an evildoer.[42]

The opposition between the alliterative and stanzaic reworkings of the Vulgate *Mort Artu* indicates the existence of two traditions concerning Lancelot, the pseudo-historical tradition in which his importance is downplayed, and the romance tradition in which he is the focus of interest. Like the stanzaic poet, later writers would draw upon the latter to establish Lancelot as the peerless hero of the British Arthurian tradition. Malory would also follow the stanzaic poet's lead in downplaying the sexual nature of the lovers' relationship in order to make it appear less blameworthy.

Lancelot and Guinevere receive incidental notice in several later works in the English tradition, which, with the notable exception of Malory, devote more space to the fostering of the image of a noble Gawain. Although not especially attracted to the Arthurian story, Chaucer, the greatest poet of the time, makes a few references in passing to Lancelot.[43] Evidencing a thorough grounding in the Vulgate, the anonymous *Early History of King Arthur* (ca. 1450–60), a prose version of the *Merlin*, represents Lancelot as the exemplar of chivalry whose love for Guinevere triggers his war with Arthur. In Henry (or Herry) Lovelich's *History of the Holy Grail* (ca. 1450), which imparts a moralistic interpretation to its major source, the Vulgate *Estoire del Saint Graal*, Lancelot appears as a traitor akin to Mordred. Thomas Chestre refers to Lancelot in passing in his *Sir Launfal* and in *Lybeaus Desconus*, based on several variant versions of Fair Unknown romances.

A revised version of the Lancelot and Guinevere story occupies several sections of Sir Thomas Malory's *Morte Darthur* (completed 1469–70, published by William Caxton in 1495).[44] Malory integrates three traditions: the English heroic tradition transmitted through the Alliterative *Morte Arthure* and Layamon's *Brut*, the French Vulgate, and the French *Tristan*.

Malory gives extended treatment to the love of Launcelot and Gwenyver in tales 3, 6, and 7.[45] Tale 3, "The Noble Tale of Sir Launcelot du Lake," traces Launcelot's rise to prominence as Arthur's most illustrious knight. Drawing from many sources, Malory develops Launcelot's qualities of self-control, rectitude, and humaneness.[46] Although largely based on the Prose *Lancelot*, the third tale concentrates on Launcelot's chivalry inspired by a yet unconsummated passion. Undertaking his quest because of Gwenyver, he becomes the best knight in the world. An episode suggesting that Launcelot's and Gwenyver's love has been consummated, found at the end of the fifth tale, "The Book of Sir Tristram de Lyones," provides an introduction to the next one. Based on the French *Queste del Saint Graal*, "The Tale of the Sankgreal" reveals a Lancelot divided between his devotion to God and his love of Gwenyver. Not allowed the full vision of the Grail of the three successful questers, he is nonetheless accorded a partial vision. Tale 7, "The Book of Sir Launcelot and Queen Gwenyver," describes a state of calm before the final destruction of Arthur's kingdom. Numerous scenes have Launcelot and Gwenyver narrowly escaping discovery.

When in the eighth and final tale, "The Morte Darthur," the lovers' adultery is at last exposed, Gwenyver is condemned to die at the stake and Launcelot unwittingly incites a chain of events that ends in the destruction of the kingdom. After he accidentally kills Gareth in coming to Gwenyver's rescue, Gawayne becomes his sworn enemy and encourages Arthur to pursue Launcelot. Established as regent during Arthur's absence, Mordred makes an attempt to seize the crown and Gwenyver. After a battle in which Arthur and Mordred inflict fatal wounds on each other, Launcelot and Gwenyver repent of their sins, enter the religious life, and die reconciled with God.

Other tales flesh out the individual portraits of the characters. In the first tale, "The Tale of King Arthur," which recounts how Arthur meets, becomes betrothed to, and marries Gwenyver in Camelot, Gwenyver appears in her customary role as Arthur's wife and queen of his splendid court. Tale 4, "The Tale of Sir Gareth of Orkney," the story of Launcelot's friendship with Gareth, Gawayne's brother, illustrates the theme of Launcelot's friendship with another knight. The final episode of tale 5, "The Book of Sir Tristram de Lyones," recounts how Launcelot is tricked into begetting Galahad with Eleyne who he believes is Gwenyver.[47]

Malory removes the focus on adultery that had marked the earlier versions of the story by downplaying the lovers' sexual relationship. The beginnings of the affair are discreetly hidden; Malory has no scene of the lovers' first kiss as in the Prose *Lancelot*, nor does their lovemaking acquire the transcendent quality of the *Charrete*'s "night of love" episode. Malory's reworked version of Chrétien's scene of one-time lovemaking occurs when Launcelot and Guinevere's affair is well underway. Adultery as such is much less a problem for Malory than maintaining chivalric bonds between men. Arthur would even have been willing to overlook the couple's transgression in order to enjoy Launcelot's company, which he recognizes as the binding force of the Round Table.

Malory portrays Gwenyver as a beautiful, courageous lady and an effective queen who assumes the function of judge and teacher of chivalry to young knights. Her rashness, however, calls down destruction on her own head; when she undergoes three public accusations of adultery, the other knights come to see her as a destroyer of men. Malory, however, excises the wholesale condemnation of her made by the *Queste* author.[48] Gwenyver's imperious attitude toward Launcelot temporarily alienates him from her. For the most part, her relationship with Launcelot is stable, with sexual attraction taking a second place to devoted affection. Malory generally presents Gwenyver in a favorable light, at least more so than her counterpart in the chronicle tradition or the Alliterative *Morte Arthure*.

Malory's depiction of Lancelot as Arthur's best knight takes its place within the context of a study centered on worldly chivalry. Since Malory chooses to omit details of Lancelot's childhood and his early love of Guinevere, his work lacks the biographical amplitude of the *Lancelot-Graal*. In presenting an anatomy of secular knighthood, Malory heightened the importance of Arthur and of other knights like Tristram, Gareth, Lamorak, and Palmydes in order to give greater depth to his portrait of the ideal knight. Magnetic and indomitable, Malory's Launcelot is the devoted lover of an admirable woman as well as the defender of the weak and the oppressed.[49] Although Malory views him as a sinner who because of his inordinate love for Gwenyver exercises poor judgment in picking battles to be fought, he does not censure his love as strongly as do the author(s) of the Vulgate. On the contrary, Malory emphasizes Launcelot's success in achieving as great an understanding of the Grail mysteries as he does.[50] Although as "an erthly synful man" he is not destined to achieve the Grail, Launcelot is nonetheless the best a secular chivalry has to offer.

Malory uses the final encounter of Launcelot and Gwenyver to illustrate one of his major themes, the potential of "erthly synful" men to accede to the spiritual life. After Gwenyver has become a nun at Almesbury following the deaths of Arthur and Mordred, her newfound generosity and spiritual commitment propel her lover to transcend his former limitations. When Gwenyver proclaims before her ladies that she and Launcelot are to blame for all that has happened and encourages her former lover to forsake her and wed another woman, Launcelot finds the strength to renounce his sinful ways and take up the religious life himself. He announces that had she not loved him carnally earlier, he would have been able to renounce earthly vanity and thus achieve higher status in the Grail quest. Although Gwenyver denies Launcelot's request that she kiss him one last time before he leaves, she faints several times, as does Launcelot. In light of prior tradition, it is significant that the lovers' most passionate embrace in Malory is the one *not* undertaken at parting.

If Malory puts the ultimate responsibility on Gwenhyver as the keeper of morality, he also shows her to be the stronger of the two in such matters. Malory's Gwenhyver fits into the patriarchal mentality underlying the religious or courtly veneration of female figures in the Middle Ages: woman exists to bring man to perfection. Given the epic flavor of the *Morte Darthur*, it is perhaps understandable that Malory's underlying message for woman is that for civilization to flower, she must keep tight hold on her sexual proclivities. Malory's influence on later Arthurian productions, especially in the modern era, has been enormous. Beginning with the Victorians, however, few subsequent writers have been as willing to downplay the question of adultery as Malory.

Composed around 1478, *Lancelot of the Laik*, the only medieval British romance besides Malory to give a prominent role to Lancelot,[51] is an adaptation in Middle Scots of Galehaut's war against Arthur.[52] It narrates a part of Lancelot's history that is prominent in the French Prose *Lancelot*, but absent in Malory—Lancelot's friendship with Galehaut and his initial meeting with Guinevere. The narrator of this tale, presented as a dream vision, states his desire to model himself on Lancelot, the ideal knight and lover, in order to win the affection and admiration of the woman he loves. Although the Scottish *Lancelot of the Laik* makes it clear that by the end of the fifteenth century Lancelot had superseded all other Arthurian knights in importance, his reputation among the British suffered a serious eclipse for several centuries afterwards for reasons to be explored in a later section.

Writers were quick to adapt parts of the Vulgate dealing with Lancelot and Guinevere into other vernaculars. A brief account of the story is made in the *Melech Artus* ("King Arthur"), a 1279 Hebrew reworking of the *Merlin* and *Mort Artu* portions of the *Lancelot-Graal*. Lancelot is mentioned along with Palamedes, Gawein, and Tristan in a Greek narrative written around 1300 concerning these knights' encounter with an aged warrior.

Lancelot was known in the Low Countries in the Middle Ages through the *Chevalier de la Charrete* and the Prose *Lancelot*. Although no adaptation of the *Charrete* was ever made, references to Chrétien's romance appear in the *Ridder metter mouwen* ("Knight with the Sleeve") and other Arthurian romances. At least three adaptations of the Prose *Lancelot* are known to have existed. The most famous renditions in Middle Dutch of Lancelot's amorous and knightly adventures were *Lantsloot vander Haghedochte* ("Lancelot of the Cave") and the *Lancelot-Compilatie* ("*Lancelot* Compilation"). The first is a free verse adaptation of the French Prose *Lancelot* written in the second half of the thirteenth century. Only fragments totaling some 6,070 lines have been preserved from a work that must have comprised over 100,000 lines in its original form. Its stylized portrait of Lancelot and Guinevere recalls the romances of Chrétien de Troyes.

The *Lancelot-Compilatie* is composed of ten Middle Dutch Arthurian verse romances. The core of the compilation is constituted by a verse translation of the French Prose *Lancelot*, the *Queste*, and the *Mort Artu*.[53] The *Lancelot-Compilatie* also contains a short Lancelot romance in verse, *Lanceloet en het hert met de witte voet* ("Lancelot and the Deer with the White Foot"). The original Middle Dutch text from which this abridged rendition was made dates probably from the first half of the thirteenth century. Initially succeeding in the challenge set by a young woman to bring her the white foot of a deer guarded by lions, Lanceloet is cheated out of his prize by another knight who leaves him severely wounded and makes off with the woman with the aid of the white foot. Walewein (Gauvain) comes to Lanceloet's rescue by defeating the arrogant impostor.[54]

Lanseloet van Denemerken ("Lancelot of Denmark") is a fourteenth-century play in Middle Dutch that concerns a prince of Denmark, his mother, and Sanderijn, a young woman of inferior birth. The mother thwarts her son's love for Sanderijn by allowing him to have sexual relations with her on the condition that he will then offend and repudiate her. Following her forcible seduction, the rejected woman finds happiness with another man. When after one year Lanseloet's servant finds the now-married woman and asks her to return to his lord, she rejects his proposal, leaving Lanseloet to die of grief. The play no longer has an Arthurian character, but it once may have, since the title may represent a corrupted form of *Lanseloet vanden Mere* ("Lancelot of the Lake"), and it may have had its origins in stories about Lancelot, Guinevere, and the Maid of Astolat.[55] Besamusca argues that the contrast between Lanseloet and his Arthurian namesake was intended: unlike Lancelot, who is totally devoted to Guinevere, Lanseloet humiliates and abuses his beloved.[56] *Lanseloet van Denemerken* is a good example of the ironic use of the usual associations of Lancelot's name.

Since Scandinavian writers made no wholesale reworking of the *Charrete* or the Vulgate and the few allusions to Lancelot and Guinevere are largely based on French originals, there is little new in the characterization of the two in Scandinavian medieval literature. Although no adaptation of the *Charrete* exists, some familiarity with the story is evident. The author of the early thirteenth-century Norwegian *Ivens saga* ("Tale of Yvain") substitutes Lancelot's name for Dodinez in the group of knights Chrétien included in the group listening to Calogrenant's (Kalebrant's) tale. Vague allusions to the abduction of the queen help explain Gawain's absence from Arthur's court at a time when his assistance was needed. The author gently chides the queen for having been foolish enough to entrust her safety to a knight of Kay's questionable chivalric prowess. Guinevere plays her customary role in the early thirteenth-century *Möttuls saga* ("Tale of the Mantle"), the Norwegian version of the tale of the chastity test conducted by means of a magic mantle. Besides the *Ivens saga*, Lancelot figures incidentally in several other works in Scandinavian medieval literature. Along with Yvain and Valvein (Gawain), Lancelot is one of Arthur's nephews in the *Breta sögur* ("Saga of the Britons"), an early- to mid-thirteenth-century translation of Geoffrey's *Historia* preserved only in Icelandic manuscripts. The epithet of the hero of the *Rémundar saga keisarasonar*, "the sick man of the cart," is reminiscent of Lancelot's cognomen as the "knight of the cart." Without mentioning the name of either Lancelot or Guinevere, the fourteenth-century Icelandic *Tristram* combines and transforms motifs from Chrétien's *Charrete* (especially those of the blood drops in the queen's bed) and other Scandinavian versions of the Tristan legend for which the Scandinavians had a particular fondness.[57]

To a greater or lesser extent depending on the country, vernacular versions of the Vulgate were influenced by recastings of Tristan material, which itself had already begun to incorporate borrowings from the Lancelot corpus. It was not unusual for the new material about Lancelot and Guinevere to include comparisons and contrasts between Lancelot and Tristan as well as between the Lancelot and Guinevere couple and Tristan and Iseut. *Lanzarote del Lago* ("Lancelot of the Lake") is a fourteenth-century Spanish translation of the *Lancelot* proper. The sections that have been preserved (in a partial mid-sixteenth-century copy containing the very end of book 1 and a long version of books 2 and 3) of this relatively well-known prose adaptation tell the story of Lancelot's departure from Arthur's court after having been made a knight and of his search for Tristan, whose adventures take their source in a lost Tristan romance.[58]

Diffusion of Arthurian material into the Hispanic peninsula had begun at an early date.[59] Many versions of the *Lancelot-Graal* Cycle were in circulation in Spain and Portugal; most are adaptations of the *Lancelot* proper, the *Queste*, and the *Mort Artu*. Sharrer surmises that King Alfonso III and his entourage brought parts of the *Lancelot-Graal* and Post-Vulgate *Roman du Graal* Cycles, along with other French romances, back to Portugal in 1245. In the fifth and final lai in the anonymous collection, the *Lais de Bretanha* ("Lays of Britain"), composed perhaps during the reign of Alfonso III's son, Dom Dinis (1279–1325), a group of young women praise Lançarote as the best man created by our Lord. The depiction of the hero is inspired by episodes of Lancelot's madness and his stay on the Isle of Joy found in the prose cycles.[60]

Of the three Spanish ballads that derive from the prose romances and are strictly speaking Arthurian, two concern Lancelot and one Tristan. As in the Middle Dutch tradition, medieval Spanish literature had its own version of the story of Lancelot and the Stag with the White Foot, *Lanzarote y el ciervo del pie blanco*. This ballad describing Lanzarote's hunt for the white stag imposed by a malevolent woman still survives in the oral tradition as "Tres hijuelos había el rey" ("The King Had Three Small Sons"). Another medieval Spanish ballad concerning Lancelot has come down to modern times. Cervantes preserved a few lines of "Nunca fuera caballero de damas tan bien servido" ("Never Was a Gallant Knight So Well Served by Women") for posterity by incorporating it into his masterpiece, *Don Quixote*. This ballad begins by telling how a lady serves Lancelot wine before he retires to the queen's bedchamber; it then goes on to recount how Lancelot defeats and kills a proud knight because he had boasted that he would become Guinevere's lover.

Lancelot is the protagonist of several Hispanic prose narratives; authors of other works presuppose knowledge of his doings. Lancelot figures in the three branches of the Post-Vulgate *Roman du Graal* ("Romance of the Grail") that were first translated into Galician Portuguese before appearing in the Spanish vernacular. The *Tragèdia de Lançalot* ("Tragedy of Lancelot") is the name given by Martí de Riquer to a Catalan reworking of the *Mort Artu*, in which the author Mossèn Gras interprets the triangle of Lancelot, Guinevere, and the Maid of Ascalot according to the conventions of fifteenth-century Hispanic sentimental romance. The characters explore their feelings of love in highly rhetorical language.[61] Garci Rodríguez de Montalvo produced a corrective refashioning of the adulterous love represented in the legends of Lancelot and Tristan by picturing the higher type of fidelity of Amadís and Oriana in *Amadís de Gaula* ("Amadis of Gaul," 1508), his reworked version of an indigenous Spanish romance originally composed at the end of the thirteenth century. Diego de San Pedro also played upon the givens of the Lancelot story in his *Cárcel de Amor* ("Prison of Love") when he borrowed elements from the episode of Lancelot's rescue of Guinevere at the stake in the Vulgate *Mort Artu*.[62]

Evidence of the diffusion of Arthurian material into Italy is found as early as the twelfth and thirteenth century. At that time, Arthurian figures appear in the decoration of cathedrals in Otranto, Modena, and Bari, and Arthurian names were popular. Dante's reference to the love of Lancelot and Guinevere in Canto 5 of the *Commedia* proves that the Prose *Lancelot* was particularly well known. Dante was not the only Italian writer to cast a disapproving eye on their adultery; Andrea da Barberino (ca. 1372–1431) was so opposed to *luxuria* that he consciously avoided undertaking an extended treatment of the legend. Even so, he occasionally refers to the characters; in his *Aspramonte* ("Aspramonte"), he tells how Lanzilotto's sword passed from one great knight to another. In line with his interest in the Matter of France, Andrea focuses on Lanzilotto's knightly attributes rather than his amorous exploits. In the *Trionfi* ("Triumphs," book 3, ll. 79–82), Petrarch disparagingly includes Lancilotto and Ginevra among a group of Arthurian characters who were conquered by love.

Recastings of the legend of Lancelot and Guinevere in Italy in the Middle Ages run the gamut from superficial allusions in lyric poetry to wholesale adaptations of the story in *cantari* ("songs") and major prose romances, whose popularity outranked that of Chrétien and the Provençal poets. Passing references to Lancelot and Guinevere in lyric poems and narrative works usually omit mention of their adulterous love affair; the two simply represent the ideal knight and the quintessential courtly lady. In Frate Stoppa de' Bostichi's ballad on Fortune, "Se la Fortuna o'l mondo" ("If Fortune or the World"), Lancelot is the epitome of the valiant knight (ll. 53–56) and Guinevere (along with Iseut) is representative of a supremely beautiful woman (ll. 79–80). In an unedited prose epic, *Ansuigi, re di Spagna* ("Ansuigi, King of Spain"), Andrea da Barberino in typical fashion praises the beauty of his heroine over that of Isotta (Iseut) and Ginevra (Guinevere).

A generic mention of Lancelot among other great knights appears in the anonymous *Cantari d'Aspramonte* ("Songs of Aspramonte"). In this late fourteenth- or early fifteenth-century Tuscan poem, Lancelotto is courtly, well-educated, and a paragon of all virtues.

More properly termed "semilearned" although originating in the oral tradition, the cantari present paraphrases of focal episodes from Old French and Italian prose romances. The two *cantari* about Lancelot associate him with Tristan. A short *cantare* of forty-two stanzas dating from the late fourteenth century, "Quando Tristano e Lanceilotto combattettero al petrone di Merlino" ("When Tristan and Lancelot Fought at Merlin's Stone"), describes the combat between Tristano and Lanceilotto. Another *cantare*, "La Vendetta che fe meser Lanzelloto de la morte de miser Tristano" ("The Revenge That Sir Lancelot Took for the Death of Sir Tristan"), describes how Lanzelloto avenges the death of Tristano. In a related fifteenth-century Venetian prose text, the *Tristano Veneto* ("Venetian Tristan"), Lancilloto exacts revenge for Tristano's death by killing King Marco. The most important of the Italian poems connected to the Arthurian cycle are the seven *Chantari di Lancellotto* ("Songs of Lancelot"), also known as *La Struzione della Tavola Ritonda* ("The Destruction of the Round Table") of the late fourteenth or early fifteenth century. The work follows the *Mort Artu* closely while introducing details from the Prose *Tristan*.[63]

Although surpassed in number by recastings of the Tristan and Iseut legend, several adaptations into Italian were made of the story of Lancelot and Guinevere. *Lancillotto del Lago* ("Lancelot of the Lake," published 1558–59) is an adaptation of the parts of the *Lancelot-Graal* dealing with Lancelot. A short fifteenth-century narrative, "La Battaglia di Tristano e Lancillotto e della Reina Isotta" ("The Battle of Tristan and Lancelot and of Queen Iseut"), describes how Lancillotto freed Tristano from the giant Barbafolta's castle. Lancialotto figures in two of the one hundred tales in the late thirteenth-century collection that nineteenth-century editors entitled *Il Novellino*: in the one in which he engages in a battle at a fountain with a knight named Alibano, Lancialotto represents the ideal knight, while in the other, a tale in which the Damigella di Scalot dies for love of him, he is rather a young woman's ideal love object. In another collection of *novelle* ("tales"), the *Conti di Antichi Cavalieri* ("Tales of Knights of Old"), Lancelocto is celebrated for his courtesy, goodness, and chivalric prowess. The late thirteenth-century *Conto di Brunor e di Galeoto sui Figlio* ("Tale of Brunor and of Galeoto His Son") explores the friendship between Galeoto (Galehaut) and Lancelotto.[64]

In the *Tristano Riccardiano* ("Riccardian Tristan," composed 1272–1300), the earliest Arthurian romance in Italian, Lancillotto, second only to

Tristano in the courtly hierarchy, appears in his traditional role as the lover of Ginevra. Including many borrowings from the *Lancelot-Graal*, the work testifies to the increasing importance of the Tristan-Lancelot relationship in the Italian tradition.

This relationship undergoes considerable development in the *Tavola Ritonda* ("Round Table"), a cyclical romance written in Italian prose in the second quarter of the fourteenth century, whose longest section is formed by the *Tristan* with interpolations from several other romances including the Vulgate *Queste*. Of the many adaptations of the Prose *Tristan* into the Spanish, Catalan, and Italian vernacular, the *Tavola Ritonda* is the most innovative. Emphasizing the love story over knightly adventures, it bases the superiority of Tristano over Lancilotto on Tristano's adherence to the paradigm of Lancelot's love service of Guinevere in Chrétien's romance, where, although adulterous, Lancelot's love, rather than being entirely antisocial, inspired knightly prowess beneficial to society. Conceived as a response to Dante's condemnation of the adulterous love of Paolo and Francesca, the *Tavola Ritonda* places the love of Tristano and Isotta, here based on Lancelot's devotion to Guinevere in Chrétien's romance, at the pinnacle of a secular hierarchy parallel to that of Christian love.[65]

Another intertwining of the stories of Lancelot and Tristan occurs in what is referred to as the *Tristano Panciatichiano* ("Panciatichian Tristan"), MS Panciatichiano 33 of the National Library of Florence (beginning of the fourteenth century). This compilation contains five fragments of Arthurian romances, two dealing with Lancelot and three with Tristan. Selecting parts of the *Queste del Saint Graal* and the *Mort Artu* that treat Lancelot's exclusive love for Guinevere, the compiler in effect "glosses" the story of one hero with events from the life of the other. Thus, Arthur's remark in the *Mort Artu* that only magic or the Devil could have made Lancelot betray him with Guinevere receives its justification in the incident of Tristan's betrayal of Mark under the influence of the potion.[66]

Later Italian authors used Lancelot and Guinevere to comment on contemporary mores. The famous lovers figure in the most influential fifteenth-century Arthurian romance, Matteo Maria Boiardo's *Orlando Innamorato* ("Orlando in Love"). Boiardo employs the characters and themes of the French prose *Lancelot-Graal* to illustrate the weaknesses of the chivalric system of the Este court.[67] Boiardo's unfinished chivalric romance was continued by Ludovico Ariosto in his early sixteenth-century *Orlando Furioso* ("Orlando Gone Mad"),[68] an enormous compendium of Arthurian lore. In including Lancelot and Guinevere among numerous victims of love, Ariosto contrasts the idealism of past chivalric tradition with the harsh realities of political and social life in contemporary Italy.

RENAISSANCE TO NINETEENTH CENTURY

The story of Lancelot and Guinevere, like Arthurian literature in general, went into such an eclipse from the sixteenth to the nineteenth century that one modern critic, Barbara Ann Gordon-Wise, has been prompted to refer to the period as a "desert" of the Arthurian myth (*The Reclamation of a Queen*, 9). Lancelot and Guinevere were neglected in English literature for several centuries following *Lancelot of the Laik* for two main reasons: first, the new moral consciousness that developed after the Reformation viewed Lancelot and Guinevere's love with disfavor; second, the historical tradition that had become increasingly popular typically depicted Guinevere as a woman of questionable virtue and had no knowledge at all of a character named Lancelot. Consequently, even though Malory had done much to improve Guinevere's reputation, writers largely ignored her for three centuries after his Arthurian epic. The only known Arthurian play of the Elizabethan age, Thomas Hughes's *The Misfortunes of Arthur* (performed by members of Gray's Inn before Elizabeth I at Greenwich in 1587) made no mention of Lancelot. With a plot based on Geoffrey of Monmouth, the play concentrates on the revenge Arthur takes on Mordred for his seduction of Guenevora (Guinevere).

Despite the infrequent appearance of Arthurian themes in literature, in the sixteenth century intense interest grew in the historical basis and moral significance of the Arthurian legend. John Leland's 1544 defense of the historical existence of Lancelot and Arthur, the *Assertio Inclytissimi Arturii Regis Britanniae* (translated by Richard Robinson in 1582 as "A Learned and True Assertion of . . . Prince Arthure, King of Great Brittaine"), cast doubt on Guenhera's (Guinevere's) reputation as an adulteress. Sometimes openly condemned for his adultery with Guinevere, as in Roger Ascham's *The Scholemaster* (published posthumously in 1570), Lancelot is more often than not formally excluded from the list of characters, as in Spenser's *Faerie Queene* (ca. 1570–99). Not only did he write Lancelot out of the Arthurian panoply in this work, Spenser portrayed Arthur as a bachelor. Shakespeare's only mention of Lancelot is in two lines of a popular ballad praising Lancelot's bravery in a battle with Sir Tarquin. Christopher Middleton gave Lancelot a prominent role in his late sixteenth-century prose romance, *The History of Chinon in England*, where, as the devoted and chaste lover of Laura, he plays a role that differs from the usual one. Works such as this one attest to the popularity of Lancelot's name rather than an understanding of the traditions associated with him.

From the seventeenth to the nineteenth century, writers paid Lancelot scant attention. His reputation declined further owing to the development of an even stronger moral and historical consciousness coupled with a general indifference to all things Arthurian. The few writers who treated Lancelot in a positive fashion depicted him as a military hero. References to Guinevere were even less frequent. In Richard Johnson's *Tom a Lincolne* (published 1607), Lancelot functioned primarily as the protagonist's lieutenant, friend, and counselor. A foil to set off another's greatness, Lancelot was an entertaining teller of love stories rather than the devoted lover of Guinevere, whose name does not even appear in the work. The first revival of interest in Lancelot after a long period of obscurity came in 1765 in Thomas Percy's *Reliques of Ancient English Poetry*, which included among its six Arthurian ballads "Sir Lancelot du Lake," a 124-line poem telling of Lancelot's battle with Tarquin.[69] In Percy's poem, Lancelot assumed his traditional role as Arthur's finest knight who excelled all others in battle. In *Arthur, or, The Northern Enchantment* (published 1789), Richard Hole presented Lancelot as the main commander of the British forces during the war against the invading Saxons. From the end of the Middle Ages to the beginning of the nineteenth century, writers tended to neglect Lancelot because he was a character who had no basis in history. Hole's contention that Arthurian material should be treated as romance rather than history prepared the way for the revival of interest in Lancelot in the century to come. (See App, 113–31, for passing references to Lancelot in English literature from 1600 to 1800.)

The Arthurian Revival in Literature

Spearheaded by developments in literature and in the visual arts in England, the nineteenth century experienced a remarkable resurgence of interest in Arthurian themes. (The visual arts are treated in a later section.) To writers and artists tired of the excesses of the Industrial Revolution, the Middle Ages appeared as an idyllic time when life was simpler and people lived in closer contact with the universe and their natural impulses. The theme of illicit love in particular afforded them the opportunity either to satirize contemporary mores or to escape the repressive atmosphere of nineteenth-century European middle-class society. The triple republication of Malory's *Morte Darthur* in the second decade of the century supplied much of the impetus behind the Arthurian revival. Taking their primary inspiration from Malory, writers looked to the Middle Ages for models of ethical conduct to help improve the present.[70]

Although the love triangle of Arthur, Guinevere, and Lancelot provided the backdrop for his *Bridal of Triermain* (1813), Walter Scott's vision of medieval times did not attain the epic intensity and ethical pertinence of later authors. Alfred, Lord Tennyson, who as Poet Laureate was the official spokesman of Victorian England, was instrumental in bringing about the extraordinary flowering of Arthurian themes in literature and art. Tennyson's career included an extended meditation on Lancelot and Guinevere; he treated each character both as part of a couple and in relation to other Arthurian figures, such as Elaine and Arthur. Well-acquainted with Malory, Tennyson reinterpreted the Arthurian saga as a moral drama that documented the rise and fall of an ideal society. An early unpublished "Sir Launcelot and Queen Guinevere" (1830) examines the nascent love of Lancelot and Guinevere. Tennyson's first published Arthurian poem, "The Lady of Shalott" (1832), takes up the heroine's tragic infatuation for Lancelot. In a second group of Arthurian poems, he devotes a piece entitled "Guinevere" to the final meeting between Arthur and Guinevere, in which he explores her complexities and her relationship to her husband seen as the ideal ruler. Torn between regal dignity and a passionate nature, Guinevere is a creature of extremes whose tragic flaw is her inability to appreciate the highest human values, which find their ultimate incarnation in her husband, Arthur. In "Elaine," Tennyson's next Arthurian poem, he emphasizes the destructive force of Guinevere's adulterous love on innocent members of the Arthurian community.[71]

In his most important Arthurian creation, *Idylls of the King,* Tennyson implies that the queen's sin is the cause of the destruction of the realm.[72] In the idyll "Lancelot and Elaine," Lancelot, whose face is symbolically marked by the love he bears the queen, is unable to appreciate the pure and honest love offered by Elaine. Like Chrétien in the *Charrete,* Tennyson leaves the Lancelot and Guinevere story without a conclusive ending. The final idyll, "The Passing of Arthur" (published 1869), whose subject is Arthur's battle with Mordred, refers in passing to Lancelot's separate campaign in which Gawain was killed. Tennyson does not reproduce Malory's scenes of the lovers' remorse at the end of the story. Tennyson's Lancelot is a generous soul divided between his passionate love of Guinevere and his loyalty to Arthur. The work illustrates the utter impossibility of being able to love Arthur's wife while remaining true to the king. A noble soul unable to resolve tremendous conflicts, Tennyson's Lancelot gains the reader's sympathy. Although it is Arthur whom Tennyson attempts to represent as the ideal knight, the king often fades in glory in comparison to Lancelot.

Tennyson's poem achieved immense success in the Victorian era and was viewed for a long period as the definitive Arthurian epic. Although often interpreted as straightforward allegory, with Arthur as the soul and

Guinevere the flesh, *Idylls of the King* was conceived primarily by Tennyson as a symbolic commentary on the ills of his time. With Lancelot and Guinevere's sin, which undermined the very foundations of honor and virtue of Arthur's realm, Tennyson registered a protest against the growing materialism and sensuality of Victorian society. The importance accorded by Tennyson to the role of Guinevere's sexual transgression in bringing about the destruction of Arthurian world would have lasting effects upon her characterization.

Dissenting voices took up Guinevere's defense almost immediately. Foremost among them was that of William Morris, who gave an unjudgmental portrait of the queen in marked contrast to Tennyson's. Morris was part of a group of Victorian artists who, by locating their stories in the remote past of the Middle Ages, were able to treat matters condemned by Victorian society, like passion and illicit love.[73] Analyzing emotions only barely suggested by Malory, his major source, Morris dedicated two of his four Arthurian poems in *The Defence of Guenevere, and Other Poems* (1858) to the lovers.[74] In the first of the two, "The Defence of Guenevere," the queen, facing imminent burning at the stake for adultery, engages in a monologue in which she attempts to defend herself against accusations of infidelity leveled by Gauwaine. Although she seems at times to sway him to her cause, Gauwaine ultimately leaves her to her fate, from which Launcelot dramatically rescues her at the end of the poem. Guenevere portrays her choice of Lancelot over Arthur as an innocent mistake in which she lost her heart to the more attractive of the two men. Ellen Sternberg comments on Guenevere's morally ambiguous but entertaining argument: "Guenevere paradoxically but most successfully uses the very sensuality of which she has been accused with Launcelot to win over her audience of accusers" (51).[75] If on the one hand Guenevere's moral confusion inadvertently reveals that she is an adulteress, on the other hand her openness convinces the reader of the validity of her passionate attachment to Launcelot.[76]

It is Guenevere's ambivalent attitudes toward both Arthur and Launcelot that come to the fore in Morris's "King Arthur's Tomb." Depicting the final meeting of the lovers at Glastonbury, where the unsuspecting Launcelot falls asleep on Arthur's tomb, the poem has Guenevere examining her feelings toward her former lover, her husband, and divine authority. When Launcelot awakens, she expresses her abiding devotion to him, while reproaching him for his lack of loyalty to Arthur, the greatest king who ever lived. Guenevere is moved to reject her lover Launcelot in favor of Christ, but since she represents the latter as an object of erotic desire her rejection of carnal passion proves unconvincing. In these two poems centered on

Guinevere's emotional reaction to the human tragedy of her situation, Morris is a perceptive precocious analyst of conflicts within the human psyche.

Algernon Charles Swinburne's Arthurian productions comment creatively on Morris's vision of the Arthur-Lancelot-Guinevere triangle. In "The Day Before the Trial" (1857–58), Arthur reflects on the beauty of a wife who was unable to love him. In the short poem (327 lines) entitled "Lancelot," Lancelot is unable to concentrate on the Grail vision because it is obscured by his memory of Guinevere's former beauty, which is in decided contrast to the queen's present "grey cheeks and waning hair." A dialogue between Lancelot and an angel, the poem is an ironic play on Morris's depiction of Galahad's successful Grail quest in his "Sir Galahad: A Christmas Mystery." Although Victorian England approved Tennyson's censure of Guinevere, it is probably Morris's more favorable presentation of the queen's perspective, little appreciated in its time, that has had the greatest influence on the twentieth-century predilection for sympathetic portraits of Guinevere and for psychological analyses of the effects of the adulterous relationship on the three members of the triangle.

TWENTIETH CENTURY

Modern English and American writers have departed from traditional representations of the lovers. T.H. White's Lancelot is a man plagued by guilt. A husband driven criminally insane by his wife's adultery, Walter Percy's protagonist in *Lancelot* evidences a mixture of traits usually associated with both Arthur and Lancelot.[77] Earlier renditions of Guinevere's story moved from Tennyson's mid-nineteenth-century negative judgment of the queen, held personally responsible for the adultery, to Morris's version, which is more favorable to Guinevere.[78] Twentieth-century portrayals of Lancelot and Guinevere are marked by the use of the first person, in which one of the two investigates aspects of his or her involvement in an adulterous relationship.[79]

Edwin Arlington Robinson's narrative poem *Lancelot* (1920) centers on the tragic consequences of Lancelot and Guinevere's love affair, especially the betrayal of the friendship between Lancelot and Gawaine. Robinson describes in detail Guinevere's condemnation to die at the stake and her rescue by Lancelot, the battle on Salisbury Plain, and the last encounter of the lovers. The author departs from the traditional ending in depicting Lancelot as an eternal wanderer. Robinson concentrates on male bonds of friendship disrupted by the intervention of women. When Guinevere is condemned to death, Arthur experiences a conflict between love for his wife and respect for the law. A pacifist, Robinson employed the mythic element associated with apocalyptic destruction to comment on the involvement of the western alliance in World War I.[80] Robinson renders a portrait of a dignified and sympathetic Guinevere in the line inaugurated by Morris. Robinson's heroine is a woman whose search for a simple vision of happiness contrasts with male ideals of honor and glory, which more often than not end in death and destruction.[81]

T.H. White's Arthurian tetralogy, later published as *The Once and Future King* (1958), the source for the hit Broadway musical *Camelot*, contains a masterly reworking of Malory's version of the legend of Lancelot and Guinevere. White depicts Lancelot as an ugly man, reluctant to engage in an affair with Guinevere. His obsession with his appearance symbolically indicates his growing attraction to her and his concomitant feelings of guilt. An important addition to the story is his prizing of his virginity, which he loses to Elaine when he fathers Galahad before succumbing to Guinevere's charms. Undertaking a number of quests in order to avoid Guinevere, he commits adultery with her only after Arthur leaves her in his care when he goes off on foreign campaigns. Lancelot's guilt is heightened by comparison with Arthur's nobility. Like the Arthur of Tennyson's *Idylls*, who magnanimously forgives his wife's adultery, for which she bears the full blame, White also emphasizes the husband's noble stance rather than the unhappy wife's plight. Arthur's kinsmen force him to take action against the adulterous couple, whose indiscretion he had benevolently ignored until that time. In White's version, the adulterous affair is not the cause of the ruin of Arthur's kingdom; it is rather the fact that it is ruled by Might rather than Right. A pacifist like Robinson, White composed a tetralogy that registered a protest against involvement in World War II.

Arguably the most original adaptation of Lancelot material in the modern era, Walker Percy's *Lancelot* (1978) enlists the Arthurian myth to contrast the search for an unholy Grail undertaken by Lancelot Lamar with the quest for a true Grail by his best friend and priest, Percival. The novel consists of a dialogue between the two men after Lancelot, having learned that his child was fathered by another man, kills several people, including his adulterous wife and her lover. Locked away in an institution for the insane a year after the crime, Lancelot pronounces a lengthy confession to Percival. His narrative changes both the teller and the listener as each experiences a crisis of self-consciousness that ultimately embodies an attempt to understand oneself and the world through dialogue with another person. Percival is the double of Lancelot's true self, the inner part of him that does not correspond to his hardened self-image. In the final exchange between the two men, Percival succeeds in making the notion of love as sacrifice and suffering impinge on Lancelot's consciousness, causing Lancelot to forgo his despair and hatred. Seeing the cynical part of himself reflected in Lancelot, Percival reasserts his commitment to the priesthood. Percy introduces major changes into the tradition: Lancelot is in many ways an Arthur figure who avenges himself on an adulterous wife who, unlike Guinevere, is not barren; Lancelot survives the final conflagration, brought about by his own hand, to tell his own story. Although Percy's novel departs in many points from the original legend, it presents a fascinating transposition of the Grail quest into the realm of modern psychology.

John Ciardi's poem "Launcelot in Hell" (1961; Lupack, ed., *Modern Arthurian Literature*, 457–59) also makes use of the first-person viewpoint to give an inside view of the Arthurian tragedy. In a stunning variation on the traditional story, it is Lancelot rather than Mordred who kills Arthur in a bloody combat on the battlefield. Covered with wounds and dismayed at the human cost of his victory, Lancelot returns to celebrate his love for Guinevere, only to be greeted by a nun who no longer returns his passion. In a novel play on many of the poem's sources, the protagonist ends up repudiating the woman who is not his equal in passion, as well as the moral codes that would deny earthly pleasure in the hope of an afterlife. In the poem's conclusion, Lancelot, reflecting on his recent encounter with Arthur in light of his disappointing reunion with Guinevere, takes pleasure in the knowledge that he has met his match at least on the battlefield, if not in bed. With the poem's obvious allusion to the *Inferno*, Ciardi, the author of a respected translation of Dante's masterpiece, multiplies the ironies in the narrator's final stance.

Modern poets tend to follow Morris's lead in letting Guinevere speak for herself, either to plead in her own defense or to provide a critical view of her past actions. In the American poet Sara Teasdale's "Guenevere" (1911), the first-person speaker complains of the social opprobrium that "branded [her] for a single fault." Her memories of Lancelot grow bitter because his love was the cause of her fall from her lofty moral position of queen. She laments: "I was a queen, and he who loved me best / Made me a woman for a night and day, / And now I go unqueened forevermore" (Lupack, ed., *Modern Arthurian Literature*, 359–60).

It is the queen's reactions following the deaths of Arthur and Lancelot that John Masefield recounts in "Gwenivere Tells" (1928) and "The Death of Lancelot as Told by Gwenivere" (1928; Lupack, ed., *Modern Arthurian Literature*, 441–45). In the first, Gwenivere (Guinevere) tells of Lancelot's delivery to her convent of a withered olive spray that he had gathered on a pilgrimage to the Holy Land with the message that he hoped it would bring her as much peace as it had brought him. Yet neither these pious sentiments, nor her sorrow at Arthur's death, nor her subsequent vows of chastity, are powerful enough to quell her passion for Lancelot. Gwenivere's love for Lancelot again appears as a manifestation of the life force in the second poem. Escaping from the convent upon hearing that Lancelot is dying, she, like Iseut, runs to join her lover. Arriving too late to speak to him before he expires, she expresses her undying love for Lancelot in the remainder of the poem.

Wendy Mnookin is another poet to give the queen a voice in her 1987 "Guenever Speaks" (which is divided into two poems in her cycle *Guenever Speaks*, published in 1991; Lupack, ed., *Modern Arthurian Literature*, 483–88). Mnookin's original contributions are framed in quotations from Malory, the first recounting how Guenever did penance at Almesbury after Arthur's death, the second telling of her wish, uttered just prior to her death, never to see Lancelot again. In the first part of Mnookin's addition, "Guenever Retreats to Almesbury," Guenever tells of the physical toll taken by the conflict between her feelings of guilt in Arthur's death and her love for Lancelot: unable to sleep or eat properly, she grows thin and weary. In the second, the former queen explains to two other nuns why she cannot bear to see Lancelot again: to lose him yet a second time would be unbearable. Mnookin manages to maintain Guenever's dignity while establishing her as a flesh-and-blood person much like us.

Contemporary writers tend to present sympathetic portraits of the queen, a remarkable development given her traditional representation as adulteress, traitor, and cause of the destruction of the Round Table.[82] The favorable view of Guinevere began with a desire to find excuses for her faults. Although Rosemary Sutcliff's *Sword at Sunset* (1963) is told from King Artos's point of view, the author takes into account the loneliness and isolation that led Queen Guenhumara to begin an adulterous affair, but here her lover is Bedwyr (Bedivere) rather than Lancelot.[83] Composed of *The Crystal Cave* (1970), *The Hollow Hills* (1973), and *The Last Enchantment* (1979), Mary Stewart's Merlin trilogy also has an engaging Guinevere begin a liaison with Bedwyr. (In giving Guinevere to Bedwyr, both Sutcliff and Stewart are reacting to the fact that Lancelot is not only a foreigner but a later addition to the Arthurian story.) Stewart attributes the queen's major flaws of shyness and insecurity to the sense of dependency fostered by the patriarchal society in which she was raised.[84] Thomas Berger's *Arthur Rex* (1978) suggests that Guinevere seduced Lancelot in an effort to obtain the power that was denied her in the Middle Ages.[85]

Parke Godwin's novels establish Guinevere in an even more positive light. Although the title of his first novel, *Firelord* (1980), refers to Arthur,

Godwin gives equal attention to Guinevere, Arthur's equal in educational background and strength of character. The inheritor of a matriarchal tradition in *Firelord*, in its sequel, *Beloved Exile* (1984), she becomes a powerful ruler in her own right after Arthur's death at the hands of Mordred, acquiring the strength of character to reign in Arthur's stead during a period as a Saxon slave.[86]

Whereas Godwin never departs from his use of the third person in his positive portrayal of the queen, Gillian Bradshaw was the first novelist to have her tell at least part of her own story. The third novel in her Arthurian trilogy, *In Winter's Shadow* (1982), is narrated in the first person by Gwynhwfar, a character who, according to Barbara Gordon-Wise, "calls into question all our inherited ideas of the traditional Arthurian woman" (*The Reclamation of a Queen*, 134). Bradshaw departs from conventional versions of the Arthurian triangle by diminishing the heroic qualities of Arthur and the queen's lover (here a one-armed Bedwyr) and by distancing Guinevere from responsibility in the destruction of the realm.

In *Guinevere* (1981), *The Chessboard Queen* (1984), and *Guinevere Evermore* (1985), Sharan Newman introduces a number of innovations into traditional representations of Guinevere. Besides being the first novelist to tell Guinevere's story entirely from the queen's point of view, she is the first to treat in detail Guinevere's life before her marriage to Arthur. Since Newman is interested in showing how Guinevere develops from a self-centered and overly protected child into a mature and even altruistic woman, she devotes the first volume of her trilogy to Guinevere's adolescence. Symbol of her desire to live in her own world is Guinevere's involvement with a unicorn that prevents her from entering into more beneficial relationships with other human beings. The unicorn disappears from her life after her wedding. At the beginning of *The Chessboard Queen*, Guinevere, married for five years to Arthur, is vaguely unhappy because she is childless and does not experience sexual satisfaction with her husband. At first disliking Lancelot, she grows to love him, and Arthur, in the hope of winning her back, gives tacit assent to their liaison, an act of generosity that does succeed in bringing Guinevere closer to her husband for a time.

In *Guinevere Evermore*, Guinevere receives some fulfillment as the foster mother of Galahad, fathered by Lancelot with Elaine, whom he mistook for Guinevere. Confronted with several personal crises, she shows an inner strength not previously seen in her character. She stands up to her sadistic second husband, Modred, and risks her own life by nursing others during an outbreak of the plague. In Newman's version of the story, Modred's treachery rather than Guinevere's adultery precipitates the downfall of Arthur's reign. It is her interest in Guinevere's personal evolution as a human being that especially distinguishes Newman from prior novelists; notable also is the care she takes to explore Guinevere's feelings for Arthur and Lancelot, each of whom she loves in different ways.[87]

A second Arthurian triptych centered on the figure of Guinevere followed quickly in Newman's wake. In the first novel of Persia Woolley's trilogy, *Child of the Northern Spring* (1987), Guinevere (Gwenhwyvaer) tells in her own words the story of her betrothal and marriage to Arthur and the establishment of the Round Table. Like Newman, Woolley invents a childhood for the heroine. Woolley's vivid depiction of the tomboy child prepares the way for a mature heroine unafraid to speak plainly and to act on her feelings, a woman able to see her husband's world with critical eyes. In the second part of the trilogy, *Queen of the Summer Stars* (1990), Guinevere grows into her role as co-regent of Camelot. The third piece in the triptych, *Guinevere: The Legend in Autumn* (1993), depicts the tumultuous final years of Arthur's reign.

Woolley devotes even more care than Newman to the feelings that Guinevere, Lancelot, and Arthur have for each other. Cognizant of his own honor and of his close bond with Arthur, Lancelot is responsible for the decision not to consummate his love for Guinevere, a decision that uncharacteristically informs his actions during the major part of the trilogy. Arthur casts an indulgent eye on Lancelot and Guinevere's close relationship. Realizing that Lancelot fulfills a need in her life for "poetry and philosophy" that he has neither the time nor the personal qualifications to satisfy, Arthur prefers to remain ignorant of the true nature of their attachment. Woolley creates characters who are innocent and guilty at different times: whereas Guinevere and Lancelot have not yet consummated their love when they are taken in compromising circumstances, after Guinevere's rescue from burning at the stake, the lovers do experience a romantic idyll together at Joyous Guard. Motivated by an altruistic desire to avoid a destructive civil war, Lancelot and Guinevere decide to part. Guinevere's deep love for Arthur propels her to enter into a bargain with Morgain that requires her to abdicate the throne and retire to a convent. When these noble actions fail to prevent the final lethal meeting between Arthur and Mordred on the battlefield, Guinevere nonetheless honors the terms of her bargain and Lancelot returns to his search for the Grail begun prior to his affair with her.

Some of Woolley's attempts to portray Lancelot and Guinevere as real people torn between altruism and passion are more successful than others. Despite the concern for his "honor" that he has managed to observe scrupulously with Guinevere, Lancelot is tricked into fathering a child by the more manipulative Elaine, undeterred by Lancelot's expressed wishes observed by Guinevere. Similarly, Guinevere departs from her own altruistic stance when confronted by Elaine, who comes to court to gloat over her triumph and humiliate the queen. Exploding in a jealous rage, Guinevere strikes her lover, causing him to leave her presence and fall into a period of temporary madness. Typical of the modern approach is Woolley's exploration of the moral and psychological ramifications of the triangular situation.

Marion Zimmer Bradley's *The Mists of Avalon* (1982) presents a reading of the Arthurian story from the point of view, not only of the queen, but of several of the female characters. Coming upon Lancelet for the first time when she strays from the cloister where she has spent some of her time as a young girl, Gwenhywfar is at first a delicate creature comfortable with the protection afforded by her Christian beliefs. Her experiences, which include a brutal rape by Meleagant and a three-way sexual relationship with Arthur and Lancelet, develop her into a more affirmative and self-aware person. Despite Guinevere's strong attraction to Lancelet, it is Arthur who proposes the liaison to his wife and best friend as a possible way to produce an heir to the throne. Tricked into a forced marriage to Elaine that produces several children before her death, Lancelet endures a long and painful separation from the company of Arthur and Guinevere. Reunited again, Lancelet and Guinevere are caught in compromising circumstances. Although Lancelet's bravery saves the day, the many knights killed in the ensuing fray provoke a rift among Arthur's followers that can never be mended.

Arthur and Morgaine, Arthur's older sister whose inadvertent coupling with him in a Celtic fertility rite had produced Gwydion (Modred), prove to be the dominant forces in Bradley's version of the legend. Gwenhywvar respects and loves the king for his magnanimity toward her and her lover. More important, she realizes that Lancelot would hate her for causing a breach between himself and the king, whose relationship with Lancelot goes far beyond mere chivalric devotion (it even has homosexual overtones). After Guinevere has made her final withdrawal to a convent, Morgaine, Celtic priestess and Great Mother, has the last word in the narrative. In Bradley's novel as in other current versions of the legend, the destructive effect of Guinevere's sexual transgression no longer forms a primary element in her characterization.

The amazing proliferation of literature dealing with Lancelot and Guinevere in modern England and America has not been matched in other countries. In France,[88] Jean-Pierre Le Dantec's *Graal-Romance* ("Grail Romance," 1985) features an older but still dashing Lancelot more intellectual than his predecessors. The most refreshing part of the novel is an excerpt from Guinevere's diary that gives her version of how she fell in love with Lancelot. Supplying insights on scantily treated parts of the legend, such as what went on during Kay's battle with Melegant, this short first-person narrative has the major effect of making the queen's actions and emotions fully intelligible to the reader. Le Dantec thus follows tendencies in modern English and American literature to give Guinevere her say. Romain Weingarten's *Roman de la Table Ronde, ou le livre de Blaise* ("The Romance of the Round Table, or the Book of Blaise," 1983) downplays the importance of the romantic triangle. More traditional in theme and treatment is the contemporary German novel *Lancelot und Ginevra* (1961) by Ruth Schirmer-Imhoff. After centuries of virtual neglect of the legend of Lancelot and Guinevere[89] (perhaps because it was not perceived as being German), contemporary German audiences have expressed a vogue for translations of modern fiction written in English.

VISUAL ARTS

Prior to the advent of the cinema in the twentieth century, the two great heydays of Arthurian topics in the visual arts were the European Middle Ages and England's Victorian era. Since visual remains are unduly subject to the vagaries of war, natural disaster, and vandalism, evidence of the undoubted popularity of Lancelot and Guinevere in the visual arts in the Middle Ages comes down to modern times in greatly reduced number. The earliest known representation of one of the two characters in monumental sculpture appears on the north portal, known as the Porta della Pescheria, of the Cathedral of Modena in northern Italy. Although the Cathedral, one of the masterpieces of Romanesque architecture, was begun in 1099, evidence suggests that the ornamental band, carved in high relief, can be dated to the second quarter of the twelfth century. Scholars agree that it depicts the abduction of Winlogee (probably Guinevere, who occupies the central position in the frieze) and her rescue by a group of knights that does not include Lancelot. Predating any known Arthurian romance, this representation of Guinevere derives from the chronicles or oral tradition. The earliest depiction of Lancelot as lover figures in a carving on a capital of St. Pierre in Caen (ca. 1350), where he is shown crossing the Sword Bridge. This is one of the most frequently seen visual images associated with Lancelot in the Middle Ages.

Written records indicate that only a small part of the entire tradition concerning the two popular characters remains. Large-scale interior decorative programs, similar to "Guenevere's Chamber" at Dover Castle (ca. 1250), once existed.[90] Images of Lancelot and Guinevere grace surviving ivory caskets, combs, and mirror-backs as well as furniture carvings, such as misericords. A late fourteenth-century Italian presentation tray depicting "The Triumph of Venus" places Lancelot (along with Tristan) among the devotees of the goddess of love. These remnants of a much larger corpus indicate that the story of Lancelot and Guinevere provided widespread iconographic motifs in the Middle Ages.

The voluminous Vulgate Cycle, of which the *Lancelot, Queste del Saint Graal*, and *Mort Artu* involve the love of Lancelot and Guinevere, exists in over 180 manuscripts, many of which are illuminated, second only in number to the thirteenth-century *Roman de la Rose*. One of the best-known images in Arthurian art is the first kiss of Lancelot and Guinevere in the Morgan copy[91] of the *Lancelot* proper. Another beautiful rendition of the same image dominates a fifteenth-century luxury manuscript once owned by Jean, duc de Berry.[92] The famous Bonn manuscript of 1286,[93] which includes another three-person representation of the kiss, was the earliest manuscript to include the image.[94]

Not all miniaturists concentrated on Lancelot's role as lover, however; many of the illustrated manuscripts of the Vulgate emphasize instead his position as Grail quester. In the copy of the *Queste* that he executed singlehandedly in Tournai in 1351, the master illuminator Piérart dou Tielt shifts the center of interest from Lancelot as representative of worldly chivalry in the first miniature to his son, Galahad, a Christologic figure, in the second and third miniatures.[95] The opposition between Galahad's spiritual chivalry and Lancelot's profane chivalry established in the iconographic program was meant to promote reflection on questions of current ecclesiastical debate. Distinguishing features of the manuscript are an extraordinary depiction of the Grail mysteries (the Christ child appears in the Grail) and abundant use of the marginal grotesques for which the Flemish school of illumination was renowned.

European countries besides France and francophone Flanders produced manuscripts illustrating stories of Lancelot and Guinevere. Whereas Flanders was known for its large-scale luxury manuscripts, Germany became a center for popular editions. The illustrations in the *Lanzelet* (dated by the scribe to 1420)[96] are similar to folk art. The many luxurious copies of vernacular versions of the Vulgate Cycle in Italy and Spain borrow from French models.

The popularity of Arthurian subjects continued with the advent of printing in the mid-fifteenth century. The *Lancelot* published by Jean Dupré in 1488 was remarkable for its elaborately detailed woodcut illustrations. The most active illustrator of Arthurian books at the turn of the century, Antoine Vérard, produced two *Lancelot* romances. With small woodcuts at the beginning of each chapter, the *Morte Darthur* printed in 1498 by Wynkyn de Worde (successor to William Caxton) displayed charming illustrations of uneven quality.[97]

From the sixteenth to the mid-nineteenth century, the popularity of Arthurian themes in the visual arts was at a low point. Following their occasional use as political propaganda during the Renaissance, the treatment of all Arthurian legends lapsed into skepticism and parody. Lancelot and Guinevere were virtually nonexistent again in the visual realm until the Victorian era.

Interest in the visual arts underwent a tremendous renewal during the Arthurian revival,[98] with artists providing interpretations of key texts, most notably those of Tennyson, Morris, and Malory. The first artist of this period to employ Arthurian themes, William Dyce, presented an allegorical interpretation of Lancelot's actions in *Generosity: King Arthur Unhorsed, Spared by Sir Lancelot* (1852), one of the frescoes that he designed to decorate the Queen's Robing Room in the new palace at Westminster (begun in 1836). Dyce choose Malory's *Morte Darthur* as the national epic that served as the basis for the allegorical representation of British history in the fresco cycle. Unlike other Pre-Raphaelites who concentrated on Arthurian topics, Dante Gabriel Rossetti, placing a private and personal rather than an ideal vision at the center of the Arthurian world, eschewed Tennyson for the more down-to-earth perspective of Malory. Rossetti's first Arthurian work, his watercolor *King Arthur's Tomb* (1854), is loosely based on Malory's account of the lovers' last meeting. The watercolor insists on the private rather than the public nature of the tragedy: a veiled nun, Guinevere refuses Lancelot's kiss as Arthur, present in effigy, interposes himself between the two former lovers. Disturbing reminders of the past appear in the serpent slithering in the background and in the tomb relief portraying the splendors of Arthur's court, destroyed through their adultery.

Rossetti returns to the private and human dimension of the Arthurian story in two of the murals he designed for the Debating Hall in the new Oxford University Union. Dominating the one completed painting, *Launcelot's Vision of the Sangrael*, is Guinevere's image as she appears to the sleeping Lancelot; her arms are draped over a tree branch from which her body sways erotically. Depicted as the temptress who, like Eve, necessitates Christ's sacrifice on the cross, her sexual transgression likewise brings about her own destruction. For Rossetti, carnal love was an integral part of human nature rather than a fault; human beings were incapable of being anything but human.[99] Rossetti provides a commentary on Malory that anticipates Freud's twentieth-century insights on civilization and its discontents:

if, as Malory had intimated, repression and/or sublimation of sexual desire was a necessary component of civilized life, these two psychological mechanisms exacted a heavy toll on the human psyche.

Guinevere is again the focus of the planned second painting, *Sir Launcelot in the Queen's Chamber*, extant today only in a pen-and-ink drawing. The work captures the feeling of panic experienced by the lovers as events lead inexorably to the downfall of the Arthurian realm. At the center of the composition, Guinevere clutches her throat as if to stifle a scream. On the left, Launcelot prepares to defend himself against Mordred and Agravaine's men, who gather noisily outside the window. Launcelot and Guinevere's seeming imprisonment in the claustrophobic chamber is expressive of their ensnarement by passion in a fatal situation.

A woman dominated William Morris's one completed painting as well as his poems. His wife, Jane Burden, served as the model for his *Queen Guenevere* (1858, also known as *La Belle Iseult*). As a self-contained, brooding beauty, Morris's queen recalls Rossetti's. Exhibiting a woman consumed by her own private vision, Morris's mood painting is an apt metaphor for extreme tendencies in the Pre-Raphaelite group of artists and writers.

One of the most important artists of the late Arthurian revival was James Archer, who made several paintings of Lancelot and Guinevere, including *Sir Lancelot and Queen Guinevere* (1864), which represents the two lovers as they had been described by Tennyson. Working in the wake of Dyce and the Pre-Raphaelites, Archer drew his inspiration from Malory as well as from Tennyson. In sculpture, Thomas Woolner's half-life-size marble statue *Guinevere* (1872) captures the dignity of Tennyson's character.[100] Usually taking their cue from developments in literature, artists of the Arthurian revival found in Lancelot and Guinevere a fertile ground for interpretation.

As in medieval manuscript books, Lancelot and Guinevere occupied a prominent place in printed book illustration. The Moxon Tennyson initiated a vogue of illustrations of Arthurian subjects. A collection of early poems illustrated by artists chosen by the writer, it was published by Edward Moxon in London in 1857 under the title *Poems*. In 1874, Julia Margaret Cameron undertook a series of photographs at the request of her close friend Tennyson. The first volume of her two-volume gift book, *Illustrations to Tennyson's "Idylls of the King" and Other Poems* (1875) contains subjects from the *Idylls* such as the famous "Parting of Lancelot and Guinevere," which was reproduced on the cover of *Harper's Weekly* for September 4, 1877.

The latent eroticism of the Arthurian legend found its fullest expression in the work of Aubrey Beardsley. In the years 1893–94 Beardsley worked on the illustrations of an edition of the *Morte Darthur* published by John Dent. Its richly embellished pages reproduced the feel of an elaborately illustrated medieval manuscript. With his effeminate men and dominant women, Beardsley ultimately created a vision that ran counter to the original spirit of the Arthurian revival. In the words of Debra N. Mancoff, "In his bizarre evocations and exotic fantasies Beardsley charted the demise of Victorian aspiration as a descent into decadence in medieval guise" (264).

In the set of drawings that she designed for the 1904 publication of William Morris's *Defence of Guenevere, and Other Poems*, Jessie M. King restores a touch of innocence to Beardsley's decadently rendered queen. As in Morris's poem, Guenevere dominates each of King's five pictures of her. The first in the series, "She Threw Her Wet Hair Backward from Her Brow," introduces a romantic figure: a long, lithe woman reminiscent of Jane Burden exhibits a magnificent mane of wavy hair. The Victorian era will be remembered for some of the most striking visual renderings of Guinevere.

Notable for his depiction of tales of Arthur and the Round Table is the American illustrator Howard Pyle (1853–1911). Among his other works, the "father of American illustration" executed *The Story of Sir Launcelot and His Companions* (1907) in a manner reminiscent of Beardsley. Despite figures like Pyle, twentieth-century book illustration has never attained the heights of the previous century, in large part because the Arthurian legend is no longer a national preoccupation as it had been in the Victorian era.[101]

FILM

In the twentieth century, the cinema has become the locus of greatest experimentation with Arthurian themes. American audiences were introduced to cinematic versions of Lancelot material in 1910 with *Lancelot and Elaine*, a free adaptation of Tennyson's poem from *Idylls of the King*. In *The Knights of the Round Table* (1953), a Hollywood extravaganza starring Robert Taylor as Lancelot and Ava Gardner as Guinevere, Lancelot is represented as foreign and a bit exotic, which harks back to his origins as a Fair Unknown. The movie presented the unusual ending of Lancelot's return to defeat Mordred. *The Sword of Lancelot* (British title: *Lancelot and Guinevere*) appeared in 1963. Directed by and starring Cornel Wilde, the film, emphasizing the tragic consequences of the love affair, lends particular weight to Lancelot's frustration with Guinevere's decision to enter a convent after Arthur's death. A great commercial success, *Camelot* (1967), based on the Lerner and Loewe Broadway play adapted from T.H. White's *The Once and*

Future King, starred Richard Harris and Vanessa Redgrave. Concentrating on the ill-fated love of Lancelot and Guinevere, the film came to symbolize the failings as well as the idealism of the Kennedy era.[102]

Although some have criticized it as a highly self-conscious piece of cinematography, many consider Robert Bresson's *Lancelot du Lac* (1974) to be the most original and powerful cinematographic retelling of the story of Lancelot and Guinevere. Winner of the 1974 International Critics Prize at the Cannes Film Festival, the film captures the sense of desolation felt by Arthur's knights after their return from their unsuccessful campaign to find the Grail. Torn between his love for Guinevere and his loyalty to Arthur, Lancelot is the focus of a world from which all former idealism has departed. Bresson introduces a final twist to the story when he has Lancelot die on the battlefield with his gaze uplifted toward Heaven and Guinevere's name on his lips. Leaving his audience with accumulated images of empty armor in the final scene, Bresson succeeds in offering a stinging critique of the validity of the Arthurian chivalric code.

The most commercially successful, albeit overly ambitious, English-language rendition of Arthurian themes is John Boorman's *Excalibur* (1981). Benefiting from stunning cinematography and a musical score that includes works by Wagner and Carl Orff as well as original pieces by Trevor Jones, the film attempts to trace the entire evolution of the Arthurian story from the reign of Uterpandragon to Arthur's death at the hand of his incestuous offspring, Mordred. With a screenplay adapted from Malory by Rospo Pallenberg, the film version has the adulterous longings of Lancelot and Guinevere form the centerpiece of a universe undermined from its very beginnings by illicit love. Despite the emphasis on the consequences of Lancelot and Guinevere's adulterous union, the distinguishing feature of the film proved to be the "commanding performance" by Nicol Williamson as Merlin (Lacy and Ashe, *The Arthurian Handbook*, 281).

First Knight (1995) provides a happy ending to the famous love triangle. Julia Ormond is the self-controlled Guinevere who, despite her resolve to remain faithful to vows made to Arthur (played by Sean Connery), cannot control her deepening attraction to Lancelot. In appearance an irreverent wanderer adept at swordplay, Lancelot (played by Richard Gere) is a man marked by witnessing the murder of his parents. Always turning up unexpectedly to rescue Guinevere, Lancelot deserves Guinevere's love in a way that the aging and ineffectual Arthur does not. When Arthur is killed by his enemies, Lancelot and Guinevere are free to marry and reign over Camelot. This version of the story is remarkable for its absence of adultery: Although Arthur is saddened by the lovers' unavoidable passion for each other, they never in fact consummate their love before his death. While making the outcome of the tale more acceptable to conventional tastes, *First Knight* trivializes its essential dilemmas.

CONCLUSIONS

Although extending its appeal far and wide, the story of Lancelot and Guinevere was especially appreciated in medieval France and England and Victorian England. From its inception, the legend opposed the private and public domains: an overwhelmingly passionate love that promised personal happiness came into irrevocable conflict with the common good. From the foregoing analysis, it is clear that the key figures in the perpetuation of the story were Chrétien de Troyes, Malory, and to a much lesser extent Tennyson. Creating Lancelot from an agglomeration of ill-defined sources, Chrétien coupled his virtually new character with a queen famous for her adultery. Lancelot and Guinevere's love—a treasonous passion that is paradoxically the most ennobling act on earth—is so great that the lovers are seemingly purified by its force. The many loose ends of Chrétien's narrative called forth interpretative commentary on the part of later writers. Whereas his work failed to predict the future of the relationship within traditional social bounds, others attempted to come to terms with the weight of prior tradition that indicated that Guinevere's adultery would lead to the downfall of the Arthurian world. Drawing much of its inspiration from the *Charrete*, the Prose *Lancelot*, which contains a conspicuous reworking of Chrétien's cart episode placed strategically in the narrative, portrays the love as source of all good; in the two succeeding romances, the *Queste* and the *Mort Artu*, it becomes the source of all evil. The savior of Arthur's kingdom in the *Charrete*, in the prose romance Lancelot is transformed into the greatest threat to the kingdom's stability.

The *Morte Darthur*, Malory's innovative reworking of French and English models, transforms the Lancelot and Guinevere story into a study of secular chivalry. In his attempt to integrate social and romantic concerns, Malory downplayed the sexual component of the tale. In setting forth a social ethic, he redefined the place of love in the moral order. He also touched upon a problem that would preoccupy the modern mentality: how much repression and/or sublimation of natural impulses is necessary to maintain civilization?

The Victorians turned to Malory for models of ethical behavior. Interpreting the legend of Lancelot and Guinevere in clear-cut moral terms, Tennyson's monolithic voice was questioned by the Pre-Raphaelites, who used the story to subject the benefits of civilization to serious scrutiny and to probe the inner recesses of the human psyche. Twentieth-century inter-preters would continue to use the time-honored tale of adulterous passion to investigate visions both public and private. Psychological analyses come to the fore in the modern era, when authors choose more often than not to tell the story from the point of view of one of the characters.

THE CONTENTS OF THIS VOLUME

This volume is composed of five original essays—by Bart Besamusca, Jane Burns, Elspeth Kennedy, Alison Stones, and Muriel Whitaker—and eleven reprinted articles, one of which is translated into English for the first time. In bringing together essays on Lancelot and Guinevere, I have privileged those studies that deal with the character of the two lovers. In contrast to scholars who study Tristan and Iseut, critics dealing with Lancelot and Guinevere tend to give greater emphasis to one of the two characters: my introduction details how throughout the long history of the transmission of the legend each character retained a measure of individuality within the unit of the couple. Accordingly, of the sixteen articles in this volume, six con-centrate on Lancelot, seven on Guinevere, and three give more or less equal weight to each character.

The essays collected in this volume begin with Derek Brewer's "The Presentation of the Character of Lancelot: Chrétien to Malory." Brewer sketches the treatment of Lancelot from his possible origins in Celtic myth to Malory. Although his emphasis is on Malory's hero, Brewer illuminates stages in Lancelot's development, especially the contribution of Chrétien, who brought the character of Lancelot to light from some nebulous mate-rial that also spawned other characters. In the *Chevalier de la Charrete*, Chrétien employed the figure of the Fair Unknown to characterize a hero who never ceased to tease the imagination of medieval poets and whose na-ture continues to elude modern critics. Chrétien's enigmatic hero provided the material for much of the *Lancelot-Graal*, the most influential Arthurian work of the thirteenth century. Malory went on to readapt this same Arthurian material in his *Morte Darthur*. According to Brewer, this work, instead of constituting a tragedy of character, alerts the reader to the inter-play of arbitrariness and design in human existence. Brewer explains the inconsistencies in Malory's depiction of Lancelot by showing that the au-thor was more interested in the moral and social implications of plot than in the naturalistic portrayal of character more typical of the modern novel. Although Malory continued Chrétien's concern with the self-contradiction inherent in Lancelot's relationship with Arthur, he, unlike Chrétien, did not avoid following it to its logical, destructive conclusion.

James Schultz argues that Ulrich von Zatzikhoven was another author who used the figure of Lancelot to illustrate something other than naturalistic concerns. In *"Lanzelet: A Flawless Hero in a Symmetrical World,"* Schultz shows that Ulrich introduced a static, ideal protagonist into German Arthurian literature. Lanzelet differs from such characters as Erec, Iwein, and Parzival, who have to atone for a mistake. Unlike the asymmetrical, bipartite narratives associated with these evolving heroes, *Lanzelet* possesses a symmetrical pattern that lacks significant character development. Consonant with this static design, Ulrich introduced a regard for political stability that had marked earlier historically oriented tales. Lanzelet, the ideal knight, later becomes the ideal king.

From Schultz's study of Lanzelet as the static German hero, the essays move to a consideration of Lancelot's paradoxical nature in Chrétien's romance. Both Joseph J. Duggan and Norris J. Lacy (*The Craft of Chrétien de Troyes*) have suggested that Chrétien intentionally left his *Chevalier de la Charrete* ambiguous. In "An Interpreter's Dilemma: Why Are There So Many Interpretations of Chrétien's *Chevalier de la Charrete?*," Matilda Bruckner, in examining the particularly obscure Immodest Damsel episode, explores how and why the *Charrete* invites multiple interpretations. This scene of the testing of Lancelot involves the problem of interpretation, which boils down to the even thornier problem of determining truth itself. Chrétien never resolves the tension between competing value systems in the *Charrete*. Involved in an adulterous relationship with his liege lord's wife, ultimately an act of treason, Lancelot becomes, because of the very depth of his devotion to the queen, the savior of her husband's kingdom. Good and evil in the public and private domains are irretrievably combined. The unresolved paradoxes in Lancelot's character provide ample material for reflection by later medieval and more recent writers.

Elspeth Kennedy's "The Figure of Lancelot in the *Lancelot-Graal*," is the first of three articles to treat the Prose *Lancelot* and its vernacular adaptations. Elspeth Kennedy considers the centrality of Lancelot to the vast cyclical compilation of the *Lancelot-Graal*. The tales of other illustrious Arthurian knights are subordinate to his own; we are told Lancelot's entire life history from birth to death. His story develops themes associated with the romance tradition in general and with earlier Lancelot material in particular: the relationship between love and prowess and the making of a name. His reputation as the best knight in the realm pales in the *Queste del Saint Graal*, in which the negative aspects of his love for Guinevere come to the fore. The reader is asked to reassess his character in light of the new values represented by the Grail. Although the events and commentary given in the

Queste put into question the romance conventions that had prevailed in the earlier parts of the cycle, Lancelot's failure as Grail seeker is accorded significance here by his position as father of Galahad, who does succeed in the quest. With Galahad's death prior to the opening of the *Mort Artu*, Lancelot's love for Guinevere acquires even greater destructive potential. Parallels with the legend of Tristan and Iseut put a new accent on the conflict between feudal loyalties that eventually leads to the destruction of the kingdom. In conclusion, Kennedy argues for a multivalent reading of the love of Lancelot and Guinevere that takes into account its glories as well as its limitations in a Christian system.

Both Elspeth Kennedy and Bart Besamusca attempt to come to grips with the thorny problem of the incorporation of the already ambiguous characters of Lancelot and Guinevere within narrative cycles. Since the phenomenon of cycle formation implies the attempt to integrate individual parts of a story within a whole, the logic of the individual tales is often at odds with that of the total narrative. The differing preexistent portraits of Lancelot and Guinevere contribute to the depiction of figures who show inconsistencies over the course of an entire cycle.[103]

In "Lancelot and Guinevere in the Middle Dutch *Lancelot* Compilation," Besamusca explores the character of Lancelot and Guinevere in the Middle Dutch *Lancelot-Compilatie*. In the textual space of the manuscript codex, the compiler has placed ten Middle Dutch verse romances, of which three are adaptations in verse of the French *Lancelot-Graal*. The compiler produces a compendium of the story of the Arthurian universe including an expanded version of the love of Lancelot and Guinevere. Unique to this manuscript, the *Lanceloet en het hert met de witte voet* is a tale in which Lancelot still loves Guinevere, but his love for her no longer provides the inspiration for all his acts. The adapter implies that Lancelot's exploits have lost much of their former glory, since Gauvain has to win battles for Lancelot and free him from a commitment to marry another powerful queen. One of the verse romances chosen for this collection is the *Ridden metter mouwen*, a second romance in which Lancelot's love for Guinevere does not entirely motivate his behavior; on the contrary, his acts even expose her to danger. If some of the verse romances added by the compiler to the core texts of the adaptations from the French prose cycle continue the criticism of Lancelot and Guinevere's relationship found in that cycle, other choices contribute to a more positive view of Lancelot's dedication to the queen. In his attempt to give a complete story of Arthurian knighthood, the compiler rounds off many of the apparent inconsistencies in the prose and verse traditions.

Alison Stones's essay, "Illustrating Lancelot and Guinevere," returns us to a consideration of the scene of Lancelot and Guinevere's first kiss in the Prose *Lancelot*, viewed ambiguously by medieval illuminators as well as by Dante. Examining representations of the kiss and the consummation of Lancelot and Guinevere's adultery in manuscripts of the Prose *Lancelot*, Stones tries to explain why these two scenes receive relatively little illustration in the extensive corpus of illuminated manuscripts of this work, even though the image of Lancelot and Guinevere's first kiss portrayed in the Prose *Lancelot* housed in the collection of the Pierpont Morgan Library is undoubtedly among the best-known images in Arthurian art. Drawing on comparisons from the illustration of religious and other secular works of the Middle Ages, Stones investigates the positive and negative resonances of these two important scenes in several manuscripts of the Prose *Lancelot*.

The next three essays are devoted to modern renditions of the Lancelot and Guinevere story. Muriel Whitaker's piece, "Unifying Makers: Lancelot and Guinevere in Modern Literature and Art," provides an overview of the depiction of the two lovers in contemporary literature and art. As in the Victorian age, twentieth-century attitudes regarding Lancelot and Guinevere expressed in literature and art derive in general from Malory's *Morte Darthur* or Tennyson's *Idylls of the King*. Writers sympathetic to Lancelot exculpate the hero's adultery and disloyalty by using such devices as psychological rationalization, fate, magic, denigration of Guinevere, the exaltation of romantic love, and plot manipulation. When their object is social satire, however, they emphasize character flaws. Whitaker provides an analysis of a number of texts, some of which, for reasons of space, I do not treat in this introduction: Chester Keith's *Queen's Knight* (1920), Lord Ernest Hamilton's *Launcelot: A Romance of the Court of King Arthur* (1926), Peter Vansittart's *Lancelot: A Novel* (1978), Robertson Davies's *The Lyre of Orpheus* (1988), and Donald Barthelme's *The King* (1990).

Although artists are constrained in time and space in comparison to authors, Whitaker shows how the viewer's recognition of a specific literary source enables the artist to develop visual narrative. Lancelot and Guinevere appear as subjects in decorative programs for architectural settings (e.g., Princeton University Chapel, Pierpont Morgan Library in New York City, King Arthur's Hall at Tintagel), the New Sculpture (e.g., works by Frampton and Reynolds-Stephens), book illustration (e.g., Jessie M. King, Charles Gere, Howard Pyle, Arthur Rackham, N.C. Wyeth), and in drawing and painting. Lancelot and Guinevere were central to the expression of moral and spiritual concepts related to the Catholic beliefs of the most important Arthurian painter of the past fifty years, David Jones.

In Walker Percy's *Lancelot* (1977), the two male protagonists' search for identity is expressed in terms of the Arthurian legend. John Bugge's article, "Arthurian Myth Devalued in Walker Percy's *Lancelot*," examines how myth functions as a source of illusion in the novel. Percy's narrator, Lancelot Lamar, casts himself as various participants in the Grail quest in order to obscure rather than to clarify a true assessment of who he is and the crimes that he has committed. His interlocutor, Harry Percival, at once priest and psychiatrist, is engaged in a search for a more positive Grail. Besides the medieval quester whose name he bears, Percival is an avatar of Percy the author and reader. The answers Harry Percival receives to the probing questions he directs to "Lance" cause him to undergo a personal transformation over the course of the narrative. The string of affirmations with which he counters Lancelot's nihilistic soliloquy conveys a note of hope to the final pages of the novel.

In "Lancelot's Last Metamorphosis," Jean-Marcel Paquette attempts to identify the sources of Robert Bresson's film *Lancelot du Lac*. Paquette believes the major one to be the *Mort Artu*, the final volume of the *Lancelot-Graal*. Paquette goes on to examine how the filmmaker adapts his source. In accordance with his typically ascetic, "Jansenist" approach, Bresson reduces his use of his source to the bare bones of the story. Bresson combines the two main themes of the *Mort Artu*, the overpowering force of love and the decline of the glory of Arthur's court. The film opens with Lancelot returning from battle in defeat. The understanding dawns slowly on him that his adulterous love for Guinevere not only is at the root of this particular failure, but will eventually cause the downfall of his entire chivalric universe. Paquette then examines Bresson's omissions from and additions to his medieval source. In conclusion, Paquette mentions two minor borrowings, one from the troubadour Bertrand de Born, and the other from a poem on Lancelot by the early twentieth-century writer Louis Aragon.

Our group of seven essays on Guinevere comprises five studies of the character in the Middle Ages and two in modern times. As others have pointed out in their studies of Lancelot, with Guinevere Chrétien also fleshed out the portrait of an intriguing figure from meager background material. In "The Character of Guinevere in the Arthurian Romances of Chrétien de Troyes," Peter Noble argues that Chrétien took very little of his character of Guinevere from the sources at hand. In all his other romances besides the *Conte du Graal*, Guinevere is a sympathetic character, often assuming a warm-hearted, maternal attitude toward others at Arthur's court. In *Perceval*, Noble finds her colorless but of irreproachable conduct. Noble attributes her reduced role in the romance to the fact that Chrétien was no longer writing for a court governed and peopled by intelligent women. According to Noble, it is in the *Charrete* that Guinevere becomes downright unattractive. He agrees with the oft-expressed belief that Marie de Champagne forced Chrétien to portray the queen as a calculating adulteress in order to illustrate the code of "courtly love" popular at the time. Noble concludes that within constraints that made Chrétien uncomfortable, the medieval author did a fine job of depicting a passionate woman determined to control the actions of her lover according to prescribed rules of courtly behavior.

In "Guinevere: A Re-Appraisal," Susann Samples examines conflicting attitudes concerning Guinevere's adultery in four texts. In contrast to the dominant tradition represented by Geoffrey of Monmouth's *Historia* and Chrétien de Troyes's *Charrete*, in Hartmann von Aue's *Erec* and Wolfram von Eschenbach's *Parzival* Guinevere is a good and faithful wife. Either because of ignorance of the *Charrete* or as a result of deliberate choice, the German writers had Guinevere conform to a German model of female acquiescence. Their depiction of Arthur's queen as a devoted and passive consort did not find much assent outside of their own national borders. It was the portrait of Guinevere given in the British and French traditions that captured popular imagination.

In "Desire, Meaning, and the Female Reader: The Problem in Chrétien's *Charrete*," Roberta L. Krueger studies Guinevere in relation to all the other female figures in the romance: Chrétien's patroness Marie de Champagne, other female characters, and female audiences both inside and outside the fictional work. Krueger sees the clerkly writer Chrétien as undermining supposed female power and authority. Even at the height of Guinevere's domination of Lancelot, for example, when she refuses to be grateful for all he has done for her, Chrétien trivializes her response to Lancelot and sets her up to function as the obstacle necessary to motivate male desire rather than as an independent agent. In the romance's concluding scene, Godefroy de Leigny, the continuator of Chrétien's unfinished narrative, reduces Guinevere to the level of a passive spectator at the final tournament, thereby nullifying the earlier threats posed by her dominant personality and her sexuality. In the final collaboration established between two male clerks, the resisting female subject vanishes from the text. Krueger ends her article by expressing her hope that the female reader outside the text understands and opposes what has been done to the female presence within the work.[104]

In "Which Queen? Guinevere's Transvestism in the French Prose *Lancelot*," Jane Burns raises directly the question of Guinevere's problematic identity. The French Prose *Lancelot* stages an issue that is central to current feminist debate: how is female identity constructed? Drawing on the work of contemporary feminist theorist Marjorie Garber, along with the performance theory of Judith Butler, Burns charts the ways in which this thirteenth-century Arthurian tale of heroism and adultery asks explicitly and repeatedly, "Who is Guinevere? How can we know, categorize, and define her?"

Numerous are the instances in the Prose *Lancelot* when Guinevere occupies male and female positions at once. What is the significance of these moments when Guinevere plays a male role? Is she simply a woman temporarily cross-dressed? Or is there something more fundamentally ambiguous about the nature of Guinevere's identity that calls into question the very categories of femaleness and maleness in this romance? Exploding convenient gender definitions, Burns contends that Guinevere's representation contributes to the questioning of fixed gender identities that characterizes the narrative.

Guinevere's metaphorical cross-dressing is an example of what Marjorie Garber calls the "transvestite effect," a phenomenon that challenges the foundations of the binary categories that purport to distinguish male from female. Based on Lacan's distinction among "having," "being," and "seeming," transvestism is an indeterminate state of "seeming" that calls into question the most basic cultural assumptions about sex and gender. In imitating gender, transvestism implicitly reveals the imitative and thus contingent structure of gender. Burns maintains that in the Prose *Lancelot* the figure of Guinevere functions as a locus of displacement between the categories of male and female, thus revealing the constructed nature of gender roles in the work.

In "Recovering Malory's Guenevere," Sarah J. Hill takes issue with the traditional view of Malory's Guinevere as the adulterous woman who prevented Lancelot from achieving the Grail quest and precipitated the destruction of Arthur's court. Hill examines Guinevere's position in the Arthurian universe: like Igraine and Iseut, the queen is caught up in the play of conflicting values where the Christian code is secondary to the physical prowess that supports chivalric honor. Subject to male desires and fantasies, women are reduced to objects of exchange between men. Hill shows that Guinevere's adultery, although not totally excusable, is nonetheless an understandable consequence of her arranged marriage to a man whom she does not love. Whereas the blame for the adultery has been placed primarily on Guinevere, Hill contends that it has to be put back on Lancelot himself and on Arthur as the person who wields ultimate power at court. Hill exposes the assumption of Guinevere's guilt as Lancelot's projection of his own transgression upon his partner. While diminishing Guinevere's responsibility for the adultery, Hill explores her positive characteristics as a moral teacher and as a courageous person. She believes that at the end of the work Guinevere becomes the standard-bearer of correct behavior. Refusing to accompany Lancelot and create another court, she rejects the contradictory values of the now-debunked Arthurian court in favor of the Christian morality that she can uphold only within the all-female community of a nunnery. Regaining her position as moral guide, Guinevere incarnates Malory's ideal of consistent Christian conduct.

Elisabeth Brewer's "The Figure of Guenevere in Modern Drama and Fiction" is the first essay in the group devoted to critical studies of modern views of the queen. Brewer documents how the transformations undergone by the figure of Guinevere in the last century reflect our changing notions of sexual morality. Beginning with three plays produced in the years around the turn of the century, Guinevere becomes the dependent woman of late Victorian convention. The disapproval accruing to her adulterous passion tends to diminish, owing to a new tolerance and understanding of the psychology of sexual relations. Rather than being impure, the lovers are seen as searching for a new, unspoiled union with nature, a wish-fulfillment fantasy about romantic love destroyed by the unpleasant realities of the First World War. The work that Brewer examines in greatest detail is T.H. White's *The Once and Future King*. Unlike the earlier plays, the novel portrays the relationship among the three principal characters with true psychological realism. Guinevere is a character with moments of anger and jealousy, increasingly neurotic with age because of her inability to bear Arthur a child.

Brewer characterizes the depiction of Guinevere since 1944 as a mixture of attractive and unattractive features. It has even undergone the influence of the images of the beautiful woman projected by modern media. From the athletic and sexually liberated young woman of the mid-1940s, Guinevere became the superwoman of the 1980s, a career woman able to lead and rule effectively. Other authors show her giving birth to a child. From her survey of Guinevere's portrayal in modern drama and fiction, Brewer concludes that by liberating Guinevere from the ambiguous moral position that she had in the Middle Ages, authors also make her less interesting as a character; moreover, her story loses much of the grandeur of the original medieval fictions.

In "Sharan Newman's Guinevere Trilogy," Harold J. Herman tells how Newman, interested in documenting Guinevere's life from before her first marriage to Arthur to her unhappy second marriage to Modred, traces her evolution from a self-centered adolescent to an altruistic woman who attains some level of self-knowledge. According to Herman, Newman is part of a growing number of contemporary writers who create sympathetic portraits of Guinevere, a difficult task when one considers that she has traditionally been charged with causing the destruction of the Arthurian universe through adultery and treason. Like numerous other twentieth-century writers, Newman accomplishes her rehabilitation of the queen by shifting the responsibility for the downfall of Arthur's realm from her adulterous relationship with Lancelot to other causes, in this case Modred's treachery.

The story of Lancelot and Guinevere remains particularly viable in the late twentieth century because each character has managed to retain a measure of individuality over the course of the long history of the legend. Guinevere had enjoyed an independent existence before Chrétien matched her with his virtually new character Lancelot in his *Chevalier de la Charrete*. Despite their coupling, each character maintained a separate status within Chrétien's romance itself. Although drawing inspiration from the adulterous couple Tristan and Iseut, Chrétien shifted the emphasis from the conflict between the demands of love and social responsibility to the dynamics of the relationship between the two members of the new couple itself. Instead of dying for their love, as do Tristan and Iseut, Lancelot and Guinevere live and grow because of their passion. Numerous are the scenes in the *Charrete* in which one lover evaluates the behavior of the other. These reflections on the part of the two lovers posit an interior life to their partners, who had begun their existence as literary types. The paradoxes of their characters are never fully resolved in the course of the narrative. With the future of the lovers' relationship in suspense at the work's conclusion, Chrétien invites reflection on how Lancelot and Guinevere will bring about further meetings and how they will negotiate problems of their interaction. The separation (whether measured as physical or mental distance or as a temporary problem of communication or misinterpretation of the other's behavior) between Guinevere and Lancelot on the one hand and Guinevere and Arthur on the other, imagined as early in the tradition as Chrétien, prepared the way for the development in later works of an existence for each character apart from that of the couple.

Starting with the revival of interest in Arthurian themes in the nineteenth century, the tradition of the individual standing of each member of the pair prompted the proliferation in the present century of first-person narratives in which either Lancelot or Guinevere ponders the complexities of his or her predicament. Since the new focus on Guinevere's feelings corresponded to the development of the feminist movement, it ultimately led to her treatment as a being with desires and ambitions different from those dictated by a patriarchal society. The tension between each lover as individual and as member of the couple inherent in the Lancelot and Guinevere story since its inception is particularly germane to the treatment of gender relations in the twentieth century. In creating characters who posed interpretive dilemmas for each other as well as for literary critics, Chrétien generated a legacy that has endured to the present day and that shows promise of continued vitality in the future.

ACKNOWLEDGMENTS

I would like to thank the many colleagues whose advice and encouragement helped make this volume possible. On the late vernacular traditions, I consulted Gloria Allaire in Italian, Harvey Sharrer in Hispanic, Susann Samples and James Schultz in German, and Marianne E. Kalinke in Scandinavian. My thanks, too, to JoAnn D. Johnson, who placed some of the articles on diskette. I am grateful to Gary Kuris and Garland Publishing for help on editorial matters. Above all, the assistance of Norris J. Lacy has been invaluable. His knowledge, tact, and unfailing good humor have stood this project in good stead.

NOTES

1. The variants of the characters' names are many: Lancelot (Launcelot, Lanzelet, Lancilotto, Lanseloet, Lançarote); Guinevere (Guenevere, Guenièvre, Gwenhwyfar, Guenhumare, Ganhumara, Ginevra, Ginevara, Ginover, Gaynore, Wehaver, Gwinfreda, Gwenda, Winlogee). When discussing the story of the lovers in a general way, I refer to the characters as "Lancelot," "Guinevere," "Arthur," "Gawain," "Kay," "Mordred," "Tristan," "Iseut," "Mark," "Galahad," but in treating a particular version, I use the form of the name adopted by the author. Whenever necessary to avoid confusion, I indicate the standard reference to the character's name within parentheses: for example, Gwenhwyfar (Guinevere).

2. The earliest extant texts recording the Tristan legend date from the last half of the twelfth century, but an earlier archetype or a collection of tales organized around a thematic nucleus had been put into circulation around 1150.

3. For a cogent discussion of matters of dating *Yvain* and the *Charrete*, see Uitti's chapter on *Yvain* in *The Romances of Chrétien de Troyes*. Uitti bases his judgment on Anthime Fourrier's remark that certain details of the *Charrete* make sense only in reference to events in *Yvain*. Jean Frappier added more evidence to the theory that Chrétien probably first began *Yvain*, interrupted it to start the *Charrete*, finished *Yvain*, and asked Godefroy de Leigny to finish the *Charrete*. See also Baumgartner.

4. Bruckner, *Shaping Romance*, 92.

5. The most complete form of the story is found in Renaut de Beaujeu's *Bel Inconnu* ("Fair Unknown," ca. 1190), where Guinglain, Gauvain's son, is the knight who plays the title role.

6. See Luttrell, *Derek Brewer (at pp. 3–28 of this volume), and *Kennedy (at pp. 79–104 of this volume) on the importance of the Fair Unknown story type.

[*Note*: Authors with asterisks have articles printed in this volume. See Select Bibliography.]

7. Korrel, 6–30; Barber, 6.

8. Gleaned from information in several triads, summaries of Welsh traditions grouped in sets of three, the queen's portrait, discussed on pp. 76–80, is qualified by Korrel as "variegated and puzzling." (For further information on the triads, see Ashe, "Triads.") Although the most important triads are found in manuscripts of the thirteenth, fourteenth, and fifteenth centuries, they contain material that predates Geoffrey of Monmouth. However, it is still an open question whether Guinevere's image as an adulteress was Geoffrey's invention or a detail that he borrowed from oral or written sources. Korrel believes that the story of Guinevere as adulteress was probably a later addition to the oldest stratum of Welsh legends. In triad 80, "The Three Faithless Wives of the Island of Britain," Gwenhwyfar is said to be more blameworthy than three other infamous ladies, including Iseut, because she shamed a better man than any of the others. Korrel contends that the mention of Gwenhwyfar as the fourth character known for her faithlessness was a comparatively late development.

9. Korrel, 84–96, cites three variations on the abduction motif: the abductor is a mortal who kidnaps a neighbor's wife; the abductor is a supernatural being who carries a mortal off to his realm; the abductor is a fairy who returns to claim a fairy whom he has loved in the other world. See also *Derek Brewer.

10. For hypotheses concerning sources for the story of Lancelot and Guinevere in the classical or medieval Latin tradition, see Micha, "Sur les sources de la *Charrette*," and Laurie.

11. Korrel, 81.

12. For other appearances of Guinevere in Welsh literature, see Ford.

13. Korrel, 124.

14. I.D.O. Arnold and M.M. Pelan, eds., *La Partie arthurienne du "Roman de Brut" (Extrait du manuscrit B.N. f. 794)* (Paris: Klincksieck, 1962).

15. "Por la vergoigne del mesfet / Et del pechié qu'ele avoit fet," ("Because of the shame of the misdeed / And of the sin that she had committed").

16. The origin of the name is still a subject of debate. On pp. 11–19 of his introduction to *Lanzelet*, Loomis stated his belief that the character of Lancelot was based on the pagan deity Lluch of the White (?) Hand, who was himself derived from the Irish sun-god Lug or Luch of the Long Hand.

17. "Devant toz les boens chevaliers / doit estre Gauvains li primiers, / li seconz Erec, li filz Lac, / et li tierz Lancelot del Lac." ("Before all the good knights / Gauvain must be the first, / the second Erec, the son of Lac, / and the third, Lancelot du Lac." ll. 1671–74). Unless otherwise noted, all references are to the CFMA editions of Chrétien's romances.

18. In the Prologue to the *Charrete*, Chrétien claims that his patroness Marie de Champagne provided him with the subject matter and overall interpretation of his new romance. The overall interpretation imparted by Marie may well have to do with the innovation of making Lancelot the queen's lover.

19. See *Bruckner.

20. See Diverres and Owen.

21. See *Krueger for a discussion of Guenièvre's contradictory explanations of her behavior.

22. For the controversy surrounding the "two steps" in the manuscript tradition of the *Charrete*, see Hult.

23. The text informs us that Chrétien left the work incomplete and that Godefroy de Leigny supplied a conclusion to the story.

24. Bruckner, *Shaping Romance*, 103.

25. In *Lancelot and the Grail*, Kennedy argues that a noncyclic Prose *Lancelot* (which could also be referred to as the independent Prose *Lancelot*), ending with the death of Galehot, preceded the cyclic version.

26. Although the *Estoire del Saint Graal* ("Story of the Holy Grail") and the *Estoire de Merlin* ("Story of Merlin") were written after these three parts, the two head the sequence in terms of narrative chronology.

27. Lancelot and Genièvre rise in estimation in the cycle in comparison to the radically altered portrait given of Arthur, depicted as irremediably lecherous for the first time in the tradition. Although unaware of what he was doing, Arthur begat Mordred with his half-sister Morgan, an action similar to Lancelot's fathering of Galaad (Galahad). Arthur moreover has sexual relations with Lisanor and the Saxon seductress, Camille. The author further mitigates Lancelot and Genièvre's transgression by having them become lovers for the first time on the same evening that Arthur sleeps with Camille.

28. Galaad was conceived when Lancelot was drugged by Pelles into thinking he was with Genièvre instead of Pelles's daughter.

29. The cycle's conclusion is more open-ended than it might first appear, for the final pages of the *Mort Artu* mention the possible return of Arthur, which constitutes an implicit invitation to later writers to continue recasting the saga of the rise and fall of the Arthurian world.

30. Combarieu claims that Lancelot proves to be a more engaging character than Perceval, the purported protagonist of the *Perlesvaus*.

31. See Busby.

32. The last parts of this work are often referred to as the *Meliadus* and *Guiron* (or *Gyron*) *le Courtois* ("Guiron the Courteous").

33. See Lacy, "Convention and Innovation in *Le Chevalier du Papegau*," and Taylor. Comparisons with the original Lancelot narrative are easily recognizable through allusions to the cart, the perilous bridge, the lady's commands to her beloved to perform ignobly in a tournament, and the night of love, here extended to an entire week of lovemaking.

34. See Kalinke.

35. Samples, "Guinevere: A Germanic Heroine."

36. The German narrative lacks the episode of the Black Cross and several others following the cart scene.

37. See Blamires.

38. As recounted in the Prose *Lancelot*, Guinevere had persuaded her nephew Giomar to leave Morgan after having surprised the two together in bed.

39. Carolyn Dinshaw develops this argument in *Straight Is the Gate: Heterosexual Subjects of Middle English Narrative* (Raleigh: Duke University Press, forthcoming).

40. See App. In the Alliterative *Morte Arthure*, Lancelot's name appears with the alternate spellings Launcelott, Lancelott, Launcelotte, Launcelot, Lawncelot de Lake, and Lawncelott.

41. See App, 43.

42. See App, 31–45. See also Wertime.

43. See App, 45–46.

44. Malory entitled it *The Hoole Book of King Arthur and of His Noble Knyghts of the Round Table*, but it has been referred to as the *Morte Darthur* ever since Caxton, the producer of the first printed edition of the work (a manuscript version also exists), mistook the title of the last tale for that of the entire work.

45. It is now usual to divide Malory's work into eight tales. See Field and Bert Dillon, *A Malory Handbook* (Boston: Hall, 1978) for a discussion of the division of the work into sections by Malory and Caxton. In my treatment of Malory, I use the divisions of the work found in Eugène Vinaver's edition as cited by Dillon on pp. 15–16.

46. See Hartung.

47. Based on the French Prose *Tristan*, the fifth tale takes up about a third of the entire *Morte Darthur*. With the positioning of the Tristan story at the heart of a compilation of tales about Arthur's court, Malory acknowledges the indebtedness of

his romance centered on Launcelot and Gwenyver (as well as prior romances about the lovers) to the Tristan legend.

48. See Ihle, 148.

49. See Wimsatt, 209–13.

50. See Ihle, 148.

51. A late ballad, "Sir Lancelot du Lake," which survives in fragmentary form, is in all likelihood based on Malory.

52. References to Arthurian subjects in late-medieval Scottish literature could be either negative or positive. See Edward Donald Kennedy on this issue.

53. See *Besamusca at pp. 105–124 of this volume for a more complete description of the works in the compilation.

54. Besamusca, "Lanceloet en het hert met de witte voet."

55. Reiss, Reiss, and Taylor, eds., 280.

56. "Lancelot in the Middle Dutch Play Lanseloet van Denemerken."

57. See Kalinke, 99–100 and 206–7.

58. See vol. l of Sharrer, A Critical Bibliography of Hispanic Arthurian Material, for other Hispanic renditions of the Vulgate.

59. Sharrer, "Spain and Portugal," cites David Hook's study that indicates a familiarity with Arthurian names in the northern Hispanic peninsula prior to Geoffrey of Monmouth.

60. Sharrer, "The Acclimatization of the Lancelot-Grail Cycle," 175–79.

61. Sharrer, "The Acclimatization of the Lancelot-Grail Cycle," 184–85.

62. Sharrer, "Spanish and Portuguese Arthurian Literature," and Entwistle.

63. See Gardner.

64. See Gottzmann, 248–53.

65. See Grimbert and Hoffman.

66. See Gardner and Heijkant.

67. See Mazzocco.

68. Ariosto published a series of versions of the work between 1516 and 1532.

69. Whitaker, "Thomas Percy."

70. I limit myself here to dealing with the most significant writers of the Arthurian revival. For a more complete description of the movement in literature and the visual arts, see Mancoff.

71. Tennyson's largely pejorative view of Guinevere does contain some nuances: the author makes it clear that Modred and Arthur both victimize the queen, and Guinevere's love for Lancelot finds its complement in Arthur's devotion to the queen despite her transgressions. See Sylvia.

72. An idyll is "a small picture of a character or of a mood, dominated by a simple emotional impulse." Mancoff, 166.

73. Gordon-Wise, The Reclamation of a Queen, 20.

74. The remaining two poems center on the Grail quest.

75. In Sternberg's view, Guenevere represents the figure of the artist who succeeds in imposing her unique vision of the world on others.

76. See chapter 2 of Silver for a detailed analysis of Guenevere's position in this poem and the following one.

77. Modern writers have produced some unusual variations on the traditional givens of Lancelot's story. In his short story, Lance, Vladimir Nabokov develops the analogy between space exploration and Lancelot's crossing of the Sword Bridge. Nicholas Seare's Rude Tales and Glorious (1983) depicts Lancelot as an emaciated beggar who lives to tell his own tale after having been kept alive for centuries thanks to an enchantment.

78. For reasons of space, I cannot deal with all the anomalous representations of Guinevere in the modern era. To take just one example, in Richard Hovey's verse drama, "The Birth of Galahad," part of an unfinished cycle entitled Launcelot and Guenevere: A Poem in Dramas, Guinevere becomes Galahad's mother.

79. I omit a discussion of Charles Williams, one of the most important twentieth-century interpreters of the Arthurian saga, because he concentrates more on the Grail quest than on Lancelot and Guinevere.

80. See Lagorio.

81. Gordon-Wise, *The Reclamation of a Queen*, 96–98.

82. For some of the more negative portrayals of Guinevere in the modern era, see *Whitaker at pp. 159–180 of this volume. Victor Canning, not discussed by Whitaker, paints the portrait of a promiscuous Guinevere in *The Crimson Chalice* (1978).

83. Gordon-Wise, *The Reclamation of a Queen*, 98–100.

84. Gordon-Wise, *The Reclamation of a Queen*, 100; see 103 for a short discussion of Peter David's *Knight Life*, a modern fantasy that transposes the Arthurian court to Manhattan.

85. Berger portrays Lancelot and Guinevere as lovers who have little enthusiasm for each other; at times disdainful and self-righteous, Guinevere is often unattractive.

86. Gordon-Wise, *The Reclamation of a Queen*, 122–23.

87. Newman introduces the detail that Guinevere was buried at Glastonbury alongside Lancelot instead of Arthur.

88. Jean Cocteau wrote a three-act play entitled *Les Chevaliers de la Table Ronde* ("The Knights of the Round Table," 1937), which ends with the death of Guenièvre and her lover.

89. An exception is the *Lanzelot und Ginevra* (1860) of Wilhelm Hertz.

90. Loomis and Loomis, *Arthurian Legends in Medieval Art*, 5, make reference to a fresco featuring Lancelot in Tamworth Castle in England that was destroyed in 1783 when it was painted over with a coat of whitewash.

91. New York, J. Pierpont Morgan Library, M 805, f. 67.

92. Paris, Bibliothèque Nationale francaise 118, f. 219v.

93. Bonn, Universitätsbibliothek 526, f. 220.

94. See *Stones at pp. 125–158 of this volume for a detailed study of the representations of Lancelot and Guinevere's first kiss.

95. In Paris, Bibliothèque de l'Arsenal, 5218, Piérart's signature is accompanied by the statement that he transcribed, illuminated, and bound the volume (f. 91v.). For a study of the manuscript, see Walters's "Wonders and Illuminations."

96. Heidelberg, University of Heidelberg, Bibliothek Palzgermanden 371; Stones, "Manuscripts, Illuminated," 304.

97. Lacy and Ashe, *The Arthurian Handbook*, 228–31.

98. Although the revival in literature began early in the nineteenth century, the revival in art coincided approximately with the beginning of Queen Victoria's reign (1837–1901).

99. See Mancoff, 159.

100. J. Stephens Thompson executed a standing statue entitled *Guinevere Repentant* in the 1870s.

101. See *Whitaker at pp. 159–180 of this volume for more recent developments in the visual arts.

102. See Harty, "Cinema Arthuriana," *Arthurian Interpretations* 2.1 (Fall 1987), 95–113, for other films in which Lancelot and Guinevere figure incidentally.

103. See in particular Kennedy's contribution to *Cyclification*, ed. Besamusca et al.

104. Krueger has reworked the essay included in this volume in *Women Readers and the Ideology of Gender in Old French Verse Romance* (Cambridge: Cambridge University Press, 1993). In chapter 2, "The Question of Women in *Yvain* and *Le Chevalier de la Charrete*," she enlarges her inquiry to include the *Charrete*'s partner narrative, *Yvain*. Krueger centers her inquiry on two related tendencies in these romances: the displacement of women from the center to the margins of power, and the depiction of female characters and readers as posing dilemmas for courtly society. Krueger concludes that in displacing the female reader in his romances, Chrétien inaugurates a debate on gender roles in literature and in life.

Note: This bibliography does not list primary sources, nor does it include every title cited in notes. Articles designated by an asterisk (*) are reprinted in this volume, some in translation or revised form, as noted.

I. Useful Reference Works

Dictionnaire des Lettres Françaises: Le Moyen Age, ed. Robert Bossuat, Louis Picard Robert, and Guy Raynaud de Lage; rev. ed. by Geneviève Hasenohr and Michel Zink. 1964; Paris: Fayard, 1992.

Lacy, Norris J., Geoffrey Ashe, Sandra Ness Ihle, Marianne E. Kalinke, and Raymond H. Thompson, eds. *The New Arthurian Encyclopedia.* New York: Garland, 1991.

Reiss, Edmund, Louis Horner Reiss, and Beverly Taylor, eds. *Arthurian Legend and Literature: An Annotated Bibliography.* Vol. I: *The Middle Ages.* New York: Garland, 1984.

Sharrer, Harvey L. *A Critical Bibliography of Hispanic Arthurian Material.* 2 vols. London: Grant and Cutler, 1977.

II. Critical Studies

Accarie, Maurice. "Guenièvre et son chevalier de la charrete: L'Orgasme des anges." In *Et c'est la fin pour quoy sommes ensemble: Hommage à Jean Dufournet,* ed. Jean-Claude Aubailly, Emmanuèle Baumgartner, Francis Dubost, Liliane Dulac, and Marcel Faure. 3 vols. Paris: Champion, 1993, III, 45–54.

Adderley, C.M. "Malory's Portrayal of Sir Lancelot." *Language Quarterly* 29 (1991), 47–65.

Adler, Alfred. "A Note on the Composition of Chrétien's *Charrette.*" *Modern Language Review* 45 (1950), 33–39.

App, August J. *Lancelot in English Literature: His Role and Character.* 1929; New York: Haskell House, 1965.

Arden, Heather. "Chrétien de Troyes's *Lancelot* and the Structure of Twelfth-Century French Romance." In *King Arthur Through the Ages,* ed. Valerie M. Lagorio and Mildred Leake Day. 2 vols. New York: Garland, 1990, I, 80–98.

Ashe, Geoffrey. "Triads." In Lacy et al., eds., *The New Arthurian Encyclopedia,* 461–62.

Barber, Richard. *King Arthur: Hero and Legend.* Woodbridge, Suffolk: Boydell, 1986.

Baron, F. Xavier. "Love in Chrétien's *Charrette:* Reversed Values and Isolation." *Modern Language Quarterly* 34 (1973), 377–84.

Barrett, Deborah J. "Discourse and Intercourse: The Conversion of the Priest in Percy's *Lancelot.*" *Critique: Studies in Contemporary Fiction* 23.2 (Winter 1981–82), 5–11.

Baumgartner, Emmanuèle. *Chrétien de Troyes: Yvain, Lancelot, la charrette et le lion.* Paris: Presses Universitaires de France, 1992.

Beattie, Susan. *The New Sculpture.* New Haven: Yale University Press, 1983.

Beltrami, Pietro G. "Lancelot entre *Lanzelet* et *Eneas:* Remarques sur le sens du *Chevalier de la Charrete.*" *Zeitschrift für Französische Sprache und Literatur* 99 (1989), 234–60.

Bennett, J.A.W., ed. *Essays on Malory.* Oxford: Clarendon, 1963.

Benson, C. David. "Gawain's Defense of Lancelot in Malory's 'Death of Arthur.'" *Modern Language Review* 72 (1983), 267–72.

Besamusca, Bart. "*Lanceloet en het hert met de witte voet.*" In Lacy et al., eds., *The New Arthurian Encyclopedia,* 269.

————. "Lancelot in the Middle Dutch Play *Lanseloet van Denemerken*: An Example of Generic Intertextuality." In *The Arthurian Yearbook* 5 (1996), forthcoming.

————, Willem P. Gerritsen, Corry Hogetoorn, and Orlanda S.H. Lie, eds. *Cyclification: The Development of Narrative Cycles in the Chansons de Geste and the Arthurian Romances. Proceedings of the Colloquium, Amsterdam, 17–18 December, 1992.* Amsterdam: Royal Netherlands Academy of Arts and Sciences, 1994.

Bezzola, Reto. *Le Sens de l'aventure et de l'amour.* Paris: La Jeune Parque, 1947.

Blamires, David. "The German Arthurian Prose Romances in Their Literary Context." In *The Changing Face of Arthurian Romance: Essays on Arthurian Prose Romances in Memory of Cedric E. Pickford*, ed. Alison Adams, Armel H. Diverres, Karen Stern, and Kenneth Varty. Cambridge: Brewer, 1986, 66–77.

Bogdanow, Fanni. "Post-Vulgate Cycle." In Lacy et al., eds., *The New Arthurian Encyclopedia*, 364–66.

————. "The Love Theme in Chrétien de Troyes's *Chevalier de la Charrette*." *Modern Language Review* 67 (1972), 50–61.

————. "The Treatment of the Lancelot-Guenevere Theme in the Prose *Lancelot*." *Medium Ævum* 41 (1972), 110–20.

Boos, Florence. "Justice and Vindication in William Morris's 'The Defence of Guenevere.' " In *King Arthur Through the Ages*, ed. Valerie M. Lagorio and Mildred Leake Day. 2 vols. New York: Garland, 1990, II, 83–104.

Brault, Gerard J. "Chrétien de Troyes's *Lancelot*: The Eye and the Heart." *Bibliographical Bulletin of the International Arthurian Society* 24 (1972), 142–53.

————. "Isolt and Guenevere. Two Twelfth-Century Views of Women." In *The Role of Woman in the Middle Ages: Papers of the 6th Annual Conference of the Center for Medieval and Renaissance Studies, State University of New York at Binghamton, 6–7 May, 1972*, ed. Rosmarie Thee Morewedge. Albany: State University of New York Press, 1975, 41–64.

Brewer, Derek. "Malory's 'Proving' of Sir Launcelot." In *The Changing Face of Arthurian Romance: Essays on Arthurian Prose Romances in Memory of Cedric E. Pickford*, ed. Alison Adams, Armel H. Diverres, Karen Stern, and Kenneth Varty. Cambridge: Brewer, 1986, 123–36.

*————. "The Presentation of the Character of Lancelot: Chrétien to Malory." *Arthurian Literature*, III, ed. Richard Barber (Totowa, N.J.: Barnes and Noble, 1983), 26–52 [reprinted at pp. 3–28 of this volume].

*Brewer, Elisabeth. "The Figure of Guenevere in Modern Drama and Fiction." In *Arturus Rex*, II, ed. W. Van Hoecke, Gilbert Tournoy, and Werner Verbeke. Louvain: Louvain University Press, 1987, 478–90 [reprinted at pp. 279–290 of this volume].

————, and Beverly Taylor. *The Return of King Arthur: British and American Arthurian Literature Since 1900* [for 1800]. Cambridge: Brewer, 1983.

Broughton, Panthea Reid. *The Art of Walker Percy.* Baton Rouge: Louisiana State University Press, 1979.

Bruce, James Douglas. *The Evolution of Arthurian Romance: From the Beginnings Down to the Year 1300.* 2 vols. Göttingen: Vanden Hoech & Ruprecht, 1923.

*Bruckner, Matilda Tomaryn. "An Interpreter's Dilemma: Why Are There So Many Interpretations of Chrétien's *Chevalier de la Charrette*?" *Romance Philology* 40 (1986), 159–80 [reprinted at pp. 55–78 of this volume].

————. "*Le Chevalier de la Charrette (Lancelot)*." In *The Romances of Chrétien de Troyes: A Symposium*, ed. Douglas Kelly. Lexington, Ky.: French Forum, 1985, 132–81.

————. *Shaping Romance: Interpretation, Truth, and Closure in Twelfth-Century French Fictions.* Philadelphia: University of Pennsylvania Press, 1993.

*Bugge, John. "Arthurian Myth Devalued in Walker Percy's *Lancelot*." In *The Arthurian Tradition: Essays in Convergence*, ed. Mary Flowers Braswell and John Bugge. Tuscaloosa: University of Alabama Press, 1988, 175–87 [reprinted at pp. 181–192 of this volume].

———. "Merlin and the Movies in Walker Percy's *Lancelot*." *Studies in Medievalism* 2.4 (Fall 1983), 39–55.

Burns, E. Jane. *Arthurian Fictions: Rereading the Vulgate Cycle*. Columbus: Ohio State University Press, 1985.

Busby, Keith. *Gauvain in Old French Literature*. Amsterdam: Rodopi, 1980.

Buschinger, Danielle. "Le personnage de Lancelot dans la littérature allemande du Moyen Age (à l'exception du *Lanzelet* et du *Prosa-Lancelot*)." In *Lancelot: Actes du Colloque d'Amiens des 14 et 15 janvier, 1984, Université de Picardie*, ed. Danielle Buschinger. Göppingen: Kümmerle, 1984, 17–28.

Chandès, Gérard. "Lancelot dans *Excalibur* de John Boormann: L'ombre du roi." In *Lancelot: Actes du Colloque d'Amiens des 14 et 15 janvier, 1984, Université de Picardie*, ed. Danielle Buschinger. Göppingen: Kümmerle, 1984, 29–38.

Christian, John, ed. *The Last Romantics: The Romantic Tradition in British Art, Burne-Jones to Stanley Spencer*. London: Lund Humphries, 1989.

Cherewatuk, Karen. "The Saint's Life of Sir Lancelot: Hagiography and the Conclusion of Malory's *Morte Darthur*." *Arthuriana* 5.1 (Spring 1995): 62–78.

Cochran, Rebecca. "Swinburne's 'Lancelot' and Pre-Raphaelite Medievalism." *The Victorian Newsletter* 74 (1988), 58–62.

Combarieu, Micheline de. "Le Personnage de Lancelot dans le *Perlesvaus* ." In *Lancelot, Yvain, Gauvain (Colloque arthurien belge de Wégimont)*. Paris: Nizet, 1984, 85–112.

Condren, Edmund. "The Paradox of Chrétien's *Lancelot*." *Modern Language Notes* 85 (1970), 434–53.

Cosman, Madeleine Pelner. *The Education of the Hero in Arthurian Romance*. Chapel Hill: University of North Carolina Press, 1966.

Cross, Tom Peete, and William A. Nitze. *Lancelot and Guenevere: A Study on the Origins of Courtly Love*. Chicago: University of Chicago Press, 1930.

Crotta, B. "*Lancelot du Lac*: la guerre, le simulacre de la vertu." *Camera/Stylo 5* (1985), 83–86.

Crowley, J. Donald, and Sue Mitchell Crowley. "Walker Percy's Grail." In *King Arthur Through the Ages*, ed. Valerie M. Lagorio and Mildred Leake Day. 2 vols. New York: Garland, 1990, II, 255–77.

Cugier, A. "*Lancelot du Lac* de Robert Bresson: le Moyen Age révisité ou la dimension tragique du XXe siècle." *Cahiers de la Cinemathèque* 42/43 (1985), 119–24.

Dale, Corinne. "Lancelot and the Medieval Quests of Sir Lancelot and Dante." In *Walker Percy: Art and Ethics*, ed. Jac Tharpe. Jackson: University of Mississippi Press, 1980, 99–106.

Davies, R.T. "Malory's Lancelot and the Noble Way of the World." *Review of English Studies* 6 (1955), 356–64.

Delbouille, Maurice. "Guenièvre fut-elle la seule épouse du roi Arthur?" *Travaux de linguistique et de littérature* 6 (1966), 123–34.

Demaules, Mireille, and Christiane Marchello-Nizia. "Träume in der Dictung: Die Ikonographie des *Lancelot-Graal* (13.–15 Jh.)." In *Träume im Mittelalter, Ikonologische Studien*, ed. Agostino Paravicini Bagliani and Giorgio Stabile. Stuttgart: Belser, 1989, 209–26.

Desmond, John F. "Love, Sex, and Knowledge in Walker Percy's *Lancelot*: A Metaphysical View." *Mississippi Quarterly: The Journal of Southern Culture* 39 (1986), 103–9.

Dinshaw, Carolyn. *Straight Is The Gate: Heterosexual Subjects of Middle English Narrative*. Raleigh: Duke University Press, forthcoming.

DiPasquale, Pasquale, Jr. "Malory's Guinevere: Epic Queen, Romance Heroine and Tragic Mistress." *Bucknell Review* 16 (1968), 86–102.

Diverres, A.H. "Some Thoughts on the *Sens* of *Le Chevalier de la Charrette*." *Forum for Modern Language Studies* 6 (1970), 24–36; rpt. in *Arthurian Romance: Seven Essays*, ed. D.D.R. Owen. New York: Barnes and Noble, 1971, 24–36.

Dornbush, Jean M. *Pygmalion's Figure: Reading Old French Romance*. Lexington, Ky.: French Forum, 1990.

Dover, Carol. "The Split-Shield Motif in the Old French Prose *Lancelot*." *The Arthurian Yearbook* 1 (1991), 43–61.

Draak, Maartje. *De Middelnederlandse vertalingen van de Proza-Lancelot*. Amsterdam: Koninklijke Akademie der Wetenschappen, 1954.

Entwistle, William J. *The Arthurian Legend in the Literatures of the Spanish Peninsula*. London: Dent, 1925; rpt. New York: Phaeton, 1975.

Field, Peter J.C. "Sir Thomas Malory." In Lacy et al., eds., *The New Arthurian Encyclopedia*, 294–97.

Fisher, R.W. "Ulrich von Zatzikhoven's *Lanzelet*: In Search of 'Sense.' " *Archiv für das Studium der Neueren Sprachen und Literaturen* 217 (1980), 277–92.

Ford, Patrick K. "Welsh Arthurian Literature." In Lacy, et al., eds., *The New Arthurian Encyclopedia*, 507–9.

Foulet, Alfred. "Guenevere's Enigmatic Words: Chrétien's *Lancelot*, vv. 211–23." In *Jean Misrahi Memorial Volume: Studies in Medieval Literature*, ed. Hans R. Runte, Henri Niedzielski, and William L. Hendrickson. Columbia, S.C.: French Literature Publications, 1977, I, 175–80.

Fowler, David. "L'amour dans le *Lancelot* de Chrétien." *Romania* 91 (1970), 378–91.

Frappier, Jean. *Amour courtois et Table Ronde*. Geneva: Droz, 1973.

————. *Chrétien de Troyes*. Paris: Hatier, 1957.

————. *Étude sur la "Mort le roi Artu."* 3d ed. Geneva: Droz, 1972.

Freeman, Michelle A. *The Poetics of "Translatio Studii" and "Conjointure": Chrétien de Troyes's "Cligés."* Lexington, Ky.: French Forum, 1979.

Fries, Maureen. "What Tennyson Really Did to Malory's Women." *Quondam et Futurus: A Journal of Arthurian Interpretations* 1.1 (Spring 1991), 44–55.

Fulton, Helen. "A Woman's Place: Guinevere in the Welsh and French Romances." *Quondam et Futurus: A Journal of Arthurian Interpretations* 3.2 (Summer 1993), 1–25.

Gardner, Edmund G. *The Arthurian Legend in Italian Literature*. London: Dent, 1930.

Gauville, H. "Lancelot du sang." *Camera/Stylo* 5 (1985), 100–3.

Gégou, Fabienne. "Lancelot du lac, le chevalier idéal: Confrontation des points de vue de Jean Chapelain en 1647 et du Graal-théâtre en 1978." In *Lancelot, Yvain et Gauvain (Colloque arthurien belge de Wégimont)*. Paris: Nizet, 1984.

Gordon-Wise, Barbara. "Guinevere 3." *Mid-Hudson Language Studies* 11 (1988), 6–11.

————. *The Reclamation of a Queen: Guinevere in Modern Fantasy*. Westport, Conn.: Greenwood, 1991.

Gottzmann, Carola L. *Artusdichtung*. Stuttgart: Metzlersche, 1989.

Gravdal, Kathryn. *Ravishing Maidens: Writing Rape in Medieval French Literature and Law*. Philadelphia: University of Pennsylvania Press, 1991.

Grimbert, Joan. "Translating Tristan-Love from the *Prose Tristan* to the *Tavola Ritonda*." *Romance Languages Annual* 6 (1995), 92–97.

Hardy, John Edward. *The Fiction of Walker Percy*. Urbana: University of Illinois Press, 1987.

Harf-Lancner, Laurence. "Les deux Guenièvre dans le *Lancelot* en prose." In *Lancelot: Actes du colloque d'Amiens des 14 et 15 janvier, 1984, Université de Picardie*, ed. Danielle Buschinger. Göppingen: Kümmerle, 1984, 63–74.

Hartung, Albert E. "Narrative Technique, Characterization, and the Sources in Malory's *Tale of Sir Lancelot*." *Studies in Philology* 70 (1973), 252–68.

Harty, Kevin J. "Cinema Arthuriana." *Arthurian Interpretations* 2.1 (Fall 1987), 95–113.

———. "Cinema Arthuriana: A Bibliography of Selected Secondary Materials." *Arthurian Interpretations* 3.2 (Spring 1989), 119–37.

*Herman, Harold J. "Sharan Newman's Guinevere Trilogy." *Arthurian Interpretations* 1.2 (Spring 1987), 39–55 [reprinted at pp. 291–310 of this volume].

———. "The Women in Mary Stewart's Merlin Trilogy." *Interpretations* 15 (1984), 101–14.

Heijkant, Marie-José. "La compilation du *Tristano Panciatichiano*." In *Cyclification: The Development of Narrative Cycles in the Chansons de Geste and the Arthurian Romances*, ed. Besamusca et al., 122–26.

Hicks, Edward S. *Sir Thomas Malory, His Turbulent Career*. Cambridge, Mass.: Harvard University Press, 1928.

*Hill, Sarah J. "Recovering Malory's Guenevere." *Proceedings of the Medieval Association of the Midwest* 1 (1991), 131–48 [reprinted at pp. 267–278 of this volume].

Hoberg, Tom. "In Her Own Right: The Guinevere of Parke Godwin." In *Popular Arthurian Traditions*, ed. Sally K. Slocum. Bowling Green, Ohio: Popular, 1992, 68–79.

Hobson, Linda Whitney. *Understanding Walker Percy*. Columbia: University of South Carolina Press, 1988.

Hoffman, Donald. "Radix Amoris: The *Tavola Ritonda* and its Response to Dante's Paolo and Francesca." In *Tristan and Isolde: A Casebook*, ed. Joan Tasker Grimbert. New York: Garland, 1995, 207–22.

Holichek, Lindsay E. "Malory's Gwenevere: After Long Silence." *Annuale Mediaevale* 22 (1982), 112–26.

Hook, David. "Domnus Artus: Arthurian Nomenclature in 13th-c. Burgos." *Romance Philology* 44 (1990–91), 162–64.

———. *The Earliest Arthurian Names in Spain and Portugal*. St. Albans: Hook, 1991.

Hult, David F. "Lancelot's Two Steps: A Problem in Textual Criticism." *Speculum* 61 (1986), 836–58.

Ihle, Sandra Ness. *Malory's Grail Quest: Invention and Adaptation in Medieval Prose Romance*. Madison: University of Wisconsin Press, 1983.

Imbs, Paul. "Guenièvre et le roman de *Cligès*." *Travaux de linguistique et de littérature* 8 (1970), 101–14.

———. "La Reine Guenièvre dans le *Conte du Graal* de Chrétien de Troyes." In *Mélanges de langue et de littérature du Moyen Age offerts à Teruo Sato*. 2 vols. Nagoya, Japan: Centre d'Etudes médiévales et romanes, 1973, I, 41–60.

Janssens, Jan. "Un *Fin' Amant* et l'ironie romanesque: Lancelot et la chanson de change." *Arthurian Literature* 8 (1989), 29–78.

Jesmok, Janet M. "The Function of Malory's 'Knight of the Cart.' " *Michigan Academician* 13 (1980), 107–15.

Jillings, L.G. "The Ideal of Queenship in Hartmann's *Erec*." In *The Legend of Arthur in the Middle Ages: Studies Presented to A.H. Diverres by Colleagues, Pupils and Friends*, ed. P.B. Grout, R.A. Lodge, C.E. Pickford, and E.K.C. Varty. Cambridge: Brewer, 1983, 113–28.

Jonin, Pierre. "Le vasselage de Lancelot dans le *Conte de la Charrette*." *Le Moyen Age* 58 (1952), 281–98.

Kalinke, Marianne E. *King Arthur, North-by-Northwest: The "Matière de Bretagne" in Old Norse-Icelandic Romances*. Copenhagen: Reitzel, 1981.

Kelly, F. Douglas. *"Sens" and "Conjointure" in the "Chevalier de la Charrette."* The Hague: Mouton, 1966.

Kennedy, Beverly. *Knighthood in the "Morte Darthur."* Woodbridge, Suffolk: Brewer, 1985.

———. "Malory's Lancelot: 'Trewest Lover, of a Synful Man.' " *Viator* 12 (1981), 409–56.

Kennedy, Edward Donald. "Chronicles, Scottish." In Lacy, et al., eds., *The New Arthurian Encyclopedia*, 93–94.

Kennedy, Elspeth. *Lancelot and the Grail*. Oxford: Clarendon, 1986.

———. "Le personnage de Lancelot dans le *Lancelot* en prose." In *Lancelot: Actes du Colloque d'Amiens des 14 et 15 janvier, 1984, Université de Picardie*, ed. Danielle Buschinger. Göppingen: Kümmerle, 1984, pp. 99–106.

———. "The Quest for Identity and the Importance of Lineage in Thirteenth-Century French Prose Romance." In *The Ideals and Practice of Medieval Knighthood II; Papers from the Third Strawberry Hill Conference 1986*, ed. Christopher Harper-Bill and Ruth Harvey. Woodbridge, Suffolk: Boydell, 1988, 70–86.

Kibler, William W., ed. *The Lancelot-Grail Cycle: Text and Transformations*. Austin: University of Texas Press, 1994.

Knight, Stephen. *Arthurian Literature and Society*. New York: Macmillan, 1983.

Köhler, Erich. *L'Aventure chevaleresque: Idéal et réalité dans le roman courtois*, trans. E. Kaufholz. Paris: Gallimard, 1974.

Konarski, Jamie A. "Progression Through Redemption: Guenevere in William Morris' 'Defence of Guenevere' and 'King Arthur's Tomb.' " *The Arthurian Yearbook* 3 (1992), 39–76.

Korrel, Peter. *An Arthurian Triangle: A Study of the Origin, Development and Characterization of Arthur, Guinevere and Modred*. Leiden: Brill, 1984.

Krueger, Roberta L. "Contracts and Constraints: Courtly Performance in *Yvain* and the *Charrete*." In *The Medieval Court in Europe*, ed. Edward R. Haymes. Munich: Fink, 1986, 92–104.

*———. "Desire, Meaning, and the Female Reader: The Problem in Chrétien's *Charrete*." In *The Passing of Arthur: New Essays in Arthurian Tradition*, ed. Christopher Baswell and William Sharpe. New York: Garland, 1988, 31–51 [reprinted at pp. 229–246 of this volume].

———. *Women Readers and the Ideology of Gender in Old French Verse Romance*. Cambridge: Cambridge University Press, 1993.

Lacy, Norris J. "Arthurian Film and the Tyranny of Tradition." *Arthurian Interpretations* 4.1 (Fall 1989), 75–85.

———. "Convention and Innovation in *Le Chevalier du Papegau*." In *Studies in Honor of Hans-Erich Keller*, ed. Rupert T. Pickens. Kalamazoo: Medieval Institute Publications, 1993, 237–46.

———. *The Craft of Chrétien de Troyes: An Essay on Narrative Art*. Leiden: Brill, 1980.

———. "Thematic Structure in the *Charrette*." *L'Esprit Créateur* 12 (1972), 13–18.

———, and Geoffrey Ashe. *The Arthurian Handbook*. New York: Garland, 1988.

Lagorio, Valerie M. "Edwin Arlington Robinson: Arthurian Pacifist." In *King Arthur Through the Ages*, ed. Valerie M. Lagorio and Mildred Leake Day. 2 vols. New York: Garland, 1990, I, 165–79.

Laurie, H.C.R. "*Eneas* and the *Lancelot* of Chrétien de Troyes." *Medium Ævum* 37 (1968), 142–56.

Lazar, Moshé. "Lancelot and la *mulier mediatrix*: La quête de soi à travers la femme." *L'Esprit Créateur* 9 (1969), 243–56.

Lefay-Toury, Marie Noëlle. "Romans bretons et mythes courtois: l'évolution du personnage féminin dans les romans de Chrétien de Troyes." *Cahiers de Civilisation Médiévale* 15 (1972), 193–204; 283–93.

Leupin, Alexandre. *Le Graal et la littérature*. Lausanne: L'Age d'homme, 1982.

Lie, Orlanda S.H., ed. *The Middle Dutch Prose "Lancelot": A Study of the Rotterdam Fragments and Their Place in the French, German, and Dutch "Lancelot en Prose" Tradition*. Amsterdam: Noord-Hollandsche, 1987.

Loomis, Roger Sherman. *Arthurian Tradition and Chrétien de Troyes*. New York: Columbia University Press, 1949.

———. Introduction to Ulrich von Zatzikhoven, *Lanzelet*, trans. Kenneth G.T. Webster. New York: Columbia University Press, 1951.

————. "The Modena Sculpture and Arthurian Romance." *Studi Medievali* 9 (1936), 1–17.

————, ed. *Arthurian Literature in the Middle Ages: A Collaborative History.* Oxford: Clarendon Press, 1959.

————, and Laura Hibbard Loomis. *Arthurian Legends in Medieval Art.* New York: MLA, 1938.

Lumiansky, R.M. *Malory's Originality.* Baltimore: Johns Hopkins University Press, 1964.

————. "The Relationship of Lancelot and Guinevere in Malory's 'Tale of Lancelot.' " *Modern Language Notes* 68 (1953), 86–91.

Lupack, Alan. "Modern Arthurian Novelists on the Arthurian Legend." *Studies in Medievalism* 2.4 (Fall 1983), 79–88.

————. "Beyond the Model: Howard Pyle's Arthurian Books." *The Arthurian Yearbook* 1 (1991), 215–34.

————, ed. *Modern Arthurian Literature.* New York: Garland, 1992.

Luttrell, Claude. *The Creation of the First Arthurian Romance: A Quest.* London: Arnold, 1974.

MacBain, Danielle Morgan. "The Tristramization of Malory's *Lancelot.*" *English Studies: A Journal of English Language and Literature* 74 (1993), 57–65.

Mancoff, Debra N. *The Arthurian Revival in Victorian Art.* New York: Garland, 1990.

Mandel, Jerome. "Constraint and Motivation in Malory's 'Lancelot and Elaine.' " *Papers on Language and Literature: A Journal for Scholars and Critics of Language and Literature* 20 (1984), 243–58.

————. "Elements in the *Charrette* World: The Father-Son Relationship." *Modern Philology* 62 (1964), 97–104.

————. "Proper Behavior in Chrétien's *Charrette:* The Host-Guest Relationship." *French Review* 48 (1975), 683–89.

Markale, Jean. *Lancelot et la chevalerie arthurienne.* Paris: Imago, 1985.

Mazzocco, Elizabeth H.D. "An Italian Reaction to the French Prose Lancelot-Grail Cycle: Matteo Maria Boiardo and the Knight's Quest for Identity." In *The Lancelot-Grail Cycle: Text and Transformations,* ed. William W. Kibler. Austin: University of Texas Press, 1994, 191–205.

McCarthy, Terence. "Malory's 'Swete Madame.' " *Medium Ævum* 56 (1987), 89–94.

Méla, Charles. *La Reine et le Graal: La "conjointure" dans les romans du Graal de Chrétien de Troyes au "Livre de Lancelot."* Paris: Seuil, 1984.

Micha, Alexandre. *Essais sur le Cycle du "Lancelot-Graal."* Geneva: Droz, 1987.

————. "Les manuscrits du *Lancelot* en prose." *Romania* 81 (1960), 145–87; *Romania* 84 (1963), 28–60; 478–99.

————. "Sur les sources de la *Charrette.*" *Romania* 71 (1950), 345–58.

————. "La tradition manuscrite du *Lancelot* en prose." *Romania* 85 (1964), 293–318; 478–517.

Mickel, Emanuel, Jr., "The Theme of Honor in Chrétien's *Lancelot.*" *Zeitschrift für Romanische Philologie* 91 (1975), 243–72.

Moorman, Charles. "Courtly Love in Malory." *English Literary History* 27 (1960), 163–76.

Müller, Ulrich. "Lancelot 1960–1984: Le personnage de Lancelot dans le roman, le drame, le film, le 'musical' et la musique 'pop.'" In *Lancelot: Actes du Colloque d'Amiens des 14 et 15 janvier, 1984, Université de Picardie,* ed. Danielle Buschinger. Göppingen: Kümmerle, 1984, 135–38.

Neuendorf, Fiona Tolhurst. "Negotiating Feminist and Historicist Concerns: Guenevere in Geoffrey of Monmouth's *Historia Regum Brittaniae.*" *Quondam et Futurus: A Journal of Arthurian Interpretations* 3.2 (Summer 1993), 26–44.

Nitze, William A. "*Sans* et *matière* dans les œuvres de Chrétien de Troyes." *Romania* 44 (1915–17), 14–36.

*Noble, Peter. "The Character of Guinevere in the Arthurian Romances of Chrétien de Troyes." *Modern Language Review* 67 (1972), 524–35 [reprinted at pp. 203–218 of this volume].

O'Brian, William James. "Walker Percy's *Lancelot*: A Beatrician Visit to the Region of the Dead." *Southern Humanities Review* 15 (1981), 153–64.

Oliver, Bill. "A Manner of Speaking: Percy's *Lancelot*." *Southern Literary Journal* 15 (1983), 7–18.

Owen, D.D.R. "Profanity and its Purpose in Chrétien's *Cligès* and *Lancelot*." In *Arthurian Romance: Seven Essays*, ed. D.D.R. Owen. New York: Barnes and Noble, 1971, 37–48.

*Paquette, Jean-Marcel. "La dernière métamorphose de Lancelot." *Cahiers de la Cinémathèque*, 42/43 (Summer 1985), 113–18 [reprinted at pp. 193–202 of this volume].

Paris, Gaston. "Études sur les romans de la Table Ronde: *Lancelot du Lac*, I. Le *Lanzelet* d'Ulrich de Zatzikhoven; *Lancelot du Lac*, II. Le *Conte de la Charrette*." *Romania* 10 (1881), 465–96; 12 (1883), 459–534; 16 (1887), 100–1.

Payen, Jean-Charles. "Un auteur en quête de personnage: Chrétien de Troyes à la découverte de Lancelot." *Lancelot: Actes du Colloque d'Amiens des 14 et 15 janvier, 1984, Université de Picardie*, ed. Danielle Buschinger. Göppingen: Kümmerle, 1984, 163–78.

———. "*La Charrette* avant la charrette: Guenièvre et le roman d'Erec." In *Mélanges de langue et de littérature du Moyen Age et de la Renaissance offerts à Jean Frappier*. Geneva: Droz, 1970, 419–32.

———. "Lancelot contre Tristan: La conjuration d'un mythe subversif (Réflexions sur l'idéologie romanesque au moyen âge)." In *Mélanges de langue et de littérature médiévales offerts à Pierre Le Gentil*. Paris: SEDES et CDU Réunis, 1973, 617–32.

———. "Plaidoyer pour Guenièvre: La culpabilité de Guenièvre dans le *Lancelot-Graal*." *Les Lettres romanes* 20 (1966), 103–14.

Pérennec, René. "Artusroman und Familie: das welsche buoch von Lanzelete." *Acta Germanica* 11 (1979), 1–51.

———. "*Le Livre Français de Lanzelet* dans l'adaptation d'Ulrich von Zatzikhoven: Recherche d'un mode d'emploi." In *Lancelot: Actes du Colloque d'Amiens des 14 et 15 janvier, 1984, Université de Picardie*, ed. Danielle Buschinger. Göppingen: Kümmerle, 1984, 179–90.

Perrine, Laurence. "Morris's Guenevere: An Interpretation." *Philological Quarterly* 39 (1960), 237–41.

Pickford, C.E. *L'Evolution du roman arthurien en prose vers la fin du moyen âge d'après le manuscrit 112 du fonds français de la Bibliothèque nationale*. Paris: Nizet, 1960.

Read, Benedict, and Joanna Barnes, eds. *Pre-Raphaelite Sculpture: Nature and Imagination in British Sculpture 1848–1914*. London: The Henry Moore Foundation in Association with Lund Humphries, 1991.

Reid, Margaret J.C. *The Arthurian Legend: Comparison of Treatment in Modern and Medieval Literature, A Study in the Literary Value of Myth and Legend*. Edinburgh: Oliver and Boyd, 1938.

Ribard, Jacques. *Chrétien de Troyes, Le Chevalier de la charrette: Essai d'interprétation symbolique*. Paris: Nizet, 1972.

Rockwell, Paul. "The Falsification of Resemblance: Reading the False Guenièvre." *The Arthurian Yearbook* 1 (1991), 27–42.

Rosenwald, John. "Defending Guenevere." *Avalon to Camelot* 1.4 (Summer 1984), 38–39.

Rychner, Jean. "Le Sujet et la signification du *Chevalier de la charrette*." *Vox Romanica* 26 (1968), 50–76.

Samples, Susann. "Guinevere: A Germanic Heroine." *Quondam et Futurus: A Journal of Arthurian Interpretations* 1.4 (Winter 1991), 9–22.

*————. "Guinevere: A Re-Appraisal." *Arthurian Interpretations* 3.2 (Spring 1989), 106–18 [reprinted at pp. 219–228 of this volume]

Scheps, Walter. "The Thematic Unity of *Lancelot of the Laik.*" *Studies in Scottish Literature* 5 (1967–68), 167–75.

Scherer, Margaret R. *About the Round Table.* New York: Metropolitan Museum of Art, 1945.

Schmolke-Hasselmann, Beate. *Der arthurische Versroman von Chrestien bis Froissart: Zur Geschichte einer Gattung.* Tübingen: Niemeyer, 1980.

*Schultz, James A. "*Lanzelet*: A Flawless Hero in a Symmetrical World." *Beiträge zur Geschichte der deutschen Sprache und Literatur* 102 (1980), 160–88 [reprinted at pp. 29–54 of this volume].

Scott, Mary Etta. "The Good, the Bad, and the Ugly: A Study of Malory's Women." *Mid-Hudson Language Studies* 5 (1982), 21–29.

Sharrer, Harvey L. "The Acclimatization of the Lancelot-Grail Cycle in Spain and Portugal." In *The Lancelot-Grail Cycle: Text and Transformations*, ed. William W. Kibler. Austin: University of Texas Press, 1994, 175–90.

————. "Spain and Portugal." In *Medieval Arthurian Literature: A Guide to Recent Research*, ed. Norris J. Lacy. New York: Garland, 1996.

————. "Spanish and Portuguese Arthurian Literature." In Lacy et al., eds., *The New Arthurian Encyclopedia*, 425–28.

————. "Two Lancelot Ballads." In *The Romance of Arthur III: Works from Russia to Spain, Norway to Italy*, ed. James J. Wilhelm. New York: Garland, 1988, 259–64.

Shichtman, Martin B. "Elaine and Guinevere: Gender and Historical Consciousness in the Middle Ages." In *New Images of Medieval Women: Essays Towards a Cultural Anthropology*, ed. Edelgard E. DuBruck. Lewiston, N. Y.: Mellen, 1989, 255–72.

Shirt, David J. "Chrétien de Troyes and the Cart." In *Studies in Medieval Literature and Language in Memory of F. Whitehead*, ed. W. Rothwell, W.R.J. Barron, David Blamires, and Lewis Thorpe. Manchester: Manchester University Press, 1973, 279–301.

Silver, Carole. *The Romance of William Morris.* Athens: Ohio University Press, 1982.

Sklar, Elizabeth S. "Malory's 'Lancelot and Elaine': Prelude to a Quest." In *The Arthurian Yearbook* 3 (1993), 127–40.

Soudek, Ernst. *Studies in the Lancelot Legend.* Houston: Rice University Press, 1972.

Southward, Elaine. "The Unity of Chrétien's *Lancelot.*" In *Mélanges de linguistique et de littérature romanes offerts à Mario Roques.* 2 vols. Paris: Didier, 1953, II, 281–90.

Staines, David. "Swinburne's Arthurian World: Swinburne's Arthurian Poetry and Its Medieval Sources." *Studia Neophilologica* 50 (1978), 53–70.

————. *Tennyson's Camelot: The Idylls of the King and Its Medieval Sources.* Waterloo, Ont.: Wilfrid Laurier University Press, 1982.

Starr, Nathan Comfort. "Edwin Arlington Robinson's Arthurian Heroines: Vivian, Guinevere, and the Two Isolts." *Philological Quarterly* 56 (1977), 231–49.

————. *King Arthur Today: The Arthurian Legend in English and American Literature, 1901–1953.* Gainesville: University of Florida Press, 1954.

Sternberg, Ellen W. "Verbal and Visual Seduction in 'The Defense of Guenevere.' " *The Journal of Pre-Raphaelite and Aesthetic Studies* 6.2 (May 1986), 45–52.

Stillwell, Richard. *The Chapel of Princeton University.* Princeton: Princeton University Press, 1971.

Stones, Alison. "Arthurian Art Since Loomis." In *Arturus Rex*, II. *Acta Conventus Lovaniensis 1987*, ed. W. Van Hoecke, Gilbert Tournoy, and Werner Verbeke. Louvain: Louvain University Press, 1991, 21–78.

————. "Aspects of Arthur's Death in Medieval Illumination." In *The Passing of Arthur: New Essays in Arthurian Tradition*, ed. Christopher Baswell and William Sharpe. New York: Garland, 1988, 52–101.

————. "Images of Temptation, Seduction, and Discovery in the Prose *Lancelot*: A Preliminary Note." In *Festschrift Gerhard Schmidt*, ed. M. Krieger and H. Aurenhammer. *Wiener Jahrbuch für Kunstgeschichte* 47 (1994), 533–43.

————. "Manuscripts, Illuminated." In Lacy et al., eds., *The New Arthurian Encyclopedia*, 299–308.

Sturges, Robert S. *Medieval Interpretation: Models of Reading in Literary Narrative, 1100–1500*. Carbondale: Southern Illinois University Press, 1991.

Surtees, Virginia. *The Paintings and Drawings of Dante Gabriel Rossetti (1828 to 1882): A Catalogue Raisonné.* 2 vols. Oxford: Clarendon, 1971.

Sylvia, Richard A. "Sexual Politics and Narrative Method in Tennyson's 'Guinevere.' " *Victorian Newsletter* 76 (1989), 23–31.

Takamiya, Toshiyuki, and Derek Brewer, eds. *Aspects of Malory.* Cambridge: Brewer, 1981.

Taylor, Jane H.M. "The Parrot, the Knight and the Decline of Chivalry." In *Conjunctures: Medieval Studies in Honor of Douglas Kelly*, ed. Keith Busby and Norris J. Lacy. Amsterdam: Rodopi, 1994, 529–44.

Thompson, Raymond H. *The Return from Avalon: A Study of the Arthurian Legend in Modern Fiction.* Westport, Conn.: Greenwood, 1985.

Thoran, Barbara. "Zur Struktur des *Lanzelet* Ulrichs von Zatzikhoven." *Zeitschrift für Deutsche Philologie* 103 (1984), 52–77.

Topsfield, Leslie T. *Chrétien de Troyes: A Study of the Arthurian Romances.* Cambridge: Cambridge University Press, 1981.

Uitti, Karl D. "Le *Chevalier au Lion (Yvain)*." In *The Romances of Chrétien de Troyes: A Symposium*, ed. Douglas Kelly. Lexington, Ky.: French Forum, 1985, 182–231.

————. "Remarks on Old French Narrative: Courtly Love and Poetic Form." *Romance Philology* 26 (1972–73), 77–93; 28 (1974–75), 190–99.

Vance, Eugene. "Le Combat érotique chez Chrétien de Troyes." *Poétique* 12 (1972), 544–47.

Vesce, Thomas E., ed. and trans. *The Marvels of Rigomer (Les Mervelles de Rigomer)* by [Jehan]. New York: Garland, 1988.

Walsh, John Michael. "Malory's 'Very Mater of *Le Chevalier du Charyot*': Characterization and Structure." In *Studies in Malory*, ed. James W. Spisak. Kalamazoo: Medieval Institute Publications, 1985, 199–226.

Walters, Lori. "Wonders and Illuminations: Piérart dou Tielt and the *Queste del saint Graal*." *The Arthurian Yearbook* 4 (1996), 232–78.

Webster, Kenneth G.T. *Guinevere: A Study of Her Abductions.* Milton, Mass.: The Turtle Press, 1951.

Welz, Dieter. "Lanzalet im Schoenen Walde: Uberlegungen zu Struktur und Sinn des Lanzelet Romans (mit einem Exkurs im Anhang)." *Acta Germanica: Jahrbuch des Sudafrikanischen Germanistenverbandes* 13 (1980), 47–68.

Wertime, Richard A. "The Theme and Structure of the Stanzaic *Morte Arthur*." *PMLA* 87 (1972), 1075–82.

Weston, Jessie L. *The Legend of Sir Lancelot du Lac.* 1901; New York: AMS, 1970.

Whitaker, Muriel. *The Legends of King Arthur in Art.* Woodbridge, Suffolk: Brewer, 1990.

————. "Thomas Percy." In Lacy et al., eds., *The New Arthurian Encyclopedia*, 357.

White, Colin. *The Enchanted World of Jessie M. King.* Edinburgh: Canongate, 1989.

Wimsatt, James I. "The Idea of a Cycle: Malory, the Lancelot-Grail, and the Prose Tristan." In *The Lancelot-Grail Cycle: Text and Transformations*, ed. William W. Kibler. Austin: University of Texas Press, 1994, 206–18.

Winters, Yvor. *Edwin Arlington Robinson*. Norfolk, Conn.: New Directions, 1946.

Wood, Charles T. "The Thrice-Unburied Guinevere." *Avalon to Camelot* 1.4 (Summer 1984), 9–12.

Yarborough, Stephen R. "Walker Percy's *Lancelot* and the Critic's Original Sin." *Texas Studies in Literature and Language* 30 (1988), 272–94.

Zaddy, Z.P. *Chrétien Studies: Problems of Form and Meaning in "Erec," "Yvain," "Cligés" and the "Charrette."* Glasgow: University of Glasgow Press, 1973.

LANCELOT
AND GUINEVERE

1 THE PRESENTATION OF THE CHARACTER OF LANCELOT

CHRÉTIEN TO MALORY

Derek Brewer

I

In the development of Arthurian story Lancelot seems as it were to spring fully-formed from the mind of Chrétien de Troyes in the late twelfth century. Compared with Kay, Gawain and others, he is a newcomer to Arthur's company. Yet, by the first quarter of the thirteenth century he seems to have achieved that pre-eminence which he has held ever since. This suddenness is not the least of the puzzles and paradoxes which surround the figure of Lancelot, and which contribute to the lasting interest that is attached to him.

Though Lancelot is interesting, he is not interesting as a 'character', that is, as an individual personality, such as we expect to find in a good novel. In some versions he has some 'inwardness', some specific, idiosyncratic contour of personality, and even in Chrétien, as will be noted, he is recognisable if only for the extravagance of his feelings, but he is primarily the type, the example, representative in its very extremity, of the good knight. In considering Lancelot we must recognise that we are dealing with a figure in traditional literature, whose story exists before the named character, whose adventures are recounted by numerous different authors, in works which develop out of each other, with multiple similarities and variations. Being the hero of many such related narratives gives him a status both less and more than that of a fully realised character in a single novel, and even makes it possible to speak of a 'biography' of Lancelot, a history of his development as a figure, which should be as it were a biography of his biographies, of the stories about him. A modern version of the admirable but outdated study by Jessie L. Weston is much to be desired. The present essay attempts only to point to one literary aspect, mainly in Malory, that such an account would include.[1]

Reprinted from *Arthurian Literature*, III, ed. Richard Barber (Totowa, N.J.: Barnes and Noble, 1983), 26–52, with permission.

II

The elements from which Chrétien built the structure (which is all the present essay is concerned with) of his story have long been recognised as partly derived from Celtic stories of the abduction of a woman, usually to the Otherworld, and her rescue. To this we shall return. The other main element has been less sharply focussed. It is the theme known to folklorists as that of the Fair Unknown, which was coming into prominence in the twelfth century in Western Europe in a variety of versions. It became probably the most frequent of themes in medieval romance. The living survivors are those folktales known as 'fairy tales', which evoke the sense of mysterious origins, describe the emergence of the individual into the adult world through various tests, establish the protagonist's sense of his own identity, and usually signalise both self-identification and emergence by successful marriage. I consider the theme of the Fair Unknown first.

It will be recalled that the name of Lancelot is referred to by Chrétien several times in poems apparently earlier than his Lancelot poem, *Le Chevalier de la Charrette* and his existence, apart from Chrétien's invention, is suggested by Ulrich von Zatzikhoven's *Lanzelet*, written in High German verse probably around 1200 in Switzerland.[2] This poem claims plausibly to be based on an Anglo-Norman original, and was composed perhaps twenty years earlier, apparently in ignorance of Chrétien's *Charrette*. The origin of the name Lancelot is still uncertain. Whatever the origin of the name, Ulrich's poem is a relatively simple romance of the Fair Unknown type. The hero is the son of King Pant, but the father dies and the child as a baby is stolen by a fairy from the sea, variously called 'a lady', 'a wise mermaid', 'a queen'. She brings him up lovingly, and has him trained in various exercises, but keeps him ignorant of his name and rank, and of chivalric practices, in a land somehow lost in the sea, inhabited solely by women. At the age of fifteen he insists on departure, so the fairy gives him fine white armour, and a horse which he does not know how to control. He rides forth, and the story tells how he meets a succession of knights with beautiful daughters. The knights he kills, the daughters he mostly sleeps with, to the number of four, all the while being praised by the poet for his bravery and nobility. The lady he finally stays with and marries is actually the third in this agreeable series. The hero is ashamed that he does not know who he is (3165–3232). It is significant that as soon as he has killed his main antagonist, Iweret (whom it turns out that the water-fairy has reared him in order to kill), and has promptly had sexual intercourse with his daughter, Yblis (who had luckily fallen in love with him in a dream the previous night), a messenger arrives from the water-fairy to tell him his name and rank. Full adulthood is expressed in sexual maturity, knowledge of one's identity, and a stable loving relationship. Lanzelet has several more adventures, including some at Arthur's court, and strays with another lady, though against his will. Despite the episodic nature of the story, which has probably been amplified by the stringing together of various similar stories, the underlying structure is a clear version of that family drama embodied in so many medieval romances, which I have discussed fully elsewhere.[3] The pattern of the mysterious origin, the testing battles against various father-figures and others, the achievement of the lady as an equal, and the establishment of identity, thus solving the mystery of origin and finding a place in society, is quite unequivocal. The water-fairy as foster mother is a distinctive marker for this stage of the Lancelot story, but she is not absolutely necessary in herself for the pattern. The hero, Perceval, from whose story Ulrich probably borrowed some elements, is another form of the Fair Unknown pattern, but he knows his own mother. A dead father, never known by the hero, is more significant to the quest for identity in the Middle Ages, as for example in *Sir Degarre*.

Ulrich's *Lanzelet*, and a few other references to Lancelot, are enough to establish the existence of some sort of Lancelot story in the twelfth century, probably including Celtic antecedents, but by then an independent version of a wide-spread theme. There is more precise evidence for a type of Celtic story concerning the abduction of a woman and her rescue which has a quite different pattern. The numerous Celtic analogues which must lie among the antecedents of the story have been tested and discussed by Cross and Nitze, and the theme itself frequently studied, most recently by Professor W. Haug.[4] Cross and Nitze isolate the original elements and consider that the accounts of Guinevere's abduction in various romances are based ultimately on a Celtic tale of the following type:

1. A husband is visited by a mysterious stranger. The visitor is a former lover of the lady and has come to claim her.
2. (a) The stranger claims the right to demand anything he may wish. When his claim is acknowledged, he asks for the person of the lady. (b) He snatches the lady away without ceremony.
3. He does not, however, consummate his union with her at once.
4. He is pursued by the husband (a) alone, (b) in company with a band of armed followers.
5. He resides in a supernatural realm, which the rescuer reaches after traversing a perilous passage and being entertained and directed by a 'hospitable host'.

6. The rescuer finally succeeds in recovering the lady (a) by the help of a 'wise man', (b) by a ruse.

7. The heroine is a *fée*, the former wife (or mistress) of the abductor. (*Op. cit.*, p. 61)

Although these scholars tend to reduce the origins of traditional stories to one hypothetical tale, this is to go beyond the evidence. What we have is a significant cluster or pattern of elements hanging together in a recognisable but by no means invariable shape. No one version accords with the simple hypothetical archetype, because there was almost certainly no such thing. Each has a characteristic selection and within limits of recognition a variable sequence of events, which embody the pattern which is only pre-existent in so far as it lies 'behind' or 'beneath' a variety of manifestations. It can only be traced through the verbal realisations which are the various narrated versions we possess, themselves influenced by current social and other pressures. This phenomenon is well recognised in the study of myth and folktale, but it also applies to that kind of literature I have called 'traditional'. As Cross and Nitze observe, there is no evidence that the abduction theme was connected with any particular heroine. "Like other traditional plots, it was a sort of blank check to be filled in with characters according to the predictions of the narrator" (*op. cit.*, pp. 55–6). The metaphor is too rigid for the fluidity of such clusters, but it makes the main point. Put simply, Chrétien wrote 'Lancelot' and 'Guinevere' in the blanks of the abduction story.

The story in its barest outline is powerfully resonant. It calls to mind similar tales from classical antiquity, of Orpheus and Eurydice, of Pluto and Proserpine. They all image the pain of loss and death, and the irrepressible hope with which vital societies and persons confront such loss. The stories are non-naturalistic, whatever social base they may sometimes have had in violent times. The essentially non-naturalistic structure determines certain responses, for example, the absence of shame on the part of both husband and wife (because the abductor is a supernatural being), and the failure of an apparently lustful abductor to consummate his success. It may also account for the frequent pattern in abduction stories of the rescuer being not the husband, but someone else, a young hero.

It may be this latter fact which attracted Chrétien. It is natural for a story-teller to wish to make his received story as convincing as possible. In his telling he interprets, rationalises and makes vivid his tale. Although Chrétien enjoys puzzles, symbolic mysteries, paradoxes, as much as anyone, he is greatly interested in the workings of the mind under the stress of love. For all his love of mystification Chrétien has also a vein of rationalism and an interest in motive, to which his secularism is a witness. When he contemplated the young hero, not her husband, rescuing the abducted lady, what better motive could he perceive than that the hero loved the lady? In Lancelot he knew of a young hero who had amply demonstrated his susceptibility to female charm, perhaps in several short *lais*, of the kind which Ulrich may have strung together. There was furthermore a tradition of Guinevere's unfaithfulness to Arthur: Marie de France's *Lanval* makes some play with this, and one early tradition makes Mordred, Arthur's nephew, her lover. It was natural in telling such tales as that of the abduction to make husband and wife king and queen, archetypes of humanity. The king in Chrétien's poems could only be Arthur. Arthur is blameless and who was Chrétien to hold the Queen up to scorn? For the noble Lancelot to be not the lover of several women, but devoted to Guinevere alone accounts for his rescue of her, leaves her relatively blameless, and Arthur is not made ridiculous. The intensification of Lancelot's love, if it be not the cause, is certainly the effect of the combination of Lancelot as the Fair Unknown with the abduction story; and it allows Chrétien to explore, not without a touch of satire, that obsessive passion of love which so greatly interested him, his audience, and so many readers since. This humanising and deepening of the feeling makes the relationships between the three principals more human and potentially more painful. It could ultimately lead only to tragedy, the antithesis of romance. It may be, as I have argued elsewhere,[5] that it was for this reason that Chrétien did not himself finish his poem. As now completed, the story has the happy ending intrinsic to romance, but once the situation is seen in terms of the ordinary human existence of actual people, the implications—granted medieval social conditions and assumptions about marriage, honor and loyalty—are disastrous. Chrétien may have felt this, and left the story to be conventionally finished with a happy ending by Godefroi de Leigni, with Chrétien's consent, but perhaps without his heartfelt endorsement.

Chrétien presents us in his poem with a most sophisticated and creative treatment of traditional materials. He picks and chooses, rejects, borrows from a variety of sources, gives unusual twists to what is familiar, and invents. Thus he twists the theme of the Fair Unknown to tease the reader or hearer about Lancelot, not naming him for most of the poem, though he seems to assume that the reader recognises who he is, and that he is the lover of the queen. Lancelot is at last triumphantly identified, but he is never in doubt about his own identity. His fairy foster-mother and the magic ring she gave him are briefly mentioned (2354–62) but Chrétien makes nothing of Lancelot's ignorance of his origins or of any solution of his ignorance. There is a playful element in the poem, which does not prevent Chrétien also suggesting the profounder echoes in the story. He is thus able in the first part to narrate a sequence of puzzling events which modern critics, even Frappier, have often considered feeble, yet whose power to fascinate they have been unable to resist. The second part of the poem, following Lancelot's passage of the sword-bridge, in which Lancelot and Guinevere are seen, at least occasionally, together, has been considered less illogical and improbable. It is right to recognise the convincing humanity of Lancelot's relationship here, but surely mistaken to divorce it from the illogicality of the first part. Logic is not intrinsic to powerful stories. They draw their strength from deep patterns of the mind. It seems similarly mistaken to attribute the interest that Lancelot holds for us to Chrétien's establishment of a "well-defined, clearly individualised character" (Frappier, *op. cit.*, p. 104). Realistic, personalised characterisation is by no means intrinsic to the presentation of a personage in a traditional story. Frappier himself gives a truer insight a paragraph later, when he refers to Lancelot's representative, typical, virtually archetypal character. Lancelot has two simple exemplary traits. He is the best knight in the world; he obsessively loves the Queen, which causes him occasionally to fall into a trance.

In the portrayal of Lancelot generally we recognise a vein of extravagance. He is the most obsessive of lovers, as he is the most beloved of ladies, and the greatest of fighters. Chrétien screws the tension to its highest point. When this hyperbole of character is placed in conjunction with the illogicality of events, and both are judged by the terms of what goes for commonsense nowadays, that is, according to contemporary naturalistic assumptions, the effect is as memorable as ever, but the interpretation may be confused. Some critics have seen Chrétien's portrayal of Lancelot as condemnatory or burlesque.[6] This is surely anachronistic and confuses several issues by imposing modern assumptions about behavior which there is no reason to think that Chrétien shared. One such assumption is that stories, and characters, and their standards, ought to be like ordinary life; whereas it is clear that Chrétien liked the strange, the remarkable, the extreme, as many less sophisticated readers and writers do today. Science fiction, folktale, myth, are better analogies for Arthurian romance than realistic novels. Plausibility is no more the main criterion for Arthurian literature than it is for these other forms, or even for much really modern art.

The art-historians have shown us how few strokes of a brush are enough to create an image of life. Our own imaginations do the rest. The point here is that Chrétien in both story and character of the *Charrette* builds an image of human life upon the basis of a non-naturalistic but significant story-structure, with characters who are sketched in with very few traits. It is as if the characters are serious caricatures. The lack of naturalism in the base, and the simplicity of character structure it requires and allows, are sources of power, which underlie, and often break through, the agreeable but thin surface of realistic observation and description.

If we over-emphasise the individualised quality of Lancelot's character, or demand unlimited realism, we are in danger of neglecting the more significant element of structure which Chrétien's genius evolved from his combination of the abduction motif with that of the Fair Unknown: this more significant structure lies not in characterisation but in the forces of feeling between Arthur, Guinevere and Lancelot, which depend on recognising the human implications of their situation rather than its possibly supernatural origins. The once mythic sequence of events takes on a new power when it is the loyal *rescuer*, not merely the remote or unknown abductor, who is the accepted lover of the Queen; and when the rescuer is an intimate companion of the King, to whom he owes his primary allegiance; and when marriage is held to be indissoluble in human social terms, the source of personal honor in society if maintained, of deepest shame if violated.

The 'eternal triangle', *cliché* as it once was, was rich in the possibilities of human personal heroism and tragedy. Lancelot, the best of knights, must betray the best of kings. Lancelot is beloved of many beautiful women, but obsessed with only one, the most beautiful of all. She is the one alone, of those who love him, with whom he can never achieve a public, social relationship which shall match and validate his personal feelings. A permanent self-contradiction characterises their relationship, and the stronger their feelings, the stronger the self-contradiction. It is the tragedy of the good, or rather of the best. The better a man Lancelot is, the more he loves Guinevere, the more loyal he is to Arthur, the more noble are Arthur and Guinevere, the deeper the contradiction, further reinforced by Lancelot's real public and social duty to cherish Guinevere as the Queen of his lord King Arthur. This poignantly paradoxical set of relationships, rich in sweet rewards which are embittered by conflicting imperatives, is the adult social world into which the Fair Unknown has matured. The cheerful optimism of the endings of many medieval romances, which Chrétien himself may have professed, must here be questioned. Adult life, society and marriage, are no heaven where all is happy ever after. Well may the hero find mysteries, especially as the events themselves which weave this tangled web of love and deceit retain their archaic resonances, and King and Queen, and hero, being more than individual characters, represent great responsibilities and issues of life and death. At the heart of all is the structure of tensions between Lancelot and his Queen and his King, the rescuer who is at once the loyal servant, the loyal lover, and the supreme traitor.

The attraction of this story is witnessed by its expansion into the immense prose romances in numerous languages of the thirteenth century. It may be, as Dr. Elspeth Kennedy has argued, that the primary expanded version in French prose is a non-cyclic *Lancelot do Lac*, which itself formed the basis of the cyclic romances of the Vulgate, of which those that concern Lancelot are now normally seen as a trilogy of the *Lancelot*, the *Queste del Seint Graal* and the *Mort Artu*. Frappier notes that about a hundred manuscripts of the Prose *Lancelot* survive, and many more must have been lost. It is essentially from these, or their derivatives, supplemented by some other texts, including a few in English, that Malory created his own work. These successive versions illustrate the usual processes of repetition, selection, re-interpretation, supplementation and invention which characterise traditional literature. Limitations of space allow only a few points to be briefly made here. The narrative of Lancelot's *enfances* is much expanded, according to a common method of writing traditional stories, often to be noticed in Arthurian literature (and elsewhere, as, for example, in the Gospel of St. Luke). There is a huge increase in realistic detail everywhere, and we hear much about Lancelot's upbringing, and the wars which took place in his father's kingdom around the time of his birth. The first visit to Arthur's court, in which he is clad in the dazzling white armour which became his emblem, and his first sight of Guinevere are amplified with the same rich detail. Lancelot takes with youthful serious literalism the conventional kindly words of welcome which Guinevere addresses to all young knights, and is for ever after her devoted servant. She helps him find the sword which Arthur forgets to gird him with. Their first kiss, during the interview procured by his friend, Galeholt, is one of the greatest passages of Arthurian literature, made further famous by Dante's association of it with the love of Paolo and Francesca (*Inferno*, V). The great expansion of narrative in the *Lancelot* includes much else, as for example Arthur's own amours, and the devoted friendship of Galeholt for Lancelot.

When the author of the *Queste* came to contemplate this chivalric world of miscellaneous adventure and love it was in order to condemn it in the name of a severe asceticism which exalted virginity above all other virtues even for men. In the search for the Grail Lancelot is shown to be sadly deficient because he is the carnal lover of Guinevere. Thus the relationship with Guinevere could be seen to have tragic implications, though even marriage is regarded as a state inferior to virginity, and it is not so much Lancelot's adultery as his love in itself which is condemned. This condemnation laid some grounds for the final tragedy of Arthur, related in the *Mort*

Artu. Though Arthur's fall is due immediately to the rebellion of Mordred, Lancelot's affair with Guinevere is part of the final tragedy. As noted above, in earlier versions Mordred, who is in the equivocal relation of nephew to Arthur (easily changed later to that of bastard son) was also the lover and abductor of Guinevere. He is, in a strange way, a prototype of Lancelot. These stories, including that of Lancelot himself, all give us interestingly varying versions of 'the family drama', impossible to explore further here.

The story of Lancelot, eventually followed through to the bitter end, was retold endlessly in many European languages, with many bewildering variants, but we may observe everywhere the same general characteristics of traditional literature, seen from Chrétien onwards. The reader is assumed already to have some knowledge of the story. The writer of the current variant must follow the general outline but is free to supplement the narrative from other sources, to invent new elements, and in his re-telling either to offer a new interpretation or to reinforce an old one. The basically non-naturalistic but psychologically profound structure first sketched out by Chrétien remains, but it is increasingly overladen with further episodes and more realistic details. The characters, and notably Lancelot, for all the increase of detail, remain typical or archetypal.

In all this plethora of narration and re-handling about Lancelot, itself only a part of the huge number of stories attracted to the Arthurian magnet, Malory comes late in time, a knight not a clerk, probably one who had carried out, at least in his own eyes, such deeds as had Lancelot, writing in prison in a country on the margins of European culture, in a literature which curiously enough contains relatively little Arthurian story. How does he present Lancelot?

IV

The chief characteristics of Arthurian writing in Europe in the thirteenth and fourteenth centuries were continuous amplification and a drift towards increased realism of detail. Malory reversed both trends. He had available a series of large French books containing the stories of Arthur and his knights, including those many associated with Tristan, plus two or three of the handful of English Arthurian poems. He 'reduced' the stories, as Caxton says, ruthlessly summarising the French, but taking as his general base (whether or not he translated it first), the English alliterative *Morte Arthure*, which he turned into prose and shortened to roughly half. The *Morte Arthure* gave him the basis of English history and patriotism, along with some criticism, and in narrative the two main summits of interest, the triumph of Arthur, and his downfall. Malory arrested the centrifugal tendency of the later French romances, which neglected Arthur in favour of Lancelot, Gawain, Tristan, Galahad, and others, though Malory was ready enough to portray these heroes as contributing to the glory of the great king himself. Malory's imagination, and his information, were nourished on romance, but his cast of mind was that of the historian of England (and historian, we may note, rather than mere chronicler, though chronicles were the only historical sources available to him). These generalisations need qualification in so far as Malory occasionally failed to master and sort out his bewildering variety of sources, containing many stories incompatible with each other; and in so far as Malory himself developed in artistry, being sometimes more clumsy, or less sympathetic to his material, than at his best and greatest.

At what stage Malory first conceived of his task as writing a unified summary account of the reign of Arthur and his chivalry as the great English achievement is not clear. Vinaver denied the attempt altogether, on the basis of the final paragraph to the first main section of the Winchester Manuscript, which is undoubtedly by Malory. But it is clear that Malory knew from very early on the general course of the events he would describe, and there is no doubt that the eight main sections of the Winchester Manuscript, which follow due order, constitute a sequential whole, a work, not the *Works* of the title of Vinaver's edition.[7]

Since Malory's deepest interest is in Arthur and England, the evolution of Arthurian romance has made Lancelot for him both essential and secondary. We begin the work with the establishment of Arthur, beginning from the beginning as we shall go on to the end. Lancelot is first mentioned, and it is of course significant, when the young king Arthur announces his intention of marrying Guinevere. Merlin warns him against the marriage, but without hope (all readers have always known, before reading this, that Arthur marries Guinevere). Merlin says that Arthur could find someone just as beautiful and good as Guinevere, but concedes that

> 'there as mannes herte is sette he woll be loth to returne.' 'That is trouthe', seyde kyng Arthur. But Merlyon warned the kyng covertly that Gwenyver was not holsom for hym to take to wyff. For he warned hym that Lanncelot scholde love hir and sche hym agayne. And so he turned his tale to the aventures of the Sankegreal. (Winchester MS, f. 35r: *Works*, p. 97)

Here Vinaver notes that Malory has made explicit what is obscure and only implicit in the French. The French text, moreover, says that Arthur did not understand what Merlin meant. The French text is superficially more realistic, more modern, since one might reasonably ask, in the work of naturalistic commonsense why, if Arthur did understand Merlin, he did not act differently. The French text takes such a question into account. Malory does so, if at all, merely by the word 'covertly'. This does indeed suggest the possibility that the warning was so obscure that Arthur did not understand, and therefore reasonably disregarded the words. This does not solve, but only increases the puzzle, since we then have to ask why Merlin should bother to state obscurely what could not be understood. Why not warn plainly? The French is open to this objection. A superficial realism only papers over the naturalistic chasms beneath.

Yet surely no reader with any natural understanding and love for traditional literature is disturbed by such realistic difficulties. They do not confuse, they clarify our vision of the events and issues before us. In the present case Merlin's warning is the author's evocation of the whole great story of Arthur, Guinevere, and Lancelot. Malory does not need anything but the merest gesture towards a realistic situation, he does not need to create a convincing illusion of daily life, because the story, being traditional, is known. We know that Arthur marries Guinevere and Lancelot becomes her lover. The little episode does not make us feel that Merlin is a particularly stupid old man, or Arthur especially obtuse and willful. We know the wise wizard and great king as such already and the context prevents their trivialisation just as it makes no attempt at plausible detailed characterisation, motivation or explanation. What is evoked is the general shape of the story as background to this particular passage in it, together with reflections on the mixture of volition, responsibility and unavoidable destiny, of splendour and vainglory, pride and willfulness, which characterise all our lives, and which Malory's work so richly represents both directly and indirectly.

It is important to understand this kind of traditional writing, different in its assumptions from the Neoclassical frame of reference which became dominant in the seventeenth century, and is still too often implicitly assumed even though modern art has discarded it. Traditional writing disregards the Neoclassical gap between fiction and ordinary life which allows fiction to act as a mirror to ordinary life, and within its own bounds to be subject to the same materialistic laws that post-seventeenth century commonsense assumes. Modern criticism of Malory often assumes a gap between art and life comparable to that created by the proscenium arch of the Neoclassical drama. It assumes that fictional action takes place on a stage, in a self-enclosed, framed space which mirrors the actions of ordinary life. It is well known that medieval, including Shakespearean drama, lacking the proscenium arch, but possessing a stage which obtrudes partly into the audience, at times allowing direct address to the audience, disregards the distinction between the fictional side and the actual. There is an unbroken continuum between actuality and fiction which denies the attempt at complete illusion of Neoclassical art. The characters move in and out of the fictional frame, as sometimes in narrative does the author.

The telling of a traditional tale, and Malory's telling of *Le Morte Darthur*, have something in common with the retrospective view we may take of our own lives, in which we become conscious of a mixture of arbitrary event, luck (or 'hap' as Malory calls it), obstinate willfulness, apparent design or purpose, even of a destiny beyond ourselves and our conceptions. Our remembered real selves are also the 'actors'.

To return to this first mention of Lancelot, we may note that at the historical level it fixes him firmly within that structure of husband, wife, lover; king, queen, loyal yet treacherous knight, which Chrétien seems to have first created. It also makes certain that the reader has a conspectus over the whole Arthurian story in its essence. Whether Malory actually wrote this first main section first, as I believe he did, because it is often unsure in touch, does not here concern us, since in any case we respond to the work of art which we have here clearly designed by Malory, following the chronology of Arthur's life.

The next mention of Lancelot touches on his infancy and again occurs in relation to Merlin. Merlin visits Lancelot's ancestral kingdom, sees 'yonge Launcelot', and prophesies to his mother about the child's future fame and greatness (*Works*, pp. 125–6). The reference is incidental to the narrative of Merlin's love for Ninive, whom he knows will betray and kill him, but whom he nevertheless woos continually 'to have hir maydeynhode'— the same mixture of foreknowledge and destiny which makes naturalistic characterisation an irrelevance.

At the end of the first of the eight main sections of the whole book of *Le Morte Darthur* Malory concludes with the feast of Pentecost, and gives a round-up of various knights, including Tristram, and Pelleas; the latter, he says (quite erroneously), was one of the four who achieved the Holy Grail. This reference, and the following final paragraph, contain several famous puzzles which do not concern the present argument. When Malory here writes 'this book endyth' he may well, *pace* Vinaver, be referring to his own book: and when he says that it ends 'where as sir Launcelot and sir Trystrams com to courte', though he has not actually described such a coming, we find the same blurring of the fictional border between narrative and commentary as we find in traditional writing between fiction and actuality. The way that Vinaver prints the last paragraphs of main sections, in capital letters (*Works*, p. 180, etc.), and calls them colophons, suggests greater difference between them and the narrative than actually exists. The manuscript begins a new paragraph, but it is written just like the rest of the narrative, and to print it in capitals, without drawing attention to this purely editorial device, is misleading, to say the least. It is an interesting example of how typography can affect meaning. Format gives interpretation, in this case misrepresenting the text. The word *explicit* follows separately a couple of lines after the end of the text.

As far as Lancelot is concerned, Malory has now shown him old enough to come to court. The general historical time sequence is observed, though not to pedantic detail. The second major section, which tells of Arthur's war against the Romans, begins with a brief summarising passage referring to Arthur's marriage, his successful wars, the filling of the Round Table, and the arrival of Lancelot and Tristram at court. This passage firmly binds the opening of the second section to the close of the first, as was long ago remarked. Malory cuts out, along with much else, all reference to Lancelot's magical and mysterious origins, thus continuing the secularising, realistic drift of other French redactors, though he also cuts out much of their realistic detail. He makes no mention of the knighting of Lancelot and his first sight of Guinevere. Malory's main aim was to summarise. At this stage he is more interested in, or considers more important, the establishment of Arthur as a great king, than any concern of Lancelot.

Nevertheless, Malory builds in the figure of Lancelot, though he is for the time being merely incidental, with some care, as Mary Dichmann has noted in detail.[8] Malory adapts the reference to Lancelot in the roll-call of knights who support Arthur's defiance of the Roman envoys, "Than leepe in yong Sir Launcelot de Laake with a lyght herte" (Winchester MS, f. 72v: *Works*, p. 189). Malory, as McCarthy notes, sometimes adds his own alliteration to that of his source, as here.[9] Lancelot is firmly placed as a young man and eager warrior, loyal to his king.

The next reference is preceded by a deliberate alteration of the source which allows us to see Malory firmly manipulating the material he is working on in order to achieve his own characteristic presentation of the story. Vinaver points out that in his source and in the comparable French accounts Arthur before leaving on his warlike expedition entrusts his kingdom and wife to the keeping of Mordred. Malory instead makes Arthur entrust them to two other knights, Baldwin and Constantine, the latter of whom was king after Arthur's day. He thus clearly envisages, as Dichmann argues, the general structure of his own later account of Arthur's fall, as his postponement of the actual ending of the alliterative poem, which tells of Arthur's downfall, equally clearly shows. The reference to Lancelot immediately follows that to Baldwin and Constantine, and is also original with Malory.

> And Sir Trystrams at that tyme he left with Kynge Marke of Cornvale for the loue of La Beale Isode. Where fore Sir Launcelot was passyng wrothe. (Winchester MS, f. 95v: *Works*, p. 195)

The next line tells of how great sorrow queen Guinevere made at the departure of Arthur and his lords. Malory clearly wishes to emphasise Lancelot's single-minded devotion to his king, and that he is not in love with Guinevere; otherwise, the contrast with Tristram would have no point. As Vinaver and Dichmann note, Lancelot is introduced a number of times by Malory to emphasise his warlike prowess, where he is absent from the source (e.g. *Works*, pp. 212, 214, 215, 216, 217, 220, 222–4). Finally, at the end of the section, Malory takes the opportunity to show Arthur restoring King Ban's land to Lancelot, abandoning the alliterative source but relying probably on memories of longer accounts in the Prose *Lancelot*. "Sir Launcelot and Sir Bors de Gaynys thanked the kynge fayre and sayde ther hertes and servyse sholde ever be his owne." (Winchester MS, f. 95v: *Works*, p. 245).

It is too much to say with Dichmann that a primary intention of the account of the Roman War is the 'aggrandizement of Lancelot', but the establishment of Lancelot as a great and loyal warrior is a strong subsidiary interest. And this is achieved by simple strokes of a character that are by no means, as Vinaver would have it, inconsistent with Lancelot's love of Guinevere. But, once again, to think in terms of characterisation rather than larger story-structure may be misleading. If Lancelot were *not* Arthur's principal knight, his love of Guinevere would be to that extent less significant. Malory rightly sees, as, in their way, had his French predecessors, that 'arms and love' must go hand in hand.

It is logical, once Arthur is established as the greatest of kings, to pause at the top of Fortune's wheel to survey the fortunes of the knights whose own magnificence contributes to that of Arthur. The next three main sections of *Le Morte Darthur* treat of Lancelot, Gareth and (with many others intermingled) Tristram, and it is logical to take Lancelot first. Malory's careful and well-planned introduction of Lancelot has necessarily been discussed in great detail. From section three onwards the material is too copious to allow for more than a few representative details to be discussed here.

Most of the Tale of Lancelot, as Professor Lumiansky points out, emphasises Lancelot's fighting ability,[10] but also his goodness, generosity and high sense of honour. The interesting question that immediately raises itself for any lover of Arthurian romance, is, what is Malory saying about Lancelot's relation to Guinevere? Malory is very equivocal. He tells us nothing of first sights, of amorous sighs, a ravishing first kiss. Malory summarises tersely, almost as soon as the section is started.

> Wherefore Quene Gwenyvere had hym in grete favoure aboven all other knyghtis, and so he loved the Quene agayne aboven all other ladyes dayes of his lyff. And for hir he dud many dedys of armys and saved her frome the fyre thorow his noble chevalry. (Winchester MS, f. 96v: *Works*, p. 253)

All this is Malory's own and shows that he has in mind the episodes towards the end of *Le Morte Darthur* in which Lancelot several times rescues Guinevere from the fire to which she has been adjudged, on two occasions because of adultery with himself. Lumiansky points out that of the five references to Lancelot's devotion to Guinevere in the section (*Works*, pp. 250, 257–9, 270–1, 274, 281), four are original with Malory. There are no references to Lancelot's youthfulness. He is now established.

The relationship with Guinevere, given or assumed knowledge of Lancelot's life and fame is evoked in a characteristic but to us puzzling way. It is naturally a piece of knowledge that we have from outside *Le Morte Darthur*, which is only, after all, a part of the whole Arthurian story, which itself could not be differentiated from actual life. Malory has already twice reminded us, once in the first section, once at the beginning of the Tale of Lancelot, of Lancelot's love of Guinevere. But he continues to be equivocal in the following key passage.

Lancelot is riding with a damsel under his protection, and she tells him that nearby is a knight that distresses ladies and gentlewomen. " 'What' seyde Sir Launcelot, 'is he a theff, and a knyght, and a ravyssher of women? He doth shame vnto the order of kynighthode and contrary vnto his oth. Hit is pyte that he lyvyth'." (Winchester MS, f. 104: *Works*, p. 269). So Lancelot kills the knight, and asks if he can do anything more for the lady. No, she says, but she regrets that Lancelot, so noble, has no wife, and apparently never loved a lady, and 'that is a great pity'. But, 'it is noised' that he loves Queen Guinevere, and that she has enchanted him. He replies,

> 'I may nat warne peple to speke of me what hit pleasyth hem. But for to be a weddyd man I thynke hit nat, for than I muste couche with hir and leve armys and turnamentis, batellys and adventures. And as for to sey to take my plesaunce with peramours, that woll I refuse:

in prencipall, for drede of God. For knyghtis that bene adventur[ou]s
shoulde nat be advountrers nothir lecherous, for than they be nat
happy nother fortunate vnto the werrys; for other they shall be
ouercom with a sympler knyght than they be hemself, other ellys they
shall sle by vnhappe and hir cursednesse better men than they be
hemself. And so who that vsyth peramours shall be vnhappy and all
thynge vnhappy that is about them.' And so Sir Launcelot and she
departed. (Winchester MS, f. 105: *Works*, pp. 270–1)

To what extent are we meant to believe that Lancelot is not yet the
accepted lover of Guinevere? How much enclosed within the fiction is this
speech, and therefore to what extent is it to be conceived of as a sincere naturalistic expression of what is (within the fiction) the true situation? If we take
it within the fiction as if that were a novel, must we assume that Lancelot is
telling the truth? Why does Malory raise the question at all?

There are several possible answers to these questions which in their
very existence show that we have not to do with novelistic presentation,
which would require consistency and depth of characterisation in naturalistic terms. To begin within the fiction, however, it is quite plausible to adopt
the view of Lumiansky, and associated views such as those of Moorman,[11]
and assume that we have a genuine dramatic expression of character, and
furthermore that what Lancelot says is true. We can then argue that we are
carefully shown the pre-adulterous phase of the relationship, and that this
is part of a long chain of cause and effect tracing the development of
Lancelot's character.

There are two difficulties here, one practical, one literary. To take the
practical one first, staying within the fiction as if it were a nineteenth-century
novel: what else could Lancelot have said in answer to such a question even if
he were in fully adulterous relationship with the Queen already? Could he say
in effect, "Do not worry about my love-life, dear lady, because I am in fact
the adulterous lover of my Queen"? The answer to the lady's question can only,
for an honorable man, as I long ago remarked, be a downright lie.[12] There is
in fact an illustration of this paradox actually in a nineteenth-century novel.
In the very last paragraph of George Meredith's *Evan Harrington* (1861) the
Countess de Saldar remarks, "The other day it was a question whether a lady
or a gentleman should be compromised [i.e. their adultery revealed]. It required
the grossest fib. The gentleman did not hesitate." [i.e. to tell it]. This is admittedly part of a jest at the expense of the ease with which Roman Catholics may
lie, since they can expiate the sin in the confessional. But the paradoxical point
is analogous. A gentleman is honour-bound to tell a lie if it is needed to pro-

tect a lady's honour. Lancelot cannot reply other than he does, which leaves the question of his adultery open.

The literary difficulty arises from this. Taking the question again novelistically, is Lancelot sincere or not? Whatever the answer, what would it tell us about his character? The tone of the remark is indeed characteristic of Lancelot's stern, laconic style, but as Lambert has so well remarked, the tone of all speakers, and of the narration itself, is identical.[13] The content, if sincere, reveals that disdain of marriage more commonly found in boys in early adolescence than grown men. The equivocation reveals a subtle mind, whether sincere or not. But these are not significant traits in our conception of Lancelot, which depends on simpler, nobler strokes. Nor are these traits followed through. But the main truth is that we surely do not care, for our conception of Lancelot, whether he is actually at this moment in the story the accepted lover of Guinevere or not. There is no change in Lancelot's character or in our general attitude to him when he becomes Guinevere's lover. He is just as good a knight—or even a better one, which is not a significant change. There must have been a period before Lancelot, to put it crudely, actually got into bed with Guinevere, but in Malory's telling that period does not seem at all important. The proof that it was not important to Malory is that he never shows the moment of acceptance, the moment of transition, of mutually realised love. Such a moment was important for the writer of the Prose *Lancelot* (or *Lancelot do Lac*), as witness the famous first kiss, its equivalent. Such a moment was important for Chaucer's Troilus, and such moments have been of supreme importance in the actual lives of men and women. But it was not so for Malory's presentation of Lancelot.

After the discourse with the damsel the theme of possible adultery goes, so to speak, underground. In so far as it may be said to surface at all it is not so much as mentioned in the rest of the Tale of Lancelot, nor in that of Gareth, but it comes up in the next Tale of Tristram, where the fact of adultery (without any moral obloquy) is taken entirely for granted. There has been no progressive development either of event or of Lancelot's character, nor even the simple cause and effect of the Prose *Lancelot*, let alone the long sorrows and complex intrigue recorded in that work. In the Tale of Sir Tristram La Beale Isoude sends Sir Palomydes to Queen Guinevere with the message that in this land there are but four lovers, "Sir Launcelot and dame Gwenyver, Sir Tristrames and quene Isode" (*Works*, p. 425). A few pages later there is a reference to the horn from which no woman who is untrue to her lord can drink without spilling. This horn (the *topos* is widespread in Arthurian literature) has been sent to Arthur's court to the despite of Lancelot and is now come to King Mark's court with the same effect for

Queen Isode (*Works*, pp. 249–50). In neither case does the offended king take any action. This kind of narrative does not depend on the mirroring of chains of naturalistic cause and effect. Were this folktale theme to be incorporated in some plausible chain of progressive development Arthur could not have allowed things to go on as he does.

Yet this is a negative judgment, which might be construed as adverse criticism of Malory's art, at best laying him open to Vinaver's charge of inconsistency. Malory's art is not faultless: is the creation of Lancelot's discourse about the Queen with the damsel a fault? Our empirical response shows that it is not. Analysis can show it to be meaningful and contribute to the whole.

The passage is deliberately placed where it occurs in Malory, being taken from an episode in the presumed French source which occurs well after Lancelot and Guinevere have been shown to be full lovers. Lancelot's speech itself is original with Malory. Next, we note that Lancelot does not precisely deny his relationship with Guinevere, but repudiates for himself both marriage and promiscuous affairs. His relationship with Guinevere comes into neither category. It would seem that Malory, concerned not with character but with story, and with a story well known outside his own particular version, feels that he has to meet the question of Lancelot's relation to Guinevere, because ever since Chrétien only two things have been significant about Lancelot: one, that he is the best knight in the world; the other, that he is Guinevere's accepted lover. Malory, however, wishes to play down the sexuality of the relationship, just as later, when Lancelot is attacked by Agravain and others in the Queen's chamber he refuses to speculate whether Lancelot and the Queen were abed together or passing the time otherwise, for love then was not as it is now, while the French source he is using says plainly that they were in bed together (*Works*, p. 1165). Malory at this stage, while keeping Lancelot's relationship with the Queen in view, wishes to make it as decent as possible; would prefer, like Arthur himself, who is the real centre of Malory's work, not to notice at all; and only notices it when it is forced upon him by public witness. His concern is with Lancelot's goodness and greatness as a knight. He is working at this stage to build up that aspect in broad, repetitive strokes, relying on the narrative interest of the succession of events.

We should read this passage, then, like so much else in *Le Morte Darthur*, whether pure narration of event or apparently dramatic speech, as a kind of commentary by the author, expressing that 'narrative view' of reality described by Professor Lambert. The 'commentary', though more often refracted through dialogue than directly addressed to the reader, is nevertheless primarily from author to reader, with only the slightest adjustment to the attributed speaker, and always in the same authorial style. Dialogue or single long speeches do indeed express the characters' feelings and convictions, (as well as, at need, the brief indications necessary for the continuation of the 'horizontal' line of action). But characters do not speak as internalised autonomous personalities. They tend to express general views. One of their most typical remarks, common to many types, is 'That is truth'. Malory does not attempt the self-contained personally motivated character of later fiction. Event and character are subdued to the exigencies of the total narrative pattern and purpose, rather than to the demands of a localised naturalism. The overall aim may sometimes cause the local acts or the specific characteristics evoked to be mutually incompatible or inconsistent with each other, but if the overall vision and pattern are sufficiently powerful, and the detailed verbal realisation sufficiently vivid, we are carried swiftly along on the stream, where a few individual passages of rapids and rough water merely add to the variety and excitement.

We may still wish to clarify the answer presented by this particular piece of commentary, by putting the damsel's question more brutally. Is Lancelot at this time, as people say, the Queen's accepted lover? The only clarification is that it is not clear. The reader may understand that Lancelot is not the Queen's lover, though he does not specifically deny it; or understand that he is, because he does not specifically deny it, and because the reader knows that Lancelot *is* the Queen's lover, from the story outside this version.

There is one further thing to say about this most interesting passage. It is also a piece of conventional, sententious wisdom, with primarily a 'vertical' reference, to the general narrative structure and common assumptions which derive from the cultural context; it is not a 'horizontal' reference, needed for the continuation of the story-line.[14] As we read it we are bound to give at least imaginative assent to its traditional wisdom of commonplace morality, and to recall, as Malory knows we can, the eventual history of the love of Lancelot and Guinevere: for Guinevere *is*, after all, Lancelot's paramour, though this word is never applied to her; and Lancelot *does* cause misfortune to all about him, because through him and Guinevere are the greatest king and the flower of knights destroyed.

Malory's indifference to 'characterisation' as we tend to conceive of it is further illustrated by a strange episode in the Tale of Tristram, that long, rambling fifth section of the whole work where Malory finds it evidently difficult to control his material, and where a minor passage of relative failure illustrates something of his artistic method.

A strange knight rides about the forest attacking, in one case killing other knights, some of them famous, and vilifying Arthur and the Round Table. He is eventually identified as Lancelot in disguise, for when challenged during their fight by Sir Tristram to say who he is, " 'Truly' seyde Sir Launcelot, 'and I were requyred I was never loth to tell my name' " (Winchester MS, f. 234v: *Works*, p. 569). The other characters concerned in this scene are not said to find Lancelot's escapade highly amusing: but nor are they apparently surprised, irritated or shocked, though he has killed an innocent young knight. The episode is the more curious in that in the French source the disguised knight remains unknown. Malory has chosen to identify him as Lancelot. Vinaver in commenting on the anomalous behavior attributed to Lancelot remarks that to Malory such inconsistency or oddity must have seemed a lesser evil than leaving the disguised knight unidentified. But Malory could surely have given the disguised knight some other name, if he felt that the episode illustrated some aspect of character. Why Lancelot? Professor Beverly Kennedy sees it as an example of Lancelot's growing love for the Queen, which leads him more and more vaingloriously to desire 'worship' for her sake; but there is no clue of that in the text. Malory makes no attempts to integrate this strange piece of behavior into Lancelot's character, and it is not essential to the sequence of events.

We are asking the wrong questions. This is not the kind of narrative in which character motivates actions to specific ends. In traditional narrative character may be independent of, even at odds with, the actions performed, and the core of the narration is the action, not the characters to whom it may be attributed (as noted by Cross and Nitze with reference to abduction stories). Much of the poignancy of traditional narratives arises from a certain mismatch between character and action, as indeed is the case in *Le Morte Darthur*. We cannot always read characters from the actions performed. In the present case we have a set of actions by the disguised knight which are quite consonant with the sort of actions performed by all the Arthurian heroes. On all grounds of plausibility and common sense in the ordinary world, even of the twelfth or fifteenth centuries, they are and were absurd. The source of their appeal lies not in their probability but their mystery, and the importance of mystery in art should not be underrated. But literary mysteries must have their justifications, and we may easily see how the arbitrary wanderings and conflicts of Arthurian knights symbolise much of our own deeper experience of life and its uncertainties. In the present case Malory seems for once to have miscalculated his effect. The contrast of behaviour with Lancelot's usual form is too great, but we should note that this *kind* of behaviour, better integrated into the narrative and given some superficially more plausible cause, is exactly that of Lancelot at times in the great narrative of sections seven and eight, when the Arthurian world is hastening to its end. In these later passages Lancelot in disguise attacks and wounds King Arthur's knights who are his friends and in some cases his very kin. Such episodes are an intrinsic part of the symbolic structure of Arthurian adventure which so entrances Malory, and which images the friendships and hatreds, the destructive rivalry and jealousy, the arbitrary accidents and ill-judged purposes, the heroism and the tragedy, of all human society. Our modern feeling for the strange, the arbitrary and the symbolic should be able to digest such a method without naturalistic hiccups.

The Tale of Tristram includes the begetting of Galahad by Lancelot, who is deceived into thinking he is making love to Guinevere. When Lancelot discovers that he has been with Elaine he runs mad in the woods. These events add to the traits of Lancelot but they cannot be said to characterise him. Their force is in their paradoxical significances, and in the structural device which makes Galahad a sort of Lancelot-substitute. The story of the Holy Grail in which Galahad achieves the Grail naturally follows. It is full of mysteries and inconsistencies which do not lessen power, but which cannot detain us here. It is well known that in Malory's French source Lancelot is remorselessly attacked for his sinful love of the Queen. Malory summarises this work even more rigorously than usual, but changes and develops less. Lancelot's supremacy among earthly sinful men is insisted upon as much as his sinfulness. He repents of his sin, but it is prophesied that he will return to it. The general effect is undoubtedly to reinforce the sense of the seriousness of Lancelot's love for Guinevere. In a naturalistic fiction—could such a narrative contain the story of the Grail—many results would surely flow from the experiences, but as it is the experiences take their part, without having further effects, in the total pattern.

The last two main sections of the whole *Le Morte Darthur* have a stronger sense of cause and effect, and a vivid, though generalised, presentation of their character. The traits which mark Lancelot are deepened, though not changed, and the relationships which are critical to the whole story are more complex. For example, as early as the Tale of Gareth Malory has emphasised Lancelot's special friendship towards the then unknown youth, and Gareth's corresponding devotion to Lancelot. The relationship does not develop through later books, but it is inconspicuously asserted here and there, sometimes by changing the French source. This friendship with Gareth, merely asserted, hardly evidenced after Lancelot has knighted him, is fundamental to the tragic paradox whereby Lancelot kills Gareth at the Queen's third rescue. Gareth is present but unarmed, because he does not wish to risk harming Lancelot.

Gareth's death is the cause of his elder brother Gawain's unremitting hostility to Lancelot, which goads Arthur to war. Thence flow more consequences. This longer chain of cause and effect is more characteristic of the last two sections than any of the preceding ones, and characteristic of Malory's free handling of his several sources. But even so it is not a product of characterisation, and may even go against it, since Gawain had not previously shown any fondness for Gareth.

We may take other examples which show that even these last books are based on a non-naturalistic structure. Three times (a typical folktale number) Lancelot rescues the Queen at the last moment. On the first occasion she has been falsely accused of poisoning Sir Patryse, who has accidentally eaten some fruit intended by another enemy to poison Gawain, whose idiosyncratic passion for fruit is mentioned only here (*Works*, p. 1045ff). Arthur immediately accepts his queen's guilt and agrees that she shall be burnt at the stake unless some knight can be found to prove her innocence by defeating her accuser, who is himself acting in good faith. At the last moment Lancelot turns up in disguise, champions Guinevere's cause, defeats her accuser in a joust and consequently saves her. He takes off his helmet and then is recognised. The king gravely thanks him. Lancelot replies that he ought always 'aright' to be in the king's quarrel and in the queen's because Arthur is the man who gave him the High Order of Knighthood. He says that on that same day that he was made knight Lancelot lost his sword through his hastiness. The Queen found it, hid it in her train, and gave it to Lancelot when he needed it. Therefore, he promised her at that day ever to be her knight either in right or in wrong (*Works*, p. 1058). This is the first time that Malory mentions the episode of the mislaid sword. The reference goes back to *Lancelot do Lac* and the Vulgate Prose *Lancelot*, though the actual incident there is rather different, and is subsequent to Lancelot being stricken with love for the Queen when he has first seen her. Malory has boldly, yet in a sense casually or inconsistently, but also artistically, remodeled the episode. He uses it here for purely local significance to reinforce the devotion of Lancelot to both Arthur and Guinevere, although by now, even in Malory's muted account, there is no doubt that Lancelot and the Queen are fully lovers. In one sense Lancelot's speech is expressive, but it is as usual expressive of a purely general conventional traditional theme and ethic. It is a 'vertical' reference, not a 'horizontal' reference, part of the line of actual narrative. It satisfies our need at that moment to place the rescue in an appropriate context of everlasting loyalty and devotion, and to recognise that Lancelot is their supreme exponent, but it is not an individualising motivation. It is not a device of vivid characterisation, though it evokes a vague memory of the traditional biographies of Lancelot.

A similar artistic effect is achieved by Malory's reference to the company of the Queen's Knights. He tells us about them in a paragraph that is even more muddled syntactically than usual and full of inconsistencies. He says that the Queen's Knights are young but honourable knights who normally accompany the Queen and normally carry only plain white shields. They do this because they are young and have yet to be identified as great knights with their own insignia. Lancelot himself, Malory tells us, has graduated through this company. The company has never been referred to before in Malory's stories. The reference is developed from various hints in the Vulgate, and the tradition that untried knights carried shields without devices. Yet in the present narrative it also immediately appears that those Queen's Knights who are with her are men of great worship and include many famous knights. Only Lancelot is absent. On this particular occasion, which is just before she is captured by Meliagaunt, it appears that the knights are quite unarmed apart from their swords, and certainly have no shields (*Works*, p. 1122).

What is the purpose of referring to these knights? Malory wishes to emphasise that the queen is worthily accompanied and that Lancelot had been a member of this *corps d'élite*. He wants to emphasise both their worthiness and their defenselessness. Their weakness is not culpable. He creates a picture using purely local realism without connectedness to the overall narrative. The description is part of the traditional conventional glamour of his presentation of the queen. We get a sense of long-established habit from the reference to the company. None of this seems designed to create speculation about Lancelot's place in the company, which is never mentioned again, nor his character. We are surely not meant to deduce that he was too serious-minded to bother about that Maying which is so delightful and appropriate an activity for the noble knights of those days, whose good behavior Malory has a little before commended (*Works*, pp. 1119–20). And even in this brief reference there is a notable inconsistency by naturalistic standards. Malory occasionally remarks on the superiority of the good old days, but it is the function of his narrative to show that in those good old days came war and wrack and wonder, not to speak of disaster, and destruction of the most noble band of knights that ever there was.

Examples might be multiplied, but the conclusion is clear. The work of art presents us with a series of images which are connected through verbal sequences which do not represent any underlying naturalistic structure of cause and effect. Merely superficial plausibility at most is enough. The underlying structure depends partly upon very general recognised sequences of events as they take place in human life from birth to death, and partly on traditional sequences of events which conform to psychological patterns. In the case of the Arthurian story the sequences depend also on the pattern of accepted relationships between people who are presented as quite simple types—the King, the Queen, the brave knight, the lover and so forth. These in turn are set in a network of ethical and social concepts about honor and shame, virtue and sinfulness, sometimes of great elaboration. A great verbal artist like Malory can put together his words to evoke these structures in very rich and interesting patterns which do not need to be a plausible imitation of everyday experiences, though the patterns do ultimately reflect, and enrich, our ordinary lives.

Malory gives his own interpretations of accepted events and to that extent rationalises them. He is capable of providing apparent causes that are locally effective, and of creating long-term relationships, but his work still rests upon a foundation of archaic structures which do not need rationality at all. Out of the mixture comes a fascinating work of art full of inconsistencies which not only leave his greatness unharmed but which may open our modern eyes to the strange mixture of arbitrariness and design which characterises our own lives.

Malory has not lost the essence of Chrétien's work, which is the self-contradiction inherent in Lancelot's relation to the King and the Queen, nor has he lost the structure of quest and rescue. What he has done is to follow, led by earlier authors, the implications not of character but of a story about people. The power to move lies ultimately in the pattern of relationships between people, embodying the tragedy of incompatible desires. *Le Morte Darthur* is not a study in character, nor a tragedy of character. One might say the character does not matter because it is not a character; it is the image, created in broad strokes, of a human being. In the story as a whole Malory responded to the challenge of the self-contradiction in human relationships and followed it through to the bitter end, to make a resolution, to come to a conclusion from which he, unlike Chrétien, did not shrink.

NOTES

1. Jessie L. Weston, *The Legend of Sir Lancelot du Lac*, London, David Nutt, 1901. Miss E. Gerslund, Darwin College, Cambridge, has begun such a task. The present essay is a much expanded version of "The image of Lancelot," a paper presented to the Görresgesellschaft meeting at Bonn in 1982.
2. A brief account of Chrétien is given by J. Frappier in *Arthurian Literature in the Middle Ages: A Collaborative History*, edited by R.S. Loomis, Clarendon Press, Oxford, 1959, pp. 157–191. See also his account of the Vulgate Cycle, pp. 295–318, for the later development of the story of Lancelot. Further on Chrétien see J. Frappier, *Chrétien de Troyes: The Man and his Work*, translated by R.J. Cormier, Athens, Ohio, Ohio University Press, 1982. For Ulrich see Ulrich von Zatzikhoven's *Lanzelet*, trans-

lated by K.G.T. Webster, revised and annotated by R.S. Loomis, New York, Columbia University Press, 1951.

3. Derek Brewer, *Symbolic Stories*, Cambridge, D.S. Brewer Ltd, 1980; Derek Brewer, "Medieval Literature, Folk Tale and Traditional Literature," *Dutch Quarterly Review of Anglo-American Letters*, 11, 1981, pp. 3–16.

4. T.P. Cross and W.A. Nitze, *Lancelot and Guinevere*, Chicago, the University of Chicago Press, 1930. W. Haug, " 'Das Land, von welchem niemand wiederkehrt', Mythos, Fiktion und Wahrheit im Chrétien's 'Chevalier de la Charrette', im 'Lanzelet' Ulrichs von Zatzikhoven, und im 'Lancelot Prosaroman'," *Untersuchungen zur Deutschen Literaturgeschichte*, 21, Tübingen, Max Niemeyer Verlag, VIII, 1978.

5. Derek Brewer, "The Nature of Romance," *Poetica* (Tokyo), 9 (1978), pp. 9–48.

6. For example, A.H. Diverres, "Some Thoughts on the *Sens* of *Le Chevalier de la Charrette*," *Arthurian Romance*, edited by D.D.R. Owen, Edinburgh, Scottish Academic Press, 1970, pp. 24–36, and D.D.R. Owen, "Profanity and its Purpose in Chrétien's *Cligés* and *Lancelot*," *op. cit.*, pp. 37–48.

7. *The Works of Sir Thomas Malory*, New Revised Edition, Clarendon Press, Oxford, 3 vols, 1967, revised 1971, 1973. Referred to as *Works*. Since pagination is continuous, volume numbers are not given in references. Quotations of Malory are normally taken here from the facsimile, *The Winchester Malory*, Oxford University Press, London, 1976. The view that Malory intended a connected sequence of narrative was put forward by D.S. Brewer, "Form in the *Morte Darthur*," *Medium Ævum*, XXI (1952), pp. 14–24, revised as "the hoole book," *Essays on Malory*, edited by J.A.W. Bennett, Clarendon Press, Oxford, 1963, pp. 41–63, which concentrates on the question of the final paragraphs, the colophons or so-called *explicits*. It was further supported by R.M. Lumiansky, "The Question of Utility in Malory's *Morte Darthur*," *Tulane Studies in English*, V (1955), pp. 29–35, and in the series of essays by various hands, *Malory's Originality*, edited by R.M. Lumiansky, Baltimore, Johns Hopkins Press, 1964.

8. Mary E. Dichmann, "The Tale of King Arthur and the Emperor Lucius: the Rise of Lancelot," *Malory's Originality* (see Note 7), pp. 67–98.

9. T. McCarthy, "The Sequence of Malory's Tales," *Aspects of Malory*, edited by T. Takamiya and Derek Brewer, Cambridge, D.S. Brewer Ltd, 1981, pp. 107–124.

10. R.M. Lumiansky, " 'The Tale of Lancelot': Prelude to Adultery," *Malory's Originality* (see Note 7), p. 91.

11. C. Moorman, *The Book of Kyng Arthur: the Unity of Malory's "Morte Darthur,"* Lexington, University of Kentucky Press, 1965.

12. *The Morte Darthur: Parts Seven and Eight*, ed. D.S. Brewer, York Medieval Texts, London, Edward Arnold, 1968, Introduction, p. 29.

13. M.H. Lambert, *Malory: Style and Vision in "Le Morte Darthur,"* New Haven and London, Yale University Press, 1975.

14. E. Auerbach, *Mimesis*, trans. W. Trask, Doubleday Anchor Books, New York, 1957, pp. 14–17; Derek Brewer, "Towards a Chaucerian Poetic," *Proceedings of the British Academy*, 60 (1974), pp. 219–52 (reprinted *Chaucer: the Poet as Storyteller*, London, Macmillan, 1983); Larry D. Benson, *Malory's Morte Darthur*, Cambridge, Mass., Harvard University Press, 1976, p. 73.

2 *LANZELET*

A FLAWLESS HERO IN A SYMMETRICAL WORLD

James A. Schultz

Just as the prologue to Ulrich von Zatzikhoven's *Lanzelet* provides a fore-taste of the work to follow, so one's reaction to this prologue offers a first indication of how he will react to the work as a whole. The casual reader, for instance, will find little in the prologue to arrest his attention: he will read past the reassuring, traditional *swer;* he will be carried along by unex-ceptional language past a few familiar maxims; and he will arrive without a thought at line 41, the beginning of the tale itself. Such a reader will very likely approach the whole work in the spirit of Fredrick Norman, who writes of Ulrich: "Wir tun gut daran, keinen Sinn bei ihm zu suchen und ihn unbekümmert zu lesen."[1]

A more careful reader, however, will want to investigate the ideas in Ulrich's prologue more closely. He will wonder if its sententious maxims (5–7; 12–13) might not, like *Iwein*'s *saelde und ere*, be the "Leitstern" of the entire work—but he will soon realize that they are not even the principles that organize the prologue. The prologue, it turns out, is little more than a string of shifting oppositions: *die frumen* and *die zagen* (7) are replaced by *die hübschen liute* (15) and *die boesen nidaere* (19), and these last are soon opposed to our flawless hero. Our more careful reader will soon conclude that Ulrich, who ignores his ostensible premises and argues in interchange-able extemes, is a careless and superficial thinker. And this is precisely the traditional scholarly reaction to Ulrich's work as a whole: "Nach der offiziellen Lesung der Literaturgeschichte" writes Kurt Ruh, "präsentiert sich . . . *Lanzelet* als ein Artusroman ohne Programm und Struktur."[2]

By now our more careful reader will feel entitled to dismiss the *Lanzelet* prologue so he can get on with the body of the work, just as

Reprinted from *Beiträge zur Geschichte der deutschen Sprache und Literatur* 102 (1980), 160–88, with permission.

Arthurian scholars have felt justified in ignoring Ulrich's work so they might devote more attention to those of Hartmann and Wolfram. But this is a mistake. For if we can see past the surface inconsistencies of Ulrich's prologue, then we will be able to perceive its fundamental organization; and this fundamental organization, reflecting as it does a structural prejudice of its author, will help us understand the organization of the entire work. If we can understand those special features that characterize the structure of Ulrich's *Lanzelet*, and if we can relate those features to the sense of the work, then our understanding of the entire genre will be more subtle and more accurate.

I

As I perceive it, the *Lanzelet* prologue comprises four sections of ten lines each. The first and second are closely related by content, as are the third and fourth. The first and third share the same level of abstraction, as do the second and fourth. Thus the whole prologue reveals a balanced, symmetrical structure.

The first premise of the prologue appears in the middle of the first ten-line section: He is *niht wol gemuot der al der liute willen tuot* (5–6). This maxim is preceded by a little propaganda in the form of a pedigree: we learn its source, *ein wise man*; its age, *bi alten ziten*; and its reception, *dem sit diu welt der volge jach*. Anyone who can distinguish *rehtiu wort* should keep these things in mind; naturally, it is implied, he will approve the premise. Following the statement of the maxim are four lines of elaboration: *al diu liute* are divided into *der frume* and *die zagen*, and, since the latter hate the former only from envy, he need not trouble himself over their enmity *(daz sol er mæzeclichen clagen)*.

These thoughts overflow into the second group of ten lines, but their development is interrupted by line 11: *Nu hoerent wi ich ez meine*. The most common epic structural marker, *nu*, introduces that line in which the narrator addresses the public for the first time. He and they make their appearance simultaneously, already defined by their roles and the relation these roles imply: *ir hoerent; ich meine*. I feel justified in seeing a division here not only because of the *nu* (underscored in MS. W by an indentation), and not just because of the introduction of the narrator and his public, but also because their appearance initiates a re-definition in the next ten lines of all the categories from the first ten. *Ein wise man* pronounced the first maxim; the narrating *ich* pronounces the second. The first was approved by *diu welt*; the second is received by the narrator's public. *Diu welt* or *al diu liute* could be divided into *die frumen* and *die zagen*; these correspond in the performance situation to the *hübsche liute* and *die boesen nidaere*. Where *der frume* was enviable because *sin dinc wol ze saelde stat*, the *hübsche liute* deserve *lop und ere*. Finally, the understated *maezeclichez clagen* that was appropriate for *die zagen* is transformed into *schalten* for *die boesen nidaere*, an intensification due, doubtless, to their immediate presence. Thus each of the general remarks for the first ten lines has been translated into the specific situation of the second.

The division between the second and third ten-line sections is not nearly so clear as that between the first and second. In place of the unmistakable signal *nu*, which introduced line 11, we find at the beginning of line 21 the relative pronoun *des*, which refers back to *ditz maere* in the previous line. In spite of this syntactic bond, however, line 21 marks a division at least as important as the more clearly articulated line 11. According to the formula that Hennig Brinkmann and Peter Kobbe have traced from antique into medieval rhetoric, a prologue consists of two parts: the first, the *prologus praeter rem*, treats a proverb or exemplum and establishes the narrator's relation with his audience; the second part, the *prologus ante rem*, introduces the narrative to be presented.[3] Now the first 20 lines of the *Lanzelet* prologue include two proverbs and clearly establish the relation of narrator and public, while the last 20 lines deal with the tale at hand. This change of direction is explicitly marked in line 21 with Ulrich's mention of the *maere, des ich hie wil beginnen*.

But Ulrich does not actually begin to tell his tale in line 21; he merely begins to introduce it. As always, the discussion proceeds by opposition: in the first ten lines the determining pair was *der frume* and *die zagen*; in the second, it was the narrator and his public; in the third, it is *diz liet* and *die nidaere*. In some ways the discourse has become more specific: *die nidaere* in the present audience represent the category *die zagen*; *ein ritter* is a more concrete description of *der frume*; and the performance situation gains in profile with the introduction of the epic to be performed. Yet in many ways the discussion in the third section is no less typological than in the first. The hero of the promised epic remains indefinite: *ein ritter*; and that he overcame many valiant knights (28–30) and always strove *nach staeten tugenden* distinguished him in no way from most of the traditional romance population. The laudatory adjectives with which our narrator characterizes his hero (27) come not from the epic that follows, but from the discussion that precedes: this knight is *hübsch*, like the better part of the audience (15), and *wis*, like the sage who provided the discussion with its first premise (2). The narrator, it turns out, is describing his offering not by its distinguishing features but by type. The opposition he establishes in the third part of his prologue is not *die nidaere* vs. the romance *Lanzelet* itself, but *die nidaere* vs. the type of *Lanzelet,* an epic with a flawless, knightly hero. The antipathy between the *nidaere* and such an epic hero is so total *(den frumen hazzent ie die zagen)* that it implies its automatic resolution: the *nidaere* will leave the room of their own accord.

Only in the last ten-line section does the prologue finally turn to the details of the epic at hand. Then, in a single breath (lines 31–37 are by far the longest indivisible syntactic unit in the prologue), we are told that the hero did not know his name or his family until his prowess caused them to be revealed. The prologue ends with three lines of general praise: *ze tugenden* (38) recalling line 26, *saelic* (39) as in line 10, and *wan er nie ze laster muot gewan* (40) being the negative formulation of line 26. Our particular hero, it turns out, is of the same stuff as *der frume* in the first section or the typological *ein ritter* in the third.

Of the four sections of the *Lanzelet* prologue, the first two are related by content: both consider the division of people into admirable and not admirable. The last two sections are similarly related: both have to do with the epic. Functionally, however, the first and third sections are parallel, as are the second and fourth. The first section establishes a principle for all people, the third an epic type and the reaction it necessarily provokes; they are abstract and absolute. In the second and fourth sections these general assertions are translated into particular contexts: in the second section to the performance situation, in the fourth to the epic at hand.

Our "more careful reader" quickly observed that Ulrich does not trouble himself over logical niceties: he admits only two categories, that which he admires and that which he does not; and he slips from one subject to another, not according to any rational argument, but only by loose association. Yet we have discovered beneath this apparent carelessness a striking order: the prologue falls into four equal parts, and each part corresponds to the others to form a balanced, symmetrical pattern. The whole of *Lanzelet* betrays a similar two-tiered construction: one is immediately struck by the many logical inconsistencies on the surface of the work, yet this apparent confusion is supported by a surprisingly symmetrical skeleton. Once we appreciate the cause of the inconsistency and the extent of the symmetry we will be better able to understand Ulrich's attitude to his work, to his art, and to his world.

II

Thanks to the industry of Georg Gervinus, who sought out MS. P in the Heidelberg library, *Lanzelet* was celebrated for its lack of coherence even before its first printing; Gervinus calls the work "eine Reihe langweiliger

Geschichten ohne Verbindung."[4] The charge of incoherence quickly established itself as a commonplace of *Lanzelet* criticism,[5] but, as far as I know,
no one has ever attempted to investigate the causes and extent of Ulrich's
notorious weakness. Even those scholars who have tried to rehabilitate
Lanzelet have done so by ignoring its contradictions rather than by explaining them.[6] Yet Ulrich's inconsistency will not go away if we ignore it, for it
is, as Gervinus' reaction shows, a very obvious feature of the work. If we
are to increase our understanding of *Lanzelet*, then we will have to look more
closely at these inconsistencies; for, if we can distinguish those areas in which
Ulrich is inconsistent from those in which he is not, then we will have isolated those features that are most important to the author and upon which
we must therefore base any comprehensive interpretation of the work.

The first category of inconsistencies in *Lanzelet* comprises Ulrich's
theoretical remarks, of which his pronouncements on *minne* provide the most
obvious examples. Ulrich maintains, for instance, that there is no escaping
submission to love: this is brutally clear in the behavior of Galagandreiz'
daughter (800–82; 1030–31; 1083); it is implied in remarks of Iblis (4336–
37); and it is formulated most generally by the narrator, when he says:
*nieman also kündec ist, der sich der minne müge erwern, in enwelle got
dervor ernern* (4054–56; cf.: 4597–98). Once one has succumbed to the
power of love, he acts with foolish excess: this is the opinion of Galagandreiz
(924), of Iblis (4383–84; 4398–99), of the narrator (4330–31; 6644–47), and
is the sense of the three inscriptions on the magical tent: *waz getar diu minne
niht bestan? . . . minne ist ein wernder unsin. . . . minne hat maze vertriben*
(4853–58). We readily find substantiation for the theoretical immoderation
of the lover in the actual behavior of Galagandreiz' daughter, of Iblis, of the
Lady of Pluris, and of *der stumme Gilimar*. But what of Ade's sensible devotion? And, even more important, what of Lanzelet? He says he loves Iblis
(4590–91), but can be reasonably happy without her at Pluris (5645). And,
even though he thinks of her constantly while captive (5671–73), once back
at Court he ignores her completely for 1000 lines (6816–7820). Lanzelet may
indeed appear to behave foolishly, but he certainly does not do so from excess of *minne!* Ulrich's pronouncements on the immoderation of love do not
seem to be in harmony with the behavior of his hero.

Although, in speaking of *minne*, Ulrich most often mentions its power
and immoderation, he does have other things to say on the subject. Kurt Ruh
points to several instances in which a lady is criticized for not rewarding a
knight whose service she has accepted (5998–606; 8008–12) and concludes
that they are meant to justify the sexual enthusiasm of the women in our
romance.[7] But this can hardly be the case: Galagandreiz' daughter goes

around the bedroom soliciting; Ade offers *sicherheit* to save Lanzelet's life; the Lady of Pluris holds our hero captive for a year. In each instance the woman seizes the initiative so quickly that Lanzelet could not possibly have offered his service. Here too Ulrich's theoretical remarks have little to do with the actual behavior of his characters.

Yet if Ulrich's remarks on *minne* are inconsistent with the behavior of his characters, then why has he included them at all? To answer this question let us note, first, that Ulrich does not distribute his remarks evenly throughout the work, but concentrates them in a few set pieces: the first speech of Galagandreiz' daughter (905–40); Iblis' "Minnerede" (4373–405); the decorations on the "Minnezelt" (4852–59); the messenger's remarks at the "Mantelprobe" (5868–6094). Second, we should note that the remarks found in these places are not special insights of Ulrich but, as is clearest in the quotation from Ovid (4852–53), they are bits of conventional wisdom that Ulrich has collected from a variety of sources. K.A. Hahn points out Ulrich's fondness for proverbs[8] and Albert Leitzmann has assembled a list of them.[9] Werner Richter speaks repeatedly of Ulrich's "Vorliebe für Sentenzen"[10] and Edmond Faral remarks that, according to medieval theoreticians, *amplificatio*, of which *pronuntiare sententiam* is one branch, "est la grande chose: elle est la principale fonction de l'écrivain."[11] Quite clearly Ulrich is not interested in presenting a uniform theory of *minne* but only in showing off his repertoire of conventional sayings in a few rhetorical display pieces. His sententious remarks can be inconsistent with the behavior of his characters because they are not intended to provide the theoretical key to that behavior; they are merely meant to ornament the passage in which they occur.

Ulrich is no more consistent in ascribing a motivation to his hero than he is in introducing remarks on *minne*. One tends, like Ernst Soudek,[12] to assume that Lanzelet, having been told the conditions under which he will learn his name, will constantly try to fulfill those conditions; but this is not the case at all. Of the five situations in which Lanzelet's namelessness is mentioned explicitly—at his departure from the water-fay (311–48); at Johfrit's (524–28); in connection with Arthur's court (1287; 1348–49; 2269); at Linier's (1396; 1664–88; 1880; 1903–94; 2045; 2241); and at the tournament (3226–28)—only in one, the tournament, does it affect his behavior in any way. It is true that Lanzelet leaves Moreiz when he remembers *durch waz er uz was geriten* (1363), but the desire to learn his name is only a subsidiary cause of his departure: he is originally motivated by eagerness to learn about knightly combat (304–06); and, even after his namelessness becomes an issue, he is said to leave *durch niht wan umb ere* (351). Perhaps

Lanzelet's namelessness motivates his refusal to accompany Walwein to Djofle, as well as his later unwillingness to join Arthur's court; but in each case the terms he uses—*min dinc* (2718), *miniu dinc* (3462)—do not rule out other explanations. In any case, it is quite clear that when Lanzelet finally does set off on the journey that leads him to Iwaret, and thus to his name, he thinks he is headed for Pluris (3502–05; 3526–27); and when he hears of Iwaret from the abbot he thinks not of his own name, but only of the water-fay's charge (3932–35). If Lanzelet himself can remain so completely indifferent to his namelessness that, in the 1500 lines before he finally learns his name, his lack of one does not once cross his mind, then we are hardly justified in assuming that he is motivated by his "Namensuche."[13]

But if Ulrich treats Lanzelet's namelessness so capriciously that it has no meaning as motivation, then why has he introduced it at all?[14] Doubtless because he recognized the contribution that his hero's anonymity could make to the coherence of the work. On the one hand, the statement, early in the romance, of the conditions under which Lanzelet will learn his name and the fulfillment of these same conditions several thousand lines later bracket and thus unify the intervening episodes. On the other hand, the suspense that is generated in the audience by its anticipation of the moment when Lanzelet will learn his name gives a special quality—and thus, unity—to that part of the romance in which we are kept in suspense. If you recall that Lanzelet thinks of his namelessness only very rarely but that we, thanks to the string of alternate designations that Ulrich is obliged to invent for *der ritter ane namen* (2059), are constantly reminded of it, then you will realize that namelessness has been introduced not for its effect on him but for its effect on us. It is a compositional trick meant to add coherence to the work; that it appears occasionally, and inconsistently, to motivate the hero is purely incidental.[15]

The third category of inconsistencies in *Lanzelet* concerns its hero's internal development and the relation of this development to certain progressive patterns by which Ulrich organizes his romance. There appears, for example, to be a clear progression in the first three women that Lanzelet wins: the lustful daughter of Galagandreiz, the helpful Ade, and the courtly Iblis. Rosemary Combridge notes this pattern and concludes: "the ladies . . . are graded in sensitivity."[16] Helga Schüppert investigates the same three episodes and detects "eine Entwicklungslinie, vom flüchtigen Minnegruß zur dauernden Minnegemeinschaft eines idealen höfischen Paares."[17] Lanzelet's development with regard to *minne* is paralleled by an apparent improvement in his qualities as a knight: he throws knives with Galagandreiz; he fights a giant, two lions, and a knight at Linier's; he participates in a courtly combat with Iwaret. Schüppert compares these contests and notes: "die Art des

Kampfes erfährt eine Steigerung auf ritterliche Perfektion hin und stützt damit die These von einer zunehmenden Vervollkommnung Lanzelets zum besten aller Ritter."[18] Finally, Lanzelet's growth in knightly worth appears to be reflected in his increasing integration into Arthur's court. He begins as an outsider; after his first victory, Orphilet brings news of Lanzelet's valor to the court; after his second victory, Walwein is dispatched to find the nameless hero; shortly thereafter, Lanzelet fights before the Court at Djofle; and finally, after his defeat of Valerin, Lanzelet becomes a member of the Round Table. Kurt Ruh, tracing this progress, concludes that membership in the Round Table signifies Lanzelet's attainment of "Artuswürdigkeit."[19]

While the evidence advanced to prove Lanzelet's development is itself quite legitimate, it is incomplete and thus misleading. The sorts of *minne* that Ulrich depicts may indeed seem to become more courtly up through the winning of Iblis, but what then of the Pluris episode? When Lanzelet must sleep with the Lady of Pluris, our narrator remarks coyly: *ich enweiz, ob erz ungerne tet, wan diu künegin was ein schoene maget* (5530–31); although Lanzelet thinks constantly of Iblis (5671–73) and is therefore *wilent truric* (5645), he is also *wilent fro* (5645); the Pluris episode includes the only lines in the entire work that can be construed as a direct criticism of its hero: Iblis was sick from misery *sit Lanzelet du Lac ir ze rehte niht enpflac* (5631–32). If we regard *triuwe* as an essential ingredient in romance *minne*, then Lanzelet's behavior at Pluris can only be viewed as a regression from the model behavior that he displays while winning Iblis. The same is true of Lanzelet's knightly prowess. He may indeed seem to become a more valiant and courtly knight up through his fight with Iwaret, or even through his defeat of the 100 knights at Pluris. But after this success he spends a year of complete passivity at Pluris, from which he must be rescued by the enterprise of others. And then, as if the year at Pluris had put him out of practice, Lanzelet functions at the rescue of Ginover only as an advisor (6953–71) and recruiting officer (7480–576): the rescue is accomplished by Malduc, whose help is won by the self-sacrifice of Erec and Walwein; and the latter are rescued by one of Lanzelet's recruits, the giant Esealt.[20] I am unable to reconcile Lanzelet's behavior at Pluris and at the rescue of the Queen with the notion that he increases throughout the work in knightly valor.[21] Finally, although Lanzelet does not seem to become more involved with Arthur's court, this does not mean that he grows in essential worth—"Artuswürdigkeit." For no sooner has Orphilet informed Arthur's court of Lanzelet's behavior at Moreiz than we are told: *do wunschte siner künfte Artus der schanden vrie und al diu massenie* (1354–56). And after the Linier adventure we learn: *do wart über lut verjehen obe der tavelrunde, daz man niender funde enkeinen degen so staete, der ie bezzerz getaete* (2278–82).

To judge from these passages, Lanzelet must be "artuswürdig" from the very start. In all three cases—love, knightly valor, worth in Arthur's terms—the theory that Lanzelet evolves throughout the course of the work is undermined by the clear evidence of the text itself.[22]

Yet if Ulrich does not mean to portray the internal evolution of Lanzelet, then why has he included those progressive patterns on which Combridge, Schüppert, and Ruh base their interpretations? Probably because he realized that such patterns, like the suspense generated by his hero's anonymity, could help unify the work. The limited evolution of *minne* from Galagandreiz' daughter through Iblis, and of *aventiure* from Galagandreiz through the 100 knights of Pluris, as well as the increasing prominence of Arthur all add coherence to those parts of the romance that they encompass. One could point as well to the general increase in the importance of magic —absent (Galagandreiz through Djofle), auxiliary (Iblis through combat with Valerin), essential (abduction of the Queen through Elidia)—or to the overall increase in the numbers involved in each episode—two (Galagandreiz), three (Linier), many (Djofle), 100 (Pluris), 200 ("Mantelprobe"), the whole world (Elidia). Yet these patterns, again like Lanzelet's namelessness, are simply techniques by which Ulrich organizes the surface of his romance; they cannot possibly correspond to the internal growth of his hero—to the "'Entwicklungsstand' des Helden"[23]—for, as I have tried to show, there is no evidence of internal growth. Thus, the apparent inconsistencies in Ulrich's handling of Lanzelet's development disappear as soon as we recognize the function of the progressive patterns: they are not indicators of psychological evolution; they are merely compositional tricks.

One begins to wonder whether all of *Lanzelet* cannot be reduced to two overlapping categories: inconsistencies and compositional devices; but this is not so. Ulrich does remain consistent in two matters of substance, and these we must take into account. He is consistent, first, in the evaluation of his hero. After Lanzelet's first adventure at Moreiz, we learn: *swer daz saehe . . . der spraech im wol daz beste* (1343–46); and Orphilet calls him *den tiursten degen . . . den ie getruoc dehein wip* (1332–33). After Lanzelet's second victory, over Linier, we learn: *zem besten man in uf huop* (2161); Arthur's court agrees: *in wurd nie bezzer ritter kunt* (2260). Lanzelet is called *der beste* not only at the outset of his career, but also at its conclusion. Directly after Esealt has liberated Erec and Walwein, the Court says of Lanzelet: *daz kein ritter bezzer waere* (7811); and in the following episode, Elidia proclaims him *der beste ritter, der nu lebet* (7921). If our hero can be praised in these terms immediately after his seemingly unheroic dalliance at Pluris and his non-intervention at the rescue of Ginover, Erec, and Walwein, then we must conclude that he is *der beste* not by virtue of anything he does but by definition. This essential pre-eminence of Lanzelet is clear to the water-fay's messenger, who says he is *von gebürte saelic unde groz* (4707) and to Arthur's court, who maintain that he was *von kinde . . . ein der saeligeste man über al die welt* (7800–02). The unchanging evaluation of Lanzelet is the corollary to the lack of interior development we have already noted: Lanzelet cannot possibly improve, because he is, from childhood on, *der beste*.[24]

Ulrich remains consistent not only in his evaluation of his hero, but also in the political assumptions, evident in the repeated juxtaposition of bad and good monarchs, that underlie his work. At the very beginning we learn that Lanzelet's father, Pant, fought too many wars (46–49), that he despoiled his own nobles (61–63), and that they attacked him because *er was ze grimme an sinen siten* (133). The narrator looks over the whole affair and remarks: *er belibet dicke sigelos, swer die sine verkos* (131–32). Clearly Ulrich feels that Pant deserves his fate and that the vassals' attack is justified. When Lanzelet regains his ancestral kingdom, however, and also when he ascends the throne of his acquired kingdom at Dodone, he behaves quite differently from his father: he seeks the advice of others (8337; 8703–13); he reassigns the vassals their fiefs (8378–81; 9208–11); he rewards the entertainers (8394; 9183–98) and he dispenses lavish gifts (8388–97; 9216–25). In this he follows the example of Arthur, who never acts but with the consent of his court (2276–89; 5231–32; 6975–7025) and who is a paragon of liberality (5722–32; 8667; 8714–30; 8923). From these examples we can extract Ulrich's conception of the ideal king without difficulty: he will respect traditional usages (seeking advice of his court; reassigning fiefs) and he will give generously (to entertainers, to subjects, and to guests).

Lanzelet's coronation at Genewis is not, however, the first time we see him behave as a model ruler in explicit contrast to a bad predecessor. In his very first adventure Lanzelet kills Galagandreiz, *der ie grimmekheite wielt und iuch [die ritter] unrehte hielt* (1203–04; for Pant cf. 133; 102–03); Galagandreiz was so miserly that there was little sorrow at his death (1232–35). When Lanzelet claims Galagandreiz' throne, however, he shows himself at once a model ruler: he is *vil milte* (1249–53) and he respects the advice of *wise liute* (1255). Since we observe Lanzelet behaving as an ideal king at the conclusion of his very first adventure—we do not again see him in this role until the end of the work—we realize that, with regard to kingship, as in every other regard, Lanzelet has nothing to learn: he is by nature the perfect monarch.[25]

The perfect monarch deserves equally virtuous subjects and, in Ulrich's scheme, he gets them. Pant's vassals, after all, do not establish themselves as lords of Genewis but simply hold the kingdom in trust until the rightful heir should appear. At Dodone, too, the vassals remain loyal to a lord they have never seen and willingly turn their kingdom over to Lanzelet as soon as they are able to locate him. In both cases Lanzelet proves himself worthy of this loyalty by performing at his coronation a series of traditional gestures (enfeoffment, consultation, gifts). Ulrich's political model, then, includes two elements: it requires, first, a king, slow to anger, who respects customary usages; and, second, vassals, equally devoted to these same standards, who will recognize virtue in their lord and therefore serve him gladly. The willing fulfillment of reciprocal obligations by king and vassals guarantees the stability of the state, and stability, in spite of the numerous regicides he portrays, is clearly Ulrich's political ideal.

We set out to distinguish inconsistency in *Lanzelet* from consistency and have ended up distinguishing surface from substance as well. We found out that the inconsistencies on the surface of the work result from the limited range of various compositional techniques but that, beneath this surface, Ulrich remains consistent in two matters of substance: the flawlessness of his hero and his model of political stability. Now we must turn to the structural skeleton of *Lanzelet* to determine whether these two consistent concerns are reflected in the over-all organization of the work.[26]

III

Ulrich indicates in a number of ways that the episodes leading up to the revelation of Lanzelet's name (Schatel le mort; Iwaret; the magic tent) are of special importance. Most striking, of course, is the revelation of the name itself; the major suspense of the work is resolved almost at the exact midpoint—a notable felicity in an author celebrated for his carelessness. These episodes are distinguished as well by the literary bravura with which they are composed. They include elaborate and careful descriptions of Iblis (4015–90) and Iwaret (4407–43), of Iwaret's *aventiure* (8371–919) and the Behforet (3940–4014), of the castle at Dodone (4091–189) and, especially, of the magical tent (4760–911). In these descriptions Ulrich parades his learning by including lists of stones (4118–51) and colors (4749–55), and by citing ancient heroes (4761–62) and Latin authors (4852–59). He addresses us directly with unparalleled frequency,[27] sometimes quite boldly (3674–75; 4040–41; 4556–57; 4952); he shows off his familiarity with romance tradition in Iblis' dream (4214–56) and "Minnerede" (4372–406); and he displays his authorial skill by carefully interweaving the portrayal of Iblis' love with the three gong strokes by which Lanzelet summons Iwaret to combat—a compositional equivalent to the ideological interdependence of *minne* and *aventiure.* Finally, these episodes include explicit references both to the beginning and the end of the work, which is not true of any others: Pant's name and fate are recalled (4709–10; 4726–29) as is Lanzelet's childhood with the water-fay (3566–69; 4730–31); and Lanzelet's eventual recovery of Genewis is foretold (4711–13) as is the final return to Dodone (4642–43; 4654–55).

The unusual attention that Ulrich lavishes on these episodes is evident not only in the high concentration of special effects they display, but also in the careful structural organization that supports this sparkling surface. At the center of the three episodes is the fight with Iwaret—*dem besten ritter der ie wart* (329). This is preceded by the passage in which we learn of Iblis' love of Lanzelet (4190–406) and followed by the scene in which we learn that the love is reciprocal (4563–607); the contest by which Lanzelet wins Iblis is, thus, surrounded by the exposition of their love. The entire episode is introduced and concluded by the appearance of the *wizzic abbas.* He functions as messenger—explaining the *aventiure* to Lanzelet (3838–919) and bringing news of the outcome to the people of Dodone (4637–55)—and as gravedigger—promising to bury Lanzelet when he is killed (3910–19) and appearing after the contest with the equipment to carry out his promise (4624–36). His presence, at once friendly and grim, helps impress upon us the magnitude of Lanzelet's accomplishment.

The episode at Schatel le mort, which precedes the Iwaret episode, and the arrival of the water-fay's messenger, which follows, contain several important parallels. First, they both relate directly to the water-fay: Mabuz is her son, and the messenger is her special envoy. Since Lanzelet's foster mother has been absent from the narrative ever since he left her, her explicit reappearance just as our hero reaches Schatel le mort (3565) reminds us of her charge to him; the revelation of Lanzelet's name by the messenger signals the fulfillment of this obligation. Second, both episodes are dependent on the fight that separates them: Iwaret's attacks on Mabuz are the *schamen* (322) that Lanzelet has been commissioned to avenge, and he is released from captivity to accomplish that purpose; the revelation of his name and the gift of the tent are, on the other hand, the rewards for having fulfilled his commission. Third, neither episode includes any significant combat; instead, they depend for their sense on a sort of demonstrative magic. We are told at once that anyone who enters Schatel le mort will be transformed into a coward (3542–47) and this is illustrated immediately by the fate of our hero (3618–37). Later we learn that, in accordance with the inverted logic of the place, the knight who behaves most basely within the castle must be the bravest of all outside its walls (3722–27). Thus Mabuz can conclude, on the basis of the captive Lanzelet's exemplary pusillanimity, that our hero is *der tiurste der nu lebend ist* (3762).

The splendid magic of the tent is quite different from the grim magic of Schatel le mort, but it too serves to demonstrate Lanzelet's excellence. As tangible proof that the messenger's tidings are true (4732–35) the tent substantiates the prophecy: *der man wirt nimer funden, der iu eins tages an gesige* (4714–15). According to the messenger, Lanzelet's excellence is not an acquired trait but a matter of birth: *ir sint . . . von gebürte saelic unde groz* (4706–07); and of prophecy: *ez ist ir [miner vrowen] allez vor geseit, waz wunders iu geschehen sol* (4618–19). Thus the magic of the tent, like that of Schatel le mort, serves to prove Lanzelet the best knight alive.

Considered together, the three central episodes of *Lanzelet* reveal a balanced organization and a common sense. A single, symmetrical episode devoted to combat and love is flanked by two dependent episodes that demonstrate our hero's pre-eminence with the help of magic. In the first, his cowardice within Schatel le mort proves him *der tiurste der nu lebend ist* (3762); in the second, he is the victor over *dem besten ritter der ie wart* (329); and in the third, the messenger confesses: *ich weiz neina iwern genoz* (4708). Thus the three central episodes of *Lanzelet* comprise a three-part demonstration of Lanzelet's essential supereminence: the first demonstration is negative; the second, positive; the third, prophetic.

The two episodes that adjoin the central ones—the tournament at Djofle introduced by the fight with Walwein, and the fight with Valerin in defense of Ginover—themselves form a matched pair, thus extending one step further the symmetry we have already observed. While the medial episodes take place at or near Dodone and in close connection with the water-fay, the tournament at Djofle and the fight with Valerin both take place before Arthur's court and under his aegis. Although we know, from our reading of other romances, that Arthur and his court represent the pinnacle of romance society, Ulrich goes out of his way to remind us of the fact several times in the first half of his own work (1263–86; 2468–71; 2880–85; 3411–13). The tournament at Djofle is Lanzelet's first appearance before this peerless company, and his fight against Valerin is his first service on their behalf. The important role played in both episodes by Walwein, celebrated for his virtue and prowess (2365; 2381; 2688–94; 3013; 5177–81), derives from their shared location: he is dispatched by Arthur to find Lanzelet (2283–315); he is nearly defeated in combat by Lanzelet (2582–85), who nevertheless regards his opinion as binding (2659–61); he is Lanzelet's confidant after the tournament (3502–20); and he is to be the Queen's champion against Valerin before Lanzelet arrives and replaces him (5230–33).

The presence of Arthur's court—at Djofle, at the fight with Valerin, and, by proxy, at the fight with Walwein—makes possible the shared purpose of both episodes: the demonstration of Lanzelet's prowess before the most exalted representatives of romance society. Accordingly, Lanzelet's overriding concern in these episodes is his own *ere*: he sets out looking for a fight (2338–44); he is afraid that he would appear to be captive were he simply to follow Walwein back to Arthur's (2432–33); he considers the *pris und ere* he would reap by a victory over Walwein (2503–15); he stops fighting when a messenger tells him that *maezic lop* is to be had from fighting where no one can watch (2607–09); at the tournament he sets off at once for the most challenging opponents (2880–87); Lanzelet resolves to defend Ginover directly upon learning the victor's reward: *dem wirt dicke wol gesprochen* (5023); and the result of his victory is, indeed, *ere* (5349–51). Lanzelet's victory over Iwaret is, according to the water-fay and her messenger, absolute proof of his prowess, but this proof remains hidden; in the tournament at Djofle and in the defeat of Valerin, the active demonstration of that prowess wins Lanzelet the highest praise possible in the romance world, that of Arthur's court. Walwein, speaking to the court of which he is the most admirable member, says of our hero: *uf der erden lebet niht sin gelich* (3021).

Just as the central episodes of *Lanzelet* are enclosed by its hero's two contests before Arthur's court, so these "Arthurian" episodes are, in turn, framed by another matched pair: Lanzelet's adventure at Limors and his captivity at Pluris. These two episodes share a detail of plot: in both cases a display of knightly valor results in Lanzelet's captivity; and they share a common designation: each is an established *aventiure* (1724; 1875; 5448; 5459). Along with the combat with Iwaret (3854; 3868), they are the only episodes in which Lanzelet elects to attempt a pre-established, open contest with a specific reward.

More important than coincidences of plot and nomenclature, however, are similarities that the episodes at Limors and Pluris reveal between their heroines: Ade and the Lady of Pluris. At first glance the quality of their attachment to Lanzelet seems quite different: Ade's life-saving devotion appears to spring from some unnamed altruism, so seldom is *minne* mentioned in the episode (1500; 1791; 1862; 2247), while the Lady of Pluris, *diun uz der maze minnete* (5571), is quite clearly driven by passion. Yet both share an aggressiveness uncommon among women in Arthurian romance. Three times at Limors, Lanzelet's very survival depends on Ade's active, unsolicited intercession: she rescues him from the attackers who greet him; she negotiates his release from prison; and she nurses him back to life after his victory. The Lady of Pluris is so taken with Lanzelet that she disarms him, has him closely guarded, and keeps him captive for over a year. To appreciate the extraordinary boldness of these women, we need only recall the conventional passivity of Iblis: she faints when Lanzelet fights; she forgives him at once for having killed her father; and she is willing to follow him anywhere; at the "Mantelprobe"—during the Pluris episode!—her *triuwe* is proved not by anything she does, but by the behavior of a cloak. In contrast with this passive courtliness, the aggressive devotion of Ade and the Lady of Pluris is all the more striking and serves to distinguish between the episodes at Limors and at Pluris from the rest of *Lanzelet*.[28] Whereas in the previous pair of episodes Lanzelet's pre-eminence was illustrated by the response of Arthur's court, here it is demostrated by the reaction he provokes in women. How appropriate that Lanzelet, called on his release from Schatel le mort *der sigesaelige man* (3789), should, in the Pluris episode, be dubbed *der wipsaelige Lanzelet* (5529)!

The episodes that form our next pair—the fight with Galagandreiz; the rescue of Ginover, Walwein, and Erec—seem to have more in common, structurally at least, with the episodes adjacent to them than with each other. The Galagandreiz episode, like that of Limors and Djofle, begins with an interrupted fight (Kuraus–Orphilet; Lanzelet–Linier's knights; Lanzelet-Walwein); each of these episodes finds its high point in a three-part event (Galagandreiz' daughter solicits Orphilet, Kuraus, and Lanzelet; Lanzelet fights a giant, two lions, and Linier; Lanzelet distinguishes himself at a three-day tournament). The rescue of Ginover, Walwein, and Erec, on the other hand, shares structural traits with the episodes in the second half of the romance: it, like the Pluris adventure, is a compound episode (Lanzelet's stay at Pluris encloses the "Mantelprobe"; the rescue of Ginover requires the surrender of Walwein and Erec, thus creating the need to liberate them); in each of these same two episodes captives must be rescued (Lanzelet by four Arthurian comrades; Ginover by Malduc; Erec and Walwein by Esealt) rather than fighting their way free as Lanzelet does in earlier episodes; and finally, three episodes of the second part—trial by combat with Valerin, Pluris, rescue of Ginover and the two heroes—contain nearly all of those strange, quasi-independent scenes that have so upset some of the critics (*diu Wachsende warte* [5124–62]; *der stumme Gilimar* [6563–672]; *daz Schriende mos, der wilde Dodones*, and *der Stiebende steg* [7040–151]).[29] We see, then, that the episodes that precede Schatel le mort share distinguishing traits as do those that follow the revelation of Lanzelet's name, that Ulrich unites series of adjacent episodes by structural analogy while correspondences of sense connect disjunct episodes in a symmetrical pattern.

But what are the correspondences of sense between the Galagandreiz episode and the rescue of Ginover, Erec, and Walwein? I think we will be able to answer this question only if we consider at the same time the next pair of matching episodes: Lanzelet's quick course in knightly skills with Johfrit, and his certification as the best knight alive by the serpentine Elidia. After the first,

Lanzelet is said to have been *gebezzert* (667) (only with regard to knightly technique!); in the last he is said to be *der beste ritter, der nu lebet* (7921). These two non-combat episodes mark the beginning and end of Lanzelet's series of active adventures. What of their relation to the adjacent ends of the series itself? After Lanzelet leaves Johfrit, he meets Kuraus and Orphilet, and they stop fighting at his request (698–704); at Galagandreiz, Lanzelet takes precedence over his companions (794–801); he is the one who wins the daughter and kills the host; he shows himself in the end to be a model king (1249–57); and he is praised without reservation at Arthur's (1326–56): thus the Galagandreiz episode shows us that Lanzelet, even though he has only just been taught the techniques of knightly combat, already outshines everybody else. The situation is altogether reversed in the rescue of Ginover and the two heroes. Here Lanzelet, as we have already seen, plays hardly any role at all: he is not the one to rescue the Queen nor is he more than the initiator of the rescue of Walwein and Erec. Yet immediately following this less-than-glorious performance, the Court is transported by universal admiration for Lanzelet—they agree *daz kein ritter bezzer waere* (7811)—and then the Elidia episode demonstrates conclusively that Lanzelet is without peer.[30] Thus, where the juxtaposition of Johfrit and Galagandreiz shows Lanzelet to be the best even though he is just beginning, the juxtaposition of the rescue episode with Elidia shows him to be the best even when he doesn't do a thing.[31] Once again Ulrich demonstrates the unchanging perfection of his hero.

Lanzelet's active career as a knight, the beginning and end of which are marked by the Johfrit and Elidia episodes, is enclosed within our last group of matched episodes: the fall of Pant and Lanzelet's childhood at the outset; and his double accession at the end. These four episodes show the same system of correspondences as the four parts of the prologue: one and two share a common topic (childhood) as do three and four (accession),[32] yet one is related to three (Lanzelet regains the throne his father lost) as two is to four (the charge of the water-fay leads to the throne of Dodone). Note that Lanzelet's course from the water-fay to Dodone depends on his defeat of Iwaret, and that single mention of Lanzelet's ancestral kingdom during his adventures comes immediately after the revelation of his name at midpoint (4709–29). Thus the first and last episodes of the work depend for their coherence on the all-important central episodes.

The most important function of the four episodes that begin and end *Lanzelet,* however, is to provide that "eminently political framework" of which W.H. Jackson speaks:[33] in the first episode we witness the fate of the bad king Pant; in the last episode we twice watch Lanzelet ascend a throne and behave as a model ruler. In the episode of his growing up, Lanzelet acquires those qualities that distinguish him from his father and make possible his success as king: lapidary magic renders him constantly cheerful (230–40); his guardian teaches him virtue (241–47); and she admonishes him at the last moment *daz er waere staete und ie daz beste taete* (395–96). We have already seen that Ulrich attaches considerable importance to kingly virtue and that he treats this theme with, for him, altogether uncommon consistency; the first and last episodes of his work are the ones in which this theme makes its major appearances.

Perhaps now you are willing to agree that *Lanzelet* reveals a symmetrical organization: at the center are three episodes in which Lanzelet is shown to be, absolutely, the best knight alive; these are surrounded by two episodes in which his unmatched prowess earns him the unreserved admiration of Arthur's court; the Ade and Pluris episodes reveal the aggressive devotion that Lanzelet's excellence can inspire in women; these are enclosed by episodes that show him without peer even though, at Galagandreiz, he is a knightly novice, and, at the rescue of Ginover, Erec, and Walwein, he hardly does a thing; the beginning and end of Lanzelet's adventures are marked by the non-combative Johfrit and Elidia episodes; and the entire romance is framed by episodes concerned with kingship and the celebration of Lanzelet's kingly virtue.[34] The following diagram will, perhaps, show the pattern more clearly:

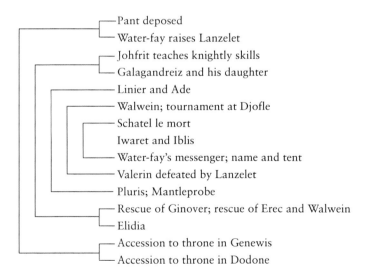

- Pant deposed
- Water-fay raises Lanzelet
- Johfrit teaches knightly skills
- Galagandreiz and his daughter
- Linier and Ade
- Walwein; tournament at Djofle
- Schatel le mort
- Iwaret and Iblis
- Water-fay's messenger; name and tent
- Valerin defeated by Lanzelet
- Pluris; Mantleprobe
- Rescue of Ginover; rescue of Erec and Walwein
- Elidia
- Accession to throne in Genewis
- Accession to throne in Dodone

Yet even if you are convinced by this evidence, you will wonder whether Ulrich's fondness for symmetry is anything more than an organizational trick, any more, that is, than those progressive patterns that we discussed earlier. The over-all symmetrical pattern does, of course, encompass the entire romance, while the progressive patterns incorporate only a few episodes; and the symmetry of the whole is, as we have seen, mirrored in the rhetorical organization of the prologue and the composition of the Iwaret and Elidia episodes. Yet you still want to know whether this inclusive symmetrical pattern is merely the imposition on Ulrich's work of a contemporary scholarly prejudice.

We concluded, after isolating the inconsistencies in Lanzelet, that Ulrich remains consistent in the evaluation of his hero and in his portrayal of political stability. Lanzelet, in spite of the various progressive patterns that tempt us to posit some internal evolution on his part, does not develop in the course of the romance; and Ulrich, in spite of behavior on Lanzelet's part that we might consider questionable, consistently regards his hero as *der beste*. A hero who is immutably excellent is a stable hero; let us call Lanzelet an instance of heroic stability. Ulrich's political theory is implied in his portrayal of kings and their vassals: those kings who are stingy and unjust will be overthrown; but those who are generous and who respect traditional usages will, on account of the loyal devotion that such behavior elicits from their vassals, guarantee harmony in their kingdoms. A harmonious kingdom is a stable kingdom; let us call Ulrich's political ideas a model of political stability. We have just seen how the sequence of episodes in *Lanzelet* is in fact organized according to a symmetrical pattern. As a symmetrical structure is a stable one, let us call our romance an example of structural stability. Taken together, then, we have abstracted three sorts of stability in *Lanzelet*: heroic, political, and structural; we have found, that is, a level of abstraction on which crucial elements of character, theme, and composition coincide, a coincidence that gives Ulrich's work its essential coherence.[35]

The extent to which Ulrich's concern with stability in form and content pervades his romance can be clearly seen in the position of the episode at Pluris and of the episode in which Ginover, Erec, and Walwein are rescued. Lanzelet's passivity at Pluris and his marginal involvement at the rescues imply a regression from his previous feats of prowess that forces us to abandon those theories that would have him improve throughout the work. Since, however, these episodes fit into our symmetrical scheme without difficulty, we must conclude that Ulrich was more eager to preserve his organizational plan than to protect the reputation of his hero; that reputation, after all, was safe by definition.[36] The timing of Lanzelet's decision to return to Genewis also testifies to Ulrich's careful harmonization of the structure of his romance with its themes. So complete is the correspondence of the perfect hero, the static world, and the stable literary form that, in spite of the information about Genewis revealed by the water-fay's messenger along with Lanzelet's name, the thought of returning to his father's kingdom does not once cross Lanzelet's mind until the precise moment when he has completed the symmetrical demonstration of his excellence. By then we have forgotten about Genewis, but Ulrich has not; he has merely been keeping it hidden until it was required by the symmetrical scheme of the work.

In isolating stasis—heroic, political, and structural—as the element that unites *Lanzelet*, we have advanced a new comprehensive interpretation of the work, replacing those we were forced to reject earlier.[37] These other interpretations tended to discover in Ulrich's work only those patterns that had already been established elsewhere: *Lanzelet* was divided in two like *Erec;* its hero was said to increase in understanding like *Parzival.* Because of their origin in the analysis of other works, these hand-me-down interpretations automatically established connections between *Lanzelet* and the rest of the Arthurian canon. Now that we have rejected the interpretations, however, we have forfeited as well the connections they established between *Lanzelet* and its literary surroundings. How, on the basis of our new understanding, shall we re-establish it in literary history?

IV

Among German Arthurian romances *Lanzelet* is unique in the strength of its political concerns. To be sure, the genre seems to require that its heroes end their careers as kings, but most authors are content with the briefest mention of the fact. Neither Erec nor Iwein, nor Gwigalois nor Meleranz nor Gauriel nor the Gawein of *Diu Crone* is anywhere portrayed in any detail as a ruler.[38] Erec and Gwigalois do organize large celebrations in connection with their coronations, but these celebrations are described most briefly: the heroes are not even said to dispense gifts.[39] Parzival is praised as the lord of Pelrapeire, but the encomium lasts only 19 lines and is couched in the most general terms.[40] Stricker's Daniel organizes a huge *hochzit* in connection with which he is praised both in general terms and, in particular, for reassigning Matur's fiefs;[41] yet only a few lines earlier, in keeping with the uncharacteristic activity King Arthur displays in this work, Arthur is the one dispensing fiefs, and he, not Daniel, reaps all the praise for liberality.[42] The pattern in *Garel* comes closest to that in *Lanzelet*: Garel enfeoffs; he is generous; he rewards the players; and he is celebrated as a model king.[43] But Garel does not seek the counsel of his vassals, and the portrayal of him as a model ruler lasts only 300 lines. The double demonstration at the end of *Lanzelet*, on the other hand, requires over 1200 lines. When we consider in addition to Ulrich's lengthy portrayal of a model king his pendant analyses of the bad kings Pant and Galagandreiz, then we realize that Ulrich attaches vastly more importance to the portrayal of kingly virtue than do the authors of other MHG Arthurian romances.[44]

The intensity of Ulrich's political interests is unusual not only among the authors of German verse romance, but also among those who treated the Lancelot material. In Chrestien's *Charrette,* of course, the hero's kingship plays no role at all. In the prose *Lancelot,* on the other hand, the loss and reacquisition of Lancelot's ancestral kingdom are of importance; yet the events are related much differently than they are by Ulrich. In the prose romance, Lancelot's father, Ban, is attacked not by his vassals but by his neighbor, the *verreter* Claudas, who has the assistance of Ban's own treasonous steward.[45] With the exception of the steward, Ban seems to have been loved by his subjects, and he dies an exemplary, pious death.[46] While in Ulrich's version the revolt against Pant was clearly the result of his own harsh government, here a beloved king is attacked from without. Much later in the prose *Lancelot* Arthur wins back Ban's country and tries to bestow it on its rightful heir; but Lancelot passes the crown on at once to several relatives. There is no demonstration of kingly virtue; there is not even mention of a celebration. Of the 2000 pages of the prose *Lancelot,* the restoration of legitimate power in Bonewig takes less than one.[47] Ulrich's work, which has long been known to differ from the orthodox Lancelot tradition in two ways—there is no adulterous love between Lanzelet and Ginover; Lanzelet does not rescue the Queen from her abductor[48]—is seen to differ as well in the attention it devotes to the political aspect of the narrative. Ulrich transforms Lanzelet's father into an exemplary bad king and turns Lanzelet's own regency into a lengthy demonstration of kingly virtue.

Yet Ulrich does not stand altogether alone in the strength of his political interests. Prior works such as the *Rolandslied* and the *Kaiserchronik* present at length active, model rulers, contrasted in the *Kaiserchronik* at least, with a series of wicked kings. Even *König Rother* and *Herzog Ernst* are, according to Ehrismann, meant to portray "die ideale Gestalt eines Fürsten."[49] One finds similar portrayals in the works of younger authors as well. In *Willehalm von Orlens* and *Alexander* Rudolf von Ems incorporates the complete catalogue of kingly virtues in the figures of his heroes, thus presenting the lessons of a *Fürstenspiegel* as part of a lengthy, coherent narrative.[50] Helmut Brackert calls this type a "Fürstenlehre."[51] *Lanzelet* differs from these "political" works, both younger and older, in two ways. First, the other works, even *König Rother,* are based on, or explicitly linked with, genuine historical material, while *Lanzelet,* as an Arthurian romance, claims no such pedigree. Second, while in the historical romances the actions of the model king dominate the narrative, in *Lanzelet* the political discussion is restricted to the beginning and the end of the work. In spite of these qualifications, however, we can recognize that Ulrich, unusual among Arthurian authors for the extent of his political interests, and unique among those who treated the Lancelot material for the same reason, does not stand altogether isolated among MHG authors. Unusual is only the extent to which he incorporated the political concerns common in historically based narrative into the world of Arthurian romance.

While Ulrich differs from the authors of other Arthurian romances in the intensity of his political interests, he is not at all unusual in presenting a flawless hero. Gwigalois, like Lanzelet, never makes a mistake, nor does the hero of *Diu Crone*.[52] Daniel often ponders two possible reactions, but he always chooses the right course in the end.[53] Tandareiz, Meleranz, and Garel are likewise without blemish. The scholarly devotion to Erec, Iwein, and Parzival has inclined us to expect all Arthurian heroes to commit some crucial mistake; yet, in spite of all the attention these erring celebrities have attracted, no one but Gauriel has followed their example. Lanzelet, then, belongs to the majority camp; in fact, viewed chronologically, he is the first of all the flawless Arthurian heroes.[54]

Just as we tend to expect all Arthurian heroes to commit some crucial mistake, so we assume that the structure of an Arthurian romance will be determined by the position of that mistake in the narrative. This assumption derives, of course, from Hugo Kuhn's analysis of *Erec*, according to which the two parts, clearly articulated by a crisis, have a necessary relation both to each other and to the meaning of the whole.[55] A number of scholars, hoping no doubt to improve Ulrich's reputation, have detected a bipartite organization in *Lanzelet*;[56] yet none of those who propose such an analysis has pointed to a scene, analogous to Erec's *verligen*, that clearly divides the work in two, nor has anyone attempted to demonstrate that the proposed two parts are rooted in the internal logic of the work. To maintain that Ulrich wrote a bipartite work without at the same time demonstrating that the sense of the work requires two parts is merely to say that Ulrich adopted a fashionable form without understanding it. This is not likely to improve his reputation.

Ulrich did not model his hero on Erec, nor was he concerned, like Hartmann, to question the ideological commonplaces of the romance world; thus he had little reason to adopt the two-part structure so suitable for Hartmann's work. Instead Ulrich conceived an unchangingly flawless hero, a paragon of kingly virtue, and employed a structure appropriate to him. The symmetrical organization of *Lanzelet* reflects, as we saw earlier, both the static perfection of its hero and its concern with political stability. *Erec* and *Lanzelet*, the first two German Arthurian romances, introduced two possible models: *Erec* with its asymmetrical, bipartite organization, its flawed hero, and its problematical theme; *Lanzelet* with a balanced, symmetrical pattern, a flawless hero, and a static theme. Yet whereas the synthesis achieved in *Erec* underlies both *Iwein* and *Parzival*, that achieved in *Lanzelet* attracted no imitators. The flawless hero, to be sure, turns up over and over, but neither the structural equivalent of that hero nor its thematic analogue, neither the symmetrical form nor the model of political stability, is to be found in any other Arthurian romance.

I do not want to claim that *Lanzelet* is the equal of *Erec,* not by any means. Doubtless we will continue to prefer Hartmann and Wolfram to Ulrich for their greater literary virtuosity as well as for the greater interest we bring both to their flawed heroes and to their thematic complexity. But this preference need not blind us to Ulrich's own accomplishments. He introduced the flawless hero to German Arthurian romance; he alone developed a model of political stability within the confines of the Arthurian world; and he, in the symmetrical structure of his work, found a formal pattern suitable both to his hero and his theme.

NOTES

1. F. Norman, "Nachwort" to: Ulrich von Zatzikhoven, *Lanzelet*, ed. K.A. Hahn, 1845; rpt. Berlin 1965, p. 292. Verse numbers in parentheses refer to this edition.

2. K. Ruh, "Der *Lanzelet* Ulrichs von Zatzikhoven: Modell oder Kompilation?" in: *Deutsche Literatur des späten Mittelalters*, Hamburger Colloquium 1973, ed. W. Harms and L.P. Johnson, Berlin 1975, pp. 48–49.

3. "Der erste Teil nimmt das Gespräch mit den Empfängern auf; der zweite Teil führt in das Werk ein" (H. Brinkmann, "Der Prolog im Mittelalter als literarische Erscheinung: Bau und Aussage," WW 14 [1964] , p. 8). "Den *prologus praeter rem* macht die mittelalterliche Poetik . . . zum Träger allgemeiner Erörterung des Proverbiums (der Sentenz), oder des Exempels"; the *prologus ante rem* "setzt dann mit dem Erzählvorhaben ein" (P. Kobbe, *Funktion und Gestalt des Prologs in der mittelhochdeutschen nachklassischen Epik des 13. Jahrhunderts*, DVjs 43 [1969], p. 414).

4. G.G. Gervinus, *Geschichte der poetischen National-Literatur der Deutschen*, Leipzig ²1840, I, 261.

5. Stefan Hofer, for example, writing 120 years after Gervinus, calls *Lanzelet* a "zusammenhangslose Aufeinanderfolge von Liebesabenteuern und ritterlicher Betätigung" (St. Hofer, "Der *Lanzelet* des Ulrich von Zatzikhoven und seine französische Quelle," ZfromPh 75 [1959], p. 35).

6. E. Soudek, "Die Funktion der Namensuche und der Zweikämpfe in Ulrich von Zatzikhovens *Lanzelet*," *Amsterdamer Beiträge zur älteren Germanistik* 2 (1972), pp. 173–82. R. Combridge, "Lanzelet and the Queens," in *Essays in German and Dutch Literature*, ed. W.D. Robson-Scott, London 1973 (Publications of the Institute of Germanic Studies 15), pp. 42–64. H. Schüppert, "Minneszenen und Struktur im *Lanzelet* Ulrichs von Zatzikhoven," in: *Würzburger Prosastudien* II: Untersuchungen zur Literatur und Sprache des Mittelalters: Kurt Ruh zum 60. Geburtstag, ed. P.

Kesting, Munich 1975 (*Medium Ævum* 31), pp. 123–38. K. Ruh (note 2), pp. 47–55.

7. "Der Minnekasus der nicht gewährten Minne . . . erscheint offensichtlich als Rechtfertigung der bereitwillig gewährten Minne im ersten Teil des Romans" (Ruh [note 2], p. 53).

8. K.A. Hahn, "Vorrede" to: *Lanzelet* (note 1), pp. v–viii.

9. A. Leitzmann, "Zu Ulrichs *Lanzelet*," *PBB* 55 (1931), pp. 300–02.

10. W. Richter, *Der 'Lanzelet' des Ulrich von Zatzikhoven*, Frankfurt a. M. 1934 (*Deutsche Forschungen* 27), pp. 216–43, here p. 221.

11. E. Faral, *Les Arts poétiques du XIIe et du XIIIe siècle*, Paris 1962, p. 61.

12. Even in his title, "Die Funktion der Namensuche . . .", Soudek (note 6) implies that Lanzelet is motivated by the desire to find his name. Soudek refers to Dodone as "das Ziel aller seiner Bestrebungen" (p. 180) and states, when Lanzelet leaves after the tournament at Djofle, that he rides off "immer auf der Suche nach seinem Namen" (p. 180)—even though Lanzelet gives his goal as Pluris (3501–05).

13. Soudek (note 6), p. 173.

14. That Lanzelet is motivated by his namelessness is the most modest claim that has been made for this feature of Ulrich's work: Ruh speaks of Lanzelet's "Namenfindung" as "Zu-sich-selber-kommen, Selbstverwirklichung" (Ruh [note 2], p. 50) and Soudek maintains that Lanzelet, in learning his name, gains "größere Einsicht in sein Wesen" (Soudek [note 6], p. 181). But how can one speak of self-realization and great insights in a hero who is happily oblivious of his supposed goal for the last third of his quest?

15. In Chrestien's *Charrette* (Chrétien de Troyes, *Le Chevalier de la Charrette*, ed. M. Roques, Paris 1975 [Les Romans de Chrétien de Troyes 3]) the question of motivation in connection with the hero's namelessness cannot arise, for there Lancelot does know his name; we, and the captives at Gorre, are the only ones kept in suspense. Ulrich, who is not so bold as Chrestien, disguises the same organizational gimmick behind the fiction of Lanzelet's own ignorance of his name.

16. Combridge (note 6), p. 48.

17. Schüppert (note 6), p. 133.

18. Schüppert (note 6), p. 130.

19. Ruh (note 2), p. 50.

20. Lanzelet is, in fact, barely visible during most of this episode. On his return from Pluris he is grouped together with his own rescuers as *die helde vermezzen* (6680) or *diu fünf degene her* (6765). Only once is Lanzelet given precedence—*sine gesellen unde Lanzelet* (6817)—but this is closely followed by: *die viere unde Walwein* (6825)! Lanzelet's name is mentioned only once (7274) from the moment he sets out with Arthur to win the aid of Malduc (7031) until he recruits the band for the rescue of Walwein and Erec (7480); that is, he is virtually ignored during the entire rescue of Ginover!

21. Lanzelet's behavior in these same two episodes would seem to undermine those interpretations that ascribe to him an increase in social self-sacrifice in the second half of the work: Luise Lerner writes of "Gemeinschaftsdienst" (L. Lerner, *Studien zur Komposition des höfischen Romans im 13. Jahrhundert*, Münster 1936 [Forschungen zur deutschen Sprache und Dichtung 7], p. 19); Ruh of "Gemeinschaftssinn" (Ruh [note 2], p. 54); Soudek of "caritas" (Soudek [note 6], p. 182). Yet there can be no talk of self-sacrifice at Pluris nor, on Lanzelet's part at least, at the rescue of Ginover. The success of this enterprise depends on the "Gemeinschaftssinn" of Walwein and Erec, who allow themselves to be taken prisoner, and on the "Gemeinschaftsdienst" of the giant Esealt, who rescues them.

22. On the basis of the same evidence I would question two interpretations of the first part of *Lanzelet*. Kuhn writes: "Dieser dreistufige Minneweg Lanzelets verschlingt sich mit den drei Stufen seines Ritterwegs zur Tafelrunde" (H. Kuhn, "Die Klassik des Rittertums in der Stauferzeit," in: *Annalen der deutschen Literatur*, ed. H.O.

Burger, Stuttgart ²1971, p. 136); yet the notion of progress that the three steps implies is not borne out by the text. Lerner entitles the first half of *Lanzelet*: "Lanzelets Erziehung zum Ritter" (Lerner [note 21], p. 17); yet Lanzelet is already the best possible knight in his first adventure. What sort of education does he need?

23. Schüppert (note 6), p. 133, note 36.

24. Ruh, who divides *Lanzelet* into two parts, states: "Programm des zweiten Teils ist Lanzelets Bewährung als *bester ritter* " (Ruh [note 2], p. 51). But, since Lanzelet shows himself to be (and is called) the best from the very start, I do not see how this definition distinguishes part two from the rest of the work.

25. For this reason I disagree with W.H. Jackson, who, while certainly right in stressing the importance of politics in *Lanzelet*, feels that "the narrative . . . is concerned at least in part with Lanzelet's education for kingship" (W.H. Jackson, "Ulrich von Zatzikhoven's *Lanzelet* and the Theme of Resistance to Royal Power," *German Life and Letters*, N. S. 28 [1975], p. 286). Similarly, I do not understand why Lerner calls the second half of the work "Lanzelets Erziehung zum Landesherrn" (Lerner [note 21], p. 17) when he is already a flawless monarch at the beginning of the first half.

26. Lerner, Kuhn, Soudek, and Ruh would all divide *Lanzelet* into two parts. Without exception they characterize each part according to the kind of development that Lanzelet makes within it. If we are right in regarding Lanzelet's development as illusory, then these characterizations are not valid, and the dependent division into two parts will collapse (see notes 12, 14, 21, 22, 24, and 25).

27. I count 46 narrator remarks in the 1032 lines between Lanzelet's departure for the Behforet (3929) and his departure for Arthur's court (4960). By contrast, there are only 17 such remarks in the first 1032 lines of the poem, 12 during the episode at Limors (1365–2249), and 25 during the first 1032 lines of the Pluris episode (5420–6451).

28. The daughter of Galagandreiz, in spite of her boldness, does not fit into this category. Lanzelet, on account of his distance from the door, is only her third choice among the knights who might still her lust, a slight for which he does not forgive her (1109–12).

29. "Dabei ist dieser Sinn in Stoff un Kompositon so überwuchert von einer verwilderten, planlosen Märchenhaftigkeit . . ." (Kuhn [note 22], p. 136). "Stoffbefangen sieht Ulrich das Wesentliche seiner Aufgabe im Außerordentlichen und Unheimlichen" (H. de Boor, *Geschichte der deutschen Literatur*, ed H. de Boor and R. Newald, Munich ⁷1966, II, 86).

30. We should note that the Elidia episode, like the Iwaret episode, is itself organized symmetrically: at the center is the kiss and transformation (7930–53); this is surrounded by two passages in which the serpent/Elidia explains the nature and meaning of the adventure (7904–29; 7954–61); these speeches are in turn surrounded by Lanzelet's journeys to and from the woods (7882–93; 7962–64), followed by the reaction of his companions/the Court (7894–903; 7965–82); the entire adventure is introduced by Iblis' account of the serpent (7817–81) and concluded by Elidia's account of her story (7983–8040).

31. I am tempted to support both my symmetrical prejudice as well as my isolation of Lanzelet's active career as a knight with a striking numerical coincidence: the first part of the adventure series, from Johfrit through the tournament, comprises 3074 lines (452–3525); while the last part, from the fight with Valerin through Elidia, comprises 3081 (4960–8040).

32. Note that the two accession episodes, in spite of their difference in length, are organized on the same pattern: messengers find their object by chance (8161; 8555); vassals who have kept order in Lanzelet's absence (8208–20; 8744–55) act out of *triuwe* (8293; 8332; 8741); they prove their good intentions by delivering money or gifts (8315–32; 8477–547); Lanzelet takes counsel (8337–39; 8703–13); Arthur and Lanzelet set out after the Court has gotten itself suitably prepared (8346–47; 8851–909); the journey is filled with joy and lots of courtly entertainment (8340–54; 9001–

86); they are suitably greeted (8355–65; 9087–198); the coronation is followed by the enfeoffment of Lanzelet's vassals, the distribution of gifts, and general happiness (8370–405; 9199–269); the episode is brought to an end by the departure of Lanzelet and Arthur (8430–61; 9270–308). These two episodes, then, are united not only by theme but also by structural analogy—like the three adjacent episodes in the first part of the work (Galagandreiz, Linier, Walwein/tourney) and the two in the second part (Pluris, multiple rescue).

33. Jackson (note 25), p. 285.

34. M. Huby also detects a symmetrical organization in *Lanzelet*, but his symmetry depends on the completely arbitrary (he calls it "très souple", p. 155) division of the "bloc" (M. Huby, "Remarques sur la structure du *Lanzelet*," in: *Mélanges pour Jean Fourquet*, ed. P. Valentin and G. Zink, Munich/Paris 1969, pp. 147–56).

35. On the limits of this kind of analogical equation see: H. Kuhn, *Tristan, Nibelungenlied, Artusstruktur*, Munich 1973 (Bayer. Akad. der Wiss., phil.-hist. Kl., SB 1973, 5), pp. 36–38.

36. For a more general discussion of the contradictions engendered by the conflicting claims of surface patterns and underlying structures see: J.A. Schultz, *The Shape of the Round Table: Structure and Genre in Middle High German Arthurian Romance*, Diss. Princeton 1977, pp. 183–98.

37. See note 26.

38. We must not confuse the brief catalogues of standard virtues addressed by their fathers to the young kings Gwigalois and Meleranz with the portrayal of the hero as king (Wirnt von Gravenberc, *Wigalois*, ed. J. M. N. Kapteyn, Bonn 1926 [Rheinische Beiträge und Hülfsbücher 9], vv. 11521–65; Der Pleier, *Meleranz*, ed. K. Bartsch, Stuttgart 1861 [Bibliothek des litterarischen Vereins 60], vv. 12614–40). Nor should we mistake Gwigalois' campaign against Lion, which is, after all, led by Gawein, with the portrayal of Gwigalois as king.

39. Mitgau's thesis was that *Wigalois* presents a new ideal of kingship more admirable than Arthur's model is surely overstated (W. Mitgau, "Nachahmung und Selbständigkeit Wirnts von Gravenberc in seinem *Wigalois*," ZfdPh 82 [1963], pp. 334–37). The brevity of Arthur's final appearance and the passing mention of Gwigalois' kindness to the poor (vv. 11621–24) do not suffice to undermine the ideological prerequisite—Arthur's ideality—of the entire genre (See: C. Cormeau, *'Wigalois' und 'Diu Crone': Zwei Kapitel zur Gattungsgeschichte des nachklassischen Aventiureromans*, Munich 1977 [MTU 57], pp. 36–38).

40. Wolfram von Eschenbach, *Parzival*, ed. A. Leitzmann, Tübingen[7] 1961 (ATB 12), 222, 10–28.

41. Der Stricker, *Daniel*, ed. G. Rosenhagen, Breslau 1894 (Germanistische Abhandlungen 9), vv. 8459–78.

42. Ibid., vv. 8305–11; 8394–97; 8444–49.

43. Der Pleier, *Garel von dem Blüenden Tal*, ed. M. Walz, Freiburg i.B. 1892, vv. 9111–19; 9289–307; 9124–28; 9331–42; 21270–86.

44. One might mention in this connection the addition to *Iwein* found in MS. f in which some later scribe has attempted to improve Hartmann's work by adding about 100 lines describing Iwein as ruler. This fifteenth century Iwein distinguished himself not only for the traditional virtues—justice, liberality, piety—but for his public works projects as well: he built good roads and bridges and outlawed tolls and taxes (Text in: Hartmann von Aue, *Iwein*, ed. and trans. T. Cramer, Berlin 1968, pp. 226–28).

45. *Lancelot*, ed. R. Kluge, Berlin 1948 (DTM 42), I, 1–12.

46. Ibid., I, 5, 22; I, 12, 8–13, 22.

47. *Lancelot*, ed. R. Kluge, Berlin 1963 (DTM 47), II, 776.

48. Jessie Weston seems to have been the first to recognize both differences (J. Weston, *The Legend of Sir Lancelot du Lac: Studies Upon its Origin, Development, and Position in the Arthurian Romantic Cycle*, London 1901, pp. 15–16; 21).

49. G. Ehrismann, *Geschichte der deutschen Literatur bis zum Ausgang des Mittelalters*, Munich 1922, 1927, II, 1, p. 308; II, 2, p. 47.

50. The "Fürstenspiegel" itself did not appear in German speaking lands until nearly 1300 (W. Berges, *Die Fürstenspiegel des hohen und späten Mittelalters*, Leipzig 1938, p. 106). Even the earliest of those works that Lucie Sandrock erroneously lables "Fürstenspiegel" (*Wartburgkrieg*, Jans Enikel's *Fürstenbuch*, Ottokar von Steiermark's *Reimchronik*) did not make its appearance until about 1260 (L. Sandrock, *Das Herrscherideal in der erzählenden Dichtung des deutschen Mittelalters*, Münster 1931, p. 59ff).

51. H. Brackert, Rudolf von Ems: *Dichtung und Geschichte*, Heidelberg 1968, p. 8; 220.

52. On the consequences of Gwigalois' and Gawein's flawlessness for the structure of their respective works see: Cormeau (note 39), pp. 48–49; 58–59; 66–68; 142–43; 164–65.

53. Der Stricker, *Daniel* (note 41), vv. 1056–110; 1159–74; 1843–73; 2167–203; 2689–93.

54. Cormeau, citing the support of de Boor and Kuhn, notes a general tendency towards static, ideal heroes that developed in the early 13th century. He suggests that this tendency is a reaction to the classical Arthurian romances, which had taught audiences to expect their heroes to achieve some sort of ideality by the end of the work. The expectation was so strong, argues Cormeau, that it affected the essential nature of the Arthurian hero; flawed heroes were no longer possible (Cormeau [note 39], p. 67). The examples of *Lanzelet* and *Gauriel*, however, would seem to undermine Cormeau's theory. Ulrich's flawless hero was certainly conceived before *Parzival* and most likely before *Iwein* as well; and if expectations aroused by the end of *Erec* are advanced to explain *Lanzelet*, as Cormeau does to explain *Wigalois*, then audiences must have been terribly disappointed with *Iwein* and *Parzival*. The erring Gauriel, on the other hand, was created after Gwigalois and the Gawein of *Diu Crone*, at which time, according to Cormeau's theory, the expectation of flawless heroes ought to have been even more binding than it was for Wirnt or Heinrich von dem Türlin. Again we see the danger of taking the works of Hartmann and Wolfram as the sole standard when, with regard to heroic flaws at least, they are clearly the exception.

55. H. Kuhn, *Erec*, in: *Dichtung und Welt im Mittelalter*, Stuttgart 1959, pp. 133–50.

56. See note 26.

3 AN INTERPRETER'S DILEMMA

WHY ARE THERE SO MANY INTERPRETATIONS OF CHRÉTIEN'S *CHEVALIER DE LA CHARRETTE?*

Matilda Tomaryn Bruckner

Lancelot's behavior provides the focus of passionate debate, not only in the romance whose very name suggests his paradoxical nature—what knight is properly to be associated with a cart?—but also in the many scholarly attempts to decide whether Lancelot is an extraordinary hero or a despicable fool, savior of Arthur's kingdom or an adulterous traitor to Arthur as king and husband. Indeed the majority of scholars working on the *Charrette* can be divided *grosso modo* into partisans and opponents of Lancelot, with Lancelot located somewhere in the middle.[1] Some recent work on the *Charrette*, however, has shifted its attention from the arguments for and against Lancelot to the ambiguity that characterizes Chrétien's narrative strategies and activates these diverging critical interpretations. Joseph J. Duggan affirms the value of ambiguity for Chrétien,[2] while Norris J. Lacy discusses his ironic techniques for obscuring narrative point of view as a means to keep open the question of meaning.[3] As Lacy also points out (1980: 58–9, 92–3), the activity of interpretation is not limited to Chrétien's critics: narrator and characters are busy throughout the *Charrette* analyzing the knotty problems that intrigue us, trying to relate actions and values—and illustrating with their own errors and misapprehensions the pitfalls that await would-be interpreters. Indeed, Chrétien's romance represents the problem of interpretation(s), as much as it does Lancelot's quest for the Queen. While 20th-century interpreters tend to see the Middle Ages as a period of "closed" texts whose meanings are determined and determinable by reference to an external ideology,[4] a close reading of Chrétien's work (and, I think, of romance in general) reveals a world where the ambiguities of signs may require an inexhaustible series of interpretations (cf. Howard Bloch 1974). We are not so very far, after all, from the modern preoccupation with "Fiction as Interpretation / Interpretation as Fiction,"[5] as I hope to demonstrate below.

© 1986 by The Regents of the University of California. Reprinted from *Romance Philology* 40 (1986), 159–80, with permission.

A careful analysis of how Chrétien's romance invites questionable interpretations should ultimately lead the reader to speculate on why he has left his public with an ambiguous *sen*, an open-ended chain of interpretations. My demonstration will thus proceed in three stages: First, a detailed study of the Immodest Damsel episode (vv. 932–2110) with its narrative and thematic analogues will allow us to follow one of the narrative strands that, woven together in the texture of the romance, lead to both positive and negative evaluations of Lancelot's conduct. A second step will focus on how Chrétien's romance forces us to move from such a single-focused reading to a more complex level of analysis, where we can follow the interplay between specific positive and negative interpretations. Finally, in a concluding section, I shall propose a way to understand the lack of closure that characterizes Chrétien's ambiguous romance. Before beginning the first part, let me explain here briefly why I have taken the Immodest Damsel episode as my point of departure. Methodologically, I believe the more complex reading of the *Charrette* to be proposed later is possible only after more specific and limited readings of the different narrative strands have signaled both the specific interpretations generated by the text and their problematic interaction; no reading is complete unless it can account for these contradictory evaluations of character, actions, and values. Since I cannot give a detailed analysis here of all the narrative components that argue for or against Lancelot, I have chosen to elaborate one partial, "exemplary" reading—a positive one that has the merit of considering the materials from a new angle, little explored by most critics of the *Charrette:* that offered by the convention of Hospitality and its recurrent sequences.

Any careful reader would agree that Hospitality is a major issue in the *Charrette*, where the custom of Gorre perverts all the traditions of hospitality by imprisoning those it "welcomes." Such is the problem raised in the opening scene of Chrétien's romance and left unresolved until Lancelot can abolish the custom and set free all the prisoner/guests. In fact, Hospitality generally functions as an important adventure for contemporary heroes of romance in the latter half of the 12th century: whether a knight accepts hospitality, how he meets its demands, how he treats his host, each of these aspects may be a test for the knight/guest. Hospitality thus participates with Combat and Love in a complex exchange of courtly services. Only correct and superlative conduct in each facet of the exchange can establish the knight's heroic identity, the proper balance between attributes and actions (Bruckner 1980). The amorous character of Lancelot's second hostess and her condition for offering hospitality have elicited strong condemnation from Jerome Mandel (1975) who ranks her with Lancelot's first hostess as the two subverters and destroyers of the guest/host relationship. My own interpretation is rather different, as it focuses on the ramifications of her *covant* and on her own evaluation of Lancelot.

It is surely appropriate that Lancelot's first two "hosts" are in fact hostesses. As the Queen's rescuer, Lancelot is proving his fitness as knight *and* lover. Hospitality in each of these cases offers Lancelot a test adventure significantly located at night—a time when Lancelot is frequently called upon to perform his most knightly feats! While there are many parallels between these two scenes (e.g. both lead to a glimpse of the Queen, either directly in person or indirectly through her comb), they operate in at least one important respect as mirror images: with his first hostess Lancelot insists on sleeping in a particular bed (and thereby demonstrates his prowess in the adventure of the Flaming Lance); with the Immodest Damsel, Lancelot prefers *not* to sleep in a particular bed (and thereby demonstrates his fidelity). Here already are evoked the well-known poles between which Lancelot operates throughout Chrétien's romance: decisive, unhesitating action—reflective, deliberating hesitation.

Mandel's criticism of the Immodest Damsel is especially aimed at her manner of offering hospitality in exchange for Lancelot's company in bed:

> Puis li dit: "Sire, mes ostex
> vos est ci pres apareilliez
> se del prandre estes conseillez;
> mes par itel herbergeroiz
> que avoec moi vos coucheroiz,
> einsi le vos ofre et presant." (vv. 940–5)[6]

While hosts are generally anxious to accommodate their guests as much as possible, it is not unusual for them to make special conditions for their hospitality. In *Partonopeu de Blois*, for example, Melior requires that Partonopeu agree not to see his hostess, even though they share the same bed rather more sociably than Lancelot and the Immodest Damsel do (Gildea ed. 1967: 1125–1311). Florimont uses the resources of the Rash Boon to force a reluctant guest to accept his hospitality for three years (Hilka ed. 1932: vv. 4389ff.; see Bruckner 1977). Within the context of Chrétien's own works there are a number of cases where hospitality leads the guest to an obligatory combat. And while the Lord of Pesme-Aventure is definitely presented in *Yvain* as a perverter of Hospitality, King Evrain in *Erec* is nonetheless described as a perfect host whose reluctance to permit his guest to seek the *joie* exonerates him from any blame that might attach to his dangerous hospitality (already fatal to quite a few knights).

The problem of a *covant* is an important one that will reappear below in a wider context. Nevertheless, attaching a condition to hospitality cannot determine in and of itself whether a host is good or bad. Though the Immodest Damsel seems to be a difficult hostess, demanding fulfillment of her agreement, she turns out to be one of Lancelot's helpers. By contrast, the accommodating host Lancelot meets in the country of Gorre, whose *ostel* will be situated just when and where Lancelot wants it (vv. 2262–78), turns out to be an enemy knight who leads his guest into a trap. Along with all the participants in Chrétien's story, we are constantly finding out that appearances are likely to be misleading.

What then is good about the Damsel's hospitality? What does it show about the quality of Lancelot's behavior beyond the usual recognition that the lover remains faithful to his lady despite powerful temptation? In one sense, Lancelot's encounter with the Damsel's men can be ranked with the dangers or obstacles that disappear before his fearless courage—the Proud Son prevented by his father from fighting, the half-hearted *sergeants* at the *Passage des Pierres*, the imaginary lions at the Sword Bridge, even the iron bars of the Queen's window. Should we include here the Immodest Damsel herself who, finally, does not insist that Lancelot spend the whole night with her in the same bed? This is tempting but, I think, misses an essential point in the episode. Lancelot is faced by a dilemma: he must choose between (1) remaining faithful to his lady and (2) living up to his word by keeping the agreement with his hostess. The narrator has indicated to us just how insistent the damsel is likely to be: "espoir tant le [Lancelot] puet ele amer, / ne l'en voldra quite clamer" (vv. 963–4). Lancelot's problem will not melt away here; he will have to resolve it.

In this episode Lancelot is not choosing between a "good" and an "evil." A simple choice like that requires no debate: Lancelot never worries about what to do with Meleagant, for example. He may obey his Lady's commands to stop fighting, but combat to the death is always clearly in order for such an evil knight. With the Immodest Damsel Lancelot must choose between two "goods," two sets of loyalties. In the society depicted in courtly romance fulfilling agreements and customs is no less incumbent on Lancelot than it is on King Arthur. In the opening scene at Arthur's court, we saw the king plunged into serious difficulty through Keu's manipulations, yet there is no narrative indication that any of the knights and ladies present thought King Arthur should renege on his word. The disapproval focuses on Keu's rashness (vv. 180–7), not on the custom of the Rash Boon itself (cf. Frappier 1969). Mention of the *covant* and the constraints it places on Lancelot recur like a leitmotif all during the tense moments that precede the guest's entry into bed (vv. 1042–4, 1049, 1057, 1074–5, 1124, 1154–5):

Covanz le vaint et si le froisse.
Donc est ce force? Autant le vaut;
par force covient que il s'aut
couchier avoec la dameisele:
covanz l'en semont et apele. (vv. 1208–12)

Against this force runs a second leitmotif: Lancelot's lack of desire for his hostess (vv. 946–8, 952–3, 1006–8, 1085–6, 1193–4, 1204–23), motivated by his exclusive love elsewhere (vv. 1223–42).

The Immodest Damsel is not unaware of Lancelot's conflicted feelings (perhaps a reason for her modestly keeping on her chemise), but sees how punctually Lancelot lives up to the letter of his agreement, as he climbs into bed, carefully avoiding any contact with his companion. When the damsel tells Lancelot that she will go spend the night in her own room, she is not simply withdrawing her condition. Lancelot has completely fulfilled his commitment:

"Or vos reposez mes enuit,
que vos m'avez randu si bien
mon covant que nes une rien
par droit ne vos puis demander." (vv. 1256–9)

Here is one of the crucial aspects of the *Charrette:* Lancelot's special heroism enables him to reconcile conflicting obligations, even conflicting "goods," without eliminating one in pursuit of the other.

This is a situation that Lancelot will meet again quite explicitly when he defeats the Orgueilleux and must satisfy the ostensibly antagonistic demands of *largece* and *pitiez* (vv. 2830–65). While Lancelot's inner debate here recalls his earlier hesitation before the Cart, when the conflicting demands of *Amors* and *Reisons* counseled him for and against stepping into such a shameful vehicle (vv. 365–77), the competing values here do not derive from two different ethical systems (as is the case with love and reason); chivalry requires both generosity and mercy from its practitioners. It is surely significant then, when Lancelot says "yes" to both these alternatives in the course of his debate (vv. 2854 and 2865)—significant, too, the whole-hearted agreement of both parties, the *pucele* (Meleagant's sister) and the Orgueilleux, to Lancelot's proposed solution. This problem of conflicting "goods" is, of course, the very one posed earlier about Lancelot's conduct with Arthur and Guenièvre. But that conflict of "goods" is not presented directly by the author of the *Charrette,* and we are not yet ready to decide if Lancelot successfully resolves it or not.

We must first explore possible analogues to the agreement between Lancelot and the Immodest Damsel, since the meaning of this episode can be fully understood only when these parallels are superimposed: in romance, meaning arises out of the play between such repetitions and variations of typical events and figures.[7] When her guest is ready to leave the next morning, the Immodest Damsel asks if he is willing to escort her according to the ancient customs of Logres (vv. 1299–1301). The narrator is careful to explain to us, just as he did earlier with the cart, exactly what the custom was in those days: a damsel unescorted was protected by virtue alone from any self-respecting knight who valued his good name, but a damsel escorted was fair game for any knight who could win her by force:

> Mes, se ele conduit eüst
> uns autres, se tant li pleüst
> qu'a celui bataile an feïst
> et par armes le conqueïst,
> sa volenté an poïst faire
> sanz honte et sanz blasme retraire. (vv. 1311–16)

Unlike the romance public, the citizens of Logres need no detailed explanation of this custom: they act with full knowledge of its conditions. When the Proud Son claims his *amie,* he refers to them quite explicitly:

> "Or ai tote ma volenté,
> quant en tel meniere vos truis
> qu'avoec moi mener[8] vos en puis
> or endroit, que n'i avrai honte." (vv. 1576–9)

The Proud Son has, however, been too eagerly counting his chickens, since Lancelot has no trouble defending his damsel against the lover's challenge; recognizing the hero's superiority, the White-Haired Knight interrupts the complete enactment of the custom by preventing any combat between his son and Lancelot.

This is a simple test case to show the application of the custom and further demonstrate Lancelot's prowess at least by implication. The notion of test cases is an important one for the *Charrette,* but before pursuing that aspect, we must note other appearances of the custom itself. This episode is not the only time the custom is enacted; it has a far more important role to play in the main plot of the romance. For what is the agreement Meleagant makes with King Arthur in the opening scene, if not precisely a variation of this custom? The Queen rides out into the forest, escorted by one of Arthur's knights—Keu, as it happens. A combat takes place; the Queen goes to the winner—Meleagant in this case—who according to the custom of Logres has won her fair and square, his honor intact. The winner, however, is prevented by his father from enjoying the fruits of the battle and the custom is replayed when a second challenger arrives. The Queen is once again at stake. She goes to the victor—this time Lancelot who, after a slight delay, does indeed complete the custom. Their night of love is, according to the custom of Logres, nothing more than Lancelot's just due: having won Guenièvre by force of arms, the knight may do as he pleases, "sanz honte et sanz blasme." Here is Lancelot's perfect justification, not in the secret value system of courtly love, not in the marvelous realm of the *pays de Gorre*, but in the time-honored customs of Arthur's own kingdom!

Of course things are not so simple, neither for the hero nor the critic evaluating his conduct. Chrétien gives no explicit recognition to such a justification for Lancelot. But then he makes no explicit comment on the problem of adultery between Lancelot and the Queen (nor do the lovers in any of their conversations or monologues). Chrétien's silences are among the most provocative features of his romance—and even his detailed explanations may raise more problems than they resolve (witness the number of articles analyzing the cart and its significance or the precise meaning of the narrator's prologue). We readers are thus enticed to fill in the gaps with our own analysis. Those successive *mises en scène* of the custom of Logres create parallels between two sets of triangular relationships—Lancelot/Immodest Damsel/Proud Son and Meleagant/Guenièvre/Lancelot—that require closer examination to reveal all the possible implications. Repetitions and variations of the basic pattern will chart the possible shades of meaning.

One of the most obvious results of these paired triangles is to put Guenièvre and the Immodest Damsel in analogous positions as objects of desire. The analogy is supported by an abundance of material, not the least of which is Lancelot's own monologue comparing his quest for Guenièvre with the quest for and defense of his villainously assaulted hostess (vv. 1097–1125). The problems of delay and hesitation,[9] of honor and blame, occupy him here as they do elsewhere before the cart or during the first battle with Meleagant. One might wonder, in fact, why the damsel sets up the rape scene. On the one hand it confirms Lancelot's valor in battle. More importantly, it emphasizes the nature of her *covant*: will her sexual favors be exchanged according to agreement or by (mis)appropriation on the part of uncourtly intruders? And finally it parallels in exaggerated terms the Queen's own situation as she is led away by Meleagant. (It might be worthwhile to recall here that medieval laws equated kidnapping a lady with rape: cf. discussions of Malory's *raptus*, e.g. in Hicks [1928].) Lancelot wins the damsel by force of arms against the combined effort of three knights and four *sergeants*. The hostess's *covant* thus moves toward a conflation with the custom of Logres.

I have already mentioned that armed force plays a key role in that custom. We can appreciate its importance by following the repeated discussions between Meleagant and his father. Bademagu advises Meleagant to *give* the Queen to Lancelot before he can ask (i.e., fight) for her (vv. 3204–5). Such generosity would, in a sense, short-circuit the custom and permit Meleagant to gain honor by honoring the best knight in the world. When that appeal fails, Bademagu tries to work on his son's selfish pride: since Lancelot wants to win the Queen in combat, since he would be shamed if he did not win her thus (vv. 3237–47), Meleagant could rob him of his *pris*,[10] if he simply gave the Queen to her anxious champion.

Only now does the reader learn something about Meleagant's motivation for going to Arthur's court. He once again refuses to follow his father's advice:

> "Je ne sui mie si hermites,
> si prodon ne si charitables,
> ne tant ne voel estre enorables
> que la rien que plus aim li doingne." (vv. 3276–9)

Where does this love come from? There is no clue about it in the opening scene. There Meleagant's proposition seems to grow rather out of sheer nastiness and boastful pride, traits that continue to unfold in later actions. I would suggest that his love for the Queen rises unavoidably from his position in the superimposable triangles. He loves Guenièvre as the Proud Son loves the Immodest Damsel—and as Lancelot himself loves the Queen.

Meleagant's position in the triangle would also contribute to the outrage he expresses upon discovering the Queen's bloody sheets. In the original configuration, Meleagant defeated Keu and carried off the prize. But Bademagu, following the Queen's own orders, has not let anyone touch the prisoner/guest, not even his son. How much more revolting then that he, the victor, has been kept away, while the defeated opponent enjoys the spoils of battle:

> "Bien savez an quel aventure,
> por le reïne, ai mon cors mis,
> dom vos [Bademagus] estes mes anemis,

que por moi le faites garder
Sire, por Deu, ne vos enuit
s'il m'an poise, et se je m'an plaing
car molt me vient a grant desdaing
qant ele me het et despit,
et Kex o li chasque nuit gist." (vv. 4806–9, 4814–18)

Yet the insults and quarreling that ensue, as well as the judiciary duel between Lancelot and Meleagant, remind us that after all Guenièvre and the damsel are not exactly alike. Damsels may be up for grabs, but not married ladies, and especially not ladies married to one's king. We need to resume the comparison of Queen and hostess, with special attention to the differences between them.

Earlier I described the rape scene as an exaggerated, more explicit version of Guenièvre's own situation vis-à-vis Meleagant. This "overstatement" is in consonance with the Immodest Damsel's general forwardness (sometimes bordering on the froward!). With Lancelot she actively volunteers her hospitality and herself: the narrator describes her as "cele qui se fet s'amie" (v. 1051). She stages the rape scene and sets up the encounter with her would-be lover (who is as aggressive an organizer as she, if not so successful). Guenièvre is, by contrast, a passive character. Both she and Lancelot participate in the custom of Logres as an unavoidable reaction to the actions of others. Her cold reception of Lancelot—much debased as a sign of her supposed cruelty to a deserving lover—may, in one sense, indicate her reluctance to be the reward in a custom having little to do with their secret love. For while the Queen early recognizes Lancelot as her *ami*, she only plays out the full measure of their love in gradual stages, precipitated by outside circumstances (e.g., the rumor of Lancelot's death).

This shared love finally marks the point of radical difference between Guenièvre and the Immodest Damsel: one is loved; the other is not; one is not loved precisely because the other is. The damsel may be worthy of any knight's desire, yet she can arouse none in Lancelot, not even when she appears "descoverte jusqu'au nonbril" (v. 1082). And yet, though the question of desire puts Guenièvre and the hostess at opposite poles, the problem of love gives each of them a special point of view from which to evaluate Lancelot's conduct, a point of view shared by the narrator and the reader, but denied to all other participants in Chrétien's story. The conjunction of Hospitality and Love that occurs in the "Night Visit"[11]—first at the damsel's castle, later at Bademagu's (and nowhere else in this romance)—may give very different results in each instance, but the repetition of the bedroom scene itself underscores the special parallels between the two relationships. From their privileged vantage points both ladies entertain the highest opinion of Lancelot. Both have tested him (or seen him tested) as knight and lover, before reaching complete satisfaction.

The Immodest Damsel is, in fact, the first character in the *Charrette* (except for the narrator) to recognize Lancelot's worth, a point in considerable doubt since his ride in the cart. The first night's hostess vigorously scolds the cart-rider, though she passes over in complete silence his successful tenure of the Perilous Bed.[12] There is no mention of Lancelot's shame during his second night of hospitality,[13] since the hostess has ample resources at her disposal for independent evaluation. After she leaves Lancelot to go back to her own bed, the narrator reports her thoughts in direct discourse:

> "Des lores que je conui primes
> chevalier, un seul n'an conui
> que je prisasse, fors cestui,
> la tierce part d'un angevin;
> car si con ge pans et devin,
> il vialt a si grant chose antendre
> qu'ainz chevaliers n'osa enprendre
> si perilleuse ne si grief;
> et Dex doint qu'il an veigne a chief." (vv. 1270–8)

She is the forerunner of those who guess or recognize Lancelot's extraordinary status and his extraordinary mission (the White-Haired Knight, the monk, the Hunting Knights and their families, Bademagu, etc.). Just as the herald at the tournament proclaims Lancelot's worth to the public domain, so the Immodest Damsel speaks in the privacy of the night. She even seems to perceive the connection between Lancelot's great enterprise and his love, if we read carefully the narrator's description of her departure from Lancelot's bed:

> . . . Lors si se lieve;
> au chevalier mie ne grieve,
> einz l'an leisse aler volentiers
> con cil qui est amis entiers
> autrui que li: bien l'aparçoit
> la dameisele, et bien le voit. (vv. 1261–6)

When she accompanies Lancelot the next morning, surely one of her objectives is to obtain more information about Lancelot's mission and identity.

Though his name remains an obstinate mystery, despite her inquiries, the episodes with the comb and at the cemetery can have left little doubt about the superlative quality of Lancelot's lady and quest.

Within the network of associations generated by the Immodest Damsel, Lancelot seems to emerge completely triumphant: valiant knight, faithful lover, honorable participant in the custom of Logres—in short, heroic reconciler of competing "goods." This is the opinion of the Immodest Damsel, stated forcefully in her own words. Unfortunately that evaluation is partial—in both senses of the word: her total endorsement of Lancelot is as extreme as the total disdain expressed by the Orgueilleux. The narrator himself takes a more distanced view of his hero, neither denying Lancelot's virtues, nor masking his faults. I cannot help but hear a slight chuckle, for example, when Lancelot's behavior in the damsel's bed is compared to that of a *convert* (lay brother):

> Ne ne dit mot ne c'uns convert
> cui li parlers est defenduz,
> quant an son lit gist estanduz. (vv. 1218–20)

The narrator mentions explicitly one aspect of the *convert*'s agreement: silence. Yet another comes inevitably to mind as we see the *convert* in his bed: chastity? Yes, Lancelot is chaste here, when many another knight would succumb to temptation. But he does not always approach the monastic ideal of chastity with such success.[14]

If I have so far given a reading of the *Charrette* from a single vantage point, Chrétien's text refuses to stop at such simple interpretations. Inasmuch as it furnishes us with data for alternate readings, this romance forces the reader to consider complex and contradictory issues. In the second stage of analysis, I shall focus on Chrétien's strategies for putting into question the completely positive evaluation of Lancelot's conduct furnished by the Immodest Damsel's point of view. The narrator's comic twists, hinted at in the quotation just given, plus his tendency to place the hero in a series of ridiculous poses, have often been taken as signals that indicate Chrétien's desire to subvert Lancelot's reputation. The lover lost in thought who rides into the ford, unconscious of his opponent's shouted challenges (vv. 711–71), the lover in ecstatic contemplation of his lady, oblivious to Meleagant's blows (vv. 3669–82), the lover who at first hesitantly at the cart (vv. 321–77)[15] and then willingly at the tournament (vv. 5653–5705, 5736–62, 5856–67) incurs shame for love of his lady. These images have led some scholars to declare Lancelot a "puppet" (Jonin 1952: 293) "emasculated" (Condren 1970:

445) by his single-minded dedication to *fin'amor*. As Douglas Kelly points out (1966: 213), Chrétien never leaves his hero in such compromising positions for long; nevertheless, such moments of apparent folly do alert the public to a possible disequilibrium among different value systems operating within the world of the *Charrette*. Before we can ultimately decide how to evaluate Lancelot's conduct, we need to find out what these ethical systems are, how they affect the characters, and how they relate to each other.

A brief description of the different value systems is quickly compiled. The feudal society represented in romance generates values of loyalty in the lord/vassal relationship, prowess in battle tempered by mercy, largess in all facets of courtly conduct. The judicial combat is one way in which such a society decides between right and wrong. Love, on the other hand, has its own decision process, its own domain of values, enthusiastically analyzed by the narrator, as well as by Lancelot and Guenièvre: absolute obedience of lover to lady, distinction of love's elite, and so on.[16] The marvelous may also be considered a source of values, since its adventures tend to reveal the special quality of the hero. Compare Lancelot's successful crossing of the *Pont de l'Espee* with Gauvain's failure at the *Pont soz Eve*, or consider Lancelot's effortless strength of ten in lifting the tombstone that seven strong men could scarcely budge. I have already referred extensively to two other sources of proper and improper conduct: the agreements between individuals and the customs accepted by an entire community. The Immodest Damsel is not the only character who offers Lancelot a bargain: the seneschal's wife gladly offered to grant Lancelot's request for a temporary release in exchange for her prisoner's love. This wife is more sympathetic hostess than cruel jailor, and by this time Lancelot knows how to pass through a fidelity test with light-hearted humor (vv. 5482–3). But he is still scrupulous in returning to prison once the tournament is over; Lancelot always keeps his word.

Customs established in romance's undatable past and sustained through memory and usage obviously play a crucial role in the *Charrette*. When the Immodest Damsel first refers to the custom of Logres, she describes it precisely in terms of its ancient standing:

> "Par les us et par les costumes
> *qui furent ainz que nos ne fumes*
> el reaume de Logres mises." (vv. 1299–1301)

These customs may have originated in individual men's actions, but are no longer subject to an individual man or woman's choice. Erich Köhler (1960:

391, 395) has described in similar terms how the Rash Boon operates: once the principle of liberality represented by the "don" becomes automatic, out of the individual's control, it works against the very order it was supposed to guarantee. Neither Arthur nor the community of knights can restore the order endangered by such customs. That is the task of a special individual, a single extraordinary hero (see also Köhler 1974).

Köhler's observations lead us directly into the way value systems and actions are coordinated in romance narrative. Values do not remain static: actions and attributes activate and validate each other. For example, the description "generous" is invariably tied to performance: giving hospitality, bestowing gifts, supplying arms, etc. Specific values will require some actions and inhibit others. Arthur's power is actually circumscribed by the Rash Boon, since once he has given his assent to Keu's unspecified request, he cannot gainsay it. Both Bademagu and the White-Haired Knight try first to advise their sons on the strength of parental authority, but when the voice of family and morality fails, only a switch to the physical force invested in their feudal positions enables them to exert control. The White-Haired Knight exercises this power directly over the person of his son, when he orders his men to bind the insistent lover. Bademagu, on the other hand, takes a softer line with Meleagant: despite the firmness of his words, he does not restrain his son. Instead he tries to protect the targets of Meleagant's aggression (with varying degrees of success, as Keu's wounds and Lancelot's imprisonment testify). Ultimately he lets parental love interfere with his duties as king, when he twice asks the Queen to stop the combat between Lancelot and Meleagant, and thus perpetuates a menace to courtly society that can finally be eliminated only away from his court in the presence of Arthur.

Occasionally different customs may converge: Meleagant gives Arthur's court the opportunity to abolish the system of "le pays dont nul ne retourne" by observing a custom of Logres (the escorted lady). The conflation of these two customs ties the prisoners' fate to Guenièvre's. Chrétien's characters repeatedly point this out and the narrative explicitly conjoins the resolution of Lancelot and Meleagant's combat (in fact, an agreement for a second duel, vv. 3875–98) to the abolition of Gorre's custom (vv. 3899–3920). On the whole, I think too much is made of the differences between Arthur's realm and Bademagu's.[17] The people of both countries seem to share the same courtly ethics (except, of course, for Meleagant). Each has its share of magic and inherited, "irrational" customs (the courteous Bademagu is no more responsible for the prisoners in his country than Arthur is for the Rash Boon—and no less). There is, to be sure, a geographical change as Lancelot moves between the two countries and some suggestion of change in nature (a tomb adventure informs Lancelot of his success in "el rëaume don nus n'eschape," v. 1936). But there are other differences between the types of competing values that seem to me more important than the distinction between countries, since conflicts arise in both kingdoms: conflicts between inherited customs and "contemporary" feudal obligations or between Lancelot and Guenièvre's private point of view and the public perspective of others.

Chrétien's text stresses quite explicitly the incompatibility of different value systems. They are often in competition with each other: Reason (and chivalric honor) demands one course of action, Love another. Even within a single system, different values may create incompatible choices, as when Pity vies with Largesse[18] and Lancelot finds his customary willingness to grant mercy to a defeated opponent is short-circuited by his equally customary granting of damsels' requests (in this case, he has promised—and so delivers—an enemy's head). The recurrence of the *débat* in Lancelot's monologues highlights these difficult choices. Even the metaphorical language reflects problems of incompatibility. Consider, for example, the repetitions of the "impossibility" topos: the sea would empty, the winds would cease, the birds would dare not sing, before "that" could ever happen (vv. 3052–9, 3316–7, 4222–3, 6941–4). Most of these conflicts are concentrated on the characterizations and actions of Lancelot, since, as I suggested earlier, he is the only character able to do the impossible, to reconcile the competing "goods." Jean Frappier (1968: 139) has admirably caught the paradoxical nature of Lancelot, without reducing him to either side of the paradox: he is ecstatic and lucid, bold and hesitating, reasonable and unreasonable, silent and outspoken. In dealing with the relation between romance and source, Jean Fourquet (1955–56: 299) has suggested that "les principes d'identité et de noncontradiction n'existent pour ainsi dire pas ici: un objet a *deux* existences, parce qu'il est engagé dans deux réseaux de relations [le chevaleresque et le mythique]." I have tried to demonstrate here that even within a single plane, that generated by courtly values, the same duality, even polyvalence, operates: many competing "goods" coexist in the romance world and complicate Lancelot's course of action.

Without suppressing the real problems involved in his conduct, the *Charrette* generally presents a view of Lancelot that strives to be as sympathetic as possible. That is the effect, I think, of including the partial viewpoints of the Immodest Damsel, Bademagu, et al., and reinforcing them by Lancelot's actual feats, as well as by narratorial comments. When Guenièvre's bloody sheets inevitably raise the issue of adultery—and thus raise at least tangentially yet other realms of values, marital and religious—Chrétien has maneuvered his plot to shield Lancelot by making Meleagant the accuser and Keu the mistaken object of complaint. The displacement signals a central problem in the *Charrette*, where the role of the Queen's defender has been shifted from Arthur to Keu to Lancelot. At the same time it de-fuses (and diffuses) the problem of adultery, not by passing over it in complete silence— that ploy might have spoken out with loud accusation—but by deflecting the question to one of misinterpretation: Meleagant has seen the signs of truth, but he has not truly read them.[19]

In Chrétien's romance the problem of interpretation is inevitably tied to that of truth itself: what is the truth, how can it be expressed, what is the process of discovery, and how can one be sure? This is a difficult problem that I can only outline here as it relates to interpreting Lancelot's conduct. That means I shall concentrate primarily on some of the obstacles that must be overcome if one is to arrive at the truth. Such a discussion is crucial here— even if it cannot be elaborated as fully as it deserves—since the problems of truth and its expression, truth and its perception, are precisely those which finally prevent us from taking sides either with the positive reading against the negative, or vice versa.[20]

The first set of obstacles may be characterized as rhetorical ones. The comb episode combines a number of these, affecting not only Lancelot, but the narrator and the reader as well. Both the narrator and the Immodest Damsel imply that telling the truth is not everywhere appropriate: the narrator at one point claims ignorance about the comb's owner ("ne sai de qui," v. 1350), just before the damsel will truthfully identify that very person at Lancelot's request ("de rien nule n'an mantirai," v. 1411). The damsel herself prefers tact to truth a moment later, when Lancelot asks her why she has run over to him:

> Ne cuidiez pas que le porcoi
> la dameisele l'an conoisse,
> qu'il an eüst honte et angoisse,
> et si li grevast et neüst,
> se el voir l'en reconeüst;
> si s'est de voir dire gueitiée,
> einz dit come bien afeitiée: . . . (vv. 1446–52)

The occasion for lying may simply be a dramatic effect, but so humorous a device points to the far more serious problem of sorting out the truth from the lies, whether intentional or not. The public is just as involved as the participants in this process of masking and unfolding the truth.

Nor is it so simple in all cases to come out and speak the truth, since that truth may not appear to be true or believable. The narrator himself warns us of such a problem, before he begins to describe Lancelot's intense reaction to several strands of the Queen's hair:

> Et por *mançongier* et por fol
> m'an tenra l'en, se *voir* an di:
> quant la foire iert plainne au Lendi
> et il i avra plus avoir,
> nel volsist mie tot avoir
> li chevaliers, c'est *voirs provez,*
> si n'eüst ces chevox trovez.
> Et, si le *voir* m'an requerez,
> ors .c^{m.} foiz esmerez
> et puis autantes foiz recuiz
> fust plus oscurs que n'est la nuiz
> contre le plus bel jor d'esté
> qui ait an tot cest an esté,
> qui l'or et les chevols veïst,
> si que l'un lez l'autre meïst. (vv. 1480–94)

In this long aside to the public, the narrator returns to a problem set up first in his prologue (vv. 7–20). One of the obstacles to truth is a standard rhetorical problem: the indescribability of truth requires the use of hyperbole. Our narrator, no less than others, must create hyperboles to speak truly; indeed, he seems particularly charmed by that figure in the passage quoted above. Two sets of hyperbole follow in quick succession, one to describe Lancelot's feeling, the second to describe the Queen's hair. The second hyperbole itself is elaborated through a double image—golden hair that makes the purest gold look like night against the brightest day of the entire year; the accumulation of details suggests a narrator engulfed by Lancelot's own passion, so carried away that he must bring himself back to the business at hand by an abrupt about-face: "Et que feroie ge lonc conte?" (v. 1495). And yet our narrator is far from naïve; he knows the dangers posed by hyperbole, the lack of belief, the charges of flattery. Like a moth around a flame, he returns again and again to the question of truth (vv. 1481, 1485, 1487). Does he wish to anticipate our accusations and secure our trust with a defensive pose? Perhaps, but it seems more likely to me that he is pointing out how we should be troubled by this narrative. These rhetorical devices are part of a strategy to make us interpret and reinterpret his text.

After all, the problem posed by hyperbole resembles one encountered earlier in this study, the extremes of opinion expressed by those critics of Lancelot, whether situated inside or outside Chrétien's romance. Correct and incorrect interpreters abound in the *Charrette*, where evaluating someone else's actions is a major occupation of all the characters presented. After the Queen's "unwelcome," Bademagu asks Lancelot why she treated him so coldly (vv. 3982–92). Arguing from Lancelot's prowess, he judges her to be wrong (vv. 3997–9)—but wrongly, since he does not understand her real motive. Lancelot, too, wonders why the Queen has acted so strangely; he even asks Keu if he can supply a reason, but the seneschal is as amazed as the others (vv. 4072–5). Lancelot knows the Queen must have a good reason, but even with his privileged point of view ends up nearly as mistaken as Bademagu, since he misinterprets Guenièvre's understanding of love (vv. 4339ff.).

This series of speculations with their focus on correct or incorrect action and, by extension, correct or incorrect interpretation, raises an issue familiar to any discussion of truth: the obstacles met in the relation between appearance and reality. On the simplest level, the outside seems to mean one thing; the inside means something else. Or, the outsiders see one thing; the insiders see another, invisible to ordinary eyes, but true nonetheless. The knights at the tournament may joke about that cowardly knight who seemed so extraordinary at first, but the real jokester is Queen Guenièvre, who not only sets up the spectacle that fools Lancelot's opponents, but also laughs to herself about the demoiselles who insist they will marry no one but Lancelot. As we have seen earlier, ladies often have a better understanding of Lancelot's worth than do his fellow knights, but even they may go off the mark with one-sided enthusiasm. When the Queen's messenger returns from her last errand, she comments on Lancelot's equal welcome for all her instructions:

> ". . . Se le voir m'an demandez,
> autel chiere tot par igal
> fet il del bien come del mal.
> — Par foi, fet ele [Guenièvre], bien puet estre." (vv. 5912–5)

The narrator, however, with his more privileged point of view, goes on to describe Lancelot as burning to show his prowess (v. 5920). There may be no contradiction between these two evaluations, but together they add up to a more nuanced picture of Lancelot.

I have so far discussed the relationship between appearance and reality as a simple equation: inside = true, outside = false. Yet the situation is far more complex, as we see again and again in the *Charrette*. I choose the verb "to see" intentionally here, since it is linked repeatedly to the truth: "le voir m'an aprendront mi oel" (v. 4828), "mes nel va lors rien decevant . . . quant il voit que c'est il por voir" (vv. 6794, 6796). "Seeing is believing," as common sense maintains. Outward signs do help establish the truth: Gauvain knows, for example, that Keu has been defeated by Meleagant, when his horse appears riderless, with broken and bloody saddle (vv. 258–65). Yet elsewhere such visible signs are ambiguous: sheets may be "ansaignes bien veraies" (v. 4774), but not everyone knows what they truly indicate. Adultery? Yes. With Keu? No. When a letter from Lancelot arrives at Bademagu's court, "si a entresaignes tes / qu'il durent croire, et bien le crurent" (vv. 5270–1). But soon all learn that "les letres fausses furent, / qui les traïrent et deçurent" (vv. 5439–40).

Visible signs are a necessary adjunct or guarantee of truth—but not always or not always in the way we expect them to be. This ambiguous situation raises further questions that can only be sketched here: When can such signs be trusted and how far? By what criteria can their truthfulness be measured? Lancelot's questions to the monk in the cemetery no longer seem so obvious or redundant, when we realize that reading a message written on a tombstone may not suffice to know the truth of its contents, but requires further confirmation. Nor does the Queen's conduct at the tournament, when she twice asks the unknown knight to fight "au noauz," seem so unnecessarily cruel. How else can she be sure that it really is Lancelot who obeyed her command and not someone accidentally presenting "true signs"—or worse, someone intentionally fabricating "true signs" to deceive? In a given work the end point for such questioning may strike us as arbitrary or mysterious, since the mediated, romance world of signs seems to open up endlessly new perspectives for interpretation: the process of testing, indeed the necessity for testing to discover the truth parallels and motivates the process of interpretation itself.

This notion of testing leads us finally to the concluding part of my analysis, as we move from the question of possible and contradictory interpretations of the *Charrette* to the more general question of what such a multiplicity of possibilities taken together might mean. We have seen something of the different interpretations *Lancelot* generates and how it does so; let us now speculate on why. Testing implies a need to measure and a standard by which to measure. "Or est venuz qui l'aunera!" (v. 5563).[21] Such is the herald's cry, concealing and announcing Lancelot's identity at the tournament. Lancelot is the one who will *measure*, but what is it precisely that he is measuring? Erich Köhler's sociological approach may help us here. He has described a difficulty posed by romance for its historical audience: the hero as solution for a community's disrupted order is possible in fiction, but not in everyday life (1960: 395). It is the merit of Chrétien's romance, I think, to pose the problem of fictional solutions within its own fictional structure. By refusing to settle into a neatly unambiguous conclusion,[22] by giving competing values expression without allowing them to cancel each other out, Chrétien has enlarged the problem of interpretation from Lancelot's own conduct to that of his society.

In Jerome Mandel's interpretation the private Lancelot is a successful lover, but the public Lancelot is a subverter of the social order:

> But as a public knight, Lancelot exists in a very particular context where the criteria for judgement have been established after the event. In this context of proper behavior, courtly love does not enhance Lancelot, and he is punished physically and spiritually for subverting order. Indeed, viewed from within the context of order, which I also understand to be Chrétien's position, Lancelot is most perfectly correct in mounting the cart. He is a malefactor—one who does evil. (1975: 689)

Based on my reading of the *Charrette*, Mandel's evaluation of Lancelot and of Chrétien's position seems reductive in a number of ways. First, it ignores the problems of disorderliness that arise in romance society independently of courtly love—for example, the clash between feudal values and pre-established customs. Secondly, it overestimates the clarity of the "criteria for judgement" that have been shown to be more problematic than Mandel's "right or wrong" approach allows. And finally this evaluation identifies Chrétien's own opinion with a single point of view—a reduction that his narrative strategies specifically prevent.

If Lancelot is to be the one who measures, he will not do so in the standard way of Gauvain, the second-best-after-the-hero who conventionally measures the other knights' achievements in Arthurian society.[23] Lancelot figures as a touchstone whose contact reveals the positive and negative alloys of the society itself. Chrétien's romance thus operates like one of André Jolles's "simple forms": the Case (Jolles 1972: 137–57).[24] In the Case, a situation arises in which we cannot measure only the conduct of an individual; we must also measure the norm by which we usually judge his conduct. As an incident unfolds, for example, a given law may be shown to produce good and bad results: the weight itself is not giving true weight. One must then judge between norms, evaluating each in turn by a superior one. But the Case does not conclude; it poses a question: where are the weight and the norm necessary for that evaluation? While it imposes on us the obligation to decide, the Case does not contain the decision itself. If it does contain such a decision, it ceases to be a Case and becomes a different form, the Nouvelle, in which the positive decision abolishes the necessity to decide.

The temptation to make a decision is, of course, very strong in the *Charrette*, where we are constantly asked to interpret and evaluate Lancelot's behavior and its impact on Arthurian society. Sometimes, as we have seen in the Immodest Damsel episode and its whole chain of analogues, Lancelot himself appears to be the superior norm, the only one who succeeds to an extraordinary degree on the different scales of values, public and private. But, if on these same scales he is shown to be a traitor and an adulterer, there is possibly something faulty in the system of measuring the society's values. Chrétien does not cut the Gordian knots posed within his text. He does not reject the Arthurian world and its chivalric values, nor does he remain uncritical of those ideals in the praxis of romance adventures. Though medieval Christianity might offer elsewhere an ultimate measure for all such competing norms, he keeps such truth outside the boundaries of *Lancelot*.[25] Within the *Charrette*, the process of interpretation continues, since the next text continues to supply more elements than can be worked into any of the systems it contains within itself.[26]

Most importantly, Chrétien does not resolve the paradox of Lancelot's characterization. His accomplishments are inextricably tied to conflicting values: Lancelot is not the savior of Arthur's Queen and kingdom *in spite of* being an adulterous traitor; he redeems them *because* he is Guenièvre's secret lover and Arthur's best knight. Chrétien demonstrates sufficient courage to face the complexity of man's position, not beyond good and evil, but entwined in both. We readers need a similar courage to grasp the essential paradox of a Lancelot in whom conflicting values do not eliminate each other. Luckily we have an excellent model to help us, since this paradoxical Lancelot forms an essential aspect of later Arthurian tradition: the seed planted in Chrétien's work blooms full-blown in the Vulgate Cycle of the 13th century[27] and even later in Malory's *Morte d'Arthur*. The paradox may take on sharper contours, but Lancelot, lover and knight, still furnishes the bittersweet tension of these Arthurian stories.

NOTES

1. A brief sample of critical opinions reveals the following partisans, for example: Alfred Adler (1950), F. Xavier Baron (1973), F. Douglas Kelly (1966), Emanuel Mickel (1975), Jean Rychner (1968). Among the adversaries are found Edmund Condren (1970), David C. Fowler (1970), Pierre Jonin (1952), Jerome Mandel (1964),

D.W. Robertson, Jr. (1951). Gaston Paris in his influential study of 1883 sets the stage for the middle position, characterized more recently by Jean Frappier (1968: 133–142): Chrétien may be unhappy about his commission from Marie de Champagne, but the attraction of Lancelot's character wins over the author's—and scholar's—reservations.

2. Duggan (1977: 136–149). Nevertheless, he would still interpret Chrétien's use of ambiguity as an expression of his dissatisfaction with Marie de Champagne's assignment (141–2).

3. Lacy (1980: 56–60) maintains total neutrality for Chrétien, since ambiguity does not necessarily indicate subversion, in his view.

4. See, for example, Juri M. Lotman (1967: 33–5) or Umberto Eco (1965: 19–20): Paul Zumthor (1977: 314) has referred to such constructions as "les rêves ordonnés, ces nostalgies d'époques à sens plein, closes sur elles-mêmes, ce mythe d'un équilibre perdu . . . ce moyen âge-là n'exista jamais." Cf. also Peter Haidu (1980), whose analysis points out the gap between traditional interpretations of the *Couronnement*, based on optimistic views of the French monarchy, and the more complex, even contradictory view of the king presented by the text itself. His conclusion calls for a semiotic approach in which "the analyst's attitude toward the modes of production of meaning in the texts will not be determined by the ideologically determined meta-semiotic theory of the period and its appeals to transcendent symbolic meanings, whether knowable or not. Such theory originates from concrete, institutional positions and represents specific political and class interests. Instead, the complexities of the text will be seen to answer to its insertion in the larger socio-historical text of the period . . ." (167).

5. This is the title of Naomi Schor's essay (1980). Her brief discussion of secondary characters as interpretants, whose interpretations function as a form of persecution, in which the object/hero becomes a scapegoat (169n) recalls the situation of Lancelot within the *Charrette*. I would like to thank Sarah Melhado White, Franklin and Marshall College, for bringing this essay to my attention.

6. Roques ed. 1967. All subsequent references are to this edition.

7. Cf. Lacy's notion of thematic analogues (1969), Vance's discussion of "*dispositio associative*" (1972), and Bruckner (1980: 177–82).

8. The verb *mener* recurs like a leit-motif throughout his scene (vv. 1569, 1578, 1591, 1607, 1609). It recalls the similar usage (also with the verb *ramener*) in the opening scene with Meleagant and Keu leading away the Queen (vv. 73, 79, 194, 196, 211, 221). Such repetition reinforces the parallels between the two episodes. Cf. also the use of *mener* associated with the cart (vv. 335, 357, 387, 420, 440).

9. For a brief discussion of the hesitation and humiliation themes, see Lacy (1980: 90–2). For a more detailed analysis of Lancelot's (and Chrétien's) tendency to delay, and the open-ended character of Chrétien's romance, see my chapter on the *Charrette* in Kelly 1985.

10. In v. 3242 Bademagu is referring to the renown Lancelot would gain when his exploit was recounted, but another meaning of *pris* comes readily to mind in the larger context, since Guenièvre is clearly the *prize* at stake.

11. Hospitality sequences in the 12th c. typically divide into four fundamental subunits; I, Welcome; II, Dinnertime; III, Bedtime; IV, Departure. Additional subunits offer possibilities for variation, as when "Preliminary Arrangements" (I*) precede the Welcome. A "Night Visit" (III*) often occurs between III and IV, when a hostess mixes Love and Hospitality. See Bruckner (1980: 26–35, 60–94).

12. At least one other hostess in the romances I have worked with most closely has a similarly sharp tongue: see Hue de Rotelande's *Ipomedon* (Kölbing & Koschwitz, eds. 1889: vv. 8179 ff.), when Ismeine is dissatisfied with her guest and champion (Ipomedon is disguised as a fool).

13. An interesting ABBA pattern appears in relation to Hospitality and Lancelot's reputation subsequent to the cart scene: the second and third host (and this includes the fourth night of hospitality that passes by in brief summary) ignore the

problem of Lancelot's shame; the first and especially the fifth host run into it head on. It is during the fifth night, when the Orgueilleux taunts and challenges him, that Lancelot's reputations as savior and cart-rider converge.

14. Conversation is a common euphemism in 12th-century texts for sexual intercourse. See, for example, Speer 1977.

15. In a pair of articles (1973a and 1973b), David Shirt suggests two ways to interpret the cart episode: (1) a veiled condemnation of Lancelot; (2) a way to underline Lancelot's paradoxical situation as devoted lover and loyal vassal; but not both at the same time—a double standard possible only in the fictive world of romance. Ultimately Shirt leans toward the negative (Chrétien must disapprove of Lancelot), since he sees the two "goods" of Lancelot's characterization cancelling each other out.

16. The domain of religious values appears in the *Charrette* primarily as a way to enhance Lancelot's prowess—e.g., at the cemetery (vv. 1837–48) or on the Sword Bridge (vv. 3105–16, 3358)—or his love for the Queen (e.g., vv. 1460–75, 4652–3, 4717–8).

17. Cf. Sarah Melhado White's discussion of boundaries in relation to the fluid boundaries of a chessboard (1977: 106; 108n).

18. Sydney Painter (1940) distinguishes three separate conceptions of chivalry operating in medieval France: the ideal knight would thus change according to different points of view—feudal, religious, courtly love. He points out that medieval people fully realized the incompatibility of these three sets of chivalric ideas, though they did form composite ideals by combining elements of each.

19. The bloody sheets in the flour episode of the Tristan legend, which undoubtedly furnishes a model for Chrétien's variation in the *Charrette*, also introduce the problem of "true signs" and their possible (mis)interpretations. See, for example, Beroul's version (1970: vv. 643–826), especially v. 778: "Trop par a ci *veraie enseigne*."

20. Cf. Lacy (1980: 93) for a brief discussion of perception as a second important system of analogues in the *Charrette*, whose relation to the other major system of hesitation and humiliation is "less than entirely clear."

21. Paule Le Rider (1978: 403) first analyzes later appearances of this proverb, where *auner* is used in the sense of giving an exact measure "de justice ou de justesse." She then speculates that the expression's metaphorical resonance might have followed from its popular usage among merchants at the fairs of Champagne (405–6). Charters of the 12th and 13th c. attest to a tax (*droit d'aunage*, 405) collected from merchants, presumably to pay for the official control and standardization of weights and measures, especially important since the length of the *aune* varied from one province to the next (405–6). The formal structure of the phrase, "Or est venu qui . . . ," suggests the cry used at fairs or in merchant streets to announce the arrival of the person charged with verifying all measures and especially those used in selling cloth (405).

22. Cf. the controversy attached to Chrétien's ending and the effort to interpret Godefroi de Leigny's role. Despite his recognition of the unresolved ambiguity in the *Charrette*, Duggan (1977: 141–2) still interprets Godefroi's role as an indication of Chrétien's discontentment with his assignment. Vinaver (1980: 21–2), on the other hand, gives an eloquent plea for allowing contradictions to stand unresolved, precisely in regard to the *Charrette*.

23. Le Rider (1978: 407) cites Chrétien's *Cligés* where Arthur's knights, Gauvain in particular, are described by Cligés as the touchstone by which he wants to measure his own worth: "An Bretaigne, se je sui preuz,/ Me porrai tochier a la quez / Et a l'essai fin et verai, / O ma proesce esproverai" (1968: vv. 4208–10).

24. In the course of his discussion, Jolles refers to "love questions" debated in the Middle Ages (153–4). The lyric *jeux-partis* and *tensons* are also particularly relevant here. The *Charrette* itself contains a brief reference to *jeu-parti* (vv. 685–96).

25. Only with his last romance and its Grail quest does Chrétien explicitly introduce a Christian perspective, but even there the unfinished state of the *Conte du graal* poses more problems than it resolves.

26. Cf. C.S. Lewis's discussion of the medieval dilemma between systematic thought and encyclopedic accumulation of knowledge (1976: 10–11).

27. I should perhaps exclude the *Queste du Saint Graal* from this tradition of a paradoxical Lancelot, since its point of view is usually interpreted as a unitary Christian (even Cistercian) one that simply condemns Lancelot for his lust and locates all positive value in his son Galahad. Nevertheless, an argument may be made for locating esteem for Lancelot and ambiguity even in this part of the Vulgate: see Grace Armstrong Savage (1977: 1–16).

References

Adler, Alfred. 1950. "A Note on the Composition of Chrétien's *Charrette*." *MLR* 45: 33–9.

Baron, F. Xavier. 1973. "Love in Chrétien's *Charrette*: Reversed Values and Isolation." *MLQ* 34: 377–83.

Bloch, Howard. 1974. "Tristan, the Myth of the State and the Language of the Self." *YFS* 51: 61–8.

Bruckner, Matilda Tomaryn. 1977. "Florimont: Extravagant Host, Extravagant Guest." *SMC* 11: 57–63.

———. 1980. *Narrative Invention in Twelfth-Century French Romance: The Convention of Hospitality (1160–1200)*. Lexington, Ky.: French Forum Publications.

Condren, Edmund. 1970. "The Paradox of Chrétien's *Lancelot*." *MLN* 85: 434–53.

Duggan, Joseph J. 1977. "Ambiguity in Twelfth-Century French and Provençal Literature: A Problem or a Value?" *Jean Misrahi Memorial Volume: Studies in Medieval Literature*, ed. H.R. Runte, H. Niedzielski, W.L. Hendrickson. Columbia, S.C.: French Literature Publications Co. 136–49.

Eco, Umberto. 1965. *L'Oeuvre ouverte*. Tr. Chantal Roux de Bézieux. Paris: Seuil.

Fourquet, Jean. 1955–56. "Le rapport entre l'oeuvre et la source chez Chrétien de Troyes et le problème des sources bretonnes." *RPh* 9: 298–312.

Fowler, David C. 1970. "L'amour dans le *Lancelot* de Chrétien." *Romania* 91: 378–91.

Frappier, Jean. 1968. *Chrétien de Troyes*. Paris: Hatier.

———. 1969. "Le motif du 'don contraignant' dans la littérature du Moyen Age." *TLL* 7: 7–46.

Gildea, Joseph. O.S.A., ed. 1967. *Partonopeu de Blois, a French Romance of the Twelfth Century*. 2 vols. Villanova, Pa.: Villanova UP.

Haidu, Peter. 1980. "Towards a Sociohistorical Semiotics: Power and Legitimacy in the *Couronnement de Louis*." *Kodikas Code* 2: 155–69.

Hicks, Edward S. 1928. *Sir Thomas Malory, His Turbulent Career*. Cambridge, Mass.: Harvard UP.

Hilka, Alfons, ed. 1932. Aimon de Varennes, *Florimont: Ein altfranzösisches Abenteuerroman*. Göttingen: Max Niemeyer Verlag.

Jolles, André. 1972. *Formes simples*. Tr. Antoine Marie Buguet. Paris: Seuil.

Jonin, Pierre. 1952. "Le vasselage de Lancelot dans le *Conte de la Charrette*." *MA* 58: 281–98.

Kelly, F. Douglas. 1966. *"Sens" and "Conjointure" in the "Chevalier de la Charrette."* The Hague: Mouton.

Kelly, F. Douglas, ed. 1985. *The Romances of Chrétien de Troyes, A Symposium*. Edward C. Armstrong Monographs on Medieval Literature, 3. Lexington, Ky: French Forum, Publishers.

Köhler, Erich. 1960. "Le rôle de la 'coutume' dans les romans de Chrétien de Troyes." *Romania* 81: 386–97.

———. 1974. *L'Aventure chevaleresque. Idéal et réalité dans le roman courtois*. Tr. E. Kaufholz. Paris: Gallimard.

Kölbing, Eugen and Eduard Koschwitz, eds. 1889. Hue de Roteland, *Ipomedon*. Breslau: Verlag von Wilhelm Koebner.

Lacy, Norris J. 1980. *The Craft of Chrétien de Troyes. An Essay on Narrative Art.* Davis Mediaeval Texts and Studies, 3. Leiden: Brill.

———. 1969. "Thematic Analogues in *Erec.*" *ECr* 9: 267–74.

Lerider, Paule. 1978. "*Or est venuz qui l'aunera* ou la fortune littéraire d'un proverbe," in *Mélanges Jeanne Lods*. Collection de l'Ecole Normale Supérieure de Jeunes Filles, 10. Paris. I: 393–409.

Lewis, C.S. 1976 (1964). *The Discarded Image.* Cambridge: CUP.

Lotman, Juri M. 1967. "Problèmes de la typologie des cultures." *Information sur les Sciences Sociales.* April–June: 33–5.

Mandel, Jerome. 1964. "Elements in the *Charrette* World: The Father-Son Relationship." *MP* 62: 97–104.

———. 1975. "Proper Behavior in Chrétien's *Charrette*: The Host-Guest Relationship." *FR* 48: 683–9.

Micha, Alexandre, ed. *Les Romans de Chrétien de Troyes, II. Cligès.* CFMA, 84. Paris: Champion.

Mickel, Emanuel. 1975. "The Theme of Honor in Chrétien's *Lancelot.*" *ZRPh* 91: 243–72.

Muret, Ernest, ed. 1970. Béroul, *Le Roman de Tristan.* CFMA, 12. Paris: Champion.

Painter, Sydney. 1940. *French Chivalry. Chivalric Ideas and Practices in Mediaeval France.* Baltimore, Md.: Johns Hopkins UP.

Paris, Gaston. 1883. "Etudes sur les romans de la Table Ronde, Lancelot du Lac, II. *Le Conte de la Charrette.*" *Romania* 12: 459–534.

Robertson, D.W., Jr. 1951. "Some Medieval Literary Terminology with Specific Reference to Chrétien de Troyes." *SP* 48: 669–92.

Roques, Mario, ed. 1967. *Les Romans de Chrétien de Troyes, III. Le Chevalier de la Charrette.* CFMA, 86. Paris: Champion.

Rychner, Jean. 1968. "Le sujet et la signification du *Chevalier de la Charrette.*" *VR* 27: 50–76.

Savage, Grace Armstrong. 1977. "Father and Son in the *Queste del Saint Graal.*" *RPh* 31: 1–16.

Schor, Naomi. 1980. "Fiction as Interpretation / Interpretation as Fiction." *The Reader in the Text. Essays on Audience and Interpetation*, ed. Susan R. Suleiman and Inge Crosman. Princeton: PUP. 165–82.

Shirt, David J. 1973a. "Chrétien de Troyes and the Cart." *Studies in Medieval Literature and Language in Memory of F. Whitehead*, ed. W. Rothwell et al. Manchester: Manchester UP. 279–301.

———. 1973b. "Chrétien de Troyes et une coutume anglaise." *Romania* 94: 178–95.

Speer, Mary. 1977. Rev. of "T.B.W. Reid, *The "Tristan" of Béroul: A Textual Commentary.*" *RP* 30: 635–40.

Vance, Eugene. 1972. "Le combat érotique chez Chrétien de Troyes." *Poétique* 12: 544–71.

Vinaver, Eugene. 1980. "Landmarks in Arthurian Romance." *The Expansion and Transformations of Courtly Literature*, ed. Nathaniel B. Smith and Joseph T. Snow. Athens, Ga.: Univ. of Georgia Press. 17–31.

White, Sarah Melhado. 1977. "Lancelot on the Gameboard: The Design of Chrétien's *Charrette.*" *FrF* 2: 99–109.

Zumthor, Paul. 1977. "Médiéviste ou pas." *Poétique* 31: 306–21.

4 THE FIGURE OF LANCELOT IN THE *LANCELOT-GRAAL*

Elspeth Kennedy

The character of Lancelot is central to the whole of the *Lancelot-Graal* cycle, apart from the first two branches (an early history of the Grail and a *Merlin*) that were added later.[1] The romance tells the story of Lancelot from his earliest childhood "en la marche de Gaule" to his death at the end of *La Mort Artu*: "Si se test ore atant Gautier Map de l'Estoire de Lancelot." This centrality is emphasized in a number of ways, both through narrative techniques and through thematic structures.

A number of narrative devices are used to remind us that Lancelot is the dominant figure in the romance. In the first place, he alone of all Arthur's knights has no unexplained gaps in his history. We are given an account of his upbringing in the lake before he appears as a Fair Unknown figure at the court of King Arthur. In contrast, Gauvain has an unnarrated past before his first, brief appearance in the story in an episode at Arthur's court immediately preceding the account of Lancelot's decision to leave the Lake to become a knight (*LK*, 136–38); but there are a number of references to past adventures of the king's nephew that appear to refer to events occurring before Lancelot first came to Camelot.[2] Galahad's life is also not told in full. Although an account is given of his conception, no detailed explanation is given of his upbringing, nor are all his adventures on the quest related.[3]

What is relevant or irrelevant to "le conte Lancelot" provides the basis for the formulae used to justify inclusion or exclusion of material in the narration of Lancelot's adventures up to his installation as a knight of the Round Table. Thus Gauvain's adventures on his unsuccessful quest with forty knights for Lancelot are not related because, like those of his companions, they do not lead him to Lancelot: "Ne de nule aventure qui lor avenist en la qeste ne parole li contes ci, por ce que il faillirent tuit a lor qeste" ("The tale says nothing here of any of the adventures which they encountered in the quest because they failed to achieve their quest," *LK*, 299). On the other hand, Gauvain's adventures on his renewed quest for Lancelot are related, because he finds the object of his search and the subject of the tale, but those of his unsuccessful companions are here left untold, although they each have their own tale (*LK*, 365–66). The dominant position of Lancelot's tale in relation to those of all the other knights is made clear in the following passage, which describes the recording of the adventures of Arthur's knights by his wise clerks:

> *Cil quatre mestoient en escrit qanque li compaignon lo roi faisoient d'armes, si mistrent en escrit les avantures monseignor Gauvain tot avant, por ce que c'estoit li commancemenz de la queste, et puis les Estor, por ce que do conte meïsmes estoient branche, et puis les avantures a toz les dis huit compaignons. Et tot ce fu del conte Lancelot, et tuit cist autre furent branches de cestuit. Et li contes Lancelot fu meïsmes branche del Greal, si qu'il i fu ajostez.*

> (These four recorded all the deeds of arms that the king's companions performed, and they recorded Sir Gauvain's adventures first, because he started the quest, and then those of Hector, because they were a branch of the same story, and then the adventures of all the eighteen companions. And all that was part of the story of Lancelot, all the others being branches of that one, while the story of Lancelot was itself a branch of the Grail story, so that it was set beside it. *LK*, 571)[4]

The importance of Lancelot's tale in comparison with any of the others is taken up at a later point in the development of the cycle in somewhat different terms, when it is said that Lancelot's adventures are recorded in a book separate from that in which are set down those of all the other knights:

> *Einsinc com Lanceloz ot dites ses aventures furent eles mises en escrit, et pour ce que li fet estoient greingnor que nus de çaux de laienz, les fist li rois mestre par lui seul si que des fez et des ovres trova l'an .I. grant livre en l'aumaire le roi Artu après qu'il fu navrez a mort en la bataille Mordret, si com li contes vos devisera apertement.*

> (Lancelot's adventures were set down in writing as he had recounted them; and because his exploits were greater than those of anyone else, the king had them recorded separately, so that a large book giving

all his exploits and deeds of arms was found in King Arthur's cupboard after he was mortally wounded in the battle against Mordret, as the tale will recount. *LM*, LXXXIV, 72)

Lancelot's preeminent position as the greatest knight at the very center of the narrative is therefore clearly marked by these references to the subordination of the recounting of all other tales to the telling of that of Lancelot in this particular romance. At the same time, a number of allusions also set the story of Lancelot firmly within the context of the whole Arthurian tradition. This thirteenth-century romance was never meant to be isolated from the existing twelfth-century literature, and Lancelot's role within the cycle can be properly appreciated only if account is taken of the importance of intertextuality and intratextuality as it is manifested in the system of pairing Lancelot with other Arthurian heroes both within and without the text.[5] Such pairings and such resonances help to structure a romance where authorial intervention or comment is rare. The interplay with existing texts serves to create links with past knights and lovers and with the familiar themes associated with them; it underlines two main themes, the quest for identity and the relationship between love and chivalry, both of which are already typical of twelfth-century Arthurian romance in general and of the earlier Lancelot tradition in particular.

The themes of the making of a name and of chivalry inspired by love intertwine in the account of Lancelot's childhood and adventures up to his installation as a knight of the Round Table; they link up with Lancelot's literary past, but are given a new form and meaning within each stage of the development of the thirteenth-century romance.[6] Already in the twelfth-century romances, Lancelot was associated with a childhood in a lake and with the discovery of the name of the hero. In Chrétien's *Le Chevalier de la Charrete*, there is a reference to the fairy who brought Lancelot up in a lake and has given him a ring which uncovers enchantments.[7] In this romance, Lancelot raises a slab in a Perilous Cemetery (*Charrete*, ll. 1856–1936) and thus shows that he is the hero destined to rescue the queen and free the prisoners of Gorre, but his name is withheld in the narrative until halfway through the romance, when the queen reveals it during his fight with Meleagant (*Charrete*, l. 3660). In the *Lanzelet* of Ulrich von Zatzikhoven,[8] an account is given of the hero's upbringing in a lake and of his learning his name; this has a number of elements in common with that in the Prose *Lancelot*, but there are also some important differences that help to throw into relief two of the characteristic features of the treatment of the theme of the young unknown hero in the thirteenth-century romance: first, the tension between the importance given to heredity as a qualification for great knighthood and the need to make one's name through one's own achievements without the help of the reputation of one's ancestors;[9] second, a tendency to rationalize the supernatural in thirteenth-century terms.[10]

Thus the unjust king who causes the withdrawal of the child into the lake is no longer, as in *Lanzelet*, the father of the hero but the persecutor of his noble and loyal parents, whose great ancestry on both sides befits a boy with a great destiny, while at the same time, his very ignorance of his parentage spurs him on to greater efforts to prove himself worthy of knighthood (*LK*, 110–11).[11] Upbringing by a supernatural being might also seem incompatible with the appropriate preparation for true chivalric achievement, so that while the Lady of the Lake is still described as a fairy, her magic powers are carefully explained: she took a course in magic from Merlin, who, as a son of a devil, a fallen angel, inherited a knowledge of spells, but the diabolical element in her learning was neutralized when he was imprisoned by her in a rock.

It is, however, with another twelfth-century account of a young hero whose childhood was spent shielded from any contact with the world of knights that the most significant pattern of intertextual allusions is to be found: that is the interplay with the Perceval of Chrétien's *Le Conte del Graal*.[12] Lancelot's father, like that of Perceval, lost his land during the troubles after Uther's death, and both young boys were brought up in ignorance of their own names, but whereas Perceval received no tuition in knightly skills[13] and set off for Arthur's court clad in rustic homespun, Lancelot was taught all knightly and courtly skills and set off for Camelot well equipped with armor, warhorse, and fine robes. The Lady of the Lake loved Lancelot as if he were her own son and grieved like Perceval's mother when the youth decided to leave to become a knight, but she was aware of his great destiny as the best of all knights, went herself with him to the court, asked Arthur to knight the lad in the armor she had given him, and instructed Lancelot to insist on being knighted the very next day. Lancelot contrives to receive his sword from Guinevere rather than from the king (indeed, the word "knight" is not applied to him in the narrative until he receives the sword from the queen), so that, again unlike Perceval (knighted by Gornemant), the inspiration behind his knighthood comes, from the beginning, from women rather than from men. The parallels with Perceval that lead up to the arrival at court and the knighting, therefore, serve also to bring out the contrast between the carefully prepared and the rustic, unprepared youth, both nameless and both destined for greatness.

The narrative pattern of the Fair Unknown seems to have been well known in the twelfth century, and echoes from it are to be found in a number of Chrétien's romances.[14] There is interplay with a version such as that of Renaut de Beaujeu[15] in relation to the episodes immediately following Lancelot's first arrival at Camelot. Like the hero of Renaut's poem, Lancelot insists on taking the first adventure that presents itself at court: a messenger arrives with a request from a lady for a champion for a judicial duel. In both texts, the youth, just knighted, is awarded the task, and the emissary doubts the worth of the young champion who is made to undergo a series of tests on the way to the battle.[16] During these tests, the network of resonances with *Le Conte del Graal* continues, when Lancelot, lapsing for a moment from the youth carefully educated to be a courteous knight and, after his first sight of Guinevere, already in love with her, most uncharacteristically insists on seeing a damsel in a tent, as Perceval had done on his way to Arthur's court.[17]

The "making of a name" theme continues to be underlined throughout Lancelot's early adventures in a series of episodes that evoke memories of other romances where this theme is important. Lancelot discovers who he is when he achieves the adventure of the Dolorous Guard and raises the tombstone in the cemetery attached to the castle (*LK*, 194). Underneath the slab is written his name and that of his father. There is again a contrast with Perceval, who guesses his name at the moment when his failure at the Grail castle is revealed to him by his cousin (*Le Conte del Graal*, ll. 3572–82), whereas Lancelot learns his name at the moment of success.[18] The raising of the slab also recalls the episode in Chrétien's Lancelot romance when the Knight of the Cart, object of scorn, is also revealed to be the hero destined to free the prisoners from the land from which no traveler returns and who will finally lie in this tomb (*Charrete*, ll. 1900–7, 1934–36). His name is withheld from the reader, although there is no suggestion in the text that the hero himself is ignorant of his own name. In the prose romance, Lancelot may have found his name inscribed beneath the slab, and one damsel from the lake may have seen it, but he has still to establish a reputation as knight in the world; he proceeds to do this under a series of different names, White Knight, Red Knight, Black Knight, a variation on the situation of Yvain who had made one name for himself, lost it and his own identity, and had to remake his name as knight and lover under the title of the Knight of the Lion. In the prose romance, once Lancelot has left the lake, his name is not used in the narrative, even though Gauvain brings back to the court news of the identity of the White Knight, until the hero admits to his various exploits as White Knight, Red Knight, Black Knight to the queen and she then pronounces his name (*LK*, 344), again a variation on the situation in Chrétien's *Charrete*, where the name appears in the text only from the point where

Guinevere identifies the champion fighting on her behalf against Meleagant as Lancelot of the Lake (*Charrete*, ll. 3660–61). White Knight, Red Knight, and Black Knight come together for Arthur only under the name of Lancelot of the Lake when Gauvain, completing his quests for the Red Knight and the Black Knight, presents the king with his deliverer from the Saxons (*LK*, 566), the youth brought up in the lake and son of the vassal whose dispossession and death Arthur had been unable to prevent.[19] Then Lancelot, having established his reputation as the greatest living knight, is made a companion of the Round Table.

During the course of this account of the events leading up to Lancelot's triumphant entry into Arthur's court, there are a number of narrative sequences in which the progress of the young man toward the making of a great name is compared and contrasted with the need for the established knight to prove himself worthy of the name he has already won. This is often done in terms that recall the parallels and oppositions between the adventures of Perceval and Gauvain in *Le Conte del Graal* and on occasion also link up with other Chrétien romances presenting variations on the narrative pattern of the Fair Unknown. For example, Hector is contrasted with Gauvain, the established knight, when he plays the role of young knight and lover in the process of making a chivalric reputation while Lancelot has been withdrawn from the action into concealment in Sorelois. The Lady of Roestoc has sent a dwarf, accompanied by his niece with whom Hector is in love, to bring back Gauvain as her champion in a judicial duel. The unrecognized Gauvain is accepted as a poor substitute for the knight the lady's emissary believes he has failed to find. On the way to Roestoc, Gauvain is doubted and scorned by the dwarf, who makes him stand by while Hector succeeds in winning a series of battles against increasingly large groups of knights encountered on the road (*LK*, 376–82). This is an intratextual allusion as it recalls the tests Lancelot had to go through on the way to his first judicial duel as a very young knight (*LK*, 166–74, 178), but it also works on the intertextual level, for the form of the tests reminds us of the sequence of battles Erec had to fight when he set off to regain his good name as a knight in a romance that Claude Luttrell links closely with an early version of the tale of the Fair Unknown.[20]

Echoes from Chrétien also serve to bring out the love theme in a text in which there are no lovers' monologues or authorial comments on love, and at first sight the emphasis on adventure seems to leave little place for love. However, by a series of lover's trances such as are to be found in the *Charrete* or in *Le Conte del Graal*, the idea that all Lancelot's deeds are inspired by his love for Guinevere is conveyed.[21] His first sight of the queen reduces him to silence, with the result that when he is unable to tell her his name, she suspects that this comes from the confusion of a youth overcome by love at first sight, although in fact he does not know who he is (*LK*, 157). Lancelot's first major trance takes place by the river, where he is roused from deep thought when he fails to respond to the challenge of a knight at the ford, who claims quite falsely to be the queen's knight (*LK*, 179–81). The subject of his meditation is not made explicit, but there is no need, for the whole episode evokes Lancelot's meditation by the river in Chrétien's poem (*Charrete*, ll. 22–28). A later trance by the water also brings in Yvain, another of Chrétien's great lovers, to whom Arthur had entrusted the young squire on his arrival at court and who now rescues the still unidentified Lancelot from drowning (*LK*, 266–67) and shortly afterwards witnesses his victory over two giants (*LK*, 270), an episode that recalls a similar victory by Yvain (*Le Chevalier au Lion*, ll. 4139–4250) and also one by another lover, Erec (*Erec*, ll. 4280–4541). Parallels with another famous twelfth-century lover, Tristan, in love with the wife of his uncle and king, are at this stage in the evolution of the Lancelot romance kept at arm's length; at this point the person who suffers because of Lancelot's love for Guinevere is his friend Galehot, not Arthur.[22]

As with the quest for identity, pairing within the romance keeps in mind the theme of Lancelot's love for Guinevere as an inspiration for chivalry during Lancelot's stay in Sorelois. Once again, it is Hector who plays the role of the young knightly lover, but in a way that serves to emphasize the positive force of Lancelot's love for Guinevere, which never represents an obstacle to his chivalric achievement, in contrast with Hector's love for his lady, which stands in his way because she doubts his prowess and does not want him to undertake a dangerous battle or wish to allow him to depart on a quest for Gauvain (*LK*, 375, 398–406). Hector's meditation upon love, which is rudely and unsuccessfully interrupted by Gauvain's companions, including Kay (*LK*, 368–70), evokes both those of Lancelot and that of Perceval, meditating over the drops of blood on the snow (*Le Conte del Graal*, ll. 4164–4500); it thus picks up the network of intertextual and intratextual resonances linking and contrasting Lancelot with Perceval and with Hector. Many of the adventures undertaken by Hector on his quest for Gauvain concern the relationship between love and chivalry, and serve again to underline by contrast the difference between these inferior loves and the supreme love of Lancelot for Guinevere.[23] It is through the inspiration of his love for the queen that Lancelot saves Arthur and his throne three times, twice from Galehot and once from the Saxons. Indeed, he makes it clear, in the scene leading up to the lovers' first kiss, that she has been the inspiration behind all his achievements, when he explains that her words to him when he first left Camelot, "Adieu, biaus douz amis," had given him the strength to perform all his feats:

> "Dame, fait il, ge ving devant vos qant ge oi pris congié de monseignor lo roi, toz armez fors de mon chief et de mes mains, si vos commandai a Deu et dis que j'estoie vostre chevaliers an quel qe leu que ge fusse. Et vos deïstes que vostre chevaliers et vostre anmis voloiez vos que ge fusse. Et ge dis: 'A deu, dame.' Et vos deïstes: 'A Deu, biaus douz amis.' Ne onques puis do cuer ne me pot issir. Ce fu li moz qui prodome me fera se gel suis. Ne onques puis ne vign an si grant meschief que de cest mot ne me manbrast. Cist moz m'a conforté an toz mes anuiz, cist moz m'a de toz mes maus garantiz et m'a gari de toz periz; cist moz m'a saolé an otes mes fains, cist moz m'a fait riche an totes mes granz povretez."

("My lady," he said, "I came to you when I had taken leave of my lord the king, fully armed except for my head and hands, and I commended you to God and said that I was your knight wherever I might be. And you said that you wished me to be your knight and your friend. And I said: 'Go with God, my lady.' And you said: 'Go with God, dear friend.' That has never been out of my heart since. Those were the words which will make me a man of valor, if I am ever to be one. Since then I have never been in such dire straits that I did not remember those words. Those words have comforted me in all my troubles, those words have protected me from all ills and saved me from all dangers, those words have satisfied me in my great hunger, those words have made me rich in my great poverty." LK, 346–47)

This is one of the few passages in the romance where Lancelot is articulate about his love and uses phrases such as the series of antitheses that have resonances of the courtly lyric and of some of the monologues in Chrétien.

The pattern of Lancelot's progress as a hero in the account of his adventures culminating with his acceptance at court under his own name (LK, 566) is very different from that of a Chrétien hero. There is no early success followed by a crisis that casts doubt upon this achievement and suggests a failure in comprehension on the part of the hero, as is to be found in *Erec et Enide*, *Le Chevalier au Lion*, *Le Chevalier de la Charrete*, and *Le Conte del Graal*; but there is an ever-mounting series of achievements culminating in Lancelot saving Arthur and his kingdom for the third time and the establishment of his reputation at Arthur's court as the greatest of all knights.[24] His love for the queen has not constituted a threat to the kingdom, but has rather been a source of strength, an inspiration for success in every adventure, in contrast with the loves of other knights encountered in the romance. However, the situation changes once the Grail is no longer mentioned only as part of a system of allusions to Arthurian stories existing outside the romance, but a Grail Quest is incorporated within a cycle that also embraces the other main twelfth-century Arthurian themes, namely a rewriting of the Chrétien *Charrete* and an account of the death of Arthur.[25]

The first clear allusion to a failure by Lancelot and to a Grail Quest still to be completed, in which the chief Grailwinner will be not Perceval but a descendant of Lancelot yet to be born, occurs in the cyclic version of the Journey to Sorelois and the False Guinevere episode (*LM*, IV, 35, 42). It is at this point too that the first unqualified condemnation of Lancelot's love for Guinevere occurs and that we learn that it is to prove the insurmountable obstacle to the achievement of the greatest adventure of all. One of Arthur's wise clerks tells Galehot:

> "*Cist (Lancelot) ne porroit recovrer les taiches que cil avra qui l'aventure del Graal achevera, kar il covient tot premierement qu'il soit de sa nativité jusqu'a sa mort virges et chastes si entierement qu'il n'ait amor n'a dame n'a damoisele.*"

> ("This man could not regain the qualities that the one destined to achieve the adventure of the Grail will have, for from birth to death, he must before all else be virgin and chaste so completely that he has no love for lady or damsel." *LM*, IV, 37)

This superseding of the father by the son will be linked to the making of a name theme as well as the love theme as will be seen, but will still keep Lancelot's role at the center of the romance.

Lancelot, however, will still be the greatest knight until the beginning of *La Queste*, when it is announced before all the court that he has lost his position of greatest knight. The love has been condemned in relation to the Grail Quest, but it will still inspire Lancelot to great achievement. The tension between the positive and negative aspects of the love relationship is demonstrated in a series of episodes in which an adventure at which Lancelot the lover is destined to succeed is paired with one at which, as lover, he is destined to fail. There is a good example of this in the prose-romance version of the prose *Charrete* story, where Lancelot is confronted by two tomb slabs. One slab, that of Galaad son of Joseph of Arimathea, according to its inscription, can be raised only by the knight destined to free the prisoners in the Roiaume sans Retor; the other, that of Symeu, according to its inscription, can be raised only by the knight destined to bring to an end the enchantments of the Royaume Aventureus and all its adventures and to achieve the Perilous Seat at the Round Table *(LM*, XXXVII), that is to say the Grailwinner.[26] Lancelot is able to raise the first slab but fails at the second.

This episode has a double resonance: it evokes both the scene in Chrétien's *Le Chevalier de la Charrete* and the raising of the slab in the cemetery of the Dolorous Guard, itself setting off echoes in the reader's memory of Chrétien's Lancelot, lover of Guinevere, and thus interlacing the theme of love with that of the making of a name. Lancelot himself recalls the Dolorous Guard when he sees the tombs in the cemetery *(LM*, XXXVII, 32). Episodes such as these form part of a gradual preparation for a reassessment both by hero and reader of Lancelot's earlier actions, a rereading that will be required within the context of the Grail adventures of *La Queste*. Lancelot is deeply ashamed at his fear of the flames coming out of the tomb of Symeu and at his failure to raise the slab *(LM*, XXXVII, 36–37). A voice (that of Symeu) reminds Lancelot that he is still the greatest knight until the coming of the one destined to surpass him *(LM*, XXXVII, 38–40). But here greater emphasis is given to the sins of the flesh of Lancelot's father rather than to his own as the reason for his failure at an adventure he had originally been meant to achieve. The part played by Lancelot's adulterous love in making it impossible for him to achieve the Grail adventure is made clearer by the inscription on another tomb, which says that the only knight who should enter the cemetery where the tomb is found is the wretched knight who for his carnal sin ("maleurose luxure") will be prevented from success in the Grail adventures *(LM*, LXV, 25). This knight is identified in another inscription as the son of the grieving queen *(LM*, LXV, 32), a name in the form "la Reine as Granz Dolors" used to designate the mother of Lancelot in the account of his father's death and his own disappearance into the lake *(LK*, 16). Yet at this stage, Lancelot's failures are rare compared with his successes as the great knightly lover. Thus, he rescues Guinevere from Meleagant and can put an end to the *carole*, a magic dance into which are drawn those who love or have loved and which can only be ended with the arrival of the most loyal, the best, and the fairest of knights *(LM*, LXXXIII, 8).

As the Grail adventures approach, the number of indications of Lancelot's future failure and of the damage inflicted on his prospects by his love for Guinevere increases. The queen herself becomes deeply disturbed at the high price he is to pay for her love, but he refuses to accept this and, in one of the few passages in which he is articulate about his love, declares that it has been his great desire to be worthy of her love that has inspired him and given him the strength to accomplish the chivalric deeds that have won him fame (*LM*, LXXXV, 3).

Lancelot's experiences during his first visit to Corbenic illustrate both his triumphs (linking with past achievements which he still ascribes to his love for Guinevere) and his future displacement as the greatest knight. He is able to save a damsel from a tub of hot water, an adventure at which Gauvain had failed (*LM*, LXVI, 4–8); he then raises the slab on a tomb that, according to its inscription, will not be raised before the leopard sets his hand to it, the leopard from whom the great lion is to come who will raise it easily, and then will be engendered the great lion in the beautiful daughter of le Roi de la Terre Forainne (*LM*, LXVIII, 45–47). By achieving this adventure, Lancelot is identified as the leopard to be surpassed by his own son, the lion (as was foretold in the vision interpreted for Galehot by Arthur's clerks, *LM*, II, 10, IV, 34–35). He is given a glimpse of the Grail; then follows the episode of the conception of Galahad, which is central to the new interpretation given to the making of a name theme as the narrative moves towards the Grail adventures. There is, in a sense, a paradox here: the very love for Guinevere, that sinful passion that disqualifies Lancelot from the supreme Grail achievement, drives him on, when under the illusion that Pelle's daughter is the queen, and prompts him to commit the carnal act, that act which, through an involuntary betrayal of his love, is to engender Galahad, destined to be the pure and virgin knight.

Lancelot's intentions, unlike those of Pelle's daughter, who is fulfilling her destiny, are sinful, but the outcome is good, for it is made clear in the text at this point through an explanation coming from the tale that by this act the name Galahad, lost by Lancelot through *luxuria*, is recovered in the chaste son, the fruit of this union (*LM*, LXXVIII, 58).[27] The hero (and the reader) had thought that the name Lancelot had been won through earthly love; we now learn that the discovery of the name Lancelot in the cemetery of the Dolorous Guard represented a loss rather than a gain, yet the very love that has been condemned plays an ambiguous role in the restoration of the name Galahad in the person of Lancelot's son. It is significant too that the prose romance, which is picking up here a theme to be found in Chrétien (the hero's loss of his name through some failure on his part) does not give Lancelot the opportunity to redeem himself and recover this lost name, as did Yvain in *Le Chevalier au Lion*.

It is indeed noticeable that intertextual resonances linking Lancelot with other twelfth-century lovers are used to different effect once the Grail theme is given importance within the romance and the negative aspects of

Lancelot's love for Guinevere begin to receive some emphasis. For example, before Lancelot is known at court and becomes a knight of the Round Table, he goes mad when imprisoned by the Saxons, is set free and is cared for by Guinevere, is quietened when he wears the split shield representing the progress of his love for Guinevere, and is healed by an ointment brought by the Lady of the Lake (*LK*, 551–57). The ointment recalls the healing of Yvain, but the madness is not caused by his being banished by his beloved as was that of Yvain. However, in the branch of the romance that leads up to *La Queste*, Guinevere, as in Chrétien and like the lady in the courtly love lyric, is prepared to doubt the quality of her knight's love. There, his period of madness arises like that of Yvain because he has been banished by his lady, but the use of the Grail rather than a magic ointment for the healing suggests a new attitude toward a love that by this stage is being represented as above all potentially destructive (*LM*, CV, 38, CVII, 1–30).

In addition, for the first time, similarities between Lancelot and Tristan are to be found in an episode in which Lancelot, in order to comfort himself during his imprisonment by Morgain, paints past scenes of his life, including the scene of the lovers' first kiss (*LM*, LXXXVI, 21–23, LXXXVIII, 1). Just as Tristan too had sought comfort from images of Iseut during his period of exile, Lancelot kisses his picture of Guinevere as Tristan had kissed the image of Iseut.[28] Lancelot has no thought of any possible disruptive consequences stemming from his activities, and the role of love in transforming a knight into an artist is underlined by Morgain (*LM*, LXXXVI, 22);[29] but it is made clear that Morgain intends to use these paintings to make trouble between Arthur and Guinevere, and when she shows them to Arthur in *La Mort Artu*, as will be seen, she uses them to reinterpret earlier events in the most damaging way possible. These first parallels with Tristan bring out the potentially destructive element in this love of Lancelot for Arthur's wife, an aspect of the love that had been carefully kept at arm's length before the rewriting of the False Guinevere episode and the first condemnation of the relationship. The episode of the paintings prepares the way for the more violent evocations of the Tristan story in *La Mort Artu*. Yet, in spite of all this, Lancelot is still the greatest knight, the object of admiration and of quests by the companions of the Round Table, and the account of his adventures is given pride of place above all others. He still sees Guinevere as the inspiration for all his achievement, has not accepted the reinterpretation of his past that the inscriptions on tombs and his inability to achieve certain adventures have urged upon him, and has not renounced his love for Guinevere or his belief in its positive value on the very eve of the Grail adventures.

With the knighting of Galahad at the beginning of *La Queste*, however, the situation is transformed, as had been predicted in the inscriptions
and prophecies, and Lancelot's status has radically changed. He shows his
awareness of this immediately by refusing to attempt to draw the sword from
the floating stone, which can only be drawn out by the best knight. Then
Galahad comes to court and takes his seat, the Perilous Seat, at the Round
Table, and draws out the sword. At this point a damsel rides up and announces that yesterday Lancelot was the greatest knight, but today this is
no longer true; she presents his demotion in terms of "li changemenz et li
muemenz de vostre nom" (*La Queste*, 13: "the change in your name"). Once
again the intertextual element is significant; the damsel's public declaration
and the reference to a change of name provide a combined allusion to two
episodes in *Le Conte del Graal* as well as linking up with developments in
the making of a name theme earlier in the cycle. In the first of these episodes,
Perceval meets a damsel who declares herself to be his cousin; she asks him
about his visit to the Grail Castle and discovers that he has failed to ask the
questions that would have healed the Fisher King; at that point, Perceval
guesses his name, Perceval li Galois, but immediately loses it again as she
declares angrily: "Tes nons est changiés, biax amis." / —"Coment?"
—"Perchevax li chaitis!" (*Le Conte del Graal*, ll. 3581–82).

In the second episode, Perceval, having made a triumphant appearance at Arthur's court, is denounced publicly before everyone by the loathly
damsel (*Le Conte del Graal*, ll. 4611–83). *La Queste* thus combines a reference to the change of name of the first scene and another to the public
denunciation of the second. In the earlier examples of intertextual allusions
to the young Perceval of Chrétien's romance, the contrast between Lancelot's
careful preparation for knighthood and Perceval's lack of preparation and
rustic simplicity was underlined, but in this interaction between the texts,
the theme of failure is common to both knights; yet there is an important
difference. Perceval is, in the first episode, a young man who has only just
discovered his name and has yet to make it at court; even in the second, he
is still young and has only just been welcomed at Arthur's court under his
own name; he may yet redeem his failure on one level at least, as is the usual
pattern in Chrétien's finished romances, even if on another level questions
may yet be left unanswered; in *La Queste* itself, on the intratextual level,
he is one of the three Grailwinners, although not the greatest. Lancelot, on
the other hand, is at this point in the *Lancelot-Graal* cycle the established
knight who is losing a good name he has already made as the best of all
knights, and he will never have the chance to redeem himself completely as
far as the Grail is concerned. The young unknown knight who, in *La Queste*,

replaces the Perceval of earlier tradition as the main Grail hero, has only to arrive at court to establish his name by taking the Perilous Seat and to demonstrate his status as the best knight in the world by drawing the sword from the stone. His quality as knight is never doubted; he has no need to go through a long period of testing before proving his identity and great destiny.

Yet, if Lancelot is no longer the best knight and it is now the company of Galahad that is sought by the others, his partial failure is, in a way, given as great a significance in the text as is Galahad's success and is closely linked to the whole thematic structure of the romance through intratextual allusions. Some of Galahad's adventures echo those of his father when a young knight. The motif of the raising of tomb slabs helps to establish a series of parallels and contrasts between Galahad's achievements in the *Queste* and with Lancelot's achievements when a young knight and his more recent failures. For example, Galahad is able to raise a slab in an abbey cemetery so that a body can be removed from it, and the diabolical marvels of the cemetery, the strange sights and sounds, are thus brought to an end (*La Queste*, 35–40). This recalls Lancelot's achievement in first conquering the Dolorous Guard (*LK*, 194), thereby learning his own name (*LK*, 194), and then his return to the castle to put an end to the enchantments of the cemetery (*LK*, 247–50).

Both Lancelot as a young knight at Dolorous Guard and Galahad at the abbey succeed in bringing peace to a troubled place through their courage and quality as the knights predestined to achieve these particular adventures. Yet their motives are very different. Lancelot is lured to the Dolorous Guard to end the enchantments by a false message that Guinevere is imprisoned there. Galahad achieves his adventure because he has no interest in earthly love but is a virgin and as pure of all sin as any man can be. Lancelot's adventure conforms to the pattern of the Arthurian marvelous characteristic of romance, with no specific Christian connotations; in Galahad's adventure, the strange sights and sounds are at first described in terms similar to those at Dolorous Guard, but it is soon made clear that Galahad has to deal with the forces of Satan, and the significance of the adventure in terms of Christian allegory is given (*La Queste*, 36–38). On a second occasion, with the lifting of the stone over a grave, thereby ending the suffering of Symeu in the burning tomb (*La Queste*, 264), Galahad's achievement is contrasted with Lancelot's failure through a reference back to Lancelot's lack of success at this tomb during the prose *Charrete* episode. Lancelot's failure there was set beside his success at the tomb whose slab could be raised only by the knight destined to rescue the prisoners of Gorre, including the queen, and where his love gives him the inspiration to pass the test. Galahad always owes his success to his purity and virginity; Lancelot, during the adventures which lead up to *La Queste*, alternates between success through his love and failure also through his love. Once the Grail adventures have begun, Lancelot's love for Guinevere can only bring him failure, and he is finally forced to renounce it, but with extreme reluctance:

> *"Sire, fet Lancelot, il est einsi que je sui morz de pechié d'une moie dame que je ai amée toute ma vie, et ce est la reine Guenievre, la fame le roi Artu. Ce est cele qui a plenté m'a doné l'or et l'argent et les riches dons que je ai aucune foiz donez as povres chevaliers. Ce est cele qui m'a mis ou grant boban et en la grant hautece ou je sui. Ce est cele por qui amor j'ai faites les granz proeces dont toz li mondes parole. Ce est cele qui m'a fet venir de povreté en richece et de mesaise a toutes les terriannes beneurtez. Mes je sai bien que par cest pechié de li s'est Nostre Sires si durement corociez a moi qu'il m'a bien mostré puis ersoir."*

("Sir," said Lancelot, "the position is that I am guilty of mortal sin with my lady whom I have loved all my life, that is Queen Guinevere, the wife of King Arthur. It is she who gave me in abundance the gold, silver and rich gifts which I have on occasion given to poor knights. It is she who raised me up and gave me my present high status. It is for love of her that I have performed the great deeds of prowess known throughout the world. It is she who brought me from poverty to riches and from hardship to great happiness on earth. But I know well that it is on account of this sin with her that I have incurred God's great wrath, as he showed me so clearly last night." *La Queste*, 66)

This echoes in rhythms and vocabulary his confession of the way he interpreted Guinevere's words of farewell when he left to undertake his first task as a knight, a confession that led up to the first kiss, as quoted earlier. A little later in *La Queste*, another hermit gives a completely new interpretation of Lancelot's first meeting with Guinevere, which he presents as part of the devil's plot to use the wiles of a woman to rob Lancelot of all the qualities he had when he entered the order of chivalry (*La Queste*, 125–26). According to this hermit, the queen was already in a state of sin, because she had not made a good confession since her marriage, and the devil entered into her so that she desired Lancelot when she first saw him. Lancelot looked at Guinevere and was aware that she took pleasure in beholding him, and (in an adaptation of the image of the arrows of love) Satan struck him with his dart so that he left the path of righteousness and entered that of lust, so that the virtue of humility that had been in him was driven out and replaced by arrogance, and he said to himself that he would set no store by anything until he had his will of her. Therefore, according to the hermit, Lancelot's confidence in the strength coming from his *joie* (*LK*, 40–41) and his conviction, expressed in the meeting leading to the kiss, that his achievements stem from that first sight of Guinevere and from her words "A Deu, biaus douz amis" are nothing but sinful arrogance.

There is a remarkably wide gap between the account provided by the tale of these earlier events, which was at that stage presented as true and authentic, and the version here given by the hermit. There is no indication, when Lancelot's first visit to Camelot was originally narrated, that the queen had a strong sexual interest in the bashful and inarticulate youth nor any sign that he set out arrogantly to obtain sinful possession of her. However, everything that happens in *La Queste* and all comments on past events made by those whose role is to interpret past and present events on the allegorical level are designed to cast doubt on all the conventions of romance and on the reality and truth of all that pertains to the ordinary Arthurian world, including, it appears, the reliability of the tale's original version of events. During the Grail adventures, happenings will have a different meaning than they had before the beginning of the adventures or, it appears, after the end of these adventures.[30]

This interplay between past and present and this constant reinterpretation of the past in the light of adventures taking place on an allegorical level, which are so characteristic of *La Queste,* integrates this branch, functioning according to a different mode, firmly within the cycle. This is indeed a branch of the work that must not be read in isolation from the whole. Lancelot, like the other knights, but unlike Galahad who begins his career as a knight with the beginning of the Grail adventures, is hampered by his own past and by his experience of earthly chivalry when he has to adapt to the unfamiliar allegorical level, where the old rules of behavior do not work and nothing is as it seems. Thus, when he goes to help the losing side, the Black Knights, against the White Knights, he suffers an unaccustomed defeat and discovers that he has unwittingly fought on the side of the devil (*La Queste*, 140–44). Yet he does better in the Grail adventures than does Gauvain, second only to Lancelot as a knight according to earlier episodes in the cycle.[31] Lancelot has a fragmentary vision of the Grail (*La Queste*, 255–58), whereas Gauvain has to return to court having achieved nothing in the Quest (*La Queste*, 161). Gauvain relies only upon his own resources and would acknowledge no debt to inspiration outside himself, whereas Lancelot, from the beginning, attributes his achievements to his love for Guinevere; the nature of this love may disqualify him from the supreme achievement in the Grail Quest, but the fact that he is a faithful and devoted lover not only, as has been seen, plays an ambiguous role in the engendering of Galahad, but also, in a way, prepares him for the need in the Quest to seek inspiration outside himself, although of a very different kind, that of heavenly love in the form of the grace of God.

On Lancelot's return to the ordinary Arthurian world of *La Mort Artu*, with Galahad now dead, he regains the position of the greatest knight, but with a reversal of roles: he who had been the savior of the kingdom now presents the greatest threat to its peace and harmony, for he has lapsed back into carnal love of an even greater intensity. Indeed, the parallels with the Tristan story, so carefully avoided in the early part of the romance,[32] play a central role in *La Mort Artu* and bring out the potentially destructive element in his relationship with Guinevere in a branch of the romance where feudal relationships are emphasized. His passion for his lord's wife threatens the peace and stability of the whole kingdom and sets two lineages at war with each other, that of Ban and that of Lot. The lovers lose all discretion so that those who are jealous of Lancelot become aware that "Lancelos amoit la reïne de fole amour et la reïne lui autresi" ("Lancelot loved the queen with wanton love and the queen loved him in the same way," *La Mort Artu*, §4, 10–18), as happened to Tristan and Iseut when they betrayed themselves to the three barons.[33] Arthur is as reluctant as Mark to believe the talebearers concerning a knight with such a heroic past who has saved the kingdom more than once, as true of Lancelot as it had been of Tristan.

The interactions with the Tristan story continue, as Morgain makes malicious use of the pictures painted by Lancelot to comfort himself when separated from his beloved, as Tristan had sought consolation in images of Iseut; and this also brings in a series of intratextual allusions. Once again, as with the hermit's account of the meetings between Lancelot and Guinevere discussed above, we have a reinterpretation of earlier events by a character in the romance, and here too there are serious discrepancies between the commentary on the events depicted (*La Mort Artu*, §52–53) and the original narrative;[34] however, as the mischiefmaking intentions of Morgain are apparent to the reader if not to Arthur, the authenticity of the tale as a true record of events is not so disturbingly undermined as it is, on one level at least, by the hermit. For Arthur, however, the combination of pictures and malevolent commentary has a devastating effect; under the guidance of

Morgain, he sees Lancelot in the same way that Mark, under the influence of the dwarf and the barons, had seen Tristan as a treacherous adulterer, and he finds in the painting "ma honte toute aparissant et la traïson Lancelot" (*La Mort Artu*, §90, 87–92). The problem is, however, both in *La Mort Artu* and in the Tristan story, that no matter how unfavorable a light is cast upon those who reveal to Arthur the *fole amor* of Lancelot and Guinevere or to Mark that of Tristan and Iseut, the fact is that there has been adultery, and in this branch of the cycle this truth is no longer kept at arms' length. In the Tristan story as presented in the so-called *version commune*,[35] the lovers consider that they cannot be held wholly responsible for their actions because of the love potion, but there is no love potion in *La Mort Artu*, although Arthur, when first told of the love by Agravain and still unwilling to believe in it, does talk of the *force d'amor* that sense and reason cannot withstand:

> "*Car ge sei bien veraiement que Lancelos nel penseroit en nule maniere; et certes se il onques le pensa, force d'amor li fist fere, encontre qui sens ne reson ne puet avoir duree.*"

> ("For I know truly that Lancelot would in no way contemplate such a thing; or indeed if he did, it would be under the compulsion of the force of love which sense and reason have no power to withstand."
> *La Mort Artu*, §6, 25–29)

However, when confronted with the evidence of the paintings combined with Morgain's explanations, he is no longer prepared to accept *force d'amor* as a justification.

Lancelot's cousin Bohort too sees only the negative aspects of this love. He reproaches Lancelot for the war that will come, once the king is certain that he has been wronged in relation to his wife, a war that will constitute a reversal of the situation early in the romance, where Lancelot saves Logres instead of threatening it. Bohort warns him:

> "*Or verroiz la guerre commencier qui jamés ne prendra fin a nos vivans. Car se li rois vos a jusques ci amé plus que nul home, de tant vos haïra il plus, des qu'il savra que vos li meffesiez tant com de lui vergonder de sa fame.*"

> ("Now you will see the war begin which will not end in our lifetime. For if the king has until now loved you more than any other man, so much the greater will be his hatred of you as soon as he learns that

you have treated him so badly as to bring shame on him with his wife." *La Mort Artu*, §90, 87–92.)

The intensity of the love and the overwhelming desire of the lovers to be together had been emphasized before the Grail theme and the first condemnations of the love were introduced, but in positive terms, as an inspiration for great deeds that would benefit the kingdom:

> *Et la reine an ce sejor l'anama tant que ele ne voit mies comment ele se poïst consirrer de lui veoir. Et li poise de ce qu'ele lo set et lo voit a si volenteïf et a si corageus, car ele ne voit mies comment sa vie poïst durer sanz la soe, s'il s'an aloit ja mais de cort. Si voudroit bien que il aüst un po mains de hardement et de proece.*

(And during this time, the queen became so much in love with him that she did not see how she could do without seeing him. And it distressed her to see and know that he was so eager and courageous, for she did not see how she could go on living without him, if he ever went away from court again. She would have liked him to have a little less bravery and prowess. *LK*, 558, 16–21)

However, she does not stand in his way, but equips him with armor so that he can defeat the Saxon army and deliver Arthur. In *La Mort Artu*, the increasing intensity of the love is also described, but with a significant use of the term *folement* in a passage that leads up to the second denunciation of the lovers by Agravain:

> *Et se Lancelos avoit devant ce amee la reïne, il l'ama orendroit plus qu'il n'avoit onques mes fet a nul jor, et ele ausint lui; et se demenerent si folement que li pluseur de leanz le sorent veraiement, et messire Gauvains meïsmes le sot tout apertement, et ausi firent tuit si quatre frere.*

(And if Lancelot had before this loved the queen, he loved her now more than ever, and the same was true of her; and they now conducted themselves with so little discretion that many people became aware of what was going on, including Gauvain himself, who gained certain knowledge of it and his four brothers as well. *La Mort Artu*, §85, 33–39)

The queen may love Lancelot *folement*, but she is also subject to fits of jealousy, and she has a tendency to suspect his fidelity to her, not a feature of the lovers' relationship in the Tristan story before the waning of the potion and their separation. Here again, the situation changes between Lancelot's early adventures, where Guinevere has complete trust and confidence in his unswerving devotion to her, and the adventures after the cyclic version of the False Guinevere episode, where she is angry with him for leaving court without her permission. Later, when she banishes him from court, he goes mad (*LM*, CV, 38, CVII, 1–30). In *La Mort Artu*, Guinevere suspects Lancelot of infidelity with the damsel of Escalot and refuses to see him. Bohort knows that rejection by the queen will destroy his cousin Lancelot and tells her that he wishes that they had never met and fallen in love, for her anger will undermine Lancelot's will to achieve great adventures and will finally bring about his death. This is a reversal of the pattern of contrasts between pairs of lovers to be found in the first branch of Lancelot's story, where within a whole system of allusions to Chrétien's romances, the relationship between Lancelot and Guinevere is presented as the ideal for the fostering of great chivalry. Now Bohort accuses Guinevere of gravely damaging the knight greatest in prowess, noblest in lineage:

> "*Mes tout einsi comme il est ores vestuz et couverz de toutes bones vertuz, tout einsi le despoilleroiz vos et desnueroiz. Et si poez par ce dire veraiement que vos osteroiz d'entre les estoiles le soleill, ce est a dire la fleur des chevaliers del monde d'entre les chevaliers le roi Artu; et par ce poez vos veoir, dame, apertement que vos domageroiz moult plus cest roiaume et maint autre que onques dame ne fist par le cors d'un sol chevalier. Et ce est li granz biens que nos atendons de vostre amor.*"

> ("But just as he is now garbed and enveloped in all the good qualities and powers, so will you strip and denude him of them. And you can therefore say truly that you will take away the sun from amongst all the stars and planets, that is to say the flower of all the knights in the world from amongst the knights of King Arthur; you can therefore see clearly, my lady, that you will inflict greater damage on this kingdom and many another than ever any lady did through the person of one knight. And this is the great benefit we expect from your love." *La Mort Artu*, §59, 73–84)

The potential for good in earthly love is here contrasted with the potential for harm, but Bohort has just given considerable stress to the negative aspect when he offered a long list of great men who had been destroyed by love, including a tragedy that had happened in the immediate past:

"Et a nostre tens meïsmes, n'a pas encore cinc anz que Tristans en morut, li niés au roi Marc, qui si loiaument ama Yseut la blonde. . . ."

("And in our time, less than five years ago, Tristan died of it who loved Yseut the Fair so faithfully. . . ." *La Mort Artu*, §59, 54–57)

Once again, a Tristan allusion is used to underline the destructive nature of Lancelot's love.

Those who come into contact with the lovers may also suffer as did some of those who came near Tristan and Iseut in the forest. The damsel of Escalot dies for love of Lancelot. Poisoned fruit is sent to court, and Guinevere, unaware of its nature, gives it to the brother of Mador de la Porte, who eats it and dies as a result; only Lancelot is prepared to defend the queen against the charge of murder. Finally, like the three barons in Beroul, Agravain lays a trap for Lancelot, who escapes as did Tristan; Lancelot has to return to rescue the queen from being burned, but by a tragic accident, kills Gauvain's beloved brother, Gaheriet. This death disturbs another well-established pairing of knights, that of Lancelot and Gauvain, often contrasted, but always linked in the comradeship of two great knights. Lancelot's love for Guinevere, resulting as it does in the loss of Gaheriet, leads to an unrestrained desire for revenge on Gauvain's part. The break-up of this longstanding comradeship between Lancelot and Gauvain, one already to be seen in Chrétien's *Le Chevalier de la Charrete* and emphasized throughout the whole cycle until this point, leads to the destruction of the Round Table and to the death of Arthur, because it is the cause of the absence of both Lancelot and Gauvain from the battle against Mordred.

Lancelot takes Guinevere away to safety as Tristan had escaped with Iseut, to Joyous Guard (the renamed Dolorous Guard), not to a forest, and not alone, apart from Governal, but with the support of his kinsmen and their men. From this point on, now that the war has started between the lineage of Ban and that of Lot, as prophesied by Bohort (*La Mort Artu*, §90, 87–92), the emphasis is no longer on Lancelot's unrestrained passion, which had set these events in motion, but on Gauvain's unbridled desire for revenge, arising from his great love for his brother. It is not that at this stage interplay with the Tristan story ceases, but rather that the allusions are to a later phase in that tale, where the passion was less violent. After the force of the potion waned and recognition of social and feudal obligations resurfaced,

Tristan, who had always been careful not to put Mark's life in jeopardy, became aware of his loss of status as a knight and his obligations to his uncle and king, and agreed with Iseut that she should return to Mark.

Lancelot, like Tristan, will not raise his hand against his king and in sparing his life revives, momentarily at least, Arthur's admiration for him (*La Mort Artu*, §116, 5–13). When Arthur receives a message from the pope that the land will be under interdict if he does not take back his wife, who has been condemned without trial (like Iseut), he is prepared to accept her but not to stop the war against Lancelot. The queen is prepared to agree to this, provided that Lancelot be allowed to return to his own land. Lancelot too is willing to surrender Guinevere to Arthur. Yet there is an ambiguity reminiscent of the *Tristan* of Beroul in Lancelot's repudiation of the idea that there had been *fole amor* between him and Guinevere (the term is applied to their love more than once in *La Mort Artu*; §4, 17–18, §85, 33–39, for example) and in his insistence that it was only the condemnation to death without trial, urged by *li desleial* (*La Mort Artu*, §119, 23–38), that had persuaded him to carry her off, where the reader/listener is aware that adultery has occurred, even if the motive of those who would condemn the queen without trial can be questioned.[36]

Lancelot, like Tristan, is sent into exile. Before he goes, by means of allusions to his heroic past (a recurrent theme in relation to Tristan in Beroul),[37] he reminds the king of what he owes him: the saving of his kingdom from Galehot, who would certainly have defeated Arthur had it not been for Lancelot (*La Mort Artu*, §119, 93–104). The king is therefore reminded of what might have been the cost of Lancelot's absence—a preparation for the tragic consequences of Lancelot's absence at the battle of Salisbury. Gauvain too is reminded of his debt to Lancelot, who delivered him from the prison of Karados, but Gauvain replies that the death of his brother at the hands of Lancelot cancels all previous debts. Finally, Lancelot says to Arthur:

> "*Sire, je m'en irai demain fors de vostre terre en tel maniere que pour tous les services que je vous ai fais, puis que je fu primes chevaliers, n'emporterai del vostre vaillant un esperon.*"

> ("Sire, I will depart tomorrow from your land in such a way that in return for all the services I have done you since I first became a knight, I will not take away with me anything of yours worth even one spur."
> *La Mort Artu*, §129, 132–36)

The allusions to the king's past debt to the knight he is sending into exile recall those to Tristan's heroic past, when he saved Cornwall from the

Morholt, but with an important difference. Tristan's great deeds for Mark and for Cornwall *preceded* his love for Iseut, caused by a potion; Lancelot's love for Guinevere has no justification in a love potion, but his great deeds in defense of Arthur and his kingdom *followed* falling in love with Guinevere, and it was his desire to prove himself worthy of her love that inspired him to save the king on several occasions. In the end, in *La Mort Artu*, it is Arthur's debt to Lancelot and the damage that the king suffers because of Lancelot's absence that is stressed, whatever part Lancelot's love for Guinevere may have played in setting in motion the events that ended with the death of Arthur. Finally, it is Lancelot and his two cousins who avenge Arthur's death against the sons of Mordret, and it is Lancelot who is buried in the same tomb as Galehot, the prince who would have defeated Arthur but for Lancelot.

The allusions to Tristan serve also to bring out the contrasts between the two knights and lovers and to remind us perhaps not to try to impose a simple, unqualified overall reading of Lancelot's role in the whole cycle as suggested by the reinterpretation of Lancelot's past and the part played in it by Lancelot's love urged upon him and us by the hermit in *La Queste*. The tensions between different presentations of this love, whether by the tale or by characters within the romance, as are to be found in the cycle as a whole, should not, I think, be resolved neatly and tidily in terms of spiritual and social condemnation. No one branch should be analyzed in isolation, but it should also be remembered that there is no single voice to be accepted unquestioningly as giving a truthful interpretation of the events in Lancelot's life that would necessarily be valid for the whole cycle. The meaning lies rather in the maintenance of these tensions between the positive and negative in relation to a love such as that of Lancelot for Guinevere, as the pattern of intertextual and intratextual allusions suggests.

NOTES

1. I refer to the following editions of the different branches of the *Lancelot-Graal: Lancelot: Roman en prose du XIIIe siècle*, ed. Alexandre Micha (Paris: Droz, 1978-83), 9 vols., abbreviated to *LM*; the roman numerals refer to chapters, the arabic to paragraphs. *Lancelot do Lac: The Non-cyclic Old French Prose Romance*, ed. Elspeth Kennedy (Oxford: Oxford University Press, 1980), 2 vols., abbreviated to *LK*; this covers the same part of the text as vols. 7 and 8 of *LM* but is based on an earlier and better manuscript. *La Queste del saint Graal*, ed. Albert Pauphilet (Paris: Champion, 1923), abbreviated to *La Queste. La Mort le roi Artu*, 3rd ed., ed. Jean Frappier, (Paris: Droz, 1964), abbreviated to *Mort Artu*. The translations are my own except where they are based on *Lancelot of the Lake*, trans. Corin Corley, Oxford World's Classics (Oxford: Oxford University Press, 1989), a translation of parts of *LK*.

2. The first example of an unnarrated adventure of Gauvain that precedes Lancelot's arrival at court refers to a wound he had received in a battle against Gasoain

d'Estrangot, who had accused him of *desleiauté* before all the court (*LK*, 149). There is also in an explanation of the name Gué la Roine, a reference to the part Gauvain played in a battle at the beginning of Arthur's reign (*LK*, 181), and a mysterious allusion to an incident connected with "la damoiselle chaitive" (*LK*, 362 and note). These allusions serve to give Gauvain a past outside the romance.

3. When Galahad's adventures are not told, it is not because, according to the traditional phrase, they are not worth telling and therefore irrelevant to the tale ("sanz aventure trover qui face a amentevoir en conte"), but because he has so many great ones that the book would be too long which told all those worth telling (*La Queste*, 95). As a type of Christ, he seems at times to be a figure operating within a different concept of time and one whose actions cannot be contained within the tale.

4. The allusion to the Grail forms part of a whole pattern of allusions outwards from the text to the twelfth-century Arthurian tradition. The references to the Grail up to Lancelot's installation as a knight of the Round Table are not to a Grail Quest yet to take place, but to an existing tradition in which Perceval is the Grailwinner who accomplished the adventure of the Perilous Seat. See Kennedy, *Lancelot and the Grail: A Study of the Prose Lancelot* (Oxford: Oxford University Press, 1986), 143–55.

5. On the importance of pairing in the *Lancelot-Graal*, see Kennedy, *Lancelot and the Grail*, 218–35; Kennedy, "Le Rôle d'Yvain et de Gauvain dans le *Lancelot* en prose, version non-cyclique," in *Yvain-Lancelot-Gauvain: Colloque arthurien belge de Wégimont* (Paris: Nizet, 1984), 19–27; Kennedy, "Le personnage de Lancelot dans le *Lancelot* en prose," in *Lancelot: Actes du colloque des 14 et 15 janvier, 1984, Université de Picardie*, ed. Danielle Buschinger (Göppingen: Kümmerle, 1984), 99–106.

6. See Kennedy, *Lancelot and the Grail*. The first stage in this development of the romance is represented by the version found in a group of manuscripts that bring the story to an end with the death of Galehot (*LK*, 611–12). In the next stage, the text of this early prose *Lancelot* up to Lancelot's installation as a knight of the Round Table (*LK*, 571; *LM*, LXXIa, 49) is taken over without change, but the last two episodes, the Journey to Sorelois and the False Guinevere episode, are rewritten to prepare the way for the addition of a prose version of the *Charrete*, a Quest for the Grail with a new Grailwinner, and a Death of Arthur. In a third stage, *L'Estoire del Saint Graal* and a prose version of Robert de Boron's *Merlin*, followed by a Merlin continuation, are added. For a different view of the relative chronology of the two versions of the Journey to Sorelois and the False Guinevere episode, see Alexandre Micha, *Essais sur le cycle du Lancelot-Graal* (Geneva: Droz, 1987), 57–83.

7. Chrétien de Troyes, *Le Chevalier de la Charrete*, ed. Mario Roques (Paris: Champion, 1958), ll. 2345–53.

8. Ulrich von Zatzikhoven, *Lanzelet*, ed. K.A. Hahn (Frankfurt a. M.: Brönner, 1845).

9. See Kennedy, "The Quest for Identity and the Importance of Lineage in Thirteenth-Century French Prose Romance," in *The Ideals and Practice of Medieval Knighthood II; Papers from the Third Strawberry Hill Conference 1986*, ed. Christopher Harper-Bill and Ruth Harvey (Woodbridge: Boydell, 1988), 70–86; Kennedy, *Lancelot and the Grail*, 10–48; U. Ruberg, "Die Suche im Prosa-Lancelot," *Zeitschrift für Deutsches Altertum* 92 (1963), 122–57; Jacques Roubaud, "Enfances de la prose," *Change* 17 (1973), 348–65.

10. See Kennedy, "The Role of the Supernatural in the First Part of the Old French Prose *Lancelot*," in *Studies in Medieval Literature and Language in Memory of Frederick Whitehead* (Manchester: Manchester University Press, 1973), 173–84; Kennedy, *Lancelot and the Grail*, 111–42.

11. See also Jean Frappier, "L'*Institution* de Lancelot dans le *Lancelot en prose*," reprinted in *Amour courtois et Table Ronde* (Geneva: Droz, 1973), 169–79.

12. Chrétien de Troyes, *Le Roman de Perceval ou le Conte du Graal*, ed. William Roach (Geneva: Droz, 1956). For a study of the Lancelot-Perceval parallels and

contrasts, see Kennedy, *Lancelot and the Grail*, 10–24, and Kennedy, "Lancelot und Perceval: Zwei junge unbekannte Helden," *Wolfram-Studien* 9 (Schweinfurter 'Lancelot' Kolloquium, 1984), 228–41.

13. Lanzelet too, although he was taught to use sword and buckler by mermen, shares some of Perceval's comic awkwardness when he leaves the lake, for he never learned to ride there.

14. For a study of the influence of the Tale of the Fair Unknown on Chrétien's romances and for further bibliography, see Claude Luttrell, *The Creation of the First Arthurian Romance: A Quest* (London: Arnold, 1974).

15. Renaut de Beaujeu, *Le Bel Inconnu*, ed. G. Perrie Williams (Paris: Champion, 1967).

16. For a list of the verbal echoes between *Le Bel Inconnu* and *LK*, see notes to *LK*, 162–63. There are also parallels between the first task of Lancelot, the battle for the Lady of Nohaut, and one for the Lady of Norison undertaken by Yvain as an unknown knight in another romance with echoes of the Tale of the Fair Unknown, *Le Chevalier au Lion (Yvain)*, ed. Mario Roques (Paris: Champion, 1960), ll. 2934–45, 3142–3314; see *LK*, notes to 162–77.

17. For the damsel in the tent, compare *LK*, 167–69, 173, and *Le Conte del Graal*, ll. 681–772.

18. See Kennedy, "Failure in Arthurian Romance," *Medium Aevum* 60 (1991), 16–32.

19. There are a number of allusions in the text that remind us of Arthur's failure to fulfil his obligations to his vassal Ban; for example, *LK*, 54–56, where a monk reproaches Arthur for not avenging Ban, and *LK*, 285, where Arthur is upbraided by a holy man for Ban's death. See Kennedy, *Lancelot and the Grail*, 82–84.

20. Luttrell, 87–92, 264–68. Erec fights first three robber knights, then five, while Enide is supposed to wait passively and silently (*Erec et Enide*, ed. Mario Roques [Paris: Champion, 1953], ll. 2791–3078). There is an inversion here in *LK* of the usual pattern in the Fair Unknown romances, an inversion by which the battles serve to reinforce the dwarf's conviction that he is bringing a useless champion; see Kennedy, *Lancelot and the Grail*, 40–41.

21. See Kennedy, "Royal Broodings and Lovers' Trances in the First Part of the Prose *Lancelot*," in *Mélanges Jeanne Wathelet-Willem, Marche Romane* (Liège: 1978), 301–14.

22. See *Lancelot and the Grail*, 73–77. Jean Frappier analyzes Galehot as a tragic figure in "Le Personnage de Galehaut dans le *Lancelot* en prose," reprinted in *Amour courtois et Table Ronde*, 181–208.

23. An example of a pair whose relationship has a very negative effect compared with that of Lancelot and Guinevere is to be found in an adventure undertaken by Hector (*LK*, 519–24). He has to rescue a great beauty, Heliene sans Per, whose husband Persides has been reproached for marrying beneath him and, like Erec, for lapsing into *peresce*. Heliene, unlike Enide, reacts angrily to these reproaches and declares that her beauty is worth more than his chivalry. Enraged by this, Persides imprisons his wife until such time as a knight can prove in battle that her beauty is greater than his chivalry. See Kennedy, *Lancelot and the Grail*, 69–71.

24. For a comparison of the differing patterns of success and failure in Chrétien and in the prose romance, see Kennedy, "Failure in Arthurian Romance."

25. See note 6 above and Kennedy, *Lancelot and the Grail*.

26. To be compared with the passage early in the Prose *Lancelot* referring to Perceval or Perlesvaus as "celui qui vit apertement les granz merveilles del Graal et acompli lo Siege Perilleus de la Table Reonde et mena a fin les aventures del Reiaume Perilleus Aventureus, ce fu li regnes de Logres" (*LK*, 33). It is clear from the manuscript tradition that the readings that give "Galahad" represent corrections of a Perceval or Perlesvaus reading; see the notes and variants to the passage in *LK* and Kennedy, *Lancelot and the Grail*, 150–55. However, by the cyclic version of the Journey to

Sorelois and False Guinevere episode, as has been seen, it is already made clear by one of Arthur's wise clerks that it is a descendant of Lancelot who will achieve these adventures: "Cil qui achevera les aventures de Bretaigne sera li mieldres chevaliers de tot le monde et aemplira le deerain siege de la Table Reonde, et cela a en escripture la senefiance de lion" (*LM*, IV, 35).

27. This underlining of the Christian significance given in the cyclic romance to the winning back by the son of the baptismal name Galahad, lost by the father, prepares the way for the development of the theme in the *Queste* in terms of the Fall and the Redemption; see Pauline Matarasso, *The Redemption of Chivalry: A Study of the "Queste del Saint Graal"* (Geneva: Droz, 1979), 90, 94. See also Emmanuèle Baumgartner, *L'Arbre et le Pain: essai sur la "Queste del Saint Graal"* (Paris: SEDES, 1981), 105, n. 18, on the ambiguity of the term *aombrement* in relation to the conception of Galahad.

28. Thomas, *Le Roman de Tristan*, ed. Joseph Bédier, SATF (Paris: Firmin Didot, 1902), I, 299–332; Thomas of Britain, *Tristran*, ed. Stewart Gregory (New York: Garland, 1991), 50–53.

29. For an analysis of Lancelot's painting in terms of the "clerk-knight configuration," see Jean M. Dornbush, *Pygmalion's Figure: Reading Old French Romance* (Lexington, Kentucky: French Forum, 1990).

30. One of the interpreters of visions and events in *La Queste*, before he is prepared to give an explanation for some mysterious happening, asks if the Grail adventures have started (*La Queste*, 44). When he is assured of this, he is prepared to reveal the meaning. Once the Grail adventures are over, we move back into the ordinary Arthurian world, where the battles are again what they seem, and the more familiar narrative conventions are operating, apart from the fact that the adventures of Logres have been brought to an end, as Gauvain recalls with nostalgia (*Mort Artu*, §70, 23–24).

31. For Gauvain's place as the greatest knight bar one, see, for example, the episode in which Agravain's arm is to be healed only by the best knight's blood (i.e., Lancelot's blood), and his leg is to be healed only by the best knight after that, who turns out to be his brother Gauvain (*LK*, 410–19).

32. For example, the triangle of lady (Guinevere), lover (Lancelot), and lover's comrade-in-arms (Galehot) replaces that of wife, lover, husband; see Kennedy, *Lancelot and the Grail*, 73–74.

33. To be compared with Beroul, *The Romance of Tristran*, ed. Stewart Gregory (Amsterdam: Rodopi, 1992), ll. 572–80.

34. See Jean Frappier, *Etude sur la "Mort le roi Artu,"* 3d ed. (Geneva: Droz, 1972), 29. Morgain gives an inaccurate account of Kay's entry into the Dolorous Guard, alleging that Lancelot allowed him in because he was the queen's knight (*LK*, 214–16). She also gives a very crude version of Galehot's role in bringing the lovers together (*LK*, 336–39) and of the lovers' first kiss (*LK*, 347–48).

35. Jean Frappier, "Structure et sens du Tristan: version commune, version courtoise," *Cahiers de Civilisation Médiévale* 6 (1963), 255–80, 441–54.

36. For example, Tristan in his letter to Mark justifies his flight with Iseut to the forest because of the condemnation of Iseut to death (without trial) (Beroul, ll. 2585–88). He is prepared to fight to prove that there has been no illicit love (he here uses the term *druerie*) between him and Iseut (Beroul, ll. 2853–59).

37. In the meeting under the tree, spied on by Mark, both the lovers refer to Tristan's saving of Cornwall by his victory over the Morhout (Beroul, ll. 50–53, 135–45). Mark is reminded of this feat and of his debt to Tristan when he sees the sword that lies between the lovers (Beroul, ll. 2036–38).

5 LANCELOT AND GUINEVERE IN THE MIDDLE DUTCH *LANCELOT* COMPILATION

Bart Besamusca

Not long after Lancelot, in a man-to-man fight, kills Meleagant, the kidnapper of Guinevere, Arthur goes out hunting with a large party in the neighborhood of Camelot. During the hunt, a weeping knight tries to abduct the queen. Three of her attendants, Kay, Sagremor, and Dodinel, are unhorsed by the unknown knight, who later turns out to be Bohort. When Guinevere's fourth and last companion, Lancelot, prepares for the final duel, an aged lady enters the field and orders him to follow her. Lancelot must comply with her wishes, having earlier promised to do so in exchange for information. Before Lancelot follows the lady, he defends the queen. He unhorses the unknown knight and is seriously injured himself while doing so, but he saves his beloved.

After a short prologue, these events open the highly fascinating *pièce de résistance* of Middle Dutch Arthurian literature, the so-called *Lancelot* Compilation. This is a collection of ten Middle Dutch Arthurian romances in verse that came into being in Brabant about the year 1320. The creator of the compilation, henceforth referred to as the compiler, made use of a number of existent thirteenth century texts, most of which had been written in Flanders. The core of the *Lancelot* Compilation is made up of three romances: *Lanceloet*, *Queeste vanden Grale*, and *Arturs doet*. These works are faithful translations (in verse) of the most important parts of the Old French *Lancelot-Grail* prose cycle: the *Lancelot* proper, the *Queste del Saint Graal*, and the *Mort le roi Artu*. The compiler made use of the transitions from one text to another to insert no fewer than seven Middle Dutch Arthurian romances. The order of the texts in the compilation is the follow-

My research has been made possible by a fellowship of the Royal Netherlands Academy of Arts and Sciences. I would like to thank Frank Brandsma and Ada Postma for their comments on the first draft of this article. The Dutch version was translated into English by Josephie Brefeld.

ing, with an asterisk used to indicate the core texts: *Lanceloet**, *Perchevael*, *Moriaen*, *Queeste vanden Grale**, *Wrake van Ragisel*, *Ridder metter mouwen*, *Walewein ende Keye*, *Lanceloet en het hert met de witte voet*, *Torec, Arturs doet**.[1]

The *Lancelot* Compilation has come down to us in incomplete form. It comprised two codices, of which the first is now lost. The manuscript that has been preserved opens with Lancelot's successful attempt to prevent Bohort's abduction of the queen, an episode that in the Old French constitutes the starting point of the "Préparation à la Queste," the final part of the *Lancelot* proper. At the beginning of the French prose romance, two brothers are introduced: King Ban of Benoyc and King Bohort (or Bors) of Gaunes. Ban's only son is still a baby, who "avoit non Lanceloz en sorenon, mais il avoit non an baptaisme Galaaz."[2] It is fair to assume that the Middle Dutch translation of this opening passage was present in the lost codex.

Transitional passages link the ten romances in the *Lancelot* Compilation. For example, the following verses mark the transition from *Walewein ende Keye* to *Lanceloet en het hert met de witte voet*:[3]

> *Nu latic dese tale wesen*
> *Ende sal vorward tellen nu*
> *Van ere joncfrouwen, dat secge ic u,*
> *Die boetscap brachte ins conincs hof*
> *Daer prijs an lach ende groten lof.*

(I shall leave this story now and next tell of a maiden who, so I say to you, brought to the king's court a message by which great praise and honor were to be gained.)

This short passage was composed by the compiler who concludes *Walewein ende Keye*, "dese tale," and announces the beginning of *Lanceloet en het hert met de witte voet* in summary.

The addition of a transitional passage is not the only method used by the compiler to present the separate romances in the *Lancelot* Compilation as one coherent unity. In other places, for example, he inserted complete episodes of his own invention to round off narrative threads. He furthermore connected the romances by means of a system of cross-references. A fine example of a reference to what will come is to be found in the *Queeste vanden Grale*.[4] Both in the Old French *Queeste* and in the Middle Dutch *Queeste*, Gauvain, who in the translation bears the name Walewein (as is customary in the Middle Dutch Arthurian romances), meets a hermit who advises him to go to confession. The knight refuses, "Et il dist que de penitance fere ne porroit il la peine soffrir," whereupon the hermit realizes his efforts are in vain: "Et li preudome le let a tant, que plus ne li dit, car il voit bien que ses amonestemenz seroit peine perdue."[5] These sentences were faithfully translated into Middle Dutch. Gauvain's refusal to confess his sins is expressed in ll. 2574–76; the hermit realizes in ll. 2599–602 that his words fall on deaf ears (Jonckbloet, vol. 2, book 3). But between the reactions of Gauvain and those of the hermit, the compiler inserted a passage in which the hermit tells the knight that the chatelaine of "der Joncvrouwen Casteel" (the "Chastel as Puceles") will fall in love with him and will imprison his brother Gariet. Thereupon the narrator addresses his audience with these words: "Gi sult hier achter al die sake Wel verstaen ende oec horen, Alse die aventure comt te voren" ("You shall hear about and understand all this hereafter, when the adventure comes," Jonckbloet, vol. 2, book 3, ll. 2596–98). This is a proleptic reference to the *Wrake van Ragisel,* in which the Lady of Galestroet (the former castle of maidens) appears to be in love with Gauvain and keeps his brother Gariet (Gaheriet) as a prisoner in order to lure Gauvain to her castle.

As the compiler clearly intended the *Lancelot* Compilation to be interpreted as a coherent entity, there is no reason whatsoever to restrict thematic investigations to the separate romances of the compilation. On the contrary, for a better understanding of the *Lancelot* Compilation as a literary work it is necessary to follow the development of the various themes across the boundaries of the separate texts. One of these themes is the subject of this article: the relationship between Lancelot and Guinevere.

The love theme must have caused the compiler trouble. In the *Lancelot* Compilation he combined two literary traditions within Arthurian romance. Whereas the interpolated texts fit the pattern of the verse romances of the type composed by Chrétien de Troyes and his successors, the core of the compilation consists of translations of French prose romances. The prose romances differ from the verse romances to such an extent that one might even speak of two different genres.[6] In these two traditions, love is viewed differently: in the prose romances, love tends to be an "unheilvolle Macht" ("disastrous force"), whereas it is "stets positiv gewertet" ("always considered favorably") in the verse romances à la Chrétien (Schmolke-Hasselmann, 5). Below I shall analyze whether the compiler managed to reconcile these conflicting views of love. I shall discuss the development of the love theme in the *Lancelot* Compilation in its entirety without referring to *Walewein ende Keye* and *Torec,* two romances in which the love of Lancelot and Guinevere plays no role.

In the part of the *Lancelot* proper that precedes the "Préparation à la Queste," the love affair of Lancelot and Guinevere appears to have only positive effects. (An exception must be made for Lancelot's adventure at the grave of Symeu, which will be discussed later.) Lancelot's love for Arthur's wife inspires him to perform great deeds. Thus he manages to bring to a favorable conclusion the adventure of the Dolorous Guard, in the course of which he discovers his name. In the war against Galehot, the son of La Jaiande (the Giantess) and Lord of the Distant Isles, he saves Arthur's throne. The same happens in the war against the Saxons. Because of his love for Guinevere, Lancelot develops into the best knight alive; the adulterous character of their relationship is not emphasized.[7]

That the relationship between Lancelot and Guinevere nonetheless has its drawbacks comes to the fore expressly in the "Préparation à la Queste," the section of the *Lancelot* proper that corresponds to the *Lanceloet* in the *Lancelot* Compilation.[8] The relationship between the two lovers comes under great pressure, not only because Guinevere on repeated occasions has her doubts about Lancelot's fidelity, but also because in the course of the story it is stressed more and more that Lancelot, precisely because of his love for the queen, will not be able to bring the crucial adventure of Logres, the quest for the Grail, to a successful conclusion.[9]

Nowhere in the entire *Lanceloet* is Lancelot knowingly unfaithful to his beloved. On the contrary, even when he faces death or captivity, he is still fully dedicated to the queen. A fine example of this is offered in the episode in which he, having drunk from a spring, is poisoned (ll. 11875–13106).[10] A damsel who falls in love with him saves his life. Yet, when she is no longer able to look after him because of her unrequited love for him, his life is again at risk. Even though he has Guinevere's permission to be unfaithful to her in order to save his life, things do not reach that stage. Lancelot informs the damsel of his unconditional love for another (ll. 12945–58):

> *Hets waer, ic minne in sulker stede*
> *Daer ic meer en doe boeshede,*
> *Mar met trouwen, sonder liegen,*
> *Sal ic minnen ende sonder bedriegen.*
> *Ende die ne sal ic niet begeven,*
> *Noch om sterven, noch om leven.*
> *Ende al woudicker af staen,*
> *Ic ne soude moegen sonder waen:*

Mijn wille es gewortelt so sere
Daer an dat ic ne mach min no mere
Mijn herte keren van hare.
Slaep ic, waec ic, si es dare
Ende mijn gepens dach ende nacht,
Mijn geest, es an hare gehacht.

(It is true, I hold dear someone to whom I shall never do wrong, whom I shall truly love honestly and without deceit. And I shall not desert her for a matter of life or death. And even if I wanted to free myself from my love for her, I would certainly not be able to do so: my desire is so deeply rooted in my love for her that I can by no means separate my heart from her. Whether I sleep or am awake, she is always present, and my thoughts are bound to her day and night.)

The damsel is deeply impressed by Lancelot's words. At her suggestion Lancelot accepts her as his ladylove, on the understanding, however, that his love for her will be a chaste one, thus enabling him to love her as well as his lady Guinevere.

Yet, the Guinevere of the *Lanceloet* is not certain of Lancelot's faithfulness. This is made very clear by a dream forecasting disaster, a dream she has even before Lancelot is poisoned. In this dream she discovers Lancelot in her own bed with an extraordinarily beautiful maiden. Even though Lancelot vows that he knows nothing about this maiden, Guinevere repudiates him (ll. 11207–38).[11] This dream will come true towards the end of the *Lanceloet*. But before that point is reached, Guinevere is not steeled in her doubts. When she meets the damsel who saved the life of the poisoned Lancelot and is informed of the platonic nature of the relationship, her mind is put to rest (ll. 20383–513).[12] Moreover, she is not told that Lancelot on his visit to the Castle of the Grail slept with King Pelles's daughter. When under the influence of a magic potion Lancelot labored under the delusion that he made love with Guinevere, he fathered the future Grail hero Galaad with Pelles's daughter. When Lancelot reports on his adventures, he keeps silent about his night with her (ll. 21180–87):[13]

Mar hine gewoch niet das,
Hoe hi vans conincs dochter bedrogen was.
Dat ne liet hi te seggene niet
Om die scande die hem was gesciet;
Mar ombe siere vrowen wille,

Der coninginnen, swech hire af stille,
Darhi waende verliesen mede
Hare minne, wiste si die waerhede.

(But he did not state that he had been deceived by the king's daughter. He kept silent about it, not because of the disgrace that had been brought upon him, but because of his lady, the queen, as he expected to lose her love once she knew the truth.)

As has already been said, Guinevere's dream comes true. This happens much later in the romance, after the story of Arthur's war against Claudas, a war that ends to Arthur's advantage. To celebrate his victory, the king holds a feast at his court, at which the daughter of King Pelles and her young son Galaad are present. Again, Lancelot is deceived and finds himself in Pelles's daughter's bed. When Guinevere, who shares her room with Pelles's daughter, overhears Lancelot talking in his sleep, she concludes that he has been unfaithful to her. She wakes him up and commands him to disappear from her presence. Lancelot flees and becomes insane (ll. 35569–732).[14] The next day Guinevere regrets her harsh words, but by then it is too late. Lancelot turns out to have disappeared without a trace; the end of their love is a fact. It is only at the conclusion of the *Lanceloet* that Lancelot returns to Arthur's court after years of absence.[15] Guinevere is overjoyed at the reunion with her lover.

As we have seen earlier, the relationship between the two lovers is put under enormous pressure in another manner. In the course of the *Lanceloet* it is stressed that Lancelot will not be able to bring the adventure of the Grail to a favorable conclusion. That he was chosen to do so is evident from his baptismal name (mentioned above): Galaad. Although his name marked him out as a candidate for the completion of the Grail adventure, he threw away his chance because of his love for the queen. Lancelot's chaste son, who also bears the name Galaad, is predestined to find the Grail. This unfortunate consequence of Lancelot's love for Guinevere for the first time plays an important part in Lancelot's adventure at Symeu's grave.[16]

In quest of Guinevere, Lancelot arrives at a monastery where there are two tombs. One, that of Symeu, is to be opened only by the knight designated to bring the adventure of the Grail to a proper conclusion. Although he is at that time the best knight alive, Lancelot fails at the task and is then told the cause of his failure: he is unsuccessful because his father Ban has been adulterous (Hector was the product of this union) and, more importantly, because of Lancelot's own love for Guinevere. This love is condemned

as "luxurien" (l. 223), lust. The opening of Symeu's grave and the successful accomplishment of the Grail adventures are reserved for Galaad,
Lancelot's son, "Om dat noit geen vier van luxuren / In hem ne quam te gere
uren" ("because he was never lecherous," ll. 203–4).[17]

That Lancelot's love for Guinevere disqualifies him as Grail hero is emphasized time and again in the *Lanceloet* section of the *Lancelot* Compilation.
This point is illustrated by an adventure of Gauvain and Hector, who, in pursuit of Lancelot, come across a graveyard on which, according to a notice, they
cannot set foot because it is reserved for "die keytive ridder . . . . Die met
luxurien es gesciet Dat hi heeft verloren altemale Die avonture vanden Grale
Te hoefde te bringene" ("the good-for-nothing knight who as a result of his
lechery lost the power to successfully perform the Grail adventures," ll. 3371–
75).[18] A little later the same knight is referred to as "der drover coninginne
sone" ("the son of the sad queen," l. 3494), a clear reference to Lancelot, whose
mother is alluded to by that name. In this passage, attention is being drawn
to the tragic consequences of Lancelot's love for Guinevere: as a result of this
love the adventure of the Grail is not to be his.

Lancelot and Guinevere express conflicting feelings about their love.
In a conversation with her lover, Guinevere deplores that he, the best knight
in the world, will not be the Grail hero as a result of his love for her. She
says that it would have been better if she had never been born. Lancelot,
however, disagrees wholeheartedly. He points out that Guinevere has been
the inspiration for all his great exploits. Without his love for her, he would
never have become the unrivaled champion of Arthur's Round Table (ll.
21340–434).[19]

It is clear that the love theme in the *Lanceloet* is very closely connected
with the theme of the Grail. In the Middle Dutch text, just as in the
"Préparation à la Queste," preparations are being made for the greatest and
final adventure in Logres: the quest for the Grail. Such knights as are successful in this quest will not permit themselves to be inspired by worldly love
as Lancelot is; only chaste and pious knights will have a chance of success.
Although, as is evident from his conversation with the queen, Lancelot's love
for Guinevere is shown by implication to be tainted, this does not yet worry
him. While Guinevere already questions their love, Lancelot has no regrets
about it yet. This is as far as the love theme has developed when the compiler uses the transition from the *Lanceloet* to the *Queeste vanden Grale* to
interpolate two romances: the *Perchevael* and the *Moriaen*. Here we leave
the realm of the prose romances and enter the world of the Arthurian verse
romances written in the tradition of Chrétien de Troyes, in which love is not
considered sinful.

The *Perchevael*, one of the most fascinating romances in the *Lancelot* Compilation, differs greatly from Chrétien's *Conte du Graal*. In the Middle Dutch adaptation in the compilation, only Gauvain's adventures have been preserved, supplemented with a number of episodes on Gauvain from the First *Perceval* Continuation and some passages original to the compiler.[20] The romance that thus came into being is a story about Arthur's nephew, who comes off much better in the *Perchevael* than he does in the *Lanceloet*, where, for example, he fails at the Grail castle and is beaten at a tournament by Lancelot's half-brother, Hector.

The relationship between Lancelot and Guinevere figures only indirectly in the *Perchevael*. Lancelot makes his appearance in just one episode when incognito he challenges Keu, Dodinel, and Tristan to meet him in single combat (ll. 40787–1005). Neither Keu nor Dodinel is on a par with the unknown knight, who, however, has considerable difficulty with Tristan. When, after a fierce fight, Tristan is about to surrender, a damsel arrives who is looking for Lancelot. She recognizes the unknown knight by his voice and tells him that the Lady of the Lake has sent for him. Lancelot immediately complies with the wish of the lady who raised him. He accompanies the damsel, leaving behind the defeated knights in amazement.

In this *Perchevael* episode, Lancelot's behavior as a knight is highlighted. He shows himself to be fearless and strong. That he defeats Keu and Dodinel does not come as a surprise, their knightly qualities being inadequate. His defeat of Tristan, however, commands respect, as this opponent is known to be an exceptionally fine knight. In these fights the love theme plays an indirect role. After all, it was shown in the *Lanceloet* that all of Lancelot's exploits are inspired by his love for Guinevere. It is this aspect of the love theme that is being continued in the *Perchevael*. Here, no allusion is made to the drawbacks of Lancelot's love.

In the *Moriaen*, Lancelot does not play a prominent role, and his relationship with Guinevere comes into play only briefly. After Gauvain and Lancelot have found shelter with a hermit, Lancelot learns that Arthur has been abducted by the Saxons and that Guinevere is being besieged by the King of Ireland. His reaction to this news characterizes him as a loyal lover (ll. 4152–58):[21]

> *Des anderdages, doe Lanceloet verstont*
> *Hoet metter coninginnen es comen,*
> *Al sout hem al die werelt vromen,*
> *Hine ware daer langer bleven niet,*

Noch om wonde no om verdriet,
Want hi seide hi ware genesen
Ende hi wilde ember te stride wesen.

(The next day, when Lancelot learned of the queen's predicament, he did not want to stay there any longer, not even if it would win him the whole world, not because of his wounds and not because of his pain, for he said that he had recovered and he definitely wanted to go to battle.)

Here again, we see that Lancelot's exploits are inspired by his love for Guinevere. As it had been in the *Perchevael*, this aspect of the love theme is continued in the *Moriaen*. That Lancelot's love for Guinevere makes it impossible for him to find the Grail, is ignored in the *Moriaen* as well. This negative aspect of the love affair will only become fully apparent in the *Queeste vanden Grale*, the work that follows the *Moriaen* in the *Lancelot* Compilation.

QUEESTE VANDEN GRALE

The Middle Dutch translation of the *Queste del Saint Graal* follows its original closely, except in the translations of a number of theological discussions that have been cut short.[22] The development of the story is not propitious for Lancelot and Guinevere. Although the departure of her lover grieves Guinevere, Lancelot leaves Arthur's court in the company of Gauvain, Galaad, and all the other knights of the Round Table to seek the Grail. Whereas Galaad completes one adventure after the other, Lancelot and Gauvain are less successful.

Lancelot's quest for the Grail ends better than Gauvain's. He is, for example, given the opportunity to spend half a year with his son, during which period they complete a large number of Grail adventures, and he sees the Grail in Corbenic, the Grail castle (ll. 9680–92 and 9763–10024).[23] Lancelot is more successful than Gauvain because he renounces his sinful love for Guinevere. In a conversation with a hermit, Lancelot admits that his affair with Guinevere is "dulre minne" (l. 2976), a "foolish love," immediately adding, however, that "alle die grote preusheden, Die ic dede harentare, Quamen mi alle van hare" ("all the great heroic deeds I performed everywhere were inspired by her," ll. 2982–84). The hermit urges him to renounce his love for Guinevere and Lancelot promises to do so (ll. 3115–26):[24]

Die goede man seide doe: "Here,
Wildi die sonden nu mere

Laten vander coninginnen,
Onse here soude u minnen
Ende macht geven van dien dingen,
Dat gi te hovede sout bringen
Noch menege aventure,
Die gi niet mocht vor dese ure
Toe comen bi uwen sonden."
Lanceloet antwerde te dien stonden:
"Ic laetse in dien maniren, here,
Dat icker nembermer toe ne kere."

(The good man then said: "Lord, if you would in the future give up committing sin with the queen, Our Lord would love you and enable you to bring to a happy conclusion many adventures which you until now have not been able to perform because of your sins." Lancelot then answered: "I give up sinning, Lord, and shall do so in such a way that I shall never relapse into it.")

This is a crucial passage in the *Queeste* because Lancelot, who has always been the absolutely loyal lover of Guinevere, here breaks off his relationship with her. Their love is condemned, not only by the hermit, but by Lancelot himself as well.

A little later in the romance, another hermit interprets Lancelot's relationship with the queen as the work of the devil, who wants to ruin Lancelot. Because the devil, filled with envy, realized that Lancelot had all worldly virtues, he wanted to make him fall into sin. He saw to it that Guinevere came to be fond of Lancelot, and when Lancelot found that she was interested in him, the devil put him on the road to lechery. It was the devil's doing that put Lancelot in the queen's bed (ll. 5011–56).[25]

The hermit's explanation of their love as the devil's work implies the end of the relationship once and for all. The love theme has been developed to this point in the *Lancelot* Compilation when the compiler inserted five Arthurian verse romances between the *Queeste* and *Arturs doet*, translations in verse of parts of the *Lancelot-Grail* prose cycle. The juxtaposition of the two types of work ran the risk of putting two traditions into conflict. According to the *Queeste* all forms of worldy love are improper, and the adulterous love of Guinevere and Lancelot is very much so. This extremely negative view of love is not characteristic of the Arthurian romances in verse of Chrétien and his followers.

Even though the love of Lancelot and Guinevere is rejected in the *Queeste*, the love theme is reintroduced in the romance that immediately follows: the *Wrake van Ragisel*. In the *Wrake*, the theme of Guinevere's infidelity figures in the reworking of the story of "Le Mantel mautaillé" that appears both in the Middle Dutch romance and in its Old French source, the *Vengeance Raguidel*. Gauvain, who plays the central role in both the *Vengeance* and the *Wrake*, is told by a lad that Arthur's court has been thrown into commotion by a magical cloak with which the chastity of women can be tested. The cloak shrinks if it is put on by a woman who has been unfaithful, and becomes longer if worn by one who has been faithful. The test with the cloak has brought shame upon Guinevere, among others.[26] With this account by the lad, the love theme in the *Lancelot* Compilation is continued; that the cloak does not fit Guinevere is the result of her relationship with Lancelot. This narrative thread is picked up further on in the *Wrake*, after we have been told how Arthur gives a great feast to celebrate Gauvain's and Yder's having carried out their assignment to avenge Raguidel. Whereas the *Vengeance* ends at this point, the *Wrake* in the *Lancelot* Compilation is followed by two episodes created by the compiler in which Lancelot plays the leading role (ll. 2977–3414). In these episodes Guinevere's lover reacts to the test with the cloak.[27]

When Yder, in the company of his beloved, has left Arthur's court to return home, he meets Lancelot, who is extremely angry because of the shame that has been brought on Guinevere. He has heard that the only one on whom even greater shame was brought was Keu's mistress. Lancelot is so upset that little is needed to make him fly into a blind rage (ll. 3006–13):

> *Dit deerden doe in sinen sinne*
> *Dat hi nigerent sint ne quam*
> *Daer hi mantele dragende vernam*
> *Hine wilder om vechten secgic u*
> *Ende om dat dese vrouwe nu*
> *Enen mantel droech oec mede*
> *Soe wildi nu al hier ter stede*
> *Jegen Ydire vechten ter vard*

(This distressed him so much that wherever he came and saw a cloak being worn, he wanted to fight about it, I tell you that. And because this lady was wearing a cloak, too, he wanted to fight with Yder on the spot.)

The simple fact that Yder's mistress wears a cloak is enough reason for Lancelot to want to fight. The two knights engage in a violent combat in which they are well matched. It is fortunate for them that Bohort appears and manages to reconcile the two parties; Lancelot is ashamed of his behavior.

Even though Lancelot broke off his relationship with the queen in the *Queeste*, Guinevere is again able to inspire him to exploits in the *Wrake*. However, in this episode his love for her leads to curious conduct. As a result of the test with the cloak, Lancelot completely loses his self-control, and he starts fighting as soon as he sees any cloak. In this way a new aspect of the love theme is introduced in the *Lancelot* Compilation. At an earlier stage in the compilation, Lancelot's love for Guinevere inspired him to great deeds while at the same time preventing him from being successful in his quest for the Grail. Neither of these two aspects of love plays a role in the *Wrake*. A third element manifests itself in this romance: Lancelot loves Guinevere without being inspired thereby to accomplish successful exploits. The fact that Lancelot is willing to fight for any cloak whatsoever can scarcely be called a great deed. Following the *Queeste*, a return to the old knightly ideal of love as the inspiration for chivalric prowess is clearly impossible.

After the reconciliation with Yder, Bohort and Lancelot ride on together, whereupon Lancelot inquires after the queen's reaction to the test with the cloak. Bohort is able to reassure Lancelot: because the cloak shrank more on Keu's mistress than it did on the queen, Guinevere's disgrace passed almost unnoticed (ll. 3147–77). When the knights at the end of the romance arrive at King Arthur's court, it becomes clear that the lovers have forgotten the condemnation of their love affair in the *Queeste*. The queen receives Lancelot lovingly (ll. 3408–11):

> *Die coninginne quam vorward saen*
> *Ende ontfinc Lancelote met bliden sinne*
> *Want die over starke minne*
> *Deetse spreken buten monde*

(The queen came forward and joyfully received Lancelot, because her enormous love caused her to speak without hesitation.)

As we shall see later, in *Arturs doet*, the translation of *La Mort le Roi Artu*, Lancelot and Guinevere do not observe sufficient discretion. At the end of the *Wrake*, such indiscretion is already apparent in Guinevere's behavior.

In the *Ridder metter mouwen* ("The Knight with the Sleeve"), the work that follows the *Wrake van Ragisel*, the relationship between Lancelot and the queen plays an indirect role. In this romance, an abridged version of a Flemish original, Lancelot's love for Guinevere, which no longer inspires him, provides a sharp contrast to the relationship between Miraudijs, the Knight with the Sleeve, and Clarette of Spain, who offers him a sleeve at the beginning of the romance. Miraudijs's subsequent affection for Clarette inspires him to perform great exploits.

When Miraudijs, in pursuit of adventures, is lost in thought of his beloved, the narrator observes that Clarette is adored by many other knights. Even Lancelot's name is mentioned (ll. 717–19):[28]

> Men seit datse Lanceloet van Lac
> Minde. Dat was sceren ende een blijf:
> Hi minde Genevren Arturs wijf.

(It was said that Lancelot du Lac was in love with her. That was nonsense: he was in love with Arthur's wife, Guinevere.)

Given this emphatic statement that Lancelot is Guinevere's lover, he behaves rather oddly further on in the romance. In a quarrel with Arthur concerning whether to defend the king and Guinevere's interests or Clarette's, Lancelot, in contrast to his former dedication to Guinevere, exposes her knowingly to the dangers posed by the invasion of the Irish king (ll. 2838–900). In the *Ridder metter mouwen*, Lancelot does not prove himself the impeccable lover we know from the *Lanceloet*. Obviously, his love for Guinevere no longer completely determines his acts.

The same holds for *Lanceloet en het hert met de witte voet* ("Lancelot and the Stag with the White Foot").[29] In that romance, Lancelot responds to a powerful queen's announcement at Arthur's court that she will marry the knight who will be able to bring her the white foot of a certain stag.[30] As in the *Ridder metter mouwen*, Lancelot's behavior is not inspired entirely by his love for Guinevere. Had it been, he would never have embarked on the adventure with the stag, an adventure in which the hand of another woman is at stake. That Lancelot is not prepared to rule out a marriage with her, is apparent from the message he asks the traitor to deliver to the other queen (Draak, ll. 264–73):

> Dat hi lage inden woude
> Gewont wonderlike onsochte.
> Hi soude comen so hi irst mochte
> Ende si nembermer man ne name

Vor dat hi tote hare quame.
"Segt hare dat si wel doe
Altoes beide spade ende vroe.
Ic heb mi gepient so sere
Om die doget ende om die ere
Die ic van hare hebbe gehort."

(He was in the woods, seriously injured. He planned to come as soon as he could, and she should not take someone else as her husband before he could come to her. "Tell her that I wish her all the best. I have exerted myself so much because of her excellence and because of the honorable things that I have heard about her.")

Even though Lancelot has carried out the adventure with the stag, he renounces his reward at the end of the text when he has Gauvain proclaim that the marriage should be postponed. In the *Lai de Tyolet*, which is the probable source for *Lanceloet en het hert*, the story develops rather differently: Tyolet, after defeating the lions and acquiring the white foot, marries the damsel who had announced that she would give her hand to the successful knight. Unlike Tyolet, however, Lancelot is not a free man. When the other queen agrees to Gauvain's proposal to postpone the marriage, the narrator remarks (Draak, ll. 823–31):

Dit behagede Lancelote wel,
Want hi in nereste no in spel
Noch oec om lief no om leet
Noch om gene dinc di hem over geet,
Noch om al die werelt oec mede
En haddise niet genomen ter stede—
Ende al omder coninginnen wille
Die hi minde lude ende stille:
Dit was hem die meeste sake.

(This pleased Lancelot a great deal, because neither in seriousness nor for fun, neither for anything else that could happen to him, nor for the entire world, would he have taken her as his wife—and this was because of the queen, whom he loved unconditionally: this was the most important thing for him.)

Even though at an earlier stage in the story Lancelot had no wish to rule out a marriage with the other queen, it becomes apparent here that he has no wish to marry her because of his love for Guinevere. On the face of things, this explanation is in keeping with the view of love expressed in the *Lanceloet*, in which Guinevere determines all Lancelot's acts. In *Lanceloet en het hert*, however, this state of affairs is evidently outdated. Lancelot does love Guinevere, but his love for her no longer provides the inspiration for all his exploits. Although he is Guinevere's lover, he starts an adventure that holds out the prospect of romantic involvement with another woman.

ARTURS DOET

The love theme is taken to its conclusion in the last work in the compilation, *Arturs doet*. At the beginning of both *La Mort le Roi Artu* and its Middle Dutch translation, we read that Lancelot, soon after his return from his quest for the Grail, slips back into his old ways. In *Arturs doet* this is put as follows (Jonckbloet, vol. 2, book 4, ll. 331–36):[31]

> *Tirst dat hi te hove was comen,*
> *Ende hi die coninginne heeft vernomen,*
> *Binnen der irster maent mindi alse sere*
> *Die coninginne als hi dede noit ere;*
> *Ende hi vel weder in die sonde also saen*
> *Als hi anderwerven hadde gedaen.*

(As soon as he had come to the court and had seen the queen, within a month he loved her as much as he ever had. And fairly soon he sinned as he had done before.)

Such a statement is a repetition of information earlier given by the *Wrake van Ragisel*, in which it is indicated that Lancelot loved Guinevere. Moreover, the quotation makes it clear that we have returned to the sphere of the prose cycle, in which the love of Lancelot and Guinevere is considered sinful, an aspect stressed in *Arturs doet* and in the *Mort Artu*.[332]

Compared to their relationship prior to the quest for the Grail, Lancelot's love affair with Guinevere has changed significantly in one regard: the degree of caution the two lovers exercise. Because of their lack of discretion in *Arturs doet*, Agravain becomes aware of their affair and sets off a series of events that inevitably leads to the ruin of Arthur's realm. Agravain, seizing his chance to harm Lancelot, whom he has always hated, informs

Arthur of Guinevere's adultery, which the king does not want to acknowledge.

Later in the romance, Morgain confirms Agravain's accusation before Arthur. When the king spends the night at her castle, she shows him the wall paintings Lancelot made long ago when he was her prisoner. The drawings in which Lancelot gave expression to his love for Guinevere are quite explicit (ll. 2665–70):[33]

> Altehant sprac Artur die coninc:
> "Ic weet gnoech van deser dinc.
> Ic sie oppenbaerlike in desen
> Mine onnere ende scande wesen,
> Ende die verradenesse, sonder waen,
> Die mi Lanceloet hevet gedaen."

(King Arthur said promptly: "I know enough about this. In these drawings I clearly see my disgrace and shame and the betrayal that Lancelot without doubt has committed against me.")

Arthur, resolved to catch his wife and Lancelot in the act, vows his determination to take revenge that will forever live on in memory.

When Arthur expresses this intention, the relationship between Lancelot and Guinevere has reached its nadir. The queen, suspecting her lover of being unfaithful to her, presumes he is in love with the lady of Escalot. Only later, when Lancelot is victorious in single combat as Guinevere's champion, is she prepared to acknowledge that she was wrong. After their reconciliation, renewed passion makes them grow careless (ll. 4028–38):[34]

> Lanceloet bleef int hof tier uren
> Lange; ende al haddi te voren minne
> Geleit an die coninginne,
> Hi minnese nu vele mere
> Dan hi gedaen hadde noit ere,
> Ende si hem weder des gelike;
> Ende si hildent soe dullike,
> Dat vele liede worden geware,
> Ende dat sijt wisten al oppenbare.
> Ende Walewein wist mede al doe
> Ende sine vire brodere daertoe.

(Lancelot stayed at court for a long time. And even if he had in the past loved the queen very much, he now loved her more than ever, and so did she love him. And they acted so foolishly that many noticed it and knew it for certain. By that time Gauvain knew it, and so did his four brothers.)

Agravain and his brothers, including the treacherous Mordred, succeed only partially in their attempts to trap Lancelot and Guinevere. After the lovers are caught, Lancelot manages to escape, but Guinevere is sentenced to be burned to death. When she is being taken to the stake, Lancelot comes to rescue her with a number of supporters. In the process, Lancelot accidentally kills Gauvain's favorite brother, Gaheriet, thereby provoking a fierce hostility in Gauvain.

In the concluding episodes of *Arturs doet*, Lancelot and Guinevere's relationship is once again broken off, this time forever. Through the agency of the pope, Guinevere later on returns to her husband. Lancelot is exiled from Logres. While Lancelot after his return to Gaule must defend himself against Arthur and Gauvain, who invade his country, Mordred, Arthur's representative in Logres, tries to seize power and win the queen. With a falsified letter he leads Arthur's vassals to think that the king was fatally wounded in the fight against Lancelot, whereupon they advise Guinevere to marry Mordred. The queen takes refuge in a tower which is defended in an all-out effort. When Arthur and Mordred prepare for their final battle, Guinevere flees to a convent where she takes the veil once Arthur has died. She herself dies when Lancelot and an army come to chase away Mordred's sons from Logres. After his victory Lancelot for a number of years serves God as a hermit. He then dies too.

As these comments indicate, the love theme in the *Lancelot* Compilation evolves systematically. In the *Lanceloet* it becomes clear that the love of Lancelot and Guinevere does not have exclusively benign effects. It not only inspires Lancelot to knightly exploits, but also has its negative consequences, the most important of which is that Lancelot will be unable to complete the Grail adventures. In the two romances interpolated after the *Lanceloet*, this negative aspect is not considered, but in the *Queeste* a decisive step is taken in the development of the love theme: Lancelot himself condemns and breaks off his relationship with Guinevere. The romances that were inserted after the *Queeste* no longer treat a knighthood that is favorably inspired by love: Lancelot still loves Guinevere after the quest for the Grail, but this love no longer incites him to accomplish all his successful chivalric exploits. In *Arturs doet*, the tragic effects of the relationship become clear when the adulterous love seen in the preceding *Lanceloet* and *Queeste* brings about the decline of Arthur's realm.

There is a clear difference in the characterization of Lancelot's love for Guinevere in the interpolated romances and in the texts that constitute the core of the compilation. *Lanceloet, Queeste,* and *Arturs doet* emphasize the negative aspects of the relationship. The interpolated romances, on the other hand, neglect these destructive elements almost completely. That there is this difference need not cause surprise. After all, in the compilation we are dealing with two literary traditions within Arthurian romance, both propagating their own view on love. But even if the interpolated romances in the *Lancelot* Compilation are not seamlessly fitted to the core, it is still true that annoying inconsistencies are lacking. It is to the compiler's credit that he managed to situate his own version of Lancelot and Guinevere's love story within the larger context of Arthurian knighthood when he synthesized two profoundly differing traditions.

NOTES

1. The only complete edition of the *Lancelot* Compilation dates back to the nineteenth century: *Roman van Lancelot,* ed. W.J.A. Jonckbloet, 2 vols. ('s-Gravenhage: Van Stockum, 1846–1849).

2. *Lancelot do Lac: The Non-cyclic Old French Prose Romance,* ed. Elspeth Kennedy, 2 vols. (Oxford: Oxford University Press, 1980), I, 1, ll. 7–8. Translation: "who was called Lancelot, but his baptismal name was Galaad."

3. *Lanceloet en het hert met de witte voet,* ed. Maartje Draak, 4th ed. (Culemborg: Tjeenk Willink/Noorduijn, 1974), 31.

4. This passage is discussed in W.P. Gerritsen, *Die Wrake van Ragisel. Onderzoekingen over de Middelnederlandse bewerkingen van de Vengeance Raguidel, gevolgd door een uitgave van de Wrake-teksten* (Assen: Van Gorcum, 1963), 207–8.

5. *La Queste del Saint Graal: Roman du XIIIe siècle,* ed. Albert Pauphilet (Paris: Champion, 1949), 55, ll. 23–26. Translation: "But he said that the hardships of penance would be more than he could brook. So with that the good man let him be and held his peace, for he realized that all his admonishments would be so much wasted effort." See *The Quest of the Holy Grail,* trans. with intro. by P.M. Matarasso (Harmondsworth: Penguin, 1969), 80.

6. See Beate Schmolke-Hasselmann, *Der arthurische Versroman von Chrestien bis Froissart: Zur Geschichte einer Gattung* (Tübingen: Niemeyer, 1980), 4.

7. A fine description of the love theme is offered by Elspeth Kennedy, *Lancelot and the Grail: A Study of the Prose "Lancelot"* (Oxford: Oxford University Press, 1986), 49–78.

8. See Jonckbloet, ed., I, ll. 1–36974. From this edition I will quote ll. 16264–36974. Lines 1–16263 will be quoted from the three published volumes of the new edition in preparation: *Lanceloet. De Middelnederlandse vertaling van de Lancelot en prose overgeleverd in de Lancelotcompilatie,* Part 1 (ll. 1–5530), ed. Bart Besamusca and Ada Postma (Assen: Van Gorcum, 1996); Part 2 (ll. 5531–10740), ed. Bart Besamusca (Assen: Van Gorcum, 1991); Part 3 (ll. 10741–16263), ed. Frank Brandsma (Assen: Van Gorcum, 1992).

9. For the love theme in the "Préparation," see Kennedy, 274–91, and in the *Lanceloet,* see Brandsma, 105–28.

10. For the Old French, see *Lancelot: Roman en prose du XIIIe siècle,* ed. Alexandre Micha, 9 vols. (Paris: Droz, 1978–83), vol. IV, LXXVI, 1–39 (roman numerals refer to chapters, arabic to paragraphs), and *The Vulgate Version of the Arthurian Romances,* ed. H.O. Sommer, 7 vols. (Washington, D.C.: Carnegie Institute, 1909–13; rpt. New York: AMS, 1979), V, 71.6–84.37.

11. For the Old French, see Micha, IV, LXXIV, 2–3, and Sommer, V, 63.33–64.6. For this dream, see also Frank Brandsma, "A dream boding ill: thematic interlace in the 'Préparation à la Quête,'" *The Arthurian Yearbook* 2 (1992), 13–26.

12. For the Old French, see Micha, IV, LXXXIV, 33–36, and Sommer, V, 178.33–180.13.

13. For the Old French, see Micha, IV, LXXXIV, 70, and Sommer, V, 191.6–9.

14. For the Old French, see Micha, VI, CV, 33–38, and Sommer, V, 379.9–381.9.

15. The conclusion of the *Lanceloet* is not present because a number of leaves of the Compilation manuscript have been lost. We of course know the ending of the story because the *Lanceloet* is a faithful translation into verse of the *Lancelot* proper.

16. This event takes place in a section of the *Lanceloet* that has not come down to us in the *Lancelot* Compilation, because it was present in the lost codex. Fortunately, it was preserved in the so-called Brussels fragment of the *Lanceloet.* See Besamusca and Postma, eds., ll. 37–332 (Brussels fragment).

17. For the Old French, see Micha, III, XXXVII, 38, and Sommer, IV, 176.18–19.

18. For the Old French, see Micha, II, LXV, 25, and Sommer, IV, 339.35–36.

19. For the Old French, see Micha, V, LXXXV, 2–3, and Sommer, V, 92.42–193.37.

20. Jonckbloet, ed., I, ll. 36951–42546.

21. *Moriaen,* ed. H. Paardekooper-van Buuren and M. Gysseling (Zutphen: Thieme, 1971). For the sake of readability I quote this edition in an adapted form.

22. See J.C. Prins-s'Jacob, "The Middle Dutch Version of *La Queste del Saint Graal,*" *De nieuwe taalgids* 73 (1980), 120–32. See Jonckbloet, ed., II, book 3, ll. 1–11160.

23. For the Old French, see Pauphilet, 251.22–28, 253.3–261.22, and Sommer, VI, 177.27–32, 178.30–184.2.

24. For the Old French, see Pauphilet, 71.3–10, and Sommer, VI, 51.16–22.

25. For the Old French, see Pauphilet, 125.8–126.11, and Sommer, VI, 89.31–90.19.

26. See Gerritsen, ll. 1340–67, and Raoul de Houdenc, *La vengeance de Raguidel: Altfranzösischer Abenteuerroman,* ed. M. Friedwagner (Geneva: Slatkine, 1975), ll. 3912–61.

27. For a discussion of these episodes, see Gerritsen, 250–59.

28. *Roman van den Riddere metter Mouwen,* ed. M.J.M. de Haan et al. (Utrecht: Hes, 1983).

29. My interpretation of the love theme in this romance is based on an article by Roel Zemel: "'Hoe Walewein Lanceloet bescudde ende enen camp vor hem vacht': Over *Lanceloet en het hert met de witte voet,*" in *De ongevalliche Lanceloet: Studies over de Lancelotcompilatie,* ed. Bart Besamusca and Frank Brandsma (Hilversum: Verloren, 1992), 77–97.

30. A small dog will lead the knights to this stag, which is being guarded by lions. After a first and vain attempt by Keu, Lancelot manages to kill both the lions and the stag, but, in doing so, is wounded himself. Thereupon he is deceived by a traitor and saved by Gauvain. Having been given the white foot by Lancelot, the traitor beats him and leaves to claim the queen. Meanwhile Gauvain starts to look for Lancelot. Once he has found him, he takes him to a doctor, leaves him there and is just in time to prevent the traitor from marrying the queen. Gauvain kills the villain in single com-

bat. Once Lancelot has recovered, he and Gauvain go to the queen's castle, where Gauvain states that Lancelot wants to postpone the marriage.

31. For the Old French, see *La Mort le Roi Artu,* ed. Jean Frappier, 3d ed. (Paris: Droz, 1964), § 4.5–10, and Sommer, VI, 205.5–8.

32. For the themes in the *Mort Artu,* see Kennedy, 303–08.

33. For the Old French, see Frappier, § 53.20–22, and Sommer, VI, 240.18–19.

34. For the Old French, see Frappier, § 85.33–39, and Sommer, VI, 269.10–14.

6 Illustrating Lancelot and Guinevere

Alison Stones

There can be little doubt that the best-known image in Arthurian art is the first kiss of Lancelot and Guinevere in the Morgan copy of the *Lancelot propre*,[1] the central branch of the vast five-part prose romance, known as the Vulgate Cycle or *Lancelot-Graal*, that held so prominent a place in the book-box or on the bookshelf of the French aristocracy between about 1220 and 1475 (figure 1).[2] Already the frontispiece to the Loomises' pioneering study of Arthurian art published in 1938,[3] a detail of this embracing couple was selected in the 1990s for the front of the leaflet inviting the public to join the Friends of The Pierpont Morgan Library, and has for several decades also been sold as one of the Library's bookmarks. So familiar has the image become that it is easy to forget that the first kiss as such is most unusual in the iconographical tradition of the *Lancelot-Graal*, and, when it does occur, it displays a number of peculiarities.[4]

Not only is the kiss episode central to the development of the relationship between Lancelot and Guinevere in the text of the *Lancelot propre*, it is one of several crucial stages in that relationship that are also selected for visual emphasis as the lengthy narrative unfolds through the *Lancelot*,

Figure 1. New York, J. Pierpont Morgan Library, M 805, f. 67 (detail). Reprinted by permission of The J. Pierpont Morgan Library, New York.

Queste, and *Mort Artu;* other episodes often represented in the cycles of pic-tures that depict aspects of this relationship include the one about the split shield given to Guinevere by the Lady of the Lake,[5] the consummation of the adultery, Lancelot's affair with the daughter of King Pelles, Arthur's dis-covery of the adultery through Lancelot's pictures of it in Morgan's castle, the poisoned apple episode, and Guinevere's trial by fire.[6] But not every manuscript includes pictures of all of these; the patterns of their distribu-tion are variable, and so is the treatment of each individual subject across the pictorial tradition.[7] There is no shortcut to finding out which manu-scripts include the episode and which omit it. The present study is a pre-lude to a more complete survey of all the illustrated *Lancelot* manuscripts: the findings presented here are based on a laborious examination of all the manuscripts up to ca. 1320 and of the major examples of the later fourteenth and fifteenth centuries.

MEDIEVAL DEPICTIONS OF THE KISS AND THEIR CONTEXTS[8]

What is of course immediately striking about the Morgan kiss is the third figure, Galeholt. It is his presence above all that distinguishes this from the usual images of kissing and those, less intimate, of embracing, that medie-val viewers would have known from the long tradition of such imagery in Christian art. Among several possible examples, all with linked metaphori-cal meaning, are the kiss of righteousness and peace in the psalms, begin-ning as early as the Carolingian period;[9] or the two kissing figures that pref-aced the Song of Songs of the Old Testament and its medieval commentaries, where the couple are Christ and Ecclesia;[10] or the embrace of Hosea and Gomer that accompanied the book of Hosea.[11] By the late twelfth century, some of these embracing male-female couples depicted in a religious con-text can be read as blatantly erotic, suggesting that their formal treatment takes its impetus as much from the literature of romance as from biblical exegesis or spiritual literature.[12]

But the two-person, male-female kiss topos can also carry many other meanings, depending on its textual or illustrative context, and the other meanings may in turn refer back to those already discussed and on to still others. Examples of the kiss motif in non-religious contexts are rare before 1200, but the range of associations shortly thereafter is enormous, from the topos of domestic bliss in the Rein monastery pattern book[13] made in the southern Empire in the early thirteenth century, to an allegory of *liberalitas* in a copy of Aristotle's *Ethics* (figure 2) illustrated in northern France about 1300.[14] Other early thirteenth-century examples from the southern Empire are the couple illustrating the poem "Suscipe flos florem quia flos designat

Figure 2. Boulogne-sur-Mer, B. M. 110, f. 16. Photograph: Alison Stones. Reprinted by permission of the Bibliothèque Municipale, Boulogne-sur-Mer.

amorem" in the *Carmina Burana*. The figures face each other and hold flowers, in a frame that is placed horizontally across the text column, as though the couple were lying on the ground.[15] Whereas the figures in the *Carmina Burana* are not actually embracing, Dido and Aeneas (shown lying down, with their horses beside them) in Heinrich von Veldecke's *Eneit* in Berlin of ca.1210–20 are much more closely united beneath a single cloak.[16] Among the medieval illustrations of the classical romances in France, there is only one thirteenth-century example of an embrace, between two knights on horseback, on the detached leaves that were once part of Benoît de Sainte-Maure's version, Paris, B. N. fr. 1610, and are now in a Dutch private collection.[17] Biblical illustration of the mid-thirteenth century offered many models for the embrace between two men, notably Jacob and Esau, Joseph and Benjamin, David and Jonathan, or David and Absalom.[18] At about the same time the Chertsey tiles had adapted the motif for the kiss of fealty between Tristan and King Mark, and between Tristan and the barons.[19] Otherwise in the illustration of the French classical romances, the kiss between men and women is depicted only in the Bodmer and Madrid B. N. copies of Guido, both made in Italy in the early fourteenth century.[20] By then the kiss and embrace motifs had become widespread in the context of imagery of courtship, as in the Montpellier *Chansonnier* of the 1280s or 90s,[21] to which the images of famous lovers in the *Roman de la Poire*, Paris, B. N. fr. 2186, of uncertain but probably earlier date, are an important forerunner;[22] or, in Germany, in the Rudolf von Ems, *Wilhelm von Orlens*, of ca. 1270–75 from Strassburg,[23] and in the Weingartner and the Manessische Liederhandschriften of the early fourteenth century.[24] By this time, too, parallels for the male embrace had come to include the Christ and St. John devotional images popular in south Germany, derived from Last Supper imagery.[25]

The connotation of the kiss in all these contexts is overwhelmingly a positive one, but the kiss gesture between men could carry with it obvious negative connotations as well, as exemplified most forcefully in the kiss of betrayal bestowed on Christ by Judas, anticipated in the Old Testament by many examples, like the kiss of Joab as he kills first Abner then Amasa with his sword.[26] Other visual interpretations of the embracing couple topos were also emerging in the thirteenth century, with the selection of the embracing male and female couple as an embodiment of *luxuria*, as among the vices on the west façade of Amiens Cathedral,[27] or in various combinations of sexes and estates of man—not only men and women and men and men, but also clerics of different ranks and laymen or women—among the moralizations of the Moralized Bibles.[28]

THE TRIPLE KISS

None of these examples bears directly on the Morgan kiss because of the presence of the third figure. The illustrative tradition of the first kiss of Lancelot and Guinevere invariably includes Galeholt with Lancelot and Guinevere, and this is above all in accordance with the text.[29] It is Galeholt who engineers the kiss in the first place and who is not only present at it but even, in the Morgan manuscript's illustration, plays an active part in the realization of it: his left arm on Guinevere's back presses her towards Lancelot, while his lap receives Lancelot's left arm; his right hand gesture matches in reverse the pose of Guinevere's on Lancelot's chin; and the chiasmic arm-crossing between Lancelot and Guinevere is matched by the foot-crossing of Lancelot and Galeholt.[30]

Scholars have performed ingenious manipulations to suggest subtle formal and psychological links between this image and other topoi of embrace. Haussherr invokes the Christ-St. John group repeated in mirror-image, endowing the resulting symmetical composition with a layer of meaning that includes the Godhead,[31] while Camille, following Perella, suggests that the Morgan's threefold configuration was appropriated from a three-person Trinity in order to "elevate the illicit relationship, making it . . . a divine union of souls."[32] Perella finds kiss imagery in two images of the Holy Trinity, the Throne of Grace Trinity image in the twelfth-century Cambrai Missal, Cambrai B. M. 234 (figure 3), and the Two Persons and Dove Trinity in Jean de Berry's Petites Heures, Paris, B. N. lat. 18014, f. 137v,[33] of the late fourteenth century. In both of these, the wing tips of the dove of the Holy Spirit touch the lips of the Two Persons. In the first example, they touch the lips of God the Father and Christ Crucified, and in the second, the lips of the Two Persons of the Trinity. The analogy is then transferred to the Morgan kiss, but not without certain difficulties, as the configuration of the participants is not identical, or even very close. The poses of the figures in the Christ-St. John groups do, however, conform to this configuration, as St. John is leaning on the breast of Christ, and Christ wraps his arm round the saint, even though the figures do not kiss. And, of course, there is no denying the underlying Trinitarian symbolism inherent, to the medieval mind, in any group of three of anything, be they gold balls or French hens;[34] but the kissing lovers in the Morgan image are otherwise formally unrelated to the Two Persons of the Trinity of the Petites Heures, still less to those of the Cambrai Missal. In neither of the Trinity groups do the Persons directly embrace. Indeed, no Trinity image, even the Three Persons type[35] or the Triple Head type invoked by Camille,[36] displays a pair of embracing figures or any gesture that even remotely resembles the distinctive play of arms or feet that are so dominant in the Morgan image. The formal analogy of the Trinity works only in part; so too its metaphorical and psychological implications.

There are other triple-embrace configurations in thirteenth-century biblical imagery whose formal structure is just as close to the Morgan kiss group as the Christ-St. John or the Trinity, but that offer different, more disturbing connotations. Indeed, the "divine union of souls" interpretive model stands countered by other, quite negative topoi—such as lechery, and even incest. In the Vienna 2554 copy of the *Bible moralisée*, Lot and his daughters form a triple embrace group as Lot sits between his two fully clothed daughters, with his arms around them, while one holds his cheek and the other extends her arm toward her sister. This configuration is very similar to the Morgan kiss, but the moralizing commentary below the picture interprets it as the monk deceived by the world, the flesh, and the devil.[37] A similar negative image appears in the *Old Testament Picture Bible*, where

Figure 3. Cambrai, B. M. 234, f. 2. Photograph: Alison Stones. Reprinted by permission of the Médiathèque Municipale, Cambrai.

Absalom, seated at the center of the group, kisses his father's concubines (figure 4).[38] Though admittedly rare in thirteenth-century biblical iconography, these two subjects nonetheless offer alternative triple-embrace topoi that seem to me just as relevant to the Morgan first kiss configuration as the Christ-St. John group or the Trinity. Their negative interpretive models, coupled with the topoi of divine love, serve together to underline visually the complexity of the relationship between Lancelot and Guinevere, just as the text does—there the adultery is presented as both ennobling and destructive at the same time.

The first kiss is an image that also offers the modern interpreter a warning lesson in the multivalent ambiguity of deep structure. We know so little about exactly where our painter drew his inspiration and what iconographical knowledge his viewers—to say nothing of the modern art historian—would be likely to bring to their reception of the image.[39] Deciphering it can be a precarious business if we invoke only part of the appropriate source material.

Figure 4. Malibu, J. Paul Getty Museum, Ludwig I 66 (83.MA.55), f. 45 (detail). Reprinted by permission of The J. Paul Getty Museum, Malibu.

Two things are striking about the representation of the first kiss in *Lancelot* illustration. The first is that the motif is illustrated at all. The majority of otherwise fully illustrated copies omit the scene altogether.[40] The second is that those copies that do include the kiss are remarkably consistent in their treatment of the subject. All of them (except the images on the walls referred to earlier) include a triple group;[41] what varies is who the central figure is, whether the three are seated or standing, which way the figures are facing, and, more significantly, whether an additional figure is present. In the twin manuscripts London, B. L. Add. 10293 (figure 5), and Amsterdam B. P. H. 1 (figure 6),[42] the group is standing and the central figure is Guinevere, squeezed between Lancelot whom she embraces and Galeholt who grasps Lancelot by the wrist ("devant" taken literally), though the configuration of the figures differs from that of the Morgan kiss. In a much later manuscript, part of the three-volume set Paris, B. N. fr. 117–120, made initially for the famous fifteenth-century bibliophile Jean, duc de Berry (d. 1416), and repainted in part for his great-grandson, Jacques d'Armagnac (d. 1470), B. N. fr. 118 (figure 7),[43] Lancelot has become the central figure, with Galeholt slightly to one side as a more distant observer ("devant" taken figuratively), his leg stretching out in a strong diagonal towards the secondary group of figures, as though he were encouraging them to pay attention to the kiss. Lancelot is again the central figure in the special Arthurian compendium

Figure 5. *London, B. L. Add. 10293, f. 78. Reprinted by permission of The British Library, London.*

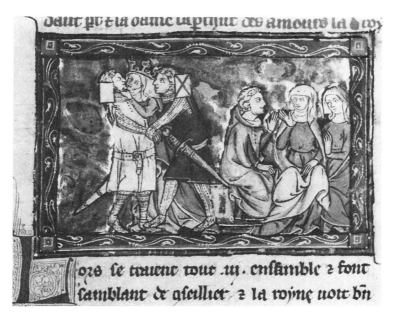

Figure 6. Amsterdam, B. P. H. 1, vol. II, f. 40. Photograph: Alison Stones. Reprinted by permission of the Biblioteca Philosophica Hermetica, Amsterdam.

written for Jacques d'Armagnac by Michel Gonnot, Paris, B. N. fr. 112 (figure 8),[44] and, with another slight alteration, in the other set of Vulgate Cycle volumes made for Jacques d'Armagnac, Paris, B. N. fr. 113–116. There, an additional female figure is added to the three-person primary group to make it a foursome. The additional lady is the Dame de Malehaut, shown standing behind Guinevere (figure 9). In the other depictions of the kiss, the Dame de Malehaut is part of the secondary group of three figures where she plays a malevolent role that counters Galeholt's efforts to conceal the kiss; only in B. N. fr. 114 does she confront the embracing couple in so direct a fashion.

If Galeholt's gaze in the Morgan manuscript image (figure 1) turns away from the kissing couple before him, it is to look over to the parallel group of three figures—two women and a man—who make up the other half (much less reproduced) of the illustration. The three figures are the Dame de Malehaut and the damoisele Lore de Carduel, accompanied by the seneschal whom Galeholt had asked to lead the ladies aside and keep them company.[45] According to the text, it is the Dame de Malehaut who sees the kiss[46] and discomforts Lancelot with her gaze.[47] The image in the Morgan manuscript departs again from the text by showing the two ladies turning away from the kiss group toward the seneschal. The text also mentions a third lady ("une soie

Figure 7. Paris, B. N. fr. 118, f. 219v. Reprinted by permission of the Bibliothèque Nationale, Paris.

damoisele"), whom other versions include in the kiss image instead of the seneschal shown here.

Elsewhere in the iconographical tradition of the first kiss the supporting group of figures is likewise a group of three people; and among the examples are cases that offer a more accurate depiction of the secondary group than the Morgan *Lancelot*. The variants are how many people are included, whether they are seated or standing, and whether they are male or female: in Amsterdam (figure 6), Morgan (figure 1), B. N. fr. 118 (figure 7), B. N. fr. 112 (figure 8), B. N. fr. 114 (figure 9), the secondary group is seated, not standing; in Additional (figure 5) the secondary group is standing, like the primary figures; and in B. N. fr. 112 there are five figures instead of the usual three. In Morgan, Amsterdam, and Additional, there are two women and one man; in the three fifteenth-century copies the secondary group is female only. Apart from M 805 and B. N. fr. 114, the other examples all place the ladies so that one of them—the Dame de Malehaut—directs her eyes to the kiss group as required by the text; in B. N. fr. 118 and fr. 112, Lancelot turns

Figure 8. Paris, B. N. fr. 112, II, f. 101. Reprinted by permission of the Bibliothèque Nationale, Paris.

his back on her, thus missing her meaningful glance, even though, in B. N. fr. 118, Galeholt's central position and his extended leg seems to link the two groups of figures; while in B. N. fr. 114, the Dame de Malehaut's position as part of the kiss group allows her to confront Lancelot much more directly than in any other example. Her presence among the primary group in B. N. fr. 114 perhaps plays on the conversation that occurs a little later in the text when she confronts Guinevere with her knowledge of the kiss.[48]

The six manuscripts discussed so far are relatively late in the development of the iconography of the *Lancelot*—after 1300, by which time sev-

Figure 9. Paris, B. N. fr. 114, f. 244v. Reprinted by permission of the Bibliothèque Nationale, Paris.

eral fairly fixed iconographical patterns, or groups of images, had become established in the illustration of the Vulgate Cycle as a whole.[49]

THE KISS IN THE BONN MANUSCRIPT

One other manuscript provides some clues about the emergence of the first kiss image. Bonn U. B. 526, written by Arnulfus de Kayo in Amiens in 1286,[50] is, so far as I know, the earliest manuscript to include an illustration of the kiss (figure 10)—but it appears to have been put in as an afterthought and is at the wrong place in the text. Along with its sister manuscript, Paris, B. N. fr. 110,[51] the Bonn copy transmits, in general, a short version of the text, and one that considerably cuts this section of the narrative.[52] But at an earlier spot,[53] at a place where other manuscripts, including B. N. fr. 110, show the Dame de Malehaut and Galeholt talking together, an apparently different hand has painted in a three-figure embrace group with the queen in the middle between

Figure 10. Bonn, U. B. 526, f. 220. Reprinted by permission of the Universitäts-bibliothek, Bonn.

Galeholt and Lancelot (without supporting ladies) (figure 10); and the rubric matches the scene.

The sequence of events that led to this placing of the kiss image could be reconstructed in several possible ways. The omission of the scene at the right place in the text could either have been an error, the need for a miniature at the right place simply overlooked by Arnulfus when he left blank spaces in his text for the pictures; or else it could have represented a deliberate desire—on his part or, more likely, on the part of his patron or his boss—to avoid depicting that scene at all. Such an omission would have been consistent with the selective pattern of illustration adopted in the other thirteenth-century copies of the *Lancelot*. But someone decided otherwise. Steps were taken to include a kiss image while the illumination was in progress, because this miniature occurs not in the margin, but in one of the deliberately planned picture-spaces left blank by the scribe.[54] The person who painted the kiss picture would appear to have been a painter other than the main artist—unless he came back and put in this image at a later stage, having modified his figure style somewhat—as one is struck by a certain difference in the drawing of the facial features and hair, although the format of the miniatures, the decorative motifs, the proportions of the figures and their draperies are broadly comparable with the work of the main painter.[55] Several other manuscripts, including B. N. fr. 110, are illustrated in a closely similar style that may or may not be the work of the same painter (depending on how one interprets minor stylistic difference in the absence of supporting documentation, as the work of another hand, or of the same painter at a different stage of artistic development).[56] Although the kiss image has been placed well before the occurrence of the incident in the text, this space must have been chosen because it offered the best option. The next image-space comes some eight and a half folios later—ninety-three pages later in Micha's edition and seventeen printed pages after the kiss. The usual sequence is for an image to precede its textual description, as a visual anticipation of the event; and so, although the substitution meant placing the picture too early and eliminating the encounter between the Dame de Malehaut and Galeholt, the kiss image took precedence. Someone clearly felt it must be included, and that person was probably not the main artist. Was it Arnulfus the scribe? The patron? The planner? The head of the production team?

The Bonn manuscript includes several indications that the process of laying out the script and pictures, writing, decorating, and illuminating was a complex one that most likely involved several individuals or several sequential stages, some of which could have been performed successively by one person. It is quite likely, though we cannot be certain, that Arnulf copied the captions in red after he had finished doing the text in brown ink; the script is closely similar. Here it is significant that the caption fits the kiss miniature and is not a caption for the encounter between the Dame de Malehaut and Galeholt, which otherwise would have filled this picture-space; and its rubric is written by the same rubricator as the rest of the captions. Following the words of the rubric, or of a now-erased note left for the rubricator, seems occasionally to have resulted in an error in the depiction of a scene, as I have shown elsewhere in relation to Galaad and his shield;[57] but one cannot be sure whether the rubrics were put in before or after the miniatures were painted.[58] There are some heads drawn in margins, in the ink of the pen flourishing, hinting that perhaps the minor initials were done by the miniature painter or painters; there are occasional words in the margins that seem to be guides for the use of colors; there are diagonal strokes in the margins next to many of the miniatures—two, three, or four strokes— that might perhaps relate to a division of labor between illuminators, were it not for the overall similarity of almost all the miniatures; but this miniature and those in the same quire lack these marks. Even with all these hints as to how things might have worked, it is difficult to reconstruct exactly what the sequence of production was and who, besides Arnulf, did what. But whatever the reasons and whatever the exact sequence of events, someone who was not the principal painter put in an image of the first kiss as an afterthought. The idea caught on in large measure: at least six later copies followed suit, enlarging, elaborating, and subtly changing the image over almost two centuries.

THE ADULTERY

If the first kiss is a relatively rare subject, so, too, is the consummation of the adultery. Nowhere in Vulgate Cycle illustrations are there scenes of lovers in bed as erotic as, for instance, the vivid depictions of King David and his amorous adventures in the *Old Testament Picture Bible*, among which the depiction of David and Bathsheba is particularly noteworthy for the splendid phallic candle behind the bed and for the suggestive poses of both figures (figure 11).[59] In non-biblical art, examples are again rare before 1300, and the *Bible moralisée* once more provides several instances of negative types among its moralizations, although scenes depicting lovemaking in bed are far less numerous than embraces.[60]

I have noted elsewhere that images of couples in bed are considerably more prevalent if those couples are married, like King Mordrain and Queen Sarracinte, who are often shown in bed together in the illustrated *Estoire*,

Figure 11. New York, J. Pierpont Morgan Library, M 638, f. 41v (detail). Reprinted by permission of The J. Pierpont Morgan Library, New York.

from the second quarter of the thirteenth century,[61] or King Ban and Queen Elaine towards the end of *Merlin*;[62] in both instances, bed is primarily a place for reflection, whether waking or sleeping and dreaming.[63] This is also the case with the first scene in the *Yvain* cycle of thirteenth-century wall-paintings at the castle of Schmalkalden in north Germany, where Arthur and Guinevere are shown in bed.[64] But the Schmalkalden cycle also includes as scene 14 an image of the wedding night of Yvain and Laudine, for which an early fourteenth-century copy of Chrétien's *Yvain* provides a parallel in the (severely rubbed) depiction of the reconciliation between the lovers that occurs at the end of the romance. The scene on f. 118 is unusual in that Chrétien speaks only in the abstract of the couple's achievement of a "peace without end" while the illustration much more explicitly depicts the couple making love in bed.[65] This and the Schmalkalden version are the only depictions of actual lovemaking in the illustrated *Yvain* tradition, whether based on Chrétien, Hartmann, or a non–text specific version.[66] Scenes of lovemaking in the illustrations of Chrétien de Troyes's romances are otherwise rare, but there is one earlier example in the Second Continuation of *Perceval* where the Montpellier manuscript showed (before its defacement) Perceval in bed with Blanchefleur, as part of a program of illustrations in which, as Walters has shown, Blanchefleur's role differs significantly from her textual role.[67] Walters points to the use of a similar visual topos for the scene of lovemaking between Jason and Medea in the Madrid copy of Guido de Columnis's version of the Troy romance,[68] though the latter is an early fourteenth-century copy, no earlier than B. N. fr. 1433. There is no guarantee that lost copies of Benoît, Guido, or other intermediaries would have depicted this incident, but Heinrich von Veldecke's *Eneit* again offers a parallel scene of Dido and Aeneas in bed,[69] and the motif occurs several times in the Munich copy of Gottfried's *Tristan* of the middle of the thirteenth century.[70] There are also a few other thirteenth-century examples in other media, such as the Forrer casket and the Bussen mirror-case, where the scenes may also be based on a version of the *Tristan* story.[71]

Despite what appears to be a general reticence in the iconographical tradition about representing lovemaking in general and adulterous lovemaking in particular, certain manuscripts stand out for their treatment of the consummation of the love between Lancelot and Guinevere. Add. 10293 (ca. 1315) is particularly remarkable for the number of times Lancelot and Guinevere are depicted in bed together. On f. 199v there are two miniatures, in which Lancelot first breaks into Guinevere's room through a barred window and then spends the night with her.[72] But the second miniature has been defaced, as though a later viewer felt it was too explicit.[73] Yet lovemaking between Lancelot and Guinevere is illustrated again in this manuscript, on f. 312v (figure 12).[74] The several bed scenes in Add. 10293 give its picture cycle an emphasis that is quite distinctive in the illustrative tradition—one would like to know more about who requested these miniatures, and for whom.[75]

In Add. 10293, scenes of Lancelot's adultery with Guinevere are matched by the inclusion of two scenes of Lancelot in bed with the daughter of King Pelles. (Lancelot, deceived into thinking that he is with Guinevere, begets his son Galaad, eventual Grail winner in the *Queste del Saint Graal*.)[76] The first of the two scenes is followed by a miniature of Lancelot's remorse, in which he raises his sword to kill King Pelles's daughter, thinking her responsible for the deception. These episodes appear to occur somewhat more frequently than depictions of the adultery. Two manuscripts that omit the adultery and include the conception of Galaad are Bonn 526 (figure 13) and Yale 229;[77] the Bonn manuscript has Lancelot threatening King Pelles's

nller
urle
our
:la
cnt
anr
rufi
aou
:falu
is
nde
nes
xla

Figure 12. London, B. L. Add. 10293, f. 312v. Reprinted by permission of The British Library, London.

daughter as a separate scene (figure 14) (he fully armed, she wearing a strik-ing red robe—often the color of guilt, selected for Mary Magdalene); the Yale manuscript acknowledges Lancelot's remorse while down-playing the whole incident by compressing the subject into a tiny historiated initial, showing King Pelles's daughter still in bed and Lancelot, half naked, raising his sword.[78] Was a pictorial emphasis on sex, even if decently covered by bedclothes, considered unsuitable for the young Guillaume de Termonde, the Yale manuscript's possible patron? Clearly the patron (planner?) of Add. 10293 thought otherwise, whereas that of Bonn 526 seems to have preferred a middle road—and this time no image of the Lancelot-Guinevere adultery was included as an afterthought.[79]

The objections to explicit lovemaking witnessed by the erasure of one such scene in Add. 10293 seem to have had an effect, as what tends to be shown in the later manuscripts are "before" and "after" scenes rather than either couple actually in bed. So in B. N. fr. 122, made for an unidentified patron probably in Tournai in 1344, Guinevere, still crowned, lies naked in bed, while Lancelot stands fully clothed beside the bed and a servant walks away (figure 15).[80] In the early fifteenth-century set made for Jean de Berry and partially repainted for Jacques d'Armagnac, B. N. fr. 117–120, the

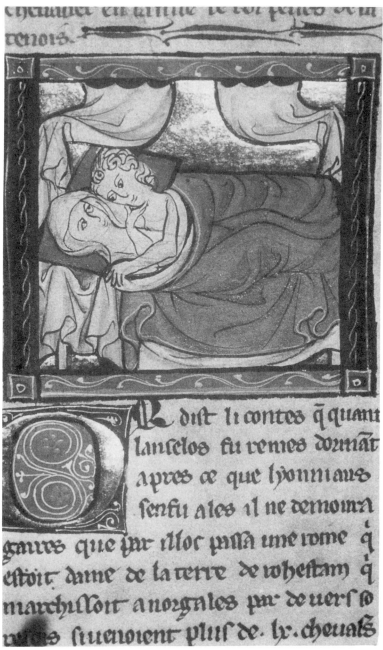

chcualicr en arine te roi peties te in
tenois.

dist li contes q̄ quant
lancelos fu venies dormāt
apres ce que hōmiaus
senfu ales il ne temoinʒ
gaires que par illoc passa une rōine q̄
estoit dame de la terre de wheffam q̄
marchissoit a norgales par deuerso
mines suenoient plus de .lx. cheuass

Figure 13. Bonn, U. B. 526, f. 352 (olim 362). Reprinted by permission of the
Universitätsbibliothek, Bonn.

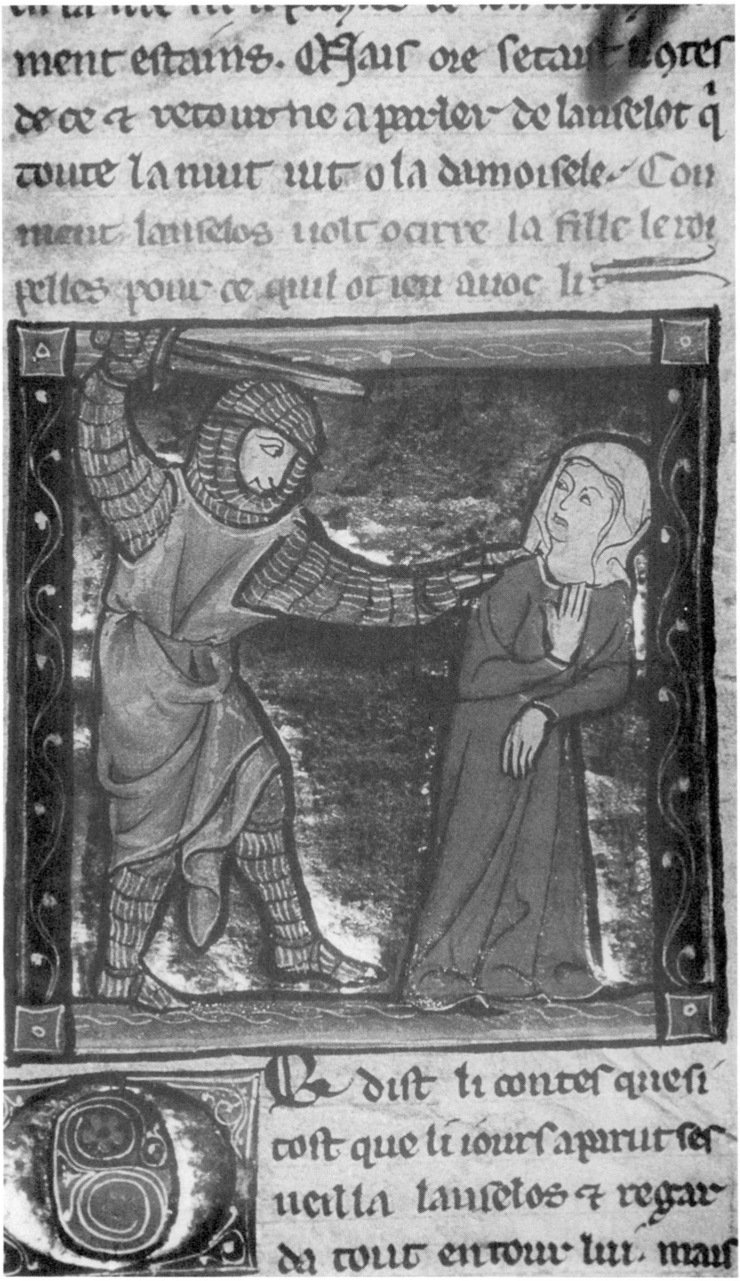

ment estains. Mais ore se taist li contes
de ce et retourne a parler de lanselot q
toute la nuit jut o la damoisele. Con
ment lanselos volt ocirre la fille le roi
pelles pour ce quil ot jeu avoec li.

dist li contes que si
tost que li jours aparut ses
veilla lanselos et regar
da tout entour lui. mais

Figure 14. Bonn, U. B. 526, f. 356v (olim 366v). Reprinted by permission of the Universitätsbibliothek, Bonn.

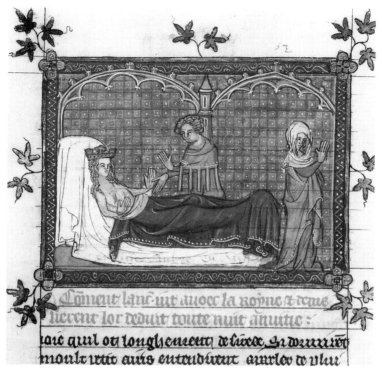

Figure 15. Paris, B. N. fr. 122, f. 147v. Reprinted by permission of the Bibliothèque Nationale, Paris.

Lancelot-Guinevere adultery is not illustrated, while the two occasions on which Lancelot was deceived by King Pelles's daughter are depicted. Both show the lady in bed and Lancelot, clothed, beside it; and both include a third figure in the composition: Brisane, who gave Lancelot the magic potion to drink, stands in the doorway in the first miniature (figure 16), while the second includes Guinevere confronting Lancelot, who has already stepped out of the bed in which King Pelles's daughter still lies (figure 17).[81] The miniatures are not identical in pictorial treatment; one striking difference is the presence, in the second, of a curiously phallic finial running the length of the roof above the room in which the scene takes place.

The confrontation scene seems to have appealed to Jacques d'Armagnac as it appears again in one of the sets he commissioned himself: B. N. fr. 115, f. 568v. This set also has Lancelot threatening to kill King Pelles's daughter, in a variant in which the lady kneels naked on the bed while Lancelot grasps her hands and raises his sword, f. 463v (figure 18). It also

par temps son malage.

Ozs entre en la chambze et fait
semblant quelle voit parler ala
royne puis revient alancelot et
li dit sire madame vous atent et vous man
de que vous ales aly et il se fait maintenant
deschauaer puis entre en la chambze tout
muds fozs de ses bzaies et de sa chemise et
vient au lit.

G se couche tout muds
auecques la damoiselle
comme cilz qui vraiement
cuide que ce soit la royne
et celle qui riens ne desi
roit fozs a auoir celui
de qui prouesce terrienne
est toute enluminee et le recoit liee et ioieu

Figure 16. Paris, B. N. fr. 119, f. 398v. Reprinted by permission of the Bibliothèque
Nationale, Paris.

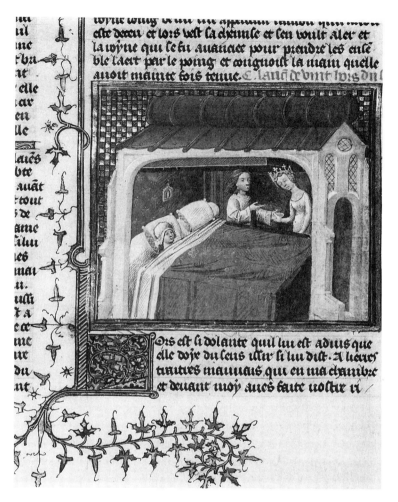

Figure 17. Paris, B. N. fr. 120, f. 493v. Reprinted by permission of the Bibliothèque Nationale, Paris.

has a scene that is not usually depicted at all: Guinevere's premonitory dream of Lancelot entering a damsel's bedchamber, on f. 446. This scene acts as a pictorial substitute for the bed scene itself, and is consistent in approach with the omission, in this set, of any representation of the Lancelot-Guinevere adultery after the first kiss. Only in the *Mort Artu* section of Armagnac's special version, B. N. fr. 112, is there a single scene of the lovemaking of Lancelot and Guinevere, chosen and placed to emphasize the role of the adultery in the imminent downfall of Arthur's kingdom, and including not a single third figure but Arthur's knights who spy.[82] The treatment of the

Figure 18. Paris, B. N. fr. 115, f. 463v. Reprinted by permission of the Bibliothèque Nationale, Paris.

lovemaking scenes in these manuscripts of the later fourteenth and fifteenth centuries seems to bear witness on the one hand to a shift in pictorial emphasis away from the adultery towards the conception of the eventual Grail winner; and on the other, through the inclusion of one or more additional characters, to allude indirectly to the pictorial and psychological complexities of the triple first kiss included much earlier in their own picture selections, while offering varying and individual interpretations of the sequel to which the first kiss was only the prelude.

NOTES

1. M 805, f. 67. The only complete description of the subjects is still the one by S.C. Cockerell in *A Descriptive Catalogue of Twenty Illuminated Manuscripts, nos. LXXV to XCIV (Replacing Twenty Discarded from the Original Hundred) in the Collection of Henry Yates Thompson* (Cambridge: Cambridge University Press, 1907), no. LXXXVIII, 94–116.

2. Some 180 manuscripts of all or parts of the cycle are listed by Brian Woledge in his indispensable *Bibliographie des romans et nouvelles en prose française* (Geneva:

Droz, 1954); Supplément, Geneva: Droz, 1975; more detailed descriptions are given in Alexandre Micha, "Les manuscrits du *Lancelot* en prose," *Romania* 81 (1960), 145–87; *Romania* 84 (1963), 28–60 and 478–99; id., "La tradition manuscrite du *Lancelot* en prose," *Romania* 85 (1964), 293–318 and 478–517; see also Micha, *Lancelot: roman en prose du 13e siècle*, 9 vols. (Geneva: Droz, 1978–83); and Elspeth Kennedy, *Lancelot do Lac: the Non-Cyclic Old French Prose Romance* (Oxford: Clarendon Press; New York: Oxford University Press, 1980). For my lists, which revise the dates proposed by these scholars, see "The Earliest Illustrated Prose *Lancelot* Manuscript?" *Reading Medieval Studies* 3 (1977), 3–44; esp. 42–44 and "Aspects of Arthur's Death in Medieval Illumination," in *The Passing of Arthur: New Essays in Arthurian Tradition*, ed. Christopher Baswell and William Sharpe (New York: Garland, 1988), 52–101, esp. 87–95. For the manuscripts of Jacques d'Armagnac, see Susan A. Blackman, "The Manuscripts and Patronage of Jacques d'Armagnac," Diss. University of Pittsburgh (1993), and forthcoming.

3. Roger Sherman Loomis and Laura Hibbard Loomis, *Arthurian Legends in Medieval Art* (New York: MLA, 1938).

4. I leave aside here the stylistic aspects of the manuscript, which I have discussed elsewhere: see "L'atelier artistique de la *Vie de sainte Benoîte d'Origny*: nouvelles considérations," in *Bulletin de la Société nationale des antiquaires de France* (no volume number) (1990), 378–400. Much literary and socio-anthropological commentary has been devoted to the kiss motif: for instance, it is one of the examples discussed in Nicolas James Perella, *The Kiss Sacred and Profane, An Interpretative History of Kiss Symbolism and Related Religio-Erotic Themes* (Berkeley: University of California Press, 1969), 128–30, figure 15; and in Michael Camille, "Gothic Signs and the Surplus: The Kiss on the Cathedral," *Yale French Studies Special Edition, Contexts: Style and Values in Medieval Art and Literature*, ed. Daniel Poirion and Nancy Freeman Regalado (New Haven: Yale University Press, 1991), 151–70, figure 10.

5. See Carol Dover, "The Split-Shield Motif in the Old French Prose *Lancelot*," in *The Arthurian Yearbook* 1 (1991), 43–61; and Dover, "*Imagines historiarum*: Text and Image in the French Prose *Lancelot*," forthcoming. The focus of the second article is four randomly selected depictions of the split-shield episode; but the illustrative tradition includes many more examples of this subject—and several interesting instances of its omission—which are not addressed.

6. For the poisoned apple and the trial by fire, and for the general background, see "Aspects of Arthur's Death" and Alison Stones, "Arthurian Art Since Loomis," in *Arturus Rex*, II, ed. W. van Hoecke, G. Tournoy, and Werner Verbeke (Leuven: Leuven University Press, 1991), 21–78, and for Arthur's discovery of the adultery, see Alison Stones, "Images of Temptation, Seduction and Discovery in the Prose *Lancelot*: a Preliminary Note," in *Festschrift Gerhard Schmidt*, ed. M. Krieger and H. Aurenhammer, *Wiener Jahrbuch für Kunstgeschichte* 47 (1994), 533–43.

7. I am grateful to Françoise Vielliard, Geneviève Hasenohr, and the staff of the Section Romane at the Institut de Recherche et d'Histoire des Textes in Paris, where the microfilm collection has been immensely helpful; to Jean-Pierre Aniel and Aleksandra Orlowska at the Bibliothèque Nationale, who have begun a database of Arthurian illustration in B. N. manuscripts; and to the many librarians who have allowed me to consult the originals. For an elaboration of my theoretical framework, see "Arthur's Death."

8. My terminology is unashamedly old-fashioned, still using words like "context" and deliberately avoiding terms like "sign," "referent," etc.; but the semiotic implications of the present examination will emerge nonetheless. For recent discussions of the semiotic approach and terminology, see Mieke Bal and Norman Bryson, "Semiotics and Art History," *Art Bulletin* 73 (1991), 174–208, and their amusing application to a medieval manuscript context by Suzanne Lewis, "Images of Opening, Penetration and Closure in the *Roman de la Rose*," *Word and Image* 8 (1992), 215–42.

9. For the Stuttgart Psalter, see my "Arthurian Art Since Loomis," figure 9; I noted there that the usual typological interpretation of this scene is the Visitation, in which, of course, the two embracing figures are the Virgin Mary and her cousin Elizabeth; but in the Stuttgart Psalter, the right-hand figure seems to me clearly male, not female.

10. For some particularly striking examples of Song of Songs illustration in Anglo-Saxon and Romanesque Bibles, see Walter Cahn, *Romanesque Bible Illumination* (Ithaca: Cornell University Press, 1982), esp. 112 and color plate on 113 (Valenciennes B. M. 10, f. 113), 199 and figure 156 (Lérida, Arch. Cap. 1, f. 299), 220 and figure 184 (Paris, B. N. lat. 16745, f. 112v); and Perella, *The Kiss*, figure 11 (Troyes B. M. 458). But it should be noted that the kiss is not the only choice for the illustration of the Song of Songs: Lyon B. M. 410–411, for instance, shows the Virgin and Christ Child embracing, in the Eleousa pose (Cahn, 273), and the Virgin and Child in various poses is also a common choice for Song of Songs illustration in the thirteenth century. See also my brief discussion in "Arthurian Art Since Loomis," 38–39, figures 10 (a seated couple), 11, and 12; and Willem Frijhoff, "The Kiss Sacred and Profane: Reflections on a Cross-Cultural Confrontation," in *A Cultural History of Gesture*, ed. Jan Bremmer and Herman Roodenburg (Ithaca, N.Y.: Cornell University Press, 1992), 210–16.

11. See "Arthurian Art," figure 13 (another seated couple). It is probably noteworthy that earlier seated couples such as the pair in Villard de Honnecourt's sketchbook, Paris, B. N. fr. 19093, f. 14, do not embrace. See Hans R. Hahnloser, *Kritische Gesamtausgabe des Bauhüttenbuches ms. fr. 19093 der Pariser nationalbibliothek*, 2d ed. (Graz: Akademische Druck und Verlagsanstalt, 1972), plate 27.

12. See particularly Troyes B. M. 1869 and Prague U. K. XIV A 17, "Arthurian Art," figures 10–12. The impact of St. Bernard's Commentary on the Song of Songs was certainly a significant factor in the development of an erotic approach in the illustration of the Song of Songs and related commentary. See Michael Camille, " 'Him whom you have ardently desired you may see': Cistercian Exegesis and the Prefatory Miniatures in a French Apocalypse," *Cistercian Art and Architecture* 3 (1987), 137–60, where the same two images are reproduced.

13. Vienna, Ö. N. B. Cod. 507, f. 1v, reproduced in F. Unterkircher, *Reiner Musterbuch*, Faksimile-Ausgabe (Codices Selecti LXIV, LXIV*) (Graz: Akademische Druck und Verlagsanstalt, 1979).

14. Boulogne-sur-Mer 110, *Catalogue général des manuscrits de bibliothèques des départements*, IV, ed. M. Michelant (Paris: Imprimerie nationale, 1872), 641, from Saint-Vaast, Arras; written in Italy for export, possibly illuminated in Paris.

15. Munich, Bayerische Staatsbibliothek Clm 4660 and 4660a (4660, f. 72v); see the facsimile ed. B. Bischoff, 2 vols. (Munich, 1967), where it is dated ca. 1230. Somewhat similar are the horizontal figures of the dead Pyramus and Thisbe on the Cambrai tympanum ("Arthurian Art," figure 6); but Pyramus and Thisbe are lying one on top of the other, both pierced by a sword, not facing each other as in the *Carmina Burana*. The Pyramus and Thisbe image in the *Roman de la Poire*, Paris, B. N. fr. 2186, f. 7v, shows the couple lying on the ground, pierced by a sword, and embracing. Full illustrations appear in Thibaut, "Le roman de la poire," ed. Christiane Marchello-Nizia (Paris: Société des Anciens Textes Français, 1984); the other embracing couples are Tristan and Isolde (f. 5v), Cligès and Fénice (f. 3v), and the anonymous couple who presumably commissioned the manuscript (f. 4v). Marchello-Nizia opts for a date of ca. 1250–60 for B. N. fr. 2186. But see now Hans-Eric Keller, "La structure du *Roman de la Poire*," in *Conjonctures: Medieval Studies in Honor of Douglas Kelly*, ed. Keith Busby and Norris J. Lacy (Amsterdam: Rodopi, 1994), pp. 205–17 at 217, where a date of 1270–1280 is proposed for B.N. fr. 2186.

16. Berlin, Staatsbibliothek, MS. germ. fol. 282, f. 11v, *Heinrich von Veldecke, Eneide. Die Bilder der Berliner Handschrift*, ed. Albert Boeckler (Leipzig: Harrassowitz, 1939). There is a parallel in the *Vergilius Romanus*, Vatican, Vat. lat. 3867, pictura XV, f. 106, facsimile ed. Carlo Bertelli et al., 4 vols. (Vatican City: Belser,

1986), where Dido and Aeneas, sheltering in a cave from the rain, sit embracing. No amorous encounters are depicted in the classical miscellany of ca. 1200 that includes the *Aeneid*, Paris, B. N. lat. 7936, discussed, with a complete list of subjects and full illustrations, by François Avril, "Un manuscrit d'auteurs classiques et ses illustrations," in *The Year 1200: A Symposium*, ed. Jeffrey Hoffeld (New York: Metropolitan Museum of Art, 1975), 261–82.

17. Hugo Buchthal, *Historia Troiana, Studies in the History of Medieval Secular Illustration*, Studies of the Warburg Institute, ed. E.H. Gombrich, 32 (London: Warburg Institute, 1971), plate 4a. Buchthal, 10, thought these illustrations are similar in *style* to the Berlin *Eneit*, a relationship I find rather implausible.

18. Sydney C. Cockerell, *Old Testament Miniatures*, rev. John Plummer (New York, 1969), esp. f. 4v, facing 40; f. 6, facing 48; f. 32, facing 150; and f. 44v (now Paris, BN n. a. lat. 2294), facing 200. In my view it was made in Flanders or Hainaut ca. 1250.

19. Reproduced in Loomis, figures 41 and 42; Perella, 27–29; and Camille, "Gothic Signs," figure 8.

20. Buchthal, plates 19a and b.

21. Ed. Yvonne Rokseth, *Polyphonies du XIIIe siècle, le ms. H 196 de la Faculté de Médecine de Montpellier*, 4 vols. (Paris, 1935–39), esp. ff. 112 and 246. The latest analysis of the date is by Mary E. Wolinski, "The Compilation of the Montpellier Codex," *Early Music History* 11 (1992), 263–301, where a date in the late 1260s or 1270s, based on stylistic parallels for the illustrations, is considered for fascicles 1 and 7, implying an early date for most of the book—a little too early in my view, as I shall argue elsewhere.

22. See note 15 above.

23. Munich, Bayerische Staatsbibliothek Cgm 63, f. 38v, reproduced in color in *Codex Manesse, Katalog zur Ausstellung*, ed. Elmar Mittler and Wilfried Werner et al. (Heidelberg: Braus, 1988), no. H 18, 300 and 612–13.

24. Stuttgart, Württembergischer Landesbibliothek HB XIII 1 (facsimile ed. Ottfried Ehrismann et al., 2 vols., Stuttgart, 1969), and Heidelberg, Univ. Bibl. Cod. Pal. Germ. 848 (facsimile Frankfurt, 1975–79), Kommentar ed. W. Koschorrek and W. Werner (Kassel, 1981) respectively.

25. For the Christ-St. John groups, see Reiner Haussherr, "Über die Christus-Johannes-Gruppen. Zum Problem 'Andachtsbilder' und deutsche Mystik," in *Beiträge zur Kunst des Mittelalters. Festschrift für Hans Wentzel zum 60. Geburtstag*, ed. R. Becksmann, U.-D. Korn, and J. Zahlten (Berlin: Mann, 1975), 79–103.

26. Mt 26:49; 2 Reg. 3:26–27; 2 Reg. 20:9–10; and the *Old Testament Picture Bible*, f. 37v, facing 172, and f. 46v, facing 208. A range of meanings and references can be found under "Kiss" in Crewden's *Concordance* (New York: Dodd and Mead, 1871); see also Perella, *The Kiss*, 27–29. Negative aspects of the embrace in the *Old Testament Picture Bible* are also conveyed by the embracing gestures of the Benjaminites as they seduce the daughters of Shiloh, f. 17, facing 90.

27. Perella, 154, and figure 16; Camille, "Gothic Signs," 53, figure 1.

28. The list is far too long to enumerate here, and includes examples from most of the books of the Bible and most of the plates in A. de Laborde, *La bible moralisée conservée à Oxford, Paris et Londres*, 5 vols., (Paris: Société française pour la reproduction de manuscrits à peintures, 1911–27), and *Bible moralisée*, ed. Reiner Haussherr, 2 vols. (Graz: Akademische Druk und Verlagsanstalt, 1973); Camille, "Gothic Signs," shows an example from Genesis 19:1 as his figure 12.

29. Except when it is discovered by Arthur on the walls of Morgan's castle, as painted by Lancelot; for some possibly sinister implications of the few representations that show the first kiss on the walls, see my "Images of Seduction."

30. Lors se traient tout .III. ensamble et font samblant de conseillier. Et la roine voit que li chevaliers [Lancelot] n'en ose plus faire, si le prent par le menton et le baise

devant Galahot. [Then the three of them draw aside together as if they were taking counsel. And the queen sees that the knight [Lancelot] dares go no further, so she takes him by the chin and kisses him in front of Galehot.] H.O. Sommer, *The Vulgate Version of the Arthurian Romances*, 7 vols. (Washington, D.C.: Carnegie Institution, 1909–13, rpt. New York: AMS, 1979), III, 267; Kennedy, *Lancelot do Lac*, I, 348; Micha, ed., *Lancelot*, VIII, 115–16. This citation is from Micha.

31. Haussherr, "Christus-Johannes." See also Jeffrey F. Hamburger, *The Rothschild Canticles, Art and Mysticism in Flanders and the Rhineland circa 1300* (New Haven: Yale University Press, 1990), 78, where the point is reiterated.

32. Camille, "Gothic Signs," 163–64.

33. Perella, 253–56, and figures 22 and 23.

34. The dowry miracle of St. Nicholas, transferred to pawnbrokers, and a popular choice in thirteenth-century illustrated lectionaries and saints' lives, is the obvious connotation for the balls; whereas, although the two turtle doves are borrowed from the Presentation, I have found no direct medieval source for the French hens.

35. E.g., *Hortus deliciarum*, ed. Rosalie B. Green, Michael Curschmann, and Michael Evans, 2 vols. (London: Warburg Institute, 1979), f. 8, plate III.

36. A precursor of the mid-fourteenth-century example cited by Camille (Toulouse, B. M. 19, f. 121), is the English thirteenth-century Trinitarian angel in Cambridge, St. John's K 26, ff. 9–10. See Nigel J. Morgan, *Early Gothic Manuscripts, II, 1250–1285* (London: Miller, 1988), cat. no. 179 with full bibliography; see also Hamburger, figures 197–202, 210–212. A splendid set of fifteenth-century variations on the Trinity occurs in the Hours of Catherine of Cleves, New York, Morgan M 945 and Guennol Collection, ca. 1440; see *The Hours of Catherine of Cleves*, ed. John Plummer (New York: Braziller, n. d.), ff. 77v–90.

37. Haussherr, *Bible moralisée*, plate 10; the text is Gn 19. This image is adjacent to Lot and his family leaving Sodom and Gomorrah, in which Lot's wife is shown completely naked with very prominent genitalia. In Oxford, Bodl., Bodl. 270b, f. 15v, Lot is shown actually in bed with his daughters—he fully clothed, including Jewish hat, on the left of the bed; they both naked on the right. On the left of the same roundel, two women (the daughters?) each hold a child, one of whom is a swaddled baby, the other an older child. The image is paired with the angel's appearance to Lot, exhorting him to leave home, and the destruction of Sodom and Gomorrah is shown as the third roundel in the left column—with Lot's wife, naked but wearing her wimple and modestly holding her hands in front of her pubis. I did not have access to illustrations of the other copies.

38. 2 Reg 16:21–22. The *Old Testament Picture Bible* includes the subject on f. 45, the leaf now in Malibu at the J. Paul Getty Museum, Ludwig I, 66. Two additional female figures are included on either side of the two around whom Absalom has his arms draped, making a total of six figures with Absalom in the middle. Three of them wear the wimple and "touret" headgear of the married woman, while two wear a simple band around their loose hair, and the other (second from the left) is bare-headed and of ambiguous sex.

39. Another discussion of Trinitarian iconography in relation to imagery in a vernacular manuscript is V.A. Kolve, "The Annunciation to Christine: Authorial Empowerment in *The Book of the City of Ladies*," in *Iconography at the Crossroads* (Papers from the Colloquium sponsored by the Index of Christian Art, Princeton University, 23–24 March, 1990), ed. Brendan Cassidy (Princeton: Index of Christian Art and Department of Art and Archaeology, Princeton University, 1993), 171–91. The visual parallel here is most workable at the level of Abraham and the Three Angels; I remain unconvinced by the additional transformations that Kolve must perform to make his interpretation work at other levels, "converting" the Three Person Trinity to a Throne of Mercy Trinity in order to interpret Christine as the Virgin Mary Annunciate. This seems to me to stretch iconographical interpretation into the realm of present-day subjectivism. Still other triple groups might also be relevant: Mary Eliza-

beth Meek suggested to me that the Temptation of Adam and Eve, with the serpent wrapped around the tree as the third element in most medieval versions of the subject, would also evoke relevant associations for the medieval viewer.

40. Examples of otherwise fully illustrated manuscripts where the kiss is lacking are Oxford, Bodl. Ash 828; Oxford, Bodl. Rawl. Q. b. 6; Paris, Ars. 3481; Paris, B. N. fr. 110; Paris, B. N. fr. 111; Paris, B. N. fr. 344; Paris, B. N. fr. 770; Rennes 255; more work is needed to complete the list. Of these, Rennes 255 dates c. 1220; B. N. fr. 770, B. N. fr. 110, and perhaps Ash. 828 in the last quarter of the thirteenth century; Oxford, Rawl. Q. b. 6, c. 1300 and Paris, Ars. 3481, in the second quarter of the fourteenth century; B. N. fr. 111 in the fifteenth century. For a detailed discussion of the dating arguments that are based on stylistic comparisons with related manuscripts, see my "The Illustrations of the French Prose *Lancelot*," diss. University of London (1970–71).

41. The only exception is the painted version of the kiss that Lancelot painted on the wall in Morgan's castle, shown in some manuscripts when Arthur discovers it. See my "Images of Temptation."

42. These are two of three surviving copies produced in St.-Omer or Ghent ca. 1315; the third member of the group, London, B. L. Royal 14.E.iii, is incomplete and lacks this section of text and pictures. For their style, see my "Another Short Note on Rylands French 1," in *Romanesque and Gothic, Essays for George Zarnecki*, ed. Neil Stratford (Bury St. Edmunds, 1987), 185–92; for the iconography of *Estoire*, see Martine Meuwese, "*L'Estoire del saint Graal*. Een studie over de relatie tussen miniaturen en tekst in het eerste deel van de Vulgaatcyclus uit de Biblioteca Philosophica Hermetica te Amsterdam," 2 vols. (Doctoraalscriptie Kunstgeschiedenis van de Middeleeuwen, Rijksuniversiteit Leiden, 1990).

43. Bought by Jean de Berry in 1405, probably from the Parisian bookdealer Regnault du Montet, and painted by an artist dubbed by Meiss the "Master of Berry's Cleres femmes" after his main work, a translation of Boccaccio. See Millard Meiss, *French Painting in the Time of Jean de Berry, I, The Patronage of the Duke* (New York and London: Phaidon, 1967), 252, 312. For Jacques d'Armagnac's manuscripts, see Blackman.

44. Ed. C.E. Pickford, *L'Évolution du roman arthurien en prose vers la fin du moyen âge d'après le manuscrit 112 du fonds français de la Bibliothèque nationale* (Paris: Nizet, 1960), and Blackman.

45. Et Galehos dist au senescal: Alés, si faites compaignie a ches damoiseles la qui trop sont seules. [And Galeholt says to the seneschal: Come on, keep these ladies company so they are not all alone.] Kennedy (cit. n. 4), 340; Micha (cit. n. 4), VIII, 104; cited from Micha.

46. si que la dame de Malohaut seit qu'ele le baise [so that the dame de Malehaut knows that she is kissing him.] Kennedy (cit. n. 4), p. 348; Micha (cit. n. 4), VIII, 116, cited from Micha.

47. si en ot teil paor et teile angoisse en son cuer que il ne pot respondre a che que la roine li disoit. Et quant il plus esgardoit la dame de Malohaut plus estoit ses cuers a malaise. [so that the fear and anguish in his heart were so great he could not reply to what the queen was saying and the more he looked at the dame de Malehaut, the more uneasy he felt.] Kennedy (cit. n. 4), 345; Micha (cit. n. 4), VIII, 110; cited from Micha.

48. She begins the conversation with the words, Ha dame, com est boine compaignie de .IIII. [Aha, my lady, what good company four make.] Micha, VIII, 118.

49. My findings for *Queste* and *Mort Artu* showed that the earliest manuscripts tended to have a single opening image only, while a "short cycle" and a "long cycle" of pictures had both emerged by ca. 1275 and continued to be copied side by side (sometimes by the same painters) into the fourteenth century; see "The Illustrations." The pattern for *Estoire* is quite different, as the earliest copy, Rennes 255, ca. 1220 (*sic*, not early fourteenth century as in Kennedy and Micha), already has a "short cycle"

of illustrations; see "The Earliest Illustrated Prose *Lancelot* Manuscript?" The pattern for the *Lancelot* Proper has still to be worked out, but the Rennes copy already has twenty-nine illustrations in its incomplete *Lancelot* and no first kiss image; the text ends at Sommer, IV, 220/33; the kiss is at III, 267.

50. Curiously, part of his colophon is in Latin, part in French: "Explicit. Arnulfus de Kayo scripsit istum librum qui est Ambianis. En l'an del incarnacion m.cc.iiii^{xx} vi el mois d'aoust le iour devant le s.iehan decolase." Arnulfus may or may not be related to another scribe of the same surname, Walterus de Kayo, who copied the *Estoire*, Le Mans MM 354, at an uncertain date, and the *Image du monde, Paris, B. N. fr.* 14962, in 1282; see Alison Stones, "The Illustrated Chrétien Manuscripts and their Artistic Context," in *Les Manuscrits de Chrétien de Troyes*, ed. Keith Busby, Terry Nixon, Alison Stones, and Lori Walters (Amsterdam: Rodopi, 1993), I, 237, where Terry Nixon is credited with discovering Walterus's signature in the *Image du monde* manuscript. In Le Mans 354, the colophon in Latin reads "EXPLICIT. Walterus de Kayo scripsit istum librum." In B. N. fr. 14962, he uses French, not Latin: "Explicit. En l'an de l'incarnation M.CC.IIII.^{XX}. et .II. l'escrit Wautiers dou Kai, foi que jou doi adeu."

51. B. N. fr. 110 may be as much as a decade later than Bonn 526, because its borders are closer to those in the *Guillaume d'Orange*, Boulogne B. M. 192, written in 1295; see Stones, "The Illustrations," ch. 5, and "Sacred and Profane," 108–10.

52. A full study of its text version is in preparation under the leadership of Daniel Poirion; I thank Mary Speer for this information.

53. At Micha, VIII, 32; the first kiss occurs on 115.

54. Examples of miniatures added later in the margins to rectify gaps in the iconography are the some twenty scenes, including such key items as Lancelot crossing the sword bridge, added in the fifteenth century to the early fourteenth-century fragments of the same set of volumes as the Amsterdam book: Manchester, Rylands French 1, and Oxford, Bodl., Douce 215. See my "Short Note on Rylands French 1 and Douce 215," *Scriptorium* 22 (1968), 41–45, figures 8a and b; and "Another Short Note," figure 8.

55. Almost all the miniatures in the Bonn manuscript, I think, are the work of the same artist; but I do see the work of the kiss painter again on f. 268v. It looks like the work of another, but contemporary, artist, trying hard to imitate the style of the main painter.

56. See "The Illustrations," ch. 5, for a list of other books by the same painter or painters, and note 40 above.

57. See "Indications écrites et modèles picturaux, guides aux peintres de manuscrits enluminés aux environs de 1300," in *Artistes, artisans et production artistique*, ed. Xavier Barral i Altet, 3 vols. (Paris: Picard, 1990), III, 322–49, and J.J.G. Alexander, *Medieval Illuminators and their Methods of Work* (New Haven: Yale University Press, 1993).

58. In the Add. 10292–94, Royal 14.E.iii, Amsterdam/Rylands/Douce volumes, the rubrics seem to have been done after the miniatures had been drawn in leadpoint— which itself would have occurred after the script had been done and miniature spaces left blank—as the pictures often have architectural details that project upwards into the rubric spaces, forcing the rubricator to add his text around them. Here there are very few pinnacles in the margins; generally they are confined to the opening miniatures of the branches. On f. 455v, for instance, the opening of *Mort Artu* shows a gap left for one decorative finial but there are two more finials that interfere with the words, or vice versa; the finials are in no way displaced in relation to the architectural frame of which they are part, but it is hard to tell whether the painter ignored existing writing or whether the scribe took no notice of existing painting or underdrawing. I could not tell which.

59. *Old Testament Miniatures*, M 638, f. 41v, facing 188; see also Amnon and Thamar, f. 43, now Paris, B. N. n. a. lat. 2294, facing 194. The iconography of David and Bathsheba in the Vienna 2554 *Bible moralisée*, f. 45, is notably more restrained, with David and Bathsheba fully clothed, sitting chastely embracing on a bed while a

nurse tends their offspring, and the moralization shows Christ standing, taking Ecclesia by the hand, both being watched by their offspring shown as tonsured male figures.

60. The gang rape and subsequent death of the wife of Dyakene by the Sodomites (Vienna 2554, f. 65) is a particularly dramatic example, discussed and reproduced in Diane Wolfthal, " 'A Hue and Cry': Medieval Rape Imagery and Its Transformation," *Art Bulletin* 75 (1993), 39–64, at 46, figure 14.

61. They are included in Rennes 255, Paris, B. N. fr. 19162, B. N. fr. 24394, B. N. fr. 770, B. N. fr. 344, Le Mans 354, Add. 10292, Roy. 14.E.iii; but are omitted in Tours 951, Bonn 526, B. N. fr. 110, B. N. fr. 95, Amsterdam B. P. H. 1; and this list is not exhaustive.

62. Sommer, II, 278, line 39. There is no study of dreams in *Merlin*; this one is not in Rennes 255, B. N. fr. 770, Bonn 526, B. N. fr. 110, B. N. fr. 95, or Add. 38117; but the list is not complete.

63. For dreams in *Estoire*, see Elizabeth Remak, *Positions des Thèses de l'École des Chartes* (1986), and for an analysis of dreams in *Lancelot, Queste*, and *Mort Artu*, see Mireille Demaules and Christiane Marchello-Nizia, "Träume in der Dichtung. Die Ikonographie des *Lancelot-Graal* (13.–15. Jh.)," in *Träume im Mittelalter, Ikonologische Studien*, ed. Agostino Paravicini Bagliani and Giorgio Stabile (Stuttgart-Zürich, 1989), 209–226.

64. Loomis, *Arthurian Legends*, 77–78, and (barely discernible) figure 161; James A. Rushing, Jr., "Adventure and Iconography: *Ywain* Picture Cycles and the Literarization of Vernacular Narrative," *The Arthurian Yearbook* 1 (1991), 91–105; Stephanie Cain Van D'Elden, "Specific and Generic Scenes: A Model for Analyzing Medieval Illustrated Texts Based on the Example of *Ywain/Iwein*," *Bulletin Bibliographique de la Société Internationale Arthurienne* 44 (1992), 255–69; and James A. Rushing, Jr., *Images of Adventure: Ywain in the Visual Arts* (Philadelphia: University of Pennsylvania, 1995, esp. pp. 91–132, with full bibliography.

65. Lori Walters, "The Creation of a *Super Romance*: Paris, Bibliothèque Nationale, fonds français, MS 1433," *The Arthurian Yearbook* 1 (1991), 3–25, esp. 15, figure 1.13. The bed episode is preceded by Yvain leaning over to embrace Laudine (not two female figures as some commentators have seen). I am grateful to Lori Walters for her careful editing of this paragraph of my study.

66. Loomis, 78, and figure 164. For the German tradition, see Rushing, 1995.

67. Montpellier, B. I., Sect. Méd. H 249, f. 172, discussed by Lori Walters in "The Image of Blanchefleur," in *Les Manuscrits de Chrétien de Troyes*, I, 437–39, at 447, figure 11, and II, figure 189; see also Angelica Rieger, "Le programme iconographique du *Perceval* montpelliérain, B. I., Sect. Méd. H 249 (M), avec la description détaillée du manuscrit," *ibid.*, I, 377–435, figure 20.

68. Madrid B. N. 17805, f. 22v, reproduced in Buchthal, 21. One might also add the rare scene of Candace and Alexander in bed in Thomas of Kent's *Roman de toute chevalerie*, Paris, B. N. fr. 24364, f. 78 (François Avril and Patricia Danz Stirnemann, *Manuscrits enluminés d'origine insulaire VIIe–XXe siècle* [Paris: Bibliothèque nationale, 1987] no. 171, 135, at plate LXIX). Both crowned, they cavort in a splendidly draped and canopied bed while ladies in niches in the margins play musical instruments that include the drum and bagpipes; Stirnemann has suggested (lecture of July 1994) that the ladies are performing a kind of charivari, earlier in date, since the manuscript was made ca. 1308–1312, than the famous charivari in the *Roman de Fauvel*, Paris, B. N. fr. 146, made after 1316.

69. On f. 13, see Boeckler; and Venus and Mars surprised by Vulcan, f. 39, reproduced in *Zimelien, Abendländische Handschriften des Mittelalters aus der Sammlungen der Stiftung Preussischer Kulturbesitz Berlin, Ausstellung 13.Dezember 1975–1.Februar 1976* (Wiesbaden: Reichert, 1975), no. 89, plate 165.

70. Gottfried von Strassburg, *"Tristan und Isolde" mit der Fortsetzung Ulrichs von Türheim*. Facsimile-Ausgabe des Cgm 51 der Bayerischen Staatsbibliothek

München, ed. Ulrich Montag and Paul Gichtel, 2 vols. (Stuttgart: Müller and Schindler, 1979). See particularly f. 10v, top left: lovemaking between Riwalin and Blanscheflur; f. 90v, top: Tristan and Isolde in bed, surprised by King Mark; f. 101v, bottom: Tristan and Isolde in bed, discovered by Antrit.

71. For the Forrer casket (late twelfth or early thirteenth century? Cologne?), see R. Forrer, "Tristan et Yseult sur un coffret inédit du XIIe s.," *Cahiers d'archéologie et d'histoire d'Alsace* 24–25 (1933), cited by Loomis, 43, where this scene is given as Mark and Ysolt in bed, with Bringvain bearing the love-potion prepared by Ysolt's mother, based on Thomas's version as reconstructed from the Norse. The bronze gilt mirror-case from Bussen (Swabia), now in the Kunstgewerbemuseum, Frankfurt, shows, on the back, a couple in bed and a harpist playing (Isolde and Mark with Tristan harping? David and Abishag?) and standing embracing lovers on the handle. It was attributed to ca. 1150 by H. Kohlhaussen, "Das Paar vom Bussen," *Festshcrift Friedrich Winkler,* ed. Hans Möhle (Berlin: Mann, 1959), 29–48, at 39, and to the first half of the thirteenth century by Hans Swarzenski in *Monuments of Medieval Art* (London: Faber, n. d. [1953?]), figure 469a, b, plate 202.

72. This is not their first sexual encounter, but it is the first one to be illustrated in this manuscript, at Sommer, IV, 209, miniatures 191 and 192; Micha, II, 75.

73. These miniatures are by the first painter. The defacement of scenes of lovemaking is not uncommon in romance manuscripts, though we cannot be sure when it occurred: see Perceval and Blanchefleur in the Montpellier manuscript, and Yvain and Laudine in B. N. fr. 1433, discussed above. Several scenes in the *Perceval,* Mons B. U. 226/331, are also erased (reproduced in Busby, Nixon, Stones, and Walters, II, figures 192–232, esp. figures 214–18, 220, 232); but here the erased scenes are not of lovemaking, and the motives for the mutilation are unclear. Another interesting instance of an erasure is in the medical compendium in Crakow, Biblioteka Jagiellonski MS. 816, f. 154, where a marginal scene shows a seated doctor performing a rectal examination of a patient who, on the curvilinear border, presents his rear: the patient has been erased, but a note in leadpoint above the scene says, "cest .i. home nu covert de .i. mantel/.i. altre home li gete .i. distere (clistere?) u cuch/a ses brees avales." For a general description of the manuscript see *Bulletin de la Société française pour la reproduction de manuscrits à peintures* 17 (1933), 39; plate VIII reproduces f. 101v; see also Zofia Ameisenowa, *Rekopisy i perwodriki iluminowane Biblioteki Jagiellonskiej* (Wroclaw-Krakow, 1958). Again there is no indication as to when the erasure occurred.

74. Sommer, V, 182, miniature 334, by the second painter; other copies shorten the text considerably here, which would help to explain the absence of parallel miniatures in other manuscripts.

75. Guilbert de Sainte-Aldegonde, who gave his Tournai Psalter, St.-Omer 270, to the Chartreuse of Longuenesse in 1323, having added to it a devotional portrait miniature by the main painter of Add. 10292–94, Roy. 14.E.iii and Amsterdam/Rylands/Douce 215, is certainly a known patron who commissioned work from one of the same artists, though we unfortunately know nothing else about his patronage. Shields on the opening pages of Add., Roy., and Amsterdam have not yielded information about original patrons. See my "Another Short Note." I am not in agreement with Judith Oliver that the origins of this style are to be sought in Verdun and reserve the question for further discussion elsewhere. A lovemaking scene also appears in the margin of a stylistically related manuscript, the psalter Oxford, Bodl. Douce 6, reproduced in Randall, *Images in the Margins,* figure 404.

76. See ff. 288 (Sommer, V, 110, miniature 299) and f. 374 (Sommer, V, 380, miniature 422); on f. 288 (Sommer, V, 111, miniature 300) Lancelot, fully armed, having realized the lady he slept with is not Guinevere, raises his sword to kill King Pelles's daughter, thinking it is she who has deceived him.

77. See "Images of Temptation," figure 15. Admittedly, the Yale manuscript only has the third part of the *Lancelot* Proper, the *Agravain* section, so the text that

would have included the first kiss and its sequel is missing; the same is true of B. N. fr. 12573, which has Lancelot's remorse on f. 48v. But lovemaking is also excluded altogether in B. N. fr. 110; and in Bonn U. B. 526 the only other example is the curious double bed scene with two couples, on f. 254, showing Arthur and Camille in one bed and Guerrehes and his "amie" in the other, with knights looking on! (Micha, VIII, 442; Kennedy, 546); in Morgan 805–6 the only bed scene is the seduction of the daughter of the King of Norgales by Gauvain on f. 99, where it is the subject of a large (and, as Cockerell remarked, somewhat touched-up) miniature. This list is not final: more looking is still needed.

78. See my "Images of Temptation," figure 15.

79. We are equally ill-informed about the owners of almost all the Vulgate Cycle manuscripts: the well-documented patronage of Jacques d'Armagnac is exceptional, see Blackman.

80. F. 147v. A full study of this important book (whose text begins with the crossing of the sword bridge) is still needed; the arms on f. 1, *or a chevron gu, 3 pennanular brooches arg* and *or a fess az, 3 besants arg*, have not been identified.

81. See the detailed tabulations of Arthurian subjects in Blackman.

82. Vol. III, f. 203v. But it should be noted that one volume of B. N. fr. 112 is missing.

7 UNIFYING MAKERS

LANCELOT AND GUINEVERE IN MODERN LITERATURE AND ART

Muriel Whitaker

The Victorian interest in Arthurian legend persisted into the twentieth century, thanks to lingering Pre-Raphaelitism and an attachment to social and moral values expressed through the image of the medieval knight. Sir Thomas Malory's *Morte Darthur* remained the chief source for writers and artists, but the Protestant ethic of Tennyson's *Idylls of the King* also affected their treatments until the mid-century. The public's obsession with the idea of the hero was stimulated by the outbreak of World War I to seek artistic expressions of valor and virility. In more than one public school the headmaster prepared students to become soldiers by reading from Malory. As the war's horrible reality pierced the chivalric camouflage, the story of Arthur's "noble knyghtes . . . layde to the colde erthe" seemed an appropriate myth for modern societies on the verge of destruction.

Lancelot retained his Malorian role as "the flower of chivalry," though the adulterous relationship with his sovereign's queen created ethical and aesthetic problems. That many were willing to gloss over, excuse, or forgive his human frailties is apparent in Alfred W. Pollard's introduction to *The Romance of King Arthur and His Knights of the Round Table* (1917):

> He is perhaps the most splendid study of a great gentleman in all our literature, generous to friend and foe, courteous to everyone, eager to set himself ever harder adventures, unwilling to be praised above his fellows . . . he is a very subtle study of a soul in which spirit and flesh, aspiration and evil habit, strive for mastery.[1]

Pollard does not mention Guinevere directly; between 1900 and 1940 most authors and editors exculpated Lancelot by diminishing or denigrating the queen.

In admitted response to the Great War, Edward Arlington Robinson, a Pulitzer Prize–winning American poet, wrote *Merlin* (1917) and *Lancelot* (1920). They were intended, he told Winfield Townley Scott, as World War poems. "If you read them with that in mind you'll get more out of them. The passing of an old order and the beginning of a new."[2] In a letter to Helen Grace Adams he suggested an underlying allegory: "Camelot representing in a way the going of a world that is now pretty much gone."[3] *Lancelot* follows the chronology of Malory's Books XX and XXI; it begins just before the lovers' entrapment and ends with the hero's departure from Almesbury. The chief narrative device consists of long dialogues or soliloquies in austere blank verse, spoken by characters who reveal their motivations and feelings. They allude to the Malorian framework, sometimes expanding the time frame and range of allusion by reminiscence, as when Lancelot recalls his first sight of Guinevere: "I saw your face and there were no more kings." Robinson intensifies the structural cohesiveness by glossing over events such as the last battle in which Lancelot does not participate.[4] The most significant conversations take place at the Joyous Gard.

Lancelot repeatedly images Guinevere as "white and gold." The emphasis that both place on the queen's appearance rather than on her moral qualities diminishes our belief in the grandeur of their passion, which fails to convey Malory's ideal of "trouthe and faythefulness." Lancelot sees the woman as a moral and spiritual obstacle: "Once I had gone / where the Light guided me, but the queen came / And then there was no Light." She perceives him as one who rejects her because she is aging and who stubbornly persists in his "slow game of empty slaughter." Picturing herself as "a blue-eyed Medusa of white and gold broken with grief and fear and fury," she uses hysteria, sarcasm, and emotional blackmail to dissuade him from "freeing" her into Camelot at the pope's command. She is incapable of understanding his intention to "see more, and I shall not be blind." Their love has deteriorated into images of crumbs, ashes, and shadows.

This is a deeply pessimistic poem. The Arthurian world is "a reign already dying, and ripe to die," its king "a sick landlord," its queen "broken with grief and fear," its greatest knight engaging in destructive wars instead of following the Light, and its God deliberately inflicting a Modred on the Camelot world to annihilate it. As in a palimpsest Robinson imposes on the traditional scenario references to the Great War. The incessant rains, fogs, mud, and the common soldiers digging graves for comrades who have died like rats because of their rulers are images from the Western Front. While Guinevere's primary role is to unsettle Lancelot and free him for his spiritual quest, her second is to voice woman's protest against war's stupid destructiveness. She asks:

How many thousand men
Are going to their death before Gawaine
And Arthur go to theirs—and I to mine? (VI, 64)

Robinson thought the most important line in the poem was "This world has paid enough for Camelot."

With his New England background, a mixture of Calvinism and Unitarianism, Robinson could not adopt Malory's closure, which promised the lovers redemption in a Catholic heaven. Guinevere is left, praying half-heartedly, to the conventional life that represents safety rather than joy and hope. Lancelot rides off into the darkness, seeking the Light. The only alternative to serving destructive political systems is the individual's lonely pursuit of moral values.

In the same year as Robinson's *Lancelot* there appeared *Queen's Knight* (1920) by the English novelist Chester Keith. The work, described as a "prose epic," makes no attempt at originality. The author follows Malory's plot, omitting the Grail Quest and the Meleagant episode, no doubt because the former was too Catholic and the latter too immoral for his sensibilities. The operation of Fate is the device that exculpates the lovers, as Keith makes clear in an epigraph from Ibsen: "There is only one gift a man may not give to his dearest friend—and that is, the woman he loves, for if he does that, he breaks the thread of fate that the Norns have spun, and two lives are ruined."[5] Although Keith does not deny the lovers' passionate attachment, he maintains the honorable natures of the central triangle. Changes made in the interests of amelioration include a wedding night scene in which Lancelot as proxy bridegroom stands in for Arthur but spends only a minute in bed; a false charge of adultery refuted by Lancelot's success in a trial by combat; a chaperoned idyll with Guenever enjoying the "absolute novelty" of the free forest life with "childlike ecstasy"; a long period of knight-errantry because the hero fears "to lose what honour I have gained" and undermine Arthur's "great scheme of unity and progress"; a Modred who acts "in the cause of virtue" when he tells his uncle (not father) about the queen's knight; and an innocent visit to Guenever's bedroom so that the hero can announce his departure to guard Arthur's northern frontiers. After Arthur's death, Lancelot supervises the funeral while the queen becomes Sister Dolorosa to spend the rest of her life praying for her husband's soul. While Keith represents the man's love as being of a higher and less selfish type than the woman's, which is based on self-gratification, nevertheless he credits Guenever with a capacity for self-sacrifice and generally makes her a sympathetic character.

Lord Ernest Hamilton takes an opposite approach in *Launcelot: A Romance of the Court of King Arthur* (1926). Launcelot's moral stature is enhanced by the author's debasement of Gueneviere. Setting his romance in the sixth century, Hamilton avoids Catholic mysticism by making Earl Pelles a Norseman who had fought with Childeric at the Battle of Bowden Hill and had subsequently been converted to Christianity. Launcelot expeditiously marries Elaine and fathers Galahad before meeting the queen. This knight follows a simple code: "Honour and love are bound together by ties which are as old as Christ." Committing adultery is "the foulest deed a man may do." To these opinions Gueneviere, sounding the sentiments of a modern woman, shrewishly and shrewdly replies,

> Oh! this never-ending honour! . . . How I weary of it! Because of this one word, the true interpretation of which no man rightly knoweth, men break poor women's hearts and fling them into the kennel to die. In this is no dishonour! Let us eat out our hearts in lonely misery. What recks it, so long as men can pin this empty word upon their breasts and puff themselves out with righteous pride?

Launcelot is tricked by Morgan's magic into sleeping with the queen, who in turn tricks him into "rescuing" her from Vortigern's tower where he finds "lying and treason which to a woman may seem honourable and seemly but to a man savoureth of villainy." Then the queen, who has no scruples about killing "any that stood in the path of my love," orders the hero to choose between herself and Elaine. Unable to deal with two women simultaneously, he jumps from the window into madness. The death of Elaine and Galahad on the same day strengthens his resistance, making him swear, "I will love no lady till the day I die!"—a vow that may reflect Hamilton's own misogyny.

The idea of male honor dominates the most sympathetic treatment of the lovers in modern literature. T.H. White (1905–1964) wrote *The Ill-Made Knight* as the third volume of his Arthurian pentateuch.[6] As he was an indefatigable correspondent who shared his creative processes with his friends, critical analysis can be illuminated by his own comments. Like Robinson's *Lancelot*, *The Once and Future King* was a response to war, in this case the Second World War, which broke out in 1939. As he wrote to David Garnett, "The epic theme is War and how to stop it . . . the Round Table was an anti-Hitler measure."[7] He justified his decision to remain *hors de combat* in Ireland by claiming that his books were his contribution to the war effort "or at any rate to the next peace effort." Having completed

The Sword in the Stone, concerned with the education of a ruler, and *The Witch in the Wood*, he turned to "the Lancelot Guenever tangle." On October 4, 1939, he set down seventeen points drawn from Malory's characterisation of Lancelot. They included sensitivity to moral issues, his relating of prowess to virginity, self-denial, devotion to honor, practicality, tolerance, humility, and humanity. White also suggested that Lancelot was sadistic and homosexual or bisexual.[8] To the Malory portrait he added ugliness—a face like an African ape. Christianity, chivalry, and self-hatred constrain the knight's sexuality.

Guenever's characterization was more difficult. Having based the poisonous Morgause on his own mother, White was reluctant to create another unattractive woman, especially if Lancelot is to love her. "Could she be a sort of tigress, with all the healthy charms of the carnivore?" (Warner, 151). By the time of his letter to L.J. Potts on March 9, 1940, he has found a motivation for the queen's jealousy, boredom, and irritability in her childlessness and the menopause. Now he thinks that she is "terrific . . . one of the realest *women* in literature."[9] Black-haired "Jenny" is normalized by providing her with feelings that are easily hurt and by perceiving her resort to dye, make-up, and gaudy dresses as a once beautiful woman's pitiable weapons against aging.

With psychological realism White increases Lancelot's self-hatred by emphasizing Arthur's virtue and Elaine's vulnerability. Because the latter is ineffectual, boring, and running to fat, the twenty-year absence of her child's father is understandable, though reprehensible. The hero's sense of his sinfulness may be his most important quality. Significantly, the novel ends with the healing of Sir Urry, the miracle that maintains Lancelot's honor by reaffirming publicly his moral and spiritual superiority.

Whatever elements of chivalric idealism and Victorian propriety survived World War I were quenched by World War II. During the past forty years, historical novelists and satirists have appropriated the lovers in order to comment ironically on chivalry and courtesy. Archaeological excavations such as those at South Cadbury, Dina Powys, and Castle Dore as well as historical studies of Dark Age Britain[10] encouraged some fiction writers to depict the places and period associated with a "real" Arthur; that is, generally south and west Britain during the fifth and sixth centuries.[11] Peter Vansittart in *Lancelot: A Novel* (1978) bases his chronology on John Morris's *The Age of Arthur* in which there are three distinct periods: the last age of Roman Britain (410–42); the conflict between Romanized Britons and Saxons ending with the southern Britons' emigration to Gaul (442–60); and the successful resistance of the British (460–95).

Arthur is not a Romanized Celt but a barbarian; known as "uncouth Artorius," he is brutal, devious, and mean, a man who "ruled through his nostrils and penis." His pernicious Round Table included Kei, a spymaster; Merlin, a charlatan; Medreut, a duplicitous thief; and Arthur's son of Welsh tradition, Anir, a scapegoat ritually sacrificed to ensure victory. The narrator of Roman Britain's decline and fall is Lancelot, known as Ker Maxim. Son of a Roman father and British mother who belonged to Roman villa society, he attaches himself first to the civilized Ambrosius and then to Arthur. Neither invincible hero, faithful lover, nor popular companion at arms, he summarized his identity as "being only in what I failed to be." Like the late Roman culture that he represents, he is a loser. Even his elegiac memoir remains uncompleted, a testimony to the unreliability of historical record.

Within his lifetime, the Romano-British culture with its Latin language and literature, urban crafts, prosperous villas, and network of roads and fortifications is replaced by a barbaric warrior culture. The family villa epitomizes the decline. At first, though overgrown orchards and diminished food supplies indicate a loss of order, Janus is still in place protecting brightly plastered walls, mosaic floors, a bird-shaped bronze lamp, and a library stacked with rolls. Returning years later, the narrator finds derelict fields, smashed monuments, rooms "dazed by spiders' webs, damp and the stealthy approach of forest." Soured by his sense of loss, he records acts of sadism and violence as the normal occurrences of Arthurian life.

Gwenhever is a cat woman with perverted sexual tastes. Her liaison with Ker Maxim occurs before her marriage and occupies one winter during which she proves "adept at playing and prolonging lust." Her lover never replaces her, not out of fidelity but from a natural asceticism that preserves his energy for useful politics, which range from administering Arthur's territories to planning the strategy that wins the Battle of Badon. His last view of the woman, who at Kei's orders has lured Lancelot into the trap, does not encourage romantic reminiscence. Her tight cheeks are caked with cracked paint, while the black artificial circles ringing her eyes fail to distract attention from her missing teeth.

The last three novelists to be discussed satirize contemporary society by assimilating medieval characters into modern life where their calculated expediency and conscious roleplaying highlight moral and spiritual failures. As a Catholic convert, Walker Percy, the author of *Lancelot* (1977), is not afraid to admit the existence of the Seven Deadly Sins. The work takes the form of a long confession of greed, lechery, anger, sloth, envy, gluttony, and pride offered by Lancelot Lamar to the priest/psychiatrist Harry Percival. Revelling in his own iniquities, Lamar ironically castigates the contemporary Waste Land. The central location is a restored antebellum mansion, Belle Isle, where Lamar, his wife Margot, his daughters, and a motley crew of movie people gather. In this perverted Otherworld castle offering food, drink, and love the chatelaine is Margot, a Guinevere/Morgan type with a fée's beauty, sexual insatiability, powers of transformation, and capacity to destroy knights-errant. According to Lancelot, she is responsible for his deterioration from football hero and idealistic liberal lawyer to self-pitying alcoholic.

In a present that lacks rules of honor his only recourse is to combat pernicious society by becoming a Knight of the Unholy Grail. Destroying the lustful woman—his wife—becomes the object of his quest, which he believes will initiate a new society whose members will not be afraid to act decisively. Like the medieval Guinevere, the adulterous wife is condemned to death by burning but not before Lamar in his guise of avenging hero has killed her lover. Ironically, while his acts of murder and arson cleanse the environment by removing a source of corruption, Lamar is ejected into the world with all his sins intact.

In another satiric view of contemporary manners and mores, the Canadian novelist Robertson Davies juxtaposes the idealized world of an Arthurian opera and the real world of academic Torontonians. *The Lyre of Orpheus* (1988) takes its title from the nineteenth-century Romantic, E.T.A. Hoffman, who wrote, "The lyre of Orpheus opens the door of the underworld." In the process of staging at the Stratford (Ontario) Festival an opera, "Arthur of Britain or the Magnificent Cuckold" (which had been composed as a doctoral dissertation), the participants reveal rampant lust, greed, anger, envy, and malice. The Canadian version of an élite society features academics at the University of Toronto and a prosperous businessman, Arthur Cornish, who presides over their Round Table deliberations and funds their "noble actes."

Each major character has an Arthurian prototype representing a "buried myth" of sufficient power to take over rather mundane lives. The beautiful graduate student, Maria Theotoky, married to Cornish, is both Guinevere (proud to be the wife of a noble character but a little bored) and Elaine (Galahad's mother). Depending on the point of view, she is a nice rich man's wife with scholarly hobbies or "one rough young broad." The opera's stage director, Geraint Powell, seduces and impregnates her after "disguising" himself as her husband by wearing Arthur's dragon-crested dressing gown. The child cannot convincingly be attributed to the husband since mumps has rendered him infertile. Like Malory's king, Arthur Cornish manages to sustain the cuckold role with patience, forgiveness, and love. Powell, however, is another debased Lancelot. His "overstated good looks" cannot conceal his sordid character. Ambitious, unscrupulous, drunken, he is described by a woman colleague as a "blathering, soapy Welsh goat." The opera's composer, a grubby graduate student called Hulda Schnakenburg, enacts the Elaine of Astolat role as her hopeless love for Geraint-Lancelot leads to attempted suicide.

Davies is at his best when satirizing academia. His sharp ear accurately catches the hectoring tones of the upwardly mobile woman professor, the American graduate student's woolly-minded jargon, and the dissertation committee's bitchiness and exhibitionism. Yet despite the dominance of the satiric mode, the author chooses a fairy-tale ending. The opera performance (its schema derived from J. Comyns Carr's *King Arthur*)[12] is a success. Arthur and Maria are accepted as genuine patrons of the arts, Schnak is "on her way" to becoming an established composer, and Powell produces a terrific "Orfeo" in Milan. Music has effected the sublimation of the base passion. As the Dodo said, "*Everybody* has won and *all* must have prizes."

A bright star of Arthurian fiction is Donald Barthelme whose *The King* (1990) wittily combines traditional story and modern allusion. The author relies on the readers' knowledge of Malory to identify characters and connect episodic scenes. Structurally the work resembles a radio script. Events and characters are created through such dramatic devices as terse stage directions, rapid dialogue generally involving only two people, and the stichomythic comments of a parodic Greek chorus. Lord Haw Haw's broadcasts from Germany detail news of British defeats and gossip about the royals:

> The invincible forces of the Reich are advancing on all fronts. Dunkirk has been completely secured. The slaughter is very great. . . . The false and miscreant king, Arthur, languishes meanwhile at Dover, according to my spies. Conspicuously alone. . . . And where is Launcelot? Where Guinevere is. . . . The war forgot. Helm and mail laid aside, hanging from the bedpost. . . . But do the ratepayers want a queen who spends all her time drinking sloe gin while dallying with one of their king's chief advisers? I think not.

Technically, Barthelme seems to have been influenced by the poet and artist David Jones. Using temporal conflation, both posit the persistence of medieval characters through linear time to the present. The result is to validate the omnipresence of legend in the modern world. Barthelme's time frame runs from the defeat at Dunkirk in 1940 to the defeat at Tobruk. Arthur knows that his tragic ending is predestined: "It will find me, never fear. No particular hurry, I suppose!" The characters retain medieval dress, weapons, activities, and chivalric speech patterns. Barry Moser's wood engravings sustain the medievalism by depicting soldiers in bascinets and plate armor and a demonically dancing Modred dressed in a scalloped houppelande as he prepares to join the Nazis. (Arthur had suggested getting rid of him by making him Governor-General of the Bahamas.)

A second device that Barthelme and Jones share is a reliance on the "actualness" of individual objects. Julian Cowley explains:

> The composition of Barthelme's stories is undisguisedly an assemblage in print of words and, on occasion, pictorial images, forming an addition to the world of things. It does not constitute a frame through which to view the processes of living, nor does it furnish a tool for the analytic detection of meaning, but the perceptibility of its mode of construction stimulates an illuminating reflexivity and may assist in our experience of the specific.[13]

Jones puts it more simply: "I have this feeling of wanting to include 'everything,' . . . the entirety or totality in a little place or space." He believed that the known provided the best "flight deck" from which to launch the imagination.[14]

Barthelme's interweaving of temporal referents produces bizarre conjunctions. A girl selling Girl Guide cookies interrupts Launcelot's joust with Sir Colgrevaunce; Launcelot tries to beat the price down from five shillings to four because "I've never had a box of Girl Guide cookies that was worth more than two shillings." Meeting a *Times* reporter in the Lamb and Flag pub to provide information for his obit, Launcelot parks his bloody mace in the men's room.

The opening chorus indicates the hero's ambiguity; he is a confused "flower of chivalry":

> "See there! It's Launcelot!"
> "Riding, riding."
> "How swiftly he goes!"
> "As if enchafed by a fiend!"
> "The splendid muscles of his horse move rhythmically under the
>   drenchèd skin of same!"
> "By Jesu, he is in a vast hurry!"

"But now he pulls up the horse and sits for a moment lost in
thought!"
"Now he wags his great head in daffish fashion!"
"He reins the horse about and puts the golden spurs to her!"
"But that is the direction from which he lately came with such
excess of speed!"

He is not unaware of his ineffectuality. As he complains to Guinevere in the
très gai Café Balalaika, "I spend my whole life *hacking* at things—Is this the
best way to exist in the world?" Inappropriate responses undermine his philosophy of "shouldness," as when a woman shoots him in the ass and when
the king is tolerant of his wife's adultery. His faith is restored only by Arthur's
refusal to manufacture the atomic bomb on the grounds that "this false Grail
is not a knightly weapon."

The most vividly conceived character is Guinevere, a hedonist who
eats buttered apples, bathes with Crabtrees' Strawberry Bath Bears, and has
"no more religion than a cat." Sharply intelligent, her psychological and strategic insights are generally ignored, condemning her to play the symbolic
roles created by the press. Loneliness incites her to fill her bed casually with
passing knights-errant, since her husband and lover are engaged in other
roles: "The one is off God knows where running the war, and the other pops
in between dragons, as it were. It's little consolation that they are both so
enormously noble and worshipful, when one's bed is empty night after night"
(p. 88).

In no previous century has the perception of Lancelot undergone such
startling revision as our own time provides. The model of fidelity, valor, and
compassion, a hero concerned with secular honor and spiritual fulfillment
is a misfit in a postmodern world rife with materialism and moral irrespon-
sibility. As Barthelme's Clarice remarks, in a nuclear world "all you good
and worshipful knights are out of work." Guinevere's representation has
remained more consistent. Drawn from such medieval works as "Sir
Launfal" and the lais, her promiscuity is a recurring trait. Malory endows
her with sufficient independence, determination, and spirit to give her legitimacy as a modern woman. Barthelme perceives her inherent possibilities
when he makes his queen affirm, "The next myth I create will be a hellacious
one, of that you may be sure. Something so wicked I can't even imagine it
now."

As an exhibition held at London's Barbican Art Gallery in 1989 asserted, the British Romantic tradition that we have been investigating in
modern Arthurian literature was also manifested in the visual arts.[15] Review-

ing "The Last Romantics" in the *Observer* newspaper, William Feaver found that "the cult of Beauty as a form of defence against reality meant cultivated sham." But the catalogue's editor, John Christian, defends the creation of autonomous visual worlds, rooted though they may be in Celticism, Symbolism, Pre-Raphaelitism, and so on. The artist who engages in visual narrative relies on the viewer's recognition of story to help decode significances. The range of images is narrow and the style idealizing. (Unlike what happened in literature, the material has seldom inspired artists to respond satirically.) Armor, arms, and heraldic devices are infallible indicators of period, rank, and role as are a woman's period dresses, crown, castle milieu, and floral attributes. If the figure is to be associated with a specific event, additional description is required, both visual (e.g., a recognizable setting and situation) and verbal (e.g., a title, quotation, or expository epigraph). The more specific the compositional details are, the more limiting in terms of time, space, and point of view.

At the end of the Victorian period the impact on Pre-Raphaelite art of French Symbolist sculpture produced an ideal style known as the New Sculpture. Reacting against "truth to nature," artists required images that could function as symbols of ideas and emotions. A desire to illustrate woman's powerful and mysterious beauty led them to choose literary heroines whose names evoked legendary or allegorical associations. Tennyson's *Idylls of the King* inspired William Ernest Reynolds-Stephens to create three small statues (approximately three feet high) that in Susan Beattie's words demonstrated a "power to convey an almost oppressive sense of stillness, isolation and silence."[16] A story in "The Last Tournament" suggested the subjects of "Sir Lancelot and the Nestling" (1899) and "Guinevere and the Nestling" (1900).[17] Lancelot has rescued from an eagle's nest a baby, naked except for a ruby necklace. This child

> Arthur pitying took,
> Then gave it to his Queen to rear: The Queen
> But coldly acquiescing, in her white arms
> Received, and after loved it tenderly,
> And named it Nestling; so forgot herself
> A moment, and her cares. (ll. 21–26)

The sculptures, following a mode that indicates how the Arts and Crafts Movement had broken down the strict division between the fine and decorative arts, combine bronze, ivory, mother of pearl, and enamel. Lancelot is dressed in flamboyant plate armor embossed with stylized roses (a symbol of love). His right arm encircles his sword, the jeweled pommel of which is surmounted by a garlanded God of Love. His left arm cradles the ivory baby. Forming the pedestal are the "roots like some black coil of carven snakes" and the oak stump with four perching eagles. Lancelot's face expresses enormous compassion tinged with regret.

The queen's long-sleeved dress and mantle are embossed with Beardsleyesque sprays of leaves and blossoming roses and, below the mother-of-pearl buckle, a jousting knight. Tenderly she holds the clothed baby upright against her shoulder, with the child's head touching her face and the little hand resting trustingly on her collar. Guinevere's closed eyes, smiling mouth, and tranquil expression suggest the brief happiness the Nestling provided.

The bronze and ivory statue "Guinevere's Redeeming" (1905, Castle Museum, Nottingham)[18] is linked more closely to literature because Reynolds-Stephens adds to the image of Guinevere in a nun's habit four labeled bas reliefs illustrating her various roles. On the back of the base, "AS QUEEN" shows her enthroned; "AS LOVER" presents her in Lancelot's embrace. The reliefs at the front illustrate her repentance "BY GIVING DOLE" to a half-naked beggar and "BY PRAYER" as she kneels at a priedieu. The major figure has clasped hands, a finely carved ivory face with downcast eyes, and a contemplative expression. The relevant lines from Tennyson are: "And so wear out in almsdeed and in prayer / The sombre close of that voluptuous day, / Which wrought the ruin of my lord the king" ("Guinevere," ll. 681–83).

Despite the influence of the French Impressionists and Post-Impressionists, the devastating physical and psychological impact of the Great War, and the view of such influential critics as Roger Fry that literary painters were "back numbers," late Romantic painters continued to choose *femme fatales*. A characteristic subject comes from Malory's Book VI, chapter 3, which Caxton entitled "How IIII quenes fonde Launcelot slepyng, and how by enchauntement he was taken and ledde into a castel." To William Frank Calderon, an English artist who founded the School of Animal Painting in 1894, it offered not only four beguiling fées but also their white mules, the escorts' destriers, and the hero's dark war-horse grazing in the foreground. The oil-on-canvas picture is a literal representation of text. Wrapped in his ermine-lined mantle of plum velvet, the dark-haired knight reclines under the apple tree's contorted branches. Calderon differentiates the fées beneath their green canopy by varying the colors of the fifteenth-century gowns. The work's exhibition at the Royal Academy in 1908 led the *Athenaeum*'s critic to comment that "the huddled group of ladies on white donkeys is pretty and full of childish romance."[19]

In 1909 Jessie M. King's watercolor "How Four Queens found Sir Lancelot" was important as the pattern for an Elise Prioleau needlework picture in blues and greens, the Aesthetes' favorite colors. Colin White describes the effect: "The finished work was astonishing in its subtlety and realism. The minute stitches were cleverly angled across the picture like brush strokes, so that the light reflected in different ways on the polished sheen of the silk and gave the scene a three-dimensional appearance."[20]

As late as 1954, Frank Cadogan Cowper exhibited his watercolor, a close-up composition that shows the ladies and knight on uneven ground against a trunk too massive to be mistaken for an apple tree. The queens' heavy make-up, spiky crowns, and décolleté gowns make no attempt at historical consistency. As they look with malign calculation at the supine knight whom they plan to force into infidelity, they have the quality of movie stars. Lancelot stretches out in monumental pose, though his faithful hound crouches at his head, not his feet. The composition somewhat resembles David Jones's watercolor on the same subject, to be discussed further on.

From the Edwardian period onward recurrent outbreaks of nostalgia for a pre-industrial, orderly society, combined with a taste for fantastic escapism, ensured that chivalric art would find a place in both private and public locations. In the United States by the early part of this century the Arts and Crafts Movement was flourishing in protest against the ever-increasing production of machine-made consumer goods. An oak chest (ca. 1900, Museum of Art, Rhode Island School of Design) designed by Sidney Burleigh, constructed by Potter and Company, Providence, Rhode Island, and carved by Julia Lippitt Mauran, exemplifies the combination of American craftsmanship and English literary sources. The chest, measuring 55.8 × 56 × 125.6 cm, has eight panels containing carved profiles and related signs, finished with green, gold, red, and cream paint. On the front, Guinevere and Arthur face each other on either side of the royal dragon. The end panel adjacent to the queen bears Lancelot's oak-encircled name, dragon coat-of-arms, and helmet. A more recent example of decorative art for the home is a set of six Royal Worcester plates that the International Arthurian Society commissioned the Yorkshire artist James Marsh to design in 1978. Though he may have been better known for the erotic women figures that he contributed to *Penthouse* and *Men Only* magazines, he successfully achieves the refinement of a fifteenth-century miniature when he shows the jousting hero on his white horse defeating the nefarious Meleagant. Watching from the battlements is the queen, a blonde-haired figure in a carmine dress that matches her lover's accoutrements.

Public buildings in the Neo-Gothic style provided another milieu in which Lancelot and Guinevere might appropriately appear. When Princeton University's new chapel was constructed in 1928, the supervising architect commissioned Charles Connick to design the stained glass. Thirteenth-century French glass was Connick's model because he believed that the workers had imparted to it "a gracious spirit of devotion."[21] To effect "glowing and colorful inspiration," the windows in the Milbank Choir were to depict narratives of man's search for God. The Malory window[22] has three tiers representing, in turn, the biography of Arthur, the adventures of secular chivalry, and the Quest of The Holy Grail. Launcelot's rescue of Guinevere exemplifies Prowess. The knight also appears wearing Elaine's ruby-red sleeve. Uniting the individual lights is a thematic inscription drawn from the medieval author's original definition of true love: "as May month flowereth and flourisheth let every man of worship flourish his heart in this world, first unto God and next unto the joy of them that he promised his faith unto."

Further evidence that chivalry as an ideal was not discredited in the postwar period is found in Tintagel's consciously moral building, King Arthur's Hall of Chivalry (1933) (Whitaker, 313–16). The concept of custard millionaire Frederick T. Glassock, every part symbolized virtues associated with Arthur. Of particular interest are Veronica Whall's splendid windows. Her father, Christopher Whall, was a pioneer of the Arts and Crafts Movement in stained glass. Deprived by the army of his male assistants, he allowed his daughter to participate in the studio. The triple windows at each end of the Hall reveal her skill in managing design so that light may pour through color—"a stupendous, every-changing force."[23] On the darker, secular wall, the right hand depicts the departure of the Grail knights; Launcelot's azure shield and the queen's blue gown denote fidelity. At the opposite end where the windows create an apocalyptic effect with their "gold pink" glass, the final light shows Arthur (in scarlet, magenta, and gold) knighting Lancelot, but Guinevere turns aside her head in a gesture foreshadowing her eventual rejection of secular love.

The most accessible form of Arthurian art is book illustration. Thanks to William Morris's concept of the book as an art object,[24] as well as to technological improvements in color printing, well-known artists were induced to illustrate both juvenile adaptations of Arthurian story and limited editions of particular texts. In America, no one more significantly shaped the chivalric imaginations of young readers than Howard Pyle. His style was a curious blend of realism and romance, the result of such diverse influences as his

Quaker upbringing in the Brandywine River valley and the literary pictorialism of the English Pre-Raphaelites. The use of the heavy black wood-cut line he learned from Albrecht Dürer, while Aubrey Beardsley inspired the eclectic headpieces and endpieces. In the third of his four Arthurian compilations, *The Story of Sir Launcelot and His Companions* (1907), the "very noble and worthy knight" is married to Elaine. Guinevere is diminished by virtual exclusion. She is not mentioned in the Foreword and appears—distantly—in only one of the thirty full-page illustrations. Pyle's Launcelot is a swarthy, bearded knight wearing impractically ornate armor. The height of his helm is increased by its crest—a busty woman whose draped headdress is two yards long. By depicting Launcelot riding in a cart, holding discourse with "Merry Minstrels," slaying a dragon, entrusting his shield to Elaine, and rescuing King Arthur, the author-artist affirms the knight's role as society's protector. The contorted sentence structure and the woodcut style produce an archaic effect, distancing the romance world from the world of experience.

Pyle's star pupil, N.C. Wyeth, provided watercolor illustrations for the 1920 edition of Sidney Lanier's *The Boy's King Arthur*. Devoted to historical authenticity, Wyeth would have preferred to bring to his romance illustration "knowledge substantiated by facts as far as possible—and above all else after a personal investigation of the country."[25] He compromised by setting romance characters in American landscapes. Color enables Wyeth to convey a greater sense of credibility and more varied moods than Pyle's black and white could encompass. His destriers are images of power that strain like farm horses and stir up the dust as Launcelot unseats Mador. Other realistic details drawn from his own terrain are brown meadow grasses beside the creek where Launcelot challenges Tarquin; the shadow-dappled boulders, sycamore trunks, and little waterfall of the mad knight's forest refuge; and the golden light of an autumn sunset that tinges the escaping lovers, their grey horse and flowery meadow embroidered with Queen Anne's lace and other wildflowers. A letter to his mother, December 5, 1908, suggests that Wyeth might have found Sir Thomas Malory temperamentally congenial: ". . . *anything* that I appreciate keenly and profoundly is always sad to the point of being tragic."[26]

Limited editions of Malory's complete text[27] provided illustrators with a wider range of characters and situations than the juveniles could accommodate. William Russell Flint painted forty-eight color illustrations for the four-volume deluxe Malory published by Philip Lee Warner for the Medici Society in 1910–11. Since Flint considered a beautiful woman to be one of the marvels of nature and gloated about his ability to get models with

"Artemisian figures," he largely ignored the adventures of knight-errantry in order to present ladies in provocative poses. Launcelot is relegated to the periphery both by the drabness of his costumes and by his place in the pictorial composition. The sequence of illustrations conveys the impression of a hero subjugated by powerful women, not only Guinevere but the aggressive fées, who make him shrink against the dungeon wall; the distressed damsel who supervises Tarquin's decapitation; a tempting Elaine stepping naked from the boiling bath (Launcelot covers his eyes); the voluptuous Dame Brisen; and the athletic huntress.

A contrast to the enervated hero is the passionate Guinevere, with the luxuriant auburn hair of the Pre-Raphaelite beauties. She swoons theatrically when Arthur departs on his Roman Wars, watches the Grail Knights' departure with a drooping emotion that lays bare her back and shoulders, writhes at the stake in revealing white satin, and lies stretched on her bier like a bride on her marriage bed. Though Flint's drawing is faulty and his ability to convey subtle characterization is limited, we are beguiled by sea-green gowns and colorful banners, snow white swans, and golden tapers into overlooking the disconcerting details; for example, as Launcelot stands beside his dead lover, he appears to be shrinking from a foul smell.

By the early 1900s, women were competing with men in decorating fine books.[28] Jessie M. King not only helped create the Glasgow Style especially associated with Charles Rennie Mackintosh, but she also devised highly individualistic linear designs of such delicacy and evocative power that she became the best Scottish illustrator of this century. When John Lane reissued William Morris's *The Defence of Guenevere and Other Poems* in 1904, King contributed the cover design, page decorations and twenty-four full-page illustrations. Her debt to Aubrey Beardsley is evident in the hand-lettered titles, the Art Nouveau line, and a repertoire of motifs . . . elongated women in japonesque gowns, dripping tapers, sardonic angels, rococo furniture, poppies, brambles, roses. King dissolved the Beardsley whiplash line into dots, the flowers into showers of petals while adding crucifixes orbed with stars and high stone walls that encourage a two-dimensional perception. The artificiality of pure decoration makes the trees, shrubs, flowers, and clouds images in a dream world unpolluted by Beardsley's cynicism.

King's Guinevere lacks the blatant sensuality and demonic energy by which some other artists have characterized her. Enclosed within a small room or walled garden, the melancholy queen offers her beauty as proof of innocence in accordance with Morris's lines in the title poem: "say no rash word / Against me, being so beautiful . . . will you dare / When you have looked a little on my brow, / To say this thing is vile?" (ll. 223–38).

The artist prefers empty white space to a massive use of black, perhaps because the former evokes the magical and mystical, enabling her to merge waking, imagining, and dreaming, as in "A Great God's Angel Standing." In the text, the queen asks her accuser, Gauwaine, to imagine that on his deathbed he must choose between two cloths, one red, one blue (representing heaven and hell). In the illustration, the white-gowned angel carrying the cloths on decorated wands illuminates the bedroom with beams that disintegrate into dots and stars. Only the ebony bedpost carved with roses and beaded interlace is substantial. Perhaps because King could not draw convincing armor, Launcelot is neglected, but he does appear in the illustration for "King Arthur's Tomb," holding a rose. Encroaching on his space are the blackness of the queen's billowing habit, headband, flower, as well as thorny branches and streaming blackbirds. One imagines that King must have enjoyed this commission, since Morris's idea of a decorated book closely resembled her own: "A page of type, beautifully set, a little ornament beautifully surrounded by type, a chapter heading, symbolic or treating of the matter in the chapter. . . is to me what book decoration means" (White, 124).

Although Romantic attitudes underlie virtually all modern art based on the Arthurian material, two more recent artists have imposed highly subjective readings to produce original interpretations. In 1983 Shelah Horvitz submitted to the *Journal of Pre-Raphaelite Studies* III/2 her drawing "I am Half-Sick of Shadows," together with an article explaining her feminist response to Tennyson's "Lady of Shalott." With her knees drawn up to protect her virginity, the naked lady sits in her prison-like tower room. The enormous mirror reflects Guinevere, with Jane Burden's face—"a thoughtless coquette"—and a naked, muscular Lancelot who resembles Barthelme's character in being a doer not a thinker. Between them is King Arthur, "the largest face in the picture because he is the greatest mind." Horvitz comments, "Had I written the story, the Lady would not have died. Indeed, she would have braved the curse, journeyed down river to find Lancelot, become his love, and resumed weaving in Camelot, where she could experience life and thereby become a better and deeper artist" (68).

The most important Arthurian artist of this century is the poet-painter David Jones. The London-born son of a Welsh father, he constructed a complex heritage of mythic and historical materials that he used in his literature and art. As well, service with the Royal Welsh Fusiliers in the Great War and his conversion to Catholicism dominated his life and art. As a link between Welsh and English tradition and as a transmitter of "recessions from the past," Malory's *Morte Darthur* was central to his image-making.[29] The subjects that it suggested permitted the "great complexity & inter-weaving, a sort of meandering (but by no means aimless meandering), strongly rhythmic but flexible, in which every peripheral part is just as essential as the more central parts, (that) comes in to our way of getting the 'wholeness' " (Davies, 89).[30] Two watercolors completed after the outbreak of World War II—"Guenever" (Tate Gallery, London, 1940) and "The Four Queens" (Tate Gallery, London, 1941)—he thought "successful and authentic." Overlays of transparent color, particularly blues, greens, and browns, effect a radiance consistent with the magical, mystical subject matter.

"Guenever" is an excellent example of modern art that functions in a medieval way through images that are both artifacts and symbols. In its literal-literary mode it illustrates a scene from the "Knight of the Cart" adventure (*Morte Darthur*, XIX, 6). Launcelot arrives at Meleagant's castle to rescue the kidnapped Guenever and her unarmed retinue. After finding a ladder and climbing to the bedroom window, the hero converses with the lady, telling her that he wishes to come in:

> "wolde ye so, madame," seyde sir Launcelot, "wyth youre harte
>   that I were with you?"
> "Ye, truly," seyde the quene.
> "Than shall I prove my myght," seyde sir Launcelot, "for youre love."

He then gains admittance by breaking the iron bars with his bare hands.

In the painting's foreground are the wounded knights. They represent a long line of war's victims: an effigy-like mailed Crusader with legs crossed to indicate death in battle; a Tommy with bayonet fixed to his rifle; an ancient Briton in his barrow. Far removed in time are the cave-dwellers huddling under the skin of the cave-bear. There are modern victims, too: Londonders taking shelter in underground stations to escape the blitz. Jones believes that his own experience of war linked him with military men of the past and with all victims who endured adversity with patience, courage, and faith. Naked except for his shield and knee cops, Launcelot hangs on the ladder. His position is that of the Christ on the crucifix above the Queen's head—hands open to display the stigmata, legs crossed, eyes closed, head dropping forward, side pierced. This is both Christ the Bridegroom of the exegetical "Song of Songs" and Christ the Redeemer.

At the center of the picture plane the naked queen reclines voluptuously, Launcelot's lover and Christ's Bride, the Church. Marian images—the crown and seven stars on the bed's headboard, roses without thorns, burning candles—confirm the allegorical identity. The sexual act about to take place symbolizes the sacrament of the mass for which the recessed altar is prepared. Other life-giving images that crowd into the plane, such as an iron soup pot hanging over the fire and the dish and gnawed bone of a sleeping dog, provide "actualness" and reinforce allegory. "Guenever" explicates the poet's conviction that sex is spiritual as well as physical. "Eros and Agape must kiss each other," he wrote to his friend Harman Grisewood.

"The Four Queens Find Launcelot Sleeping" is also both literal and anagogic, illustrating as well Jones's view that a particular landscape accumulates associations through the centuries. As in Cowper's painting, the women, medieval queens and otherworldly fées, crowd close to the knight beneath the apple tree. The source of their costumes may have been a London *Times*'s account of the dresses worn by women presented at court in 1935—"a gown of crystal & silver, hand embroidered entirely of a heavy white net over close-fitting foundation of silver tissue with a train of silver widely-bordered with embroidery of crystal diamond . . . a draped gown of lavender . . . pearl necklace, pearl earrings, pearl & diamond tiara."[31] The jeweled garter on Morgan's extended leg suggests music hall and nightclub associations. The white mules stand to the left, under the canopy that had shaded the equestriennes.

Launcelot occupies the literal time of the text and the allegorical time of the dream world when he thinks of Guinevere, symbolized by the swan. The stigma visible in the palm of the right hand and the spear wound gashing the left side identify him anagogically as Christ the Knight, a figure that Jones discovered in William Langland's fourteenth-century allegory, *Piers Plowman*. Jones's gift for attaching "confluent ideas" to a single image applies to the tree, too, for it is a literal tree providing shade, an Otherworld connection that brings a sleeper into contact with Celtic magic, and Langland's Tree of Charity, still present in the modern world, as the wire netting suggests.

The hero's effigy-like pose and fourteenth-century armor associate him with the Middle Ages, but such details as a modern German helmet and an identification disc confirm the persistence through time of the soldier/Savior. In the background, dolmens, an Iron Age chalkdown horse, a Romanesque chapel, and a graveyard reiterate the sleep of death/eternal life motif. Though belonging to different periods, all are aspects of British culture unified by the landscape that, as the contours of the hills, the chapel, and the Welsh ponies confirm, really exists in the Black Mountains area on the Welsh border.

One of Jones's last watercolors was the 1959 "Gwener." Using again the figure of a long-haired woman reclining naked on a bed, he now identifies her as Venus, whom he characterized as the goddess of fidelity. A letter to Valerie Wynne-Williams explicated the iconography that combined Greek and Roman mythology, Roman architecture, medieval weapons, Welsh costumes, and English flowers.[32]

Writing to Grisewood (Hague, 93), Jones felicitously defines lovers, along with saints, as "unifying makers." The familiarity of the Lancelot-Guinevere story with its fated lovers and cluster of associates—Arthur, the two Elaines, the fées, Gawain, Modred—has imposed on the pair an iconic status from which can resonate a wide spectrum of attitudes. Performing roles that range from images of futility to eucharistic symbols of salvation, these lovers have proved their value as "unifying makers."

NOTES

1. Alfred W. Pollard, *The Romance of King Arthur and His Knights of the Round Table*, abridged from Malory's *Morte Darthur*, ill. Arthur Rackham (London: Macmillan, 1971).

2. Winfield Townley Scott, "To See Robinson," *New Mexico Quarterly* 26 (Summer 1956), 160, cited by Laurence Perrine, "Contemporary Reference of Robinson's Arthurian Poems," *Twentieth Century Literature* 8 (1962–63), 74.

3. Perrine, 74. The suggestion that Arthur represented the British Empire, Gawaine the United States, and Lancelot Germany is not substantiated by the text.

4. Yvor Winters in *Edwin Arlington Robinson* (Norfolk, Conn.: New Directions, 1946), 61, describes *Lancelot* as "one of the most powerfully constructed long poems in English."

5. Chester Keith, *Queen's Knight: A Prose Epic* (London: Allen Unwin, 1920), 4.

6. White's Arthurian books are *The Sword in the Stone* (New York: Putnam, 1939); *The Witch in the Wood* (New York: Putnam, 1939); *The Ill-Made Knight* (New York: Putnam, 1940); *The Once and Future King*, comprising *The Sword in the Stone*, *The Queen of Air and Darkness*, *The Ill-Made Knight*, and *The Candle in the Wind* (New York: Putnam, 1958); and *The Book of Merlyn* (Austin: University of Texas Press, 1977).

7. David Garnett, ed., *The White/Garnett Letters* (New York: Viking, 1968), 86.

8. Sylvia Townsend Warner, *T.H. White: A Biography* (London: Jonathan Cape/Chatto and Windus, 1967), 148–50. Warner (93) quotes John Moore's opinion that White was "a self-tormented person and I imagine he saw himself very much as Lancelot in *The Ill-Made Knight*."

9. Françoise Gallix, ed., *T.H. White, Letters to a Friend: The Correspondence between T.H. White and L.J. Potts* (Gloucester: Sutton, 1984), 112. See also White's discussion of Elaine on 114 and his recognition that Malory's doubling of the character is more convincing psychologically.

10. Peter Vansittart in *Lancelot: A Novel* (London: Owen, 1978) indicates that his critical sources included works by R.G. Collingwood, F.M. Stenton, R.W. Stenton, R.W. Chambers, Kenneth Jackson, J.N.L. Myers, E.K. Chambers, C. and J. Hawkes, and John Morris. To these might be added Leslie Alcock, *Arthur's Britain* (London: Allen Lane, 1971).

11. For specific authors and titles see Raymond H. Thompson, *The Return from Avalon: A Study of the Arthurian Legend in Modern Fiction* (Westport, Conn.: Greenwood, 1985), 33–75.

12. Carr's *King Arthur* was produced in London's Lyceum Theatre in January, 1895, with Henry Irving as the king, Forbes Robertson as Launcelot, and Ellen Terry as Guenevere. Sir Arthur Sullivan provided music and Edward Burne-Jones the costumes and sets.

13. Julian Cowley, " 'Weeping map intense activity din': Reading Donald Barthelme," *University of Toronto Quarterly* 60/2 (1990/91), 292.

14. Aneirin Talfan Davies, ed., *David Jones: Letters to a Friend* (Swansea: Davies, 1980), 80–81.

15. John Christian, ed., *The Last Romantics: The Romantic Tradition in British Art, Burne-Jones to Stanley Spencer* (London: Lund Humphries in Association with Barbican Art Gallery, 1989).

16. Susan Beattie, *The New Sculpture* (New Haven: Yale University Press, 1983), 161.

17. They are reproduced and described in Benedict Read and Joanna Barnes, eds., *Pre-Raphaelite Sculpture: Nature and Imagination in British Sculpture 1848–1914* (London: The Henry Moore Foundation in Association with Lund Humphries, 1991), 132–34.

18. A smaller version in silver, bronze, and shell dated 1905 is in the Museum and Art Gallery, Warrington. The Harris Museum, Preston, has a bronze copy. For a reproduction of the Nottingham work, see Muriel Whitaker, *The Legends of King Arthur in Art* (Cambridge: Brewer, 1990), 234.

19. The work was offered for sale at Christie's auction of Fine Victorian Painting in London, October 25, 1991, with an estimated value of £15,000–£20,000.

20. Colin White, *The Enchanted World of Jessie M. King* (Edinburgh: Canongate, 1989), 81. The needlework panel is reproduced on 82 and a pen, ink, and bodycolor-on-vellum version belonging to the Strathclyde Department of Education on 115. Unusually, Lancelot has auburn hair.

21. Connick explained his aesthetic theories in *Adventures in Light and Color* (New York: Random House, 1937).

22. For a detailed discussion see Richard Stillwell, *The Chapel of Princeton University* (Princeton: Princeton University Press, 1971), 59–75. On Arthurian designs for Princeton's Proctor Hall by Connick and the English artist Florence Camm, see Whitaker, *The Legends of King Arthur in Art*, 298–300.

23. Veronica Whall, "Glass, Lead, and Light," *Stained Glass* 20/1 (Spring/Summer, 1935), 10–14.

24. William S. Peterson, ed., *The Ideal Book, Essays and Lectures on the Arts of the Book by William Morris* (Berkeley: University of California Press, 1982).

25. The letter of January 31, 1921, to his father. See Betsy James Wyeth, ed., *The Wyeths: The Letters of N.C. Wyeth 1901–1945* (Boston: Gambit, 1971).

26. Other well-illustrated juvenile editions of Malory adaptations include Gladys Davidson, *Lancelot and Guenevere*, ill. Innes Fripp (London: Thomas Nelson, 1913); Henry Gilbert, *King Arthur's Knights*, ill. Walter Crane (London: Bracken, 1985 [1911]); Barbara Leonie Picard, *Stories of King Arthur and His Knights*, ill. Roy Morgan (London: Oxford University Press, 1955); Alfred W. Pollard, *The Romance of King Arthur and His Knights of the Round Table*, ill. Arthur Rackham (London: Macmillan, 1979 [1917]); James Riordan, *Tales of King Arthur*, ill. Victor Ambrus (London: Hamlyn, 1982); Emma Gelders Sterne and Barbara Lindsay, *King Arthur and the Knights of the Round Table*, ill. Gustaf Tenggren (New York: Golden Press, 1962).

27. In this century these have included the Ashendene Press Malory with woodcuts by Charles and Margaret Gere (1913), the Golden Cockerel Press Malory with wood engravings by Robert Gibbings (1936), and the Folio Society of London's *Sir Thomas Malory's Chronicles of King Arthur* (1982) with Edward Bawden's linocuts. Probably the most influential illustrated Malory was the Dent Malory of 1892 with Aubrey Beardsley's 585 chapter headings, borders, initials, ornaments, and full- or double-page illustrations. On illustrated editions, see Whitaker, 263–73, 275–82.

28. Cf. Eleanor Fortescue-Brickdale, who provided twenty-one color plates for Tennyson's *The Idylls of the King* (London: Hodder and Stoughton, 1911) reproduced from the twenty-eight watercolor originals exhibited at London's Leicester Galleries, October, 1911; Phoebe Traquair, who executed an illuminated manuscript on vellum

of William Morris's *Defence of Guenevere*; Florence Harrison, who illustrated William Morris's *Early Poems* (1914) and Tennyson's *Guinevere and Other Poems* (1912). See Jan Marsh and Pamela Gerrish Nunn, *Women Artists and the Pre-Raphaelite Movement* (London: Virago, 1989).

29. See David Jones, *Epoch and Artist* (London: Faber, 1959), 202–59; René Hague, ed., *Dai Greatcoat: A Self-Portrait of David Jones in his Letters* (London: Faber, 1980).

30. Jones explicated many of his aesthetic theories in *David Jones: Letters to a Friend*, ed. Aneirin Talfan Davies (Swansea: Trishkele Books, 1980).

31. Jones paraphrased the report in letters to friends, which Thomas Dilworth quotes in *The Shape of Meaning in the Poetry of David Jones* (Toronto: University of Toronto Press, 1988), 229.

32. Whitaker, 317–25, discusses ten Arthurian art works by Jones. Many are reproduced in *David Jones: Paintings, Drawings, Inscriptions, Prints*, catalogue of an exhibition held at London's South Bank Centre, 1989 (London: Publications Office, South Bank Centre, 1989).

8 ARTHURIAN MYTH DEVALUED IN WALKER PERCY'S *LANCELOT*

John Bugge

Walker Percy's one-word title, *Lancelot,* may seem a simple, bold stroke announcing a straightforward use of Arthurian myth; but those who persevere through his narrator's shocking and vertiginous account of adultery and murderous revenge learn otherwise. The title is ironic, and so is Percy's use of the material throughout. He employs the Arthuriad only to devalue it against standards established in his own existential philosophy of cognition.

In a way, the narrative is rather too vehemently Arthurian, a pretty good hint that Percy has something ingenious planned. Made aware of the novel's Arthurian pretensions even before we turn to the first page, we must endure Lance the narrator's ostentatious lecturing of his interlocutor, Harry Percival, on the significance of their names, plus much else that is supererogatory.[1] Yet part of the appeal of the mythographic method here is that its effects are hidden and submerged, not, as we first suspect, all floating conspicuously on the surface of Lance's narrative consciousness. Not even this sometimes maniacally perceptive observer realizes how deeply his own thoughts and actions are anchored in the Arthurian myth—and this is basic to Percy's plan. For example, Lance is sure his father named him for the Arthurian hero. He prefers to believe that the middle name "Andrewes" was merely a dodge, "tacked on by him to give it Episcopal sanction." Here is a hint that it is Lance who dodges association with the morally stringent Anglican divine in favor of one with Lancelot du Lac (p. 116). Further, although Lance is relatively knowledgeable about his chosen namesake, his awareness of such mythic identification is far from complete: Percy inserts details designed to work as a kind of dramatic irony, permitting the reader to see deeper into Lance's "received" character than he himself can. His surname

"Lamar," for example, is "the pool" (*la mare*) in French, strikingly close to "du Lac," to be sure, yet with connotations of comparative shallowness and inconsequence. Again, Malory's Lancelot goes through a period of madness after his rejection by Guinevere until he is cured by being brought into the presence of "the holy vessel of the Sankgreall."[2] Correspondingly, although Lance is a patient in a mental hospital, his narrative convinces us he is sane, that he only gives himself "license to talk crazy" (p. 160). This means, of course, that he is fully responsible for the murders he has committed. As we shall see, Lance's blindness to these and other similar discrepancies between the myth and his own experience suggests that, though he may conceive of himself as Lancelot *redivivus*, we are everywhere encouraged to see his actions as a dangerous case of what Percy decries as "impersonation."

Only two other characters have names directly from the tradition: Harry Percival and Bob Merlin. Thus the three are marked as the only survivors from that grand age of heroic myth. Percy is fond of survivors among the ruins, out of place in their time and alienated from their surroundings (cf. *Love in the Ruins*); the world these three inhabit is far removed from the mythic Golden Age of Arthur. Lance's father once had shown him the nighttime sky and pointed "how far away Arcturus was," a dim star, thirty light-years away, too remote to serve as a beacon or cast its influence on the degenerate world of 1976 (pp. 56–57). Each of the survivors has lost his bearings in the modern age. Lance is a pseudo-heroic Lancelot adrift in a world that no longer provides opportunities for heroic action, whether in deeds or arms or love. Harry Percival, reflex of the tradition's pure and sensitive God-bitten ascetic, is someone whose Christian commitment has been more foppish aestheticism than substance. Bob Merlin, contemporary version of the tradition's mighty thaumaturge and seer, is reduced to the level of a filmmaker whose only magic is the disreputable and shallow illusionism of the silver screen. All are debased, failed versions of their mythic originals; their fundamentally illusory lives in the here and now illustrate Percy's favorite theme: lack of existential authenticity.

Perhaps this is clearest in Lance's relationship with Bob Merlin, who has cuckolded him and fathered the child Lance had thought his own. His discovery of his wife Margot's past adultery with Merlin propels the narrative. Merlin is now in residence at Belle Isle, Lance's estate, to oversee the making of a film; and Lance can express only well-founded contempt for the specious profundities of its scenario as mouthed by the people involved in making it. Still, he finds himself strangely drawn to Merlin. Lance feels that he, of all the eccentric movie people, is the most sensible and intelligent and, despite Merlin's offense against him, the one he finds most sympathetic (p. 47). Unwittingly, Lance draws closer to Merlin, imitating his ideas, his speech patterns, even—most telling of all—his moviemaking. Thus, an important key to Lance's predicament is his "impersonation" of Merlin; despite his boast that all the actions prompted by his catastrophic discovery of the adultery proceed from a newfound self-possession, we actually hear in the contours of his speech and thought that he has surrendered title over his own being to this modern magus. Lance's unconscious alliance with Merlin helps to certify Lance's failure to achieve authenticity.[3]

Such prominence given to the movies in the novel, together with Percy's own epistemological speculation on how "movie-going" prevents access to being, seems to invite us to draw a moral antithesis between the specious modern world of merely celluloid reality, represented by Merlin, and the ancient verities of a worthier age, as handed down through the Arthurian tradition.[4] Our own reverence for that tradition, perhaps in some way justified by the strong pull of Tennysonian pieties that have come to inform it, naturally inclines us to believe that Percy must think the Arthurian myth has value for those dwelling in alienation in the twentieth century. The author's neatest trick in *Lancelot*, however, is both to play on these sympathies for all they're worth and, at the same time, to vitiate our most fundamental assumption about the value of myth as a way of structuring reality.[5] If we prize Percy's finesse in scattering through the text so many subtle correspondences between Lance Lamar and his medieval counterpart—Lance resides along the "English Coast" of the Mississippi (Logres), separated from the "French" aristocracy of New Orleans by the river (the English Channel), in a landscape of chaste, incorrupt chapels (that of medieval romance) (pp. 14, 46, 116), and so on—we risk falling into the same trap as does the narrator, who records these parallels without consciously remarking on them. That is, we fall enthusiastically into Lance's mythographic way of seeing and thinking, only to be brought up short when we discover that Percy is using the Arthurian myth with neither sympathy nor admiration, but portraying it as a distinctly negative force and equating it with the movies as a source of illusion. Like the movies, myth, too, prevents access to true being.

The central issue of the novel, a constant theme in Percy's writings on epistemology, is the difficult one of ascertaining one's own identity.[6] Lance remarks of the movie people that they didn't seem to know who they were but were "like puffballs," blown "in and out of their roles" (p. 112). He complains about Margot, of *nouveau* oil-*riche* Texas origins, and her determination to take on the identity of the *chatelaine* of Belle Isle (p. 88). Of himself, Lance says that before the discovery he did not know who he was; it is a revelation forcibly brought home by the odd circumstance of his momentary failure to recognize his own reflection in a mirror (pp. 63–64). Purportedly, of course, he "finds himself" when he makes his discovery; but that sense of identity—the self he discovers, indeed, appropriates—comes mainly from the Arthurian myth. Just as the role Merlin's movie actor Troy Dana plays lends him an aura of authenticity while the klieg lights burn (pp. 146–48), Lance Lamar *is* someone only—and just as ironically—when he is impersonating Lancelot du Lac and attempting to find the meaning of his existence in the golden vagaries of the myth.

Lance's disposition to approach reality through the filter of the Arthurian myth is as feckless as Merlin's own obsession with a mystique of blood and roses all too obviously that of Ernest Hemingway's tight-lipped macho heroes (for example, pp. 201–205). Neither character takes reality straight. In Lance's case, his possession by the Arthurian myth of a heroic past prevents him from seeing the reality of his own existence in the present.[7] Here, Percy's own comments about true seeing are as relevant to Lance as to Merlin. In writing about a sightseer's first view of the Grand Canyon, Percy describes how such a person in fact fails to see the canyon as it is, to make noetic contact with its reality, because his act of knowing is inhibited by a pre-formed "symbolic complex" already present in his mind (through postcards, travel folders, and so on). This intervenes and prevents objective reality from being known on its own terms. The situation demonstrates what Percy, following Whitehead, would call the fallacy of misplaced concreteness: we mistakenly regard the symbol as more real than the actual concrete reality it signifies.[8] The Arthurian myth fits the definition of just such a pre-formed symbolic complex.

It is important to see that the entire myth takes possession of Lance—not just one character in the tradition. Lance cannot rest content being only Lancelot du Lac. In his moments of wildest vaticination, he plays the role of Merlin himself, of prophet and seer. In his plan to establish a new American social order in Virginia, Lance would be a reincarnation of Arthur as well, returned from a purgatorial city of the dead to reestablish the Round Table amid the American moral wilderness. In what turns out to be his most salutary role, he plays Fisher King to his old friend Percival's Percival. Shifting as he does between these various avatars, however, Lance most consistently plays Lancelot, the Great Lover of the tradition and, in consequence, the most important failure in the quest of the Holy Grail.

As Lance remembers his Malory, the number of knights who have had a glimpse of the Grail is only two, Lancelot and Percival (p. 116); now their namesakes are once again united, sharing their consternation at not having achieved the goal.[9] Lance introduces the Grail theme with typically hyperbolic, brazen posturing: "Do you know what I was? The Knight of the Un-holy Grail . . . Sexual sin was the unholy grail I sought" (pp. 138, 140). Lance's tone whenever he refers to himself in this vein threatens to drown out the quieter echoes of the Grail-quest myth with which Percy has invested the narrative, and which are so essential to his point in the novel. Never-theless, dozens of significant details override Lance's own hollow self-mock-ery, suggesting that the Grail-quester correspondence is far stronger (and more in possession of his consciousness) than he himself realizes. For ex-ample, he seems not even to realize the abbreviated form of his name is a pun connected to the phallic and vaginal symbolism of the grail articles (lance and cup). In its full form ("lance a lot"), it helps illuminate the spiritual arid-ity of his definition of "lancing" as the meaning of life (pp. 11–12, 168–69), as well as pointing up his own peculiar manic obsessiveness about sex (as seen, for example, in his weird sexual theory of history [pp. 35–36, 176–80]). His wife Margot is the holy vessel Lance seeks to be united with, spe-cifically a "sanctuary guarded by the heavy gold columns of her thighs," where, in blasphemous mimicry of the Eucharist, he reports to Percival: "That was my communion, Father—no offense intended" (p. 171). Having discovered her infidelity and embarked on his search for absolute ocular proof of her adultery—a "vision" of this unholy grail—Lance becomes the medieval knight setting out on his quest. He becomes ascetic: beginning a new life, he discovers that he "didn't need a drink. It became possible to . . . watch and wait" (p. 63). He practices mortification of the flesh, involving tests of his physical strength (p. 65). Preparatory to his quest, he bathes care-fully and ritually purifies himself (p. 66). He spends a night in vigil peering through a window of stained glass as if at devotions in a medieval chapel (p. 86). Finally, in drug-induced hallucination, he imagines he receives a sword from a woman who resembles the Lady of the Lake; it is his ritual "charge" to carry out the quest. He comes to his senses holding not a sword but a Bowie knife (pp. 225–26).

The setting, too, contributes to the theme of grail quest. Several times, Lance's ante-bellum home, Belle Isle, is likened to a boat or ship, the equiva-lent of the mysterious vessels that carry Malory's Grail knights to their des-tination. The belvedere atop the house is a captain's deck; during the hurri-cane "it rattled and rocked like the *Tennessee Belle*," a river steamer (p. 174); and from its height the river is "like the sea" (p. 171). When the storm wors-ens, Lance can hear the house creak as if it were "laboring through heavy seas" (p. 230; cf. p. 228). When the scene shifts to the interior of the dark-ened house, the imagery becomes liturgical. Lance can hear the "organ sounds" made by the wind in the loft of the house (p. 227). In the blackness he finds his way by feeling with his hand for a "cathedral chair" (p. 230). In the master bedroom he finds what he is searching for in an ornate "Gothic bed" also "like a cathedral," whose posts taper to "spires and gargoyles," and whose headboard is likened to an "altar screen" (p. 237). The bed is a perverse Grail chapel. Finally, in the explosive climax of Lance's quest, the murder of Margot's lover accomplished, he strikes a match in the house now filled with methane. "All was light and air and color and movement. . . ." Belle Isle blows up, but Lance is blown free: "When I came to myself," he says, "the fire was hot against my cheek" (p. 246). Lance's account recalls his namesake's experience in the presence of the Grail, when, in Malory, Lancelot "saw the chambir dore opyn, and there cam oute a grete clerenesse, that the house was as bryght as all the tourcheis of the worlde had bene there." Though warned not to enter the chamber, Lancelot does so anyway, attempting to come close to the Grail itself: "and whan he cam nyghe hit he felte a breeth that hym thought hit was entromedled with fyre, which smote hym so sore in the vysayge that hym thought hit brente hys vysayge" (*Works*, pp. 1015–16).

All these detailed correspondences provide more than a mere deepening mythic dimension to the action, however undeniably attractive such resonance may be. In Percy's scheme, the primary function of the correspondences is to work a colossal irony upon the "hero," who tells us all this by way of demonstrating, the seductive correspondences notwithstanding, how impossibly at variance with the true quest of the Grail is Lance's action of murderous revenge and how it must be judged when seen from any perspective other than his own solipsistic one. As Lance uses the Grail-quest theme as a source of overheated metaphor, Percy shows him in the grip of "automythography"—finding meaning in one's existence by apprehending it in mythic terms. This is no way to live a life. To engage in such misplaced concreteness is to act without authenticity.

Everyone in Percy's existentialism is capable of "the search," a concept Percy takes from Kierkegaard. To engage in it, however, one must first be aware of one's predicament, and such knowledge is not easy to acquire: for, as Kierkegaard writes (in *Sickness unto Death*, used by Percy as the epigraph to *The Moviegoer*), "the specific character of despair is precisely this: it is unaware of being despair." Nevertheless, once one has been forcibly made aware of one's own predicament through the sort of catastrophic discovery Lance makes, the search must proceed honestly and not, as it were, vicariously, seeking reality through symbolization, as in the movies. As Binx Bolling remarks in *The Moviegoer*, "The movies are onto the search, but they screw it up. The search always ends in despair."[10] Just as the movies offer no satisfaction to one alienated and in despair, however, neither does myth. The proof lies in Lance's final confession to Percival when his account of the terrible night at Belle Isle is over. He "felt nothing at all. Nothing good, nothing bad, not even a sense of discovery . . . I feel nothing now except a certain coldness" (p. 253). He seems to end where he began—in despair.

The other search, or quest, in the novel is that of Harry Percival.[11] It too is told in terms of the traditional Arthurian quest of the Grail but only because Lance is telling it, seeing it through the same mythographic filter he uses for his own experience. Lance remarks expansively that in youth Harry was called "Parsifal, who found the Grail and brought life to a dead land" (p. 10). Once again, however, although we are perhaps even more tempted here to think of such mythic correspondences as reinforcing the meaning of Percival's quest, it is absolutely necessary that we (and Percival) reject them if we are to see how the search can be successful. Lance's sketchy, elliptical account of Percival's youth reveals him to have been a "melancholy and abstracted" sort (p. 15), given to putting on "acts." Suddenly converted to Catholicism, Harry has gone "from unbeliever to priest" and had set out idealistically for Biafra to change the world. Now apparently painfully disillusioned, he has returned empty, having reached Lance's same low point of despair. Lance asks him if he has lost his faith—"or is it a woman?" (p. 61). In a way it turns out to be both.

In the mythic terms Lance prefers (but does not fully appreciate here), the entire novel comprises a single episode in the traditional account of the Grail quest—the visit of Percival to Corbenic, the castle of Malory's "Maymd Kynge." Modern America is the land mysteriously laid waste, New Orleans is "the city of the dead" (p. 254), the *uscio dei morti* of the novel's epigraph from the *Purgatorio*. Seeming to preside over everything is Lance as the Fisher King, immured and immobilized in his upper-story cell of the mental asylum, from which he looks down on the blasted cityscape below. In actuality, Lance's passive role as Fisher King is more important to us than his overt impersonation of Lancelot du Lac; but it is one of the book's central ironies that he does not realize he is playing the former role. Many details he supplies incidentally, however, support the association. For example, Lance is a "drinker," even to the point of incipient alcoholism. Perhaps we are to see his excessive thirst as implying a need to relieve the spiritual desiccation that has overtaken his life. Lance confesses that he hadn't even seen the river for years (p. 56); he's had no contact, not even visual, with the water that flows by Belle Isle (because literally, of course, it is obscured by the levee). At another point, Lance unwittingly lets flip a crucial indication of his mythical status. Like King Pellam in Malory (*Works*, pp. 84–87), rendered sexually impotent by the Dolorous Stroke, Lance has been "like a man favoring a secret wound. . . . It was that lately I had trouble making love to Margot" (p. 66).

Lance's role as Fisher King clarifies the mythic one played by Anna, the young woman in the next room, victim of a brutal sexual assault. She seems a thoroughly modern avatar of the female Grail bearer, the unidentified, almost faceless woman who carries the Grail articles silently and mysteriously before the quester. Like that figure, Anna resides "with" the wounded king, fulfilling her part in a highly enigmatic relationship that also involves the questing knight—in this case, Harry Percival himself—and which contains the promise of spiritual fulfillment. Thus it should not be surprising to the reader (though it is to Lance), when Harry announces on the last page of the novel that he knows Anna well enough to predict that she will, after all, join Lance's future in Virginia (p. 257).[12] The triangular relationship among the three principals suggests the potential for grace and renewal that exists in the similar triangle of the grail myth, involving quester, bearer, and wounded king.

In some versions of the grail myth (for example, Chrétien's *Conte del Graal*), Percival fails in his quest through his unaccountable silence when the Grail is made manifest to him.[13] True, the vocations of this Percival (he is both priest and psychiatrist) make him a professional listener less inclined to talk than listen. But it only *seems* that he shares the taciturnity of his namesake; in fact, he is full of probing questions, to which the apparent monologue that is the narrative comprises the answers. The point is crucial, of course, for it says Percival's quest will succeed. Also in Percival's favor is that, being both priest and physician, two kinds of healer, he is the only figure in the novel who seems capable of restorative action. By the end of his long and problematical interview with Lance, the questions Percival has not failed to ask appear to have revitalized him spiritually. Although we are forced to view it through the obscurantism of Lance's relentless egotism, Percival undergoes a regeneration in the encounter—"You know, something has changed in you" (p. 254)—as shown by the string of Yes's that are his only words of spoken dialogue. They are words of purest affirmation, in response now to questions from Lance (perhaps a hopeful symptom of the latter's eventual escape from the prison of the self). However tantalizing and enigmatic they may be, they are counterpoint to the hopeless negativity, the "nothingness" that has afflicted Lance's existence.

Percival is Lance's opposite in another way. As if to prove that Percival does not suffer from the delusion of modeling his own experience after the career of a mythic prototype, Percy's own more sympathetic character does not—like Malory's Percival, for instance (*Works*, pp. 1035–36)—exchange the world of action for one of cloistered contemplation of the mystery he has been privy to. Instead, he will go back into the world, to Alabama, where he will "preach the gospel, turn bread into flesh, forgive the sins of Buick dealers" (p. 256). What could be more drab and humdrum—and less mythic? Such is precisely the author's point, however. If we feel a pang of disappointment that Percival's new (and obviously genuinely spiritual) quest is no longer fitted out in Arthurian dress, then we too have been taken in by the fallacy of misplaced concreteness; we will have assumed that Percival should somehow play out the role Lance has created for him. Truly to find himself, though, to create his own self in action, Percival must impersonate no one.[14]

Perhaps the strategic triumph of the novel is that Percy puts the reader squarely in Percival's situation (which is also the author's—"Percy" being Percival for short). Both Percival and the reader listen to Lance and pose unstated questions. They find him an immensely engaging storyteller; they suspect his sanity at first but, to their horror, gradually realize that he is perfectly sane. Deprived of sympathy for Lance's mythographic sensibility by the violence and shocking nihilism of his account, the reader gets the same salutary "vision" Percival receives at the end of the novel and goes away from the book feeling that he, like Percival, has acquired a crucial insight that Lance has not yet achieved. Specifically, although he introduces it early (p. 4) and brings up the subject again at the end of his narrative (p. 250), Lance never comes to realize what a half-obscured sign located around a corner outside his window really says. He has been looking at it for a year, yet can still make out only

Free &

Ma

B

"Notice that it is impossible to see more than that," says Lance (p. 4). For him, yes; for he does not realize even now (though he may in time) that, all along, the sign has said just what he has been reading and no more, that one is "Free and Ma(y) B(e)"—but only if one can learn to see the reality there in front of one's eyes.

Lancelot is an astonishingly creative exploitation of the Arthurian myth: both a narratorial tour de force of artful correspondences that illustrates all too well the seductiveness of myth as a way of escaping reality; and a cool-handed demolition of the epistemological underpinnings of such a mythographic approach. Our admiration for the ingenuity of Percy the novelist in reshaping the Arthurian myth into so engaging a modern likeness must not allow us to forget that for Percy the philosopher, all myth is a species of illusion, in the final analysis as devastating to "the search" as films or any other type of pre-formed symbolic complex that prevents access to true being. *Lancelot* is, finally, about "impersonation" and the title character's chameleon-like quality of facile adaptability.[15] In the course of his story we observe how Lance is drawn into playing a number of roles, but his main impersonation is of the legendary figure whose name he bears. As long as Lance remains "Lancelot" in self-perception as well as in name, he will never take title to his own existence, never have a name to call his own.

NOTES

1. Walker Percy, *Lancelot* (New York: Farrar, Straus & Giroux, 1977), pp. 9–10. Further citations from this edition appear in the text in parentheses.

2. *The Works of Sir Thomas Malory,* ed. Eugène Vinaver, 2nd ed., 3 vols. (Oxford: Clarendon Press, 1967), pp. 805–24. Further citations from this edition appear in the text in parentheses.

3. John Bugge, "Merlin and the Movies in Walker Percy's *Lancelot,*" *Studies in Medievalism* 2, no. 4 (1985): 39–55.

4. On the movies as preventing access to reality, instead providing only transcendent pseudo-religious experience, see Lewis A. Lawson, "Walker Percy's Indirect Communications," *Texas Studies in Language and Literature* 11 (1969): 867–900.

5. The ambivalence toward the Arthurian reader here besetting the reader here recalls a similar strategy (if that is what it is) in Twain's *Connecticut Yankee,* where the narrator, Hank Morgan, also falls victim to a kind of myth-madness that precipitates his role in a final apocalyptic dissolution.

6. See, most recently, Walker Percy, *Lost in the Cosmos: The Last Self-Help Book* (New York: Farrar, Straus & Giroux, 1983).

7. The Arthurian past is paired and conflated with the myth of the Old South, linked in Lance's mind, as in his father's before him, with the past of his Confederate ancestors (pp. 115–16). Both seem to have been times of great deeds—of heroic enterprise, storied valor, austere integrity. In the course of the narrative, however, at least the myth of the Old South is effectively deflated, and in "Questions They Never Asked Me," a "self-interview" in *Esquire* 88 (December 1977), Percy undermines the idea of a special Southern literary mystique based on "sense of identity, tragic dimension, community, history and so forth . . . I was never quite sure," writes Percy, "what it meant" (p. 172).

8. Walker Percy, "The Loss of the Creature," in *The Message in the Bottle* (New York: Farrar, Straus & Giroux, 1975), pp. 46–63.

9. The novel's Galahad figure, Lance's unnamed son, has never set out. Unlike Lancelot's son by Elayne, Lance's son by his first wife Lucy avoids the Sege Perelous by refusing to fight in Vietnam and, in a perverse burlesque of Galahad's ethereal chastity, shuns the company of women and becomes a "mild homosexual" (pp. 17, 177).

10. Walker Percy, *The Moviegoer* (New York: Knopf, 1961; repr. 1975), p. 13.

11. On Percival's role as quester, see Robert D. Daniel, "Walker Percy's *Lancelot:* Secular Raving and Religious Silence," *Southern Review* 14 (1978): 186–94; Corinne Dale, "*Lancelot* and the Medieval Quests of Sir Lancelot and Dante,"

Southern Quarterly 18, no. 3 (1980): 99–106; and Lewis A. Lawson, "Walker Percy's Silent Character," Mississippi Quarterly 33 (1980): 123–40.

12. It is significant that Anna is named for the mother of the Virgin, in that role a "bearer" of the gift of salvation. For a similar reason, Lance's wife is named "Mary Margaret" (after the Virgin, and with the connotations of the pearl's purity), and not after Guinevere ("Gwen"?), who is less relevant—indeed, antithetical—to the Grail myth. Margot's more important mythic function is hinted at when Lance says she seemed strangely like Anna (a true Grail bearer) in her last moment alive at Belle Isle (pp. 245–46).

13. See also, Jessie L. Weston, From Ritual to Romance (first published, 1920; repr. Garden City, N.Y.: Doubleday, 1957), pp. 12–24.

14. To her credit, neither does Anna subscribe to Lance's mythmaking. For example, she rejects as the arrant nonsense it is Lance's "great secret of life . . . the ignominious joy of rape and being raped" (p. 252).

15. See Lewis J. Taylor, "Walker Percy and the Self," Commonweal 100, no. 10 (10 May 1974): 234.

9 LANCELOT'S LAST METAMORPHOSIS

Jean-Marcel Paquette

Let us begin with a paradox, which is that, for the moment, we will adopt an old and discredited method, "source criticism," in examining a very modern subject: Bresson's film.[1]

A reading of almost all the critical appraisals published at the time of the first showing of *Lancelot du Lac* in 1974 permits us immediately to give some credit to "source criticism," especially when we consider the extraordinary number of inane remarks that were made in the press at that time by usually careful pens. Indeed, we learn from these, for example, that in one instance Bresson was inspired by Chrétien de Troyes's romance and in another that he borrowed from "old chansons de gestes" [sic], and that the filmmaker modeled his script on Thomas Malory's account. And so on.

These cultural references, we believe, have been distilled from vague schoolboy memories. Ten years after the tumultuous première of the film at Cannes, it is thus important to take stock.

Let us make it clear from the beginning that nothing, in the many interviews granted to magazines and newspapers by Bresson himself, hints at what his principal source was. Even the credits of the film tell us nothing more about it. But we do know from other sources that his plan to film a *Lancelot* had already taken shape around 1954. It was then that he drafted the script—the very one, with no change in its scope, so he said—that was used in the filming. Meanwhile, for more than twenty years, Bresson had to all appearances given up his plan for want of producers who would allow him to film as he wished.

In the end, what do we know of Bresson's basic source? It could be none other than the famous *Mort le roi Artu*, which existed at that time in

Originally published as "La dernière métamorphose de Lancelot." *Cahiers de la Cinémathèque* 42/43 (Summer 1985), 113-18; translated by Marco D. Roman. Reprinted with permission.

only three editions: those of Bruce (1910), Sommer (in volume VI of his Vulgate, 1913) and Jean Frappier (1936). Of the three, the last one was the most accessible to a nonspecialist. No modern prose version of the thirteenth-century prose romance existed then except the very free adaptations of J. Boulenger (*La Mort d'Artus*, 1923). We can, therefore, reasonably assume that it is in Frappier's text, most likely through the summary of the work provided in the introduction, that Bresson first met the character of Lancelot. If our hypothesis is correct, it still remains for us to show Bresson's particular use of the text.

The plot of the medieval work is well known. Of the incessant proliferation of adventures, intrigues, fights, and discussions that make up the entire generous breadth of the medieval text, the filmmaker, in accord with his strict aesthetic that is often characterized as "Jansenist," has retained only the following skeleton:

I.   The return of Lancelot, who is the subject of the first sequences.

II.   The reunion of Lancelot and Guinevere, in the form of a meeting during which the lovers resolve not to pursue their forbidden love.

III.   The tournament, leading simultaneously to Lancelot's triumphant display of valor and to his injury.

IV.   The queen's abduction.

V.   The restoration of the queen and Mordred's revolt.

VI.   The last battle, transformed into a veritable twilight of all knights and all chivalry.

This sketch is reduced to its barest outline, but it essentially retains what Frappier had already identified as the two fundamental themes of the romance: the force of love and the fading of Arthurian glory (1964 edition, p. xiv).

In his study devoted to Bresson's work, Michel Estève correctly recognizes the specific and rigorous work that the filmmaker invested in the composition of a script; Estève maintains that Bresson "suggests the essential while eliminating what is accessory and anecdotal" (Seghers, 1964, 33). Thus, in *Lancelot*, what remains of the old medieval story in Bresson's script reveals, albeit negatively, the resolutely inessential character of what has been omitted—inessential, that is to say, to the meaning of the film. Moreover, Bresson himself explained this subject in an interview granted to the magazine *Cinéma-Québec* in May 1975: "If I chose the end of the adventures, it is because these romances are fanciful, magical . . . and then suddenly, there is an extraordinary situation: Lancelot du Lac, who went off on an adventure, returns vanquished. Suddenly, a conscience enters into play where before there was none. That is the most beautiful situation there is in the world" (IV/3,33). The appearance of a conscience is the true subject of Bresson's film. Its sudden emergence through "the force of love" is also the cause of the annihilation of the Arthurian universe; and therein the two essential themes of the romance are united. It is the conscience, supreme accession and origin of all downfalls, that represents an ethical thesis often sustained and treated since Genesis and its Tree of Knowledge.

By eliminating, for example, all the episodes in which the character Bohort appears, notably the one that opens the romance's account, the scriptwriter dissolved any links that his "story" might have had with the earlier episodes. The credits, reduced to a few lines, are the only means of succinctly recalling the events that led up to where the film begins. There is scarcely any allusion to the Grail, except to introduce the return of Lancelot as a failure anticipating the final collapse of an entire world. Between these two failures, only the "force of love" is presented as a major theme of the film text.

By omitting the entire episode of the "damsel/lady of Escalot," the film, such as it became, spares us the whole psychology of love, with its disorders, Guinevere's jealousy, and Lancelot's naïveté. However, if we look closely, something of the Escalot episode may remain in the young girl associated from the beginning with the old peasant woman. With her ear to the ground, the young girl listens to the hoofbeat of Lancelot's horse. Later, when he leaves at the end of the scene in the inn, the same girl kisses the ground on which the horse has just trod, and we hear the horse galloping off in the distance. The girl is the opposite of a psychological character type. She is the mute monitoring of Lancelot's internal drama to the extent that in one scene, which did not survive editing and was supposed to be the last scene of the film, it is she who lifts Lancelot's visor only to find an empty suit of armor.

It is Mordred and not Agravain, as in the romance, who here becomes King Arthur's main informant concerning Lancelot and Guinevere's love affairs, thus short-circuiting the path that leads from denunciation to final revolt. Whereas the romance conceived of two distinct plots—first the denunciation by Agravain and then the revelation of Mordred's love for Guinevere—that are at the root of Mordred's revolt, Bresson recognizes only one connection between denunciation and revolt. Need it be pointed out how right Bresson was to ignore the fact that Mordred, until then thought to be the king's nephew, is in reality his son born of an incestuous relationship? The film, obviously, did not need this in order to reveal Lancelot's interior drama.

Banished from the script as well is the episode of the pyre borrowed by our romance from Béroul. The scene is too spectacular, all show, and Bresson goes in for only the most tenuous signs of interiority, in other words, for their slow transformation under the influence of nascent conscience.

All the kingdoms of the romance disappear: neither Gaunes, nor Logres, nor Rome is even alluded to. Everything is confined to the single narrow space of the tragedy in which there are three points of intensity: the forest, the castle, the dueling field. Joyous Guard and Camelot no longer have names: Escalot subsumes them all. Even Salisbury, the high place of the final battle, no longer exists. No longer a plain, it is a forest, the same one as in the first scene, which closes the tragic space on itself—a forest with barely a somber clearing containing piles of suits of armor, rather than the cadavers of dead knights. None of these dead knights, except Lancelot collapsing while pronouncing Guinevere's name, is identified. Even Arthur remains unidentified, which justifies Bresson's not having fully exploited the marvelous in the romance's final scene. Thus, there is no more Excalibur, no more mysterious hand coming out of the lake to reclaim the sword, no more fairy ship. Why would Morgan be there?

A single tournament (that of Escalot) and a single battle (the last) suffice to produce the synthesis of all the tournaments of all the battles that animate the thirteenth-century story. As a result, Bresson's version has replaced the characteristic medieval technique of double or triple interlacing of episodes, by the pure and absolute linearity of film narrative.

It should be noted that the filmmaker has taken no "word," no speech verbatim from the medieval text, thereby avoiding archaic language. Besides, the cinema has only one alternative in this matter: either to do as Bresson has done or to follow the method of Rohmer, whose excellent *Perceval* is entirely taken, word for word, from Chrétien de Troyes and uttered entirely in the language of the twelfth-century writer himself.

Finally, a word about the music, which is as stark as the film narrative itself. It too has its "source." It is a bagpipe that is, by the way, "intradiagetic" since we see it during the tournament scene (the player is not shown), and a heavy roll of drums that one would say prolongs the clash of armor. The brevity of this musical interval could be found in a metaphor from the very text of Frappier's introduction. In effect, our master was making a final judgment on the artistry of the *Mort le roi Artu*:

> "For this Twilight of the Gods, we would wish for the playing of a great organ or all the resources of an orchestra. We must be content to hear a flute" (p. xxix).

At first, only two particularly significant sequences seem to constitute Bresson's additions to the medieval text.

One is the scene with the old peasant woman who begins the film's narrative with a kind of prophecy and later takes Lancelot into her home, after he has been wounded in the tournament. The other scene is the storm after which the knights, seeing Lancelot's pennant torn by the wind, believe that he is dead.

If we examine them more closely, we can easily trace these two "units" in the medieval text. Bresson, however, has transformed them so as to make them almost unrecognizable, but without altering their evident narrative function. Each of the two appearances by the old peasant woman reveals, in fact, the two attributes of a character who appears only once in the *Mort Artu*: it is the "old woman"—the one whom Frappier calls "destiny's messenger" (§ 130, 55 ff.)—whose attributes are prophecy and the condemnation of war. The first character of the film to speak, the old peasant woman predicts the death of Lancelot ("he whose footfall is heard before he is seen will die within the year"). Then, in the later scene in which she lodges and cares for the wounded Lancelot, she attempts in vain to prevent the knight from resuming his battles. (In the medieval romance, it is to Arthur and Gawain that the "old woman" appears, announcing the "heavy losses" that await them and enjoining them not to pursue their fratricidal war any longer.)

As for the storm prefiguring the death of Lancelot, should we not see in it a scene inspired by the famous "very heavy and wondrous rain" (§ 193, 32 ff.) that announces the magical ship of the "fairy women" come to reclaim the body of King Arthur? If our hypothesis turned out to be correct, Bresson would have succeeded in this extraordinary feat, characteristic of his alchemy as a filmmaker, that consists in transforming medieval marvels into specifically modern figures that reveal a realism bearing a meaning beyond reality itself. In fact, he transforms what had constituted magical signs into elements that become for us perceptible signs of the tragic.

Indeed, one scene alone is pure Bressonian invention, and it is capital: the brief chess game between Gawain and an unidentified knight. It will serve as our guide in the analysis and the more properly cinematographic reading of Bresson's *Lancelot*.

There are few works in the Middle Ages, from the *Chanson de Roland* to the *Ballades* of Villon, not to mention the prose *Tristan*, where chess is not played. This serves as proof that the "noble game" (as it was also called) is so often, in our minds as in the characters represented by its pieces, associated with the Middle Ages. However, our *Mort le roi Artu* is one of the rare works where it does not figure. By introducing this "medieval" game into a work where it did not occur, Bresson performs a significant exchange, "medievalizing" the text, so to speak, which he borrows but modernizes by means of cinematographic creation. Thereby, he accomplishes its most profound transformation.

In the most important study devoted to Bresson, well before the première of *Lancelot*, Jean Sémolué had already shown how the *Dames du Bois de Boulogne* (1945) could be read as a veritable game of chess (éd. Universitaires, 1960, 169). He could have shown, in the same way, how Bresson's chessboard was already in place beginning with his first film, *Les Anges du péché* (1943), where the flagstone that separates the nuns in the chancel from the monastery is composed of a series of black and white squares, on each side of which the drama between Thérèse and Anne-Marie is played out.

Among all those who have written on *Lancelot*, Barthélémy Amengual was alone in noting how much the chess game with Mordred, with its symbolic value and its coded language, "condenses the aesthetic formula of the work" (*Positif*, 162/1974, 55). Therefore, we suspect that the game of chess condenses *all* of Bresson's work.

Let us look at the scene and hear what is said in it. We see only the chessboard and the hands of the players. Mordred moves one chess piece and says: "Checkmate: with the queen and a rook. Where is the knight? Can't you guess? Gone, taken off. . . ."

It is understood that the king is Arthur, the queen is Guinevere, the knight is Lancelot, and the rook is the meeting place of the lovers. But that would be only a superficial decoding and, to tell the truth, quite insignificant. Bresson would not have pushed the "game" to the mannerism inherent in conceiving everything according to the strict logic of chess. But, in this scene, he was indicating how it was necessary to read literally the images of his film and the relationships that they maintain among themselves.

The "cinematograph" (to use an expression dear to Bresson), as a phenomenon, already appears as a chessboard through the alternation between the chaotic screen in front of the film and the lit screen of the projection itself. In other words, the screen already possesses the form and the attributes of the square in the game of chess. But, once the film begins, there appears in turn another alternation, a permanent dialectic of visual and audible signs. The first words of the film immediately inform us of this: "He whose footsteps are heard before he is seen . . ." Thus, at the beginning of the film and even throughout its development, we already find in place the dual articulation of the camera and the sound recorder, the two vehicles of expression through which cinematographic art produces its universe.

Let us run through the whole film in order to examine its last sequence, that of the final battle. Four shots of this sequence, the last four, interest us: (a) a white screen with the sky where a bird of prey hovers; (b) a dark screen where the dying Lancelot's armor glitters; (c) and (d) retakes of these same two shots in the same order—four image shots of equal length—which contribute to the creation of a certain rhythm, itself an indication of the direction of the reading that must take place. This reading sends us back persistently to the alternation of the white and black squares on the chessboard.

Let us now return to the very beginning of the film, before the credits, where four shots are rhythmically alternated: (a) war scenes in darkness, where sound dominates but the sign gradually penetrates; (b) the actual credits, dominated by the visual element of the text in light red, with the Grail on a white pedestal in the background; (c) and (d) retakes of these two shots in the same rhythm, this time with the white rectangle formed by the "old woman's" hovel in the background.

The whole film unfolds as an alternated regrouping of long dark sequences (Lancelot's return, the meeting with Guinevere, the hall of the Round Table, etc.) and of equally long light sequences (tournament scenes, after the storm, etc. . . .). Furthermore, within the images themselves, which are a number of signs even more than representations, as Bresson himself likes to point out, reminders of the chessboard proliferate: pennants of Escalot's jousters, pennants of the tents and pavilions, Lancelot's white shield, a white flag against a black screen introducing the scene of the return of Guinevere to Arthur, a half-black, half-white screen from the staging to the sacking of Escalot. . . . Lancelot at the tournament defeats exactly eight adversaries, the number of pawns in a chess game. The chessboard images are more subtle still: whereas the screen already forms a square, a "squared off" background sets off another square *en abîme*. Therefore, everything—castle or pavilion walls; the doors, tents, and arrow loops in the merlons; the window in Guinevere's room, the window of the tower where the lovers meet; the trap door to the upstairs through which the queen appears twice; the large square of the white linen under Guinevere's bath basin; the trees forming a square in the scene where the queen returns to Arthur, when Guinevere hesitates to pass from one side to the other; even the scene where Gawain and the queen pass in turn from one perfect square in the background to another, with the precise and slow pace of "chess pieces" being moved—everything ultimately contributes to the division of the screen into squares and the establishment of the characters' function as "game pieces." But in all this, as we have said, there is no mannerism or excess. It is not a game of chess, it is the chessboard with its infinite variety of figures and movements. The greatest subtlety and an impression of ordered chance preside over it. These two elements even include the "sound/image" dialectic established by the characteristic voice of Bresson's actors (called white voice) and, twice repeated, a close-up of the black eye of Lancelot's horse.

Why, in fact, would he have chosen to give his film the "format" of a chess game? Doubtless, first, simply because chess is a game like motion pictures—a serious game. Because this game, like the other, has the same rules as destiny and can exist only when given its freedom. Above all, it has a form and thus presupposes a consciousness that organizes it: Lancelot's consciousness is also that of the filmmaker/creator.

And finally, Bresson, the artisan of an aesthetic proceeding from a pure ethic, could have been the author of Massimo Bontempelli's famous assertion in *La Femme de Nadir*: "If the World must revert to chaos and chaos to nothingness, then the game of chess will be inscribed among the eternal Ideas."

By thus sectioning the space where the drama of any emerging consciousness is played out, the film poses a series of questions that in turn give it its meaning. It is thanks to Bresson that in Lancelot's last metamorphosis he becomes an eminently modern hero, in that he evolves in a universe devoid of all ideal and henceforth takes his very precise place, with Perceval and Tristan, at the center of an ineffable trinity where the highest lyrical abstraction that the West has ever conceived is defined. "Lancelot," Bresson likes to recall, "is Tristan without the magic potion." Indeed! And, above all, he is Perceval without the Grail.

Although we dealt with a "principal source" at the beginning of this article, it is also possible to locate the traces of two other sources in the film. Although they are minor, one of them seems to have inspired a short sequence that is among the most famous of Bresson's work; the other, the very spirit of the film. The first refers us back to our Middle Ages; the other, without distracting us completely, is more precisely contemporary for us.

Who has not been struck by this image, recurring four times (in the manner of a formulaic pattern, one could say), of a horse, without its rider, crossing the screen and the forest, as one hears its terrible gallop closer and closer? We do not believe it an exaggeration to affirm that this image, obsessive and cruel, makes us hear (as it were) the distant echo of one of the most beautiful lines of the troubadour Bertrand de Born, taken from his political *sirventés*, entitled by the editors "Eloge de la guerre." In it the poet affirms that he finds an infinite pleasure:

". . . aug dire:
Chevals voitz per l'ombratge." (éd. Bec, 10/18, 215)

That is:

". . . to hear the whinny
of the riderless horses in the woods."

With Bresson, like Bertrand, the image (in the cinematographic and linguistic sense of the term) is striking, in the sense that it does not evoke anything else but itself.

The second minor source in question here is a poem by Aragon dating from 1942 and entitled precisely "Lancelot." It is no surprise that we find in it specific references to the cinematographic world, as if the character were already clamoring for its filmmaker; some references as well to the world (ours) that from that moment on has been in a permanent state of decay, as if Lancelot were both the final incarnation and the last spectator. Here are scattered lines of this poem in which the images to come in Bresson's film are already taking shape:

Ce siècle a sur la mort quarante-deux fenêtres
. . . .
Aimant passionément les dessins animés
. . . et le film en couleur
. . . .
J'écoute les appels d'un monde qui se noie
. . . .
J'ai soupé des flonflons de cette décadence
. . . .
Je n'ai pas d'autre azur que ma fidélité
Je suis ce chevalier qu'on dit de la charrette
Qui si l'amour le mène ignore ce qu'il craint
. . . .
(Poésies complètes, vol. VII, 259–63)

Do we not almost hear the armor buckling without seeing it, and understand without yet hearing them Guinevere's merciless words: "God is not an object that one can bring back"?

If a conclusion were necessary, I would cite the judgment that the filmmaker Jean-Pierre Lefebvre pronounced on Bresson's *Lancelot* when he affirmed that it was "the inventory and the process of cinema itself" (*Cinéma Québec*, IV/3 1975, 36).

But, as I do not see the need for it, I would simply say, to take a scene from *La Mort le roi Artu*, that, all things considered, the film is the fresco of images painted by Lancelot himself on the wall of his bedroom. The prerogative of the cinematographer, Bresson states again, "is to give the past back to the present" (*Etudes cinématographiques*, 18–19/1962, 31).

NOTE

1. A note in the original French work indicates that this article represents the reworking of a paper delivered at the conference on the character of Lancelot organized by the Centre d'Etudes Médiévales at the University of Picardy (January 14–15, 1984).

10 THE CHARACTER OF GUINEVERE IN THE ARTHURIAN ROMANCES OF CHRÉTIEN DE TROYES

Peter Noble

In the Arthurian Romances of Chrétien de Troyes Guinevere emerges as a character of importance to a degree which marks a change from the writings of his predecessors who were, of course, writing for a different sort of society. In the older Arthurian stories of the Mabinogion, for example, *Rhonabwy's Dream* and *Kulhwch and Olwen* there is very little mention of her. She is presumably Gwenhwyfar, the first lady of the island, who appears in the long list of names in *Kulhwch and Olwen*, but that is all we learn about her. Geoffrey of Monmouth mentions her briefly as Arthur's Queen and Modred's accomplice, while Wace adds the information that Arthur loved her greatly but that they could have no children. In both writers she appears as a lady of ancient Roman lineage, married very largely for political reasons. From this it can be seen that Chrétien took very little of his material for this character from his predecessors, with the result that she is very largely his own creation, made necessary by the type of society for which he was writing and by the demands of the stories themselves. As Chrétien was writing during at least part of his career for the sophisticated court of Marie de Champagne at which women played a considerable social role, it would be only realistic to portray a character fulfilling such a role, even if idealized, in the romances. For this reason alone the role of Guinevere was almost certain to increase in importance. Her position in each romance is dependent on the requirements of the story although she is always a secondary character, except in *Le Chevalier de la Charrete* (and for this reason it will be the last of the romances to be considered in this article).

In *Erec and Enide*[1] the role of the Queen is that of a model consort and an inspiration to the young knights of the court. Her first ap-

Reprinted from *Modern Language Review* 67 (1972), 524–35, with kind permission of the Modern Humanities Research Association.

pearance shows her participating in the life of the court by following the hunt:

> Apres aus monte la reine; (77)

and her esteem and regard for Erec are clear from the moment he joins her:

> "Biax amis, vostre conpaignie
> aim je molt, ce saichiez de voir;
> Je ne puis pas meillor avoir." (112–14)

This affection and regard for Erec are evident throughout the poem, and when Yder comes to surrender to her at the court, she shows herself impatient for news of Erec:

> La reine plus ne se test,
> d'Erec li demande novele;
> "Or me dites, sire, fet ele,
> savez vos quant Erec vanra?" (1192–5)

Later in the same scene she describes Erec to Arthur as "le vaillant chevalier" (1213). When Erec and Enide are actually sighted approaching by the barons watching from the highest window, we are told:

> La reine Ganievre i cort . . . (1504)

and once they are in the court, the first reaction which Chrétien describes is that of the Queen:

> La reine grant joie an mainne . . . (1515)

From this it is easy to see that the Queen attaches special importance to Erec and seems to feel special affection for him, naturally enough perhaps, as he is portrayed as the most outstanding of the young knights at the court.

This regard and affection seem to be returned in full by Erec, who is first seen offering to escort the Queen as she rides after the hunt:

> "Dame, fet il, a vos seroie,
> s'il vos pleisoit, an ceste voie;

je ne ving ça por autre afere
fors por vos conpaignie fere." (107–10)

When Erec has beaten Yder, he sends him at once to the Queen "por fere son comandement" (1033). Another mark of the esteem in which Erec holds the Queen is his refusal to allow anyone else to dress Enide in a manner befitting her station. He insists on this point twice, saying first of all:

"je voel que ma dame l'atort
de la soe robe demainne," (1334–5)

and when Enide's cousin offers to dress her, Erec flatly refuses:

"ne voldroie por nule rien
qu'ele eust d'autre robe point
tant que la reine li doint." (1356-8)

Yet another point is that when Erec has been to the King and received his *congé* after the wedding celebrations, he still has to see the Queen:

La reine congie demande, (2245)

and it seems to be only with her permission that he can go:

La reine congie li done. (2247)

From this it can be seen that in the first part of the poem to some extent the Queen is Erec's lady. His real motive in fighting Yder is to avenge the Queen, and Enide is little more than a useful symbol at that point in the story; and it is only after Erec and Enide have returned to the court of Erec's father that Enide replaces the Queen as the inspiration of Erec's valour.

The Queen herself seems to be in no way jealous of Enide nor does she resent the marriage. When Erec presents Enide to her, explaining that he had refused the offer of Enide's cousin, the Queen says:

". . . Molt avez bien fait;
droiz est que de mes robes ait
et je li donrai boene et bele,
tot or androit, fresche et novele." (1563–6)

—which suggests that she is both pleased at the compliment paid to her by Erec and of a generous nature herself. The description of the clothes which she bestows on Enide more than confirms this. She does, in fact, take a great liking to Enide as is confirmed by Gauvain when he is trying to persuade Erec to come to the court:

> "de li veoir a molt ma dame
> la reine grant desirrier,
> encor parler l'en oï hier." (4146–8)

While they are at court on this brief visit, Enide shares the Queen's bed in the room next to where the wounded Erec is sleeping.

> An une chanbre par delez
> Enyde avoeques la reine,
> sor un grant covertor d'ermine,
> s'an dormirent a grant repos . . . (4248–51)

In her relationship with Enide as with Erec the Queen shows a warm, friendly, and sympathetic nature but these are not the only aspects of her character that are revealed in the course of the poem.

She is inquisitive and perhaps also aware of her responsibilities as Queen, for when she sees the strange and unknown knight approaching she wants to know who he is:

> La reine Guenievre . . .
> vialt savoir qui il sont andui. (149–52)

The imperious side of her nature is reflected in the words which she uses to her damsel when sending her to intercept the knight.

> alez dire qu'il vaigne a moi . . . (157)

and her concern for those whom it is her duty to protect as well as her anger at the insult offered to her is shown by the lines:

> La reine ne set que face,
> quant sa pucele voit bleciee;
> molt est dolante et correciee . . . (192–4)

This evidence that she is aware of her position and her own importance is confirmed by the treatment accorded to her at the court by the knights and by Arthur himself. Kay goes to tell the Queen when Yder is sighted approaching the court, which is natural enough in the circumstances but nonetheless shows that the knights were aware of her wishes and obeyed them. She also has an important role to play in the ceremonial of the court, although admittedly both episodes are in what might be called a woman's domain. She supervises the bedding of the newly-married couple:

> la reine s'est antremise
> de l'atorner et del couchier,
> car l'un et l'autre avoit molt chier. (2024–6)

The last line quoted would suggest that the Queen did not always play this role but chose to do so on this occasion because of her affection for the couple as well as from her desire to see that nothing went wrong. Another episode in which the Queen takes charge is the dressing of Enide for the coronation:

> Quanque pot, d'Enide atillier
> se fu la reine penee. (6761–3)

Here the Queen lavished so much time on the preparations that Enide is late but this does not seem to be a serious matter. Both these episodes are perhaps only to be expected in the life of a Queen but it is also clear that the Queen is not without influence at the court and her advice is sought by Arthur. It may even be offered unasked.

When the knights start to dispute as to which of their ladies should get the kiss after the killing of the White Stag, the King draws his leading barons away to a council. The Queen comes to this council without being sent for and, as far as can be seen from the text, by right. She relates the story of her adventures, culminating in the advice:

> "metez cest beisier an respit
> jusqu'a tierz jor qu'Erec revaingne." (338–9)

which is accepted without further discussion or comment. Chrétien adds a very human touch to her character because when Yder announces that Erec will shortly return, the Queen points out to the King how wise her advice was and how wise he was to follow it:

"Molt vos donai boen consoil hier,
quant jel vos loai à atandre;
por ce fet il boen consoil prandre." (1214–16)

Once Erec has returned with Enide it is Guinevere who proposes that Enide is without question the fairest at the court and should therefore have the kiss, which is accepted by all without demur. The Queen has been instrumental in rescuing the King from the very dangerous position into which his obstinacy had led him.

Chrétien's own attitude to the Queen can be seen in one or two minor points. He makes the King send to tell the Queen the news as soon as the messenger has come to the court from Guivret le Petit and Erec. He frequently couples their names as if it were natural for them always to be together:

Li rois Artus et la reine
et de ses barons li meillor
i estoient venu le jor . . . (3920–3)

There is never any physical description of the Queen but her mortal qualities are described:

La reine fu preuz et sage (1200)

and later when the Queen has taken Enide away to dress her, Chrétien calls her:

la franche dame de bon ere . . . (1612)

Taken with the fact that the Queen speaks "cortoisemant" Chrétien is clearly at pains to describe her in terms which reveal the best side of the Queen's character and justify her role and importance at the court.

Though not a major character in *Erec and Enide* the Queen is presented as more than just a stereotype. She emerges as a mature, active woman, full of sense and ingenuity whose advice is listened to and respected. She shows herself to be human with her inquisitiveness and her imperiousness and her tendency to say "I told you so." She is kind and generous, admired by the knights and, together with her husband, provides a stable and glittering background against which one of the younger knights can reveal his true greatness. There is no hint of criticism and no breath of scandal which could only detract from the importance of Erec by drawing attention to the Queen, nor does her relationship with her husband seem to be anything other than excellent. She is clearly meant to be an exemplary woman, morally as well as in every other way.

In *Cligés*[2] the role of the Queen is both more limited and more active. She does not appear at all in the part of the book devoted to the exploits of Cligés himself, despite the opportunities for her to do so at the tournament at Wallingford and at the end of the book when the lovers come to seek refuge at the court of Arthur. It would have seemed quite natural for the Queen to have appeared at the tournament and, in view of the affection which she felt for both Cligés's parents, she could well have shown some interest in his presence at court. Her presence would, however, be an unnecessary distraction from the development of the story at this point and there is no role for her to play in forwarding the plot, so Chrétien dispenses with her presence. This absence of the Queen shows very clearly that she is regarded purely as a functional character and that the portrayal of her character is not of any importance in this poem.

Nonetheless her character does emerge in the first part of the poem where her role is of considerable importance. From the start she shares in the general liking for Alexander:

> Que molt l'aimme li rois et prise,
> Et li baron, et la reine. (414–15)

Thanks to this liking she is both able and willing to take an active role in promoting the love of Alexander and Soredamors once she has realized that it exists. The Queen is observant and notices that the young couple are affected on board ship but she is misled by the conditions and attributes the change to sea-sickness, a sensible if unromantic conclusion:

> La reine garde s'an prant,
> Qui l'un et l'autre voit sovant
> Descolorer et anpalir;
> Ne set don ce puet avenir,
> Ne ne set por coi il le font
> Fors que por la mer ou il sont. (533–8)

Chrétien obviously intends the Queen to be looked upon as a shrewd and intelligent observer because he goes on to say quite clearly that it was only because of the sea that she was misled:

Espoir bien s'an aparceust,
Se la mers ne la deceust;
Mes la mers l'angingne et deçoit
Si qu'an la mer l'amor ne voit . . . (539–42)

Her affection for Alexander has already been mentioned by Chrétien but this liking is stressed:

La reine la chose set,
Qui Alexandre pas ne het,
Einz l'aimme molt et loe et prise. (1139–41)

As a result the Queen gives him the shirt which Soredamors had embroidered with her own hair, although at this point in the story the Queen does not realize the importance of this. The Queen is also present at the knighting of the new knights although her motive for being there does not seem to be altogether clear, unless it be just pure curiosity and presumably her interest in them:

La reine, si com moi sanble,
Fu au tref venue seoir,
Por ce qu'ele voloit veoir
Les noviax chevaliers venir. (1192–5)

The Queen is responsible for the further development of the love because she tells Alexander that he is wearing the shirt embroidered by Soredamors and she realizes from the reactions that they are in love. She is, however, far too tactful to let it be seen that she has guessed the secret:

Bien aparçoit et voir le sanble
Par les muances des colors
Que ce sont accident d'amors;
Mes ne lor an vialt feire angoisse
Ne fet sanblant qu'ele conoisse
Rien nule de quanqu'ele voit. (1578–83)

In the end the Queen realizes that unless she takes the initiative, the lovers will find it difficult to resolve the situation and so she arranges the marriage after persuading the lovers to admit their feelings. All this shows her sympathy and kindness towards the lovers, but these qualities are revealed in another episode which suggests that she was not without power and influence at the court. After his return to the camp with his prisoners, Alexander surrenders them to the Queen because he knows that the King would hang them at once. The King immediately sends for the Queen and demands the surrender of the prisoners:

> Car a randre li covandra
> Ou oltre son gre les tandra. (1349–50)

The wording suggests that it might just have been possible for the Queen to have kept the prisoners but she has to surrender them after speaking to the King, so clearly her political power and influence are very limited in this instance. The episode does suggest that in more favourable circumstances she might have been able to exercise both. It also shows clearly that Alexander esteems her as a person for her qualities of mercy and generosity.

The role of the Queen in *Cligés* is to unite the two lovers by taking the initiative which they were unable to take in the circumstances since they were too well brought up and too modest to do so. She provided a suitable setting against which they could meet and her presence makes it easier for Alexander to meet and see Soredamors who is in attendance on the Queen. She is only seen in relation to the lovers and so she emerges as a shrewd, observant, and tactful woman who has a kind heart and a real interest in the young people about her, but there is a decidedly motherly air about the way in which she looks after them and promotes their love. Her relationship with Arthur is barely looked at but it is worth commenting that she seems to be in more awe of Arthur than in some of the other poems and this is no doubt because Arthur is a more vigorous and forceful King, relying less on the advice and guidance of others, the Queen included.

In *Le Chevalier au Lion*[3] the role of Guinevere is even more limited because for a large part of the poem she is held in captivity in the kingdom of Bademagus. She does not accompany Arthur on his visit to the court of Laudine, however, and no reason is given for this, but one may assume that, as there were no women in Arthur's party at all (witness the flirting of Arthur's knights with Laudine's ladies), the Queen would have been out of place in a party such as this, seeking adventure and risk. Her appearances are largely confined to the beginning of the book and from the beginning it seems clear that she has influence over the King.

> Mes cel jor einsi li avint,
> Qu la reine le detint,

Si demora tant delez li,
Qu'il s'oblia et andormi. (49–52)

We can see too that she is interested in the knights and inquisitive, because she leaves the sleeping King to go listen to Calogrenant's story. She knows herself to be outspoken and sharp-tongued when rebuking Kay, but she is also able to soften Kay's rudeness to Calogrenant by making a personal appeal to Calogrenant not to be upset by Kay. Later she has to rebuke Kay even more sharply for his rudeness to Yvain and she expresses herself with great forcefulness on the subject of his tongue. We also learn that she is a skillful storyteller:

Et la reine maintenant
Les noveles Calogrenant
Li reconta tot mot a mot;
Que bien et bel conter li sot. (657–60)

After this the Queen's abduction is mentioned as is her release from prison, and her final appearance is during the duel between Yvain and Gauvain when the Queen leads the prayers of the court that the King should intervene by imposing a settlement on the elder sister. Again there is a slight difference in the picture of the Queen in this poem. She emerges as sharper-tongued and more outspoken but is respected and liked by the knights, who are ready to fulfill her requests, and she is sympathetic towards the bravery shown by the knights fighting for the sisters.

In *Perceval*[4] the role of the Queen is reduced still further. She is never called anything except *la reine* and it is perhaps significant that this is in the romance which was not written for the court of Champagne with its influential and intelligent women. Chrétien was writing for a patron and the role of the Queen is correspondingly reduced.

The first mention of the Queen is in the King's answer to Perceval when he is explaining why the Queen is not present and he is so distressed. The Queen has withdrawn to her room after being insulted by having the wine poured over her by the Vermax Chevaliers. When Clamadeus comes to court, however, the Queen is beside the King and although she is not there when Orgueilleux de la Lande arrives, she comes at the King's request and again sits beside him. There is a brief reference to the Queen's maidens:

Neis pucele n'i remaint,
Que la roine ne l'i maint
Por richesce et por seignorie. (4157–9)

—and the Queen herself speaks twice to utter conventional words of thanks. Otherwise all that we learn about her is what Perceval and Gauvain think of her. Perceval addressing her directly says

> . . . Diex doint joie et honor
> A la plus bele, a la meillor,
> De totes les dames qui soient, (4587–9)

which is really only a conventional greeting to a lady of her rank. Gauvain, on the other hand, describes her to Ygerne in terms which go far beyond the needs of mere politeness:

> "Dame, voir, ele est tant cortoise
> Et tant est bele et tant est sage
> C'ainc Diex ne fist loi ne langage
> Ou l'en trovast si bele dame . . .
> Ausi ma dame la roine
> Tot le mont ensaigne et aprent;
> Que de li toz li biens descent
> Et de li vient et de li muet.
> De ma dame partir ne puet
> Nus qui desconseilliez s'en aut.
> Ele set bien que chascuns vaut
> Et qu'ele doit por chascun faire
> Por coi qu'ele li doie plaire.
> Nus hom bien ne honor ne fait
> Qui a ma dame apris ne l'ait:
> Ja nus hom n'ert si deshaitiez
> Qui de ma dame parte iriez." (8176–98)

This is a very remarkable tribute to someone who plays such a small part in the story and presents the Queen as a character of great moral worth and influence wholly for the good. There is almost a religious note in the suggestion that all good comes from the Queen which is all the more unexpected as she seems to have had very little influence on anyone so far and to have done very little in her own right. Nor is it altogether in keeping with what we know of her from Chrétien's other romances. In view of this opinion it is not surprising that Gauvain should stress that he wants the Queen to be summoned from Orquenie as well as the King to watch his duel with Guiromelans. Despite this eulogy the Queen remains a very colourless character in *Perceval*, little more than part of the background and never emerges as a personality. She has no role to play in this poem and Chrétien is not sufficiently interested in her even to give her her name.

In *Le Chevalier de la Charrete*[5] for obvious reasons the Queen is no longer a secondary figure and inevitably her character is more fully developed than in the other poems. Many of the traits that are to be seen in the other poems are still there. Arthur asks her help when he has failed to dissuade Kay from leaving the court, and when her first request fails, she is prepared to do what the King asked and to prostrate herself before Kay:

> et la reine de si haut
> com ele estoit, as piez li chiet. (148–9)

Her affection for the knights of her husband's court is again shown by her refusal to leave the kingdom of Bademagus until she has had news of the safety of Gauvain. When Meleagant comes to Arthur's court to challenge Lancelot, the Queen is quick to warn the King of his evil nature. She feels able to advise and intervene if necessary in the affairs of the court. Similarly she is greatly admired by both sexes. The ladies ask her to preside at the tournament of Noauz and because she agrees to do so, vast numbers come:

> mes plus en ot defors assez,
> que por la reine en i ot
> tant venu que li quinz n'i pot
> ostel avoir dedanz recet . . . (5514–17)

The charming and sympathetic side of her nature which has already been seen in *Erec et Enide* and *Cligés* is to be seen again in her behavior towards Bademagus whom she embraces when she leaves him to return to Arthur's court:

> et ses deus bras au col li met . . . (5289)

She also agrees instantly to his requests to stop Lancelot fighting when he is beating Meleagant:

> Biax sire, por vostre proiere,
> le voel ge bien, fet la reine; (3788–9)

and it is in her relationship with Bademagus that she is at her most sympathetic. We see her modesty too when she blushes for shame at being accused of adultery with Kay and something of the sharp-tongued Queen of Yvain when she defends herself and Kay with spirit against the blustering attack of Meleagant:

> Ele respont: "Se Dex m'ait,
> onques ne fu, neis de songe,
> contee si male mançonge." (4836–8)

All this, however, refers to her public face, so to speak, and it is here that she tries to be seen at her best and most attractive. Her character seems warm and pleasant although never lacking in dignity, and this, coupled with her beauty, makes her attraction more comprehensible. Her beauty is never described in this or any other poem and all that we know about it is that she had golden hair because of the color of the hairs stuck in the comb which Lancelot finds so inspiring. We also learn that her grief over Lancelot's death is so great that she loses most of her beauty:

> Tel duel a de sa crualté
> que molt an pert de sa biauté. (4189–90)

No details are given, however, which is perhaps as well as in this way the reader is left to picture his own ideal of beauty.

The character that emerges in her personal relationship with Lancelot is rather less attractive to us and possibly also to Chrétien since he failed to finish the romance. To start with there is her attitude to Lancelot when he appears at the court of Bademagus. In spite of the fact that he has just crossed the sword bridge and successfully fought Meleagant, giving proof of his devotion by being unable to take his eyes off her, she shows nothing but contempt and coldness for him because he had hesitated before getting into the cart and eventually she goes to her room:

> Quant la reine voit le roi
> qui tient Lancelot par le doi,
> et c'est contre le roi dreciee
> et fet sanblant de correciee, . . .
> mes por lui grever et confondre,
> ne li vialt un seul mot respondre,
> einz est an une chanbre antree. (3937–67)

Later she almost kills herself because of the news of the death of Lancelot:

De li coirre est si estoute
que sovant se prant a la gole . . . (4180–1)

Reasonably enough she blames herself for his death. She decides that a fitting punishment is to live and to mourn Lancelot which she does for two days, revealing the depth of her passion of which there had been no evidence before. She is happy to hear that he would have killed himself for her although she is glad that it did not actually come to that. In the mood of repentance which has been brought on by the realization of how nearly she destroyed him, she is prepared to tell him what his fault had been. As a further proof of her feeling for him she invites him to come to her window although it is perfectly clear that at this point she does not intend to commit adultery:

Ceanz antrer, ne herbergier
ne porroiz mie vostre cors;
je serai anz, et vos defors
que ceanz ne porroiz venir. (4512–15)

She does, however, say:

et, s'il vos plest, jusqu'a demain
i serai por amor de vos. (4518–19)

Only her lips and hands can be touched. When he does come and proposes to remove the bars which block the window she encourages him and they become lovers, so that she is now unfaithful to Arthur. After their long separation it is understandable that she should wish to make sure that her influence over Lancelot is still as great but her command:

que "au noauz que je li mant" (5645)

does not make her seem any more attractive, especially when it is repeated on the second day, although this second order is quickly countermanded. More understandable is the pleasure which the Queen feels when she overhears the other ladies extolling Lancelot, but the calculating and intelligent side of her nature is evident again when we are told that the Queen takes care not to show too much joy at Lancelot's return and reserves it for a more private place in case the King or anyone else should see. We have already seen that she could dissemble and had had to, when she heard the news of

Gauvain's rescue from the water although Lancelot had still not been found. The second occasion suggests that she has every intention of continuing the adultery when the opportunity arises and the resulting impression is not attractive.

From this study of the treatment of Guinevere in the five romances it can be seen that Chrétien treats her in three ways. There is a marked contrast between the warm-hearted, capable and sympathetic Queen of *Erec et Enide*, *Cligés* and *Yvain*, the colorless but irreproachable Queen of *Perceval* and the calculating adulteress of the *Lancelot* and this contrast is not due entirely to the larger role allotted to the Queen in *Lancelot*. The additional features are due to the courtly code which imposes on Chrétien the stereotype of the domineering, capricious lady and it is within this framework that he has to write. He does in fact make the Queen a decidedly human person within these limitations, with good qualities as well as faults. Her attempts to remedy these faults compensate to some extent for the capriciousness which, while demanded by the code within which Chrétien was writing, is unattractive to the modern reader. It may indeed have been unattractive to Chrétien himself for he failed to finish the romance and there is very little trace in the other portrayals of Guinevere of any of these courtly characteristics, although admittedly she is not the heroine in any of the other romances. Chrétien seems to have preferred to see her as an active and kindly woman of great intelligence and understanding, taking an almost motherly interest in the knights of her husband's court and helping to smooth the path for young lovers. She herself, however, does not engage in such activities as a love intrigue in any romance except *Lancelot*, and in *Perceval* where the interest of the poem is not really focused on the Arthurian court, she is reduced to a nameless background figure. It is also noticeable how forcefully Chrétien disclaims the responsibility for the story of the *Lancelot*:

> matiere et san li done et livre
> la contesse . . . (26–7)

It seems a reasonable guess that left to himself Chrétien would not have written the story or at any rate not in that way.

In his other romances he portrays active men who are not subservient to their ladies in the way that Lancelot is to Guinevere. Neither Fénice nor Laudine, who are to some extent able to dominate their men, treat them with the capriciousness and scorn which Guinevere is able to show Lancelot. Further the other three romances, which treat the relationship of a man and a woman in love all end in marriage with the prospect of its lasting happily whether the love developed after the marriage as with Erec and Enide or before as with Cligés and Fénice. Chrétien insists on this even when he has to resort to gross improbabilities, if not magic, to solve the difficulties, as in *Cligés*. On this evidence therefore it seems not unreasonable to suggest that the study of an adulterous relationship and the characterization necessary to it were distasteful to Chrétien.

In the circumstances, with a theme which he seems to have disliked, Chrétien makes an excellent job of the character of Guinevere in the *Lancelot*, showing her both as a Queen and as a passionate woman determined to dominate and control her lover according to the rules of the courtly code. No doubt this was what Marie de Champagne wanted but, on the evidence of the other romances, Chrétien preferred to treat Guinevere as a secondary character, fulfilling her role of Queen and if necessary able to act as a *deus ex machina* but with a reputation unsullied by any hint of adultery. Her role is no doubt an idealization of the role aspired to by many women of the period, as she is admired, respected, and influential. Even in *Perceval* her greatly reduced role has something of this but Chrétien allowed Guinevere to take the centre of the stage only under pressure from his patroness. Part of his conception of her character was due to that pressure, as he had to expand on his own original creation to satisfy a situation that was not entirely of his own devising. The basic outlines of his own characterization are evident in all five romances and, despite his probable reluctance to undertake the task, the additional characteristics necessary for the role of Guinevere in *Le Chevalier de la Charrete* do not jar. The result is that the character of Guinevere has a coherence and unity throughout Chrétien's work which in the circumstances is not altogether to be expected and shows his skill both as a poet and as an observer of human nature.

NOTES

1. *Erec et Enide*, edited by M. Roques (Les Classiques français du Moyen Age [Paris, 1955]). All references are to this edition.
2. *Cligés*, edited by A. Micha (Les Classiques français du Moyen Age [Paris, 1957]). All references are to this edition.
3. *Yvain (Le Chevalier au Lion)*, edited by T.B.W. Reid (Manchester, 1952). All references are to this edition.
4. *Perceval*, edited by W. Roach (Textes littéraires français [Paris, 1959]). All references are to this edition.
5. *Le Chevalier de la Charrete*, edited by M. Roques (Les Classiques français du Moyen Age [Paris, 1958]). All references are to this edition.

11 GUINEVERE

A RE-APPRAISAL

Susann Samples

In spite of the persistent interest and significant research in Arthurian leg-
end, one notable Arthurian figure—Guinevere—continues to be viewed
ambivalently.[1] This ambivalence is demonstrated in the different ways
Guinevere is depicted in each of four important medieval works: Geoffrey
of Monmouth's *The History of the Kings of Britain* (1136), Chrétien de
Troyes's *Charrette* (c. 1164), Hartmann von Aue's *Erec* (1180–85), and
Wolfram von Eschenbach's *Parzival* (1200–10). She is a shadowy figure in
History, a principal actor in *Charrette*, and a respected member of Arthur's
court in *Erec* and *Parzival*. Each writer reshapes the characterization of
Guinevere as he presents the relationship of Guinevere to Arthur, his court,
and others associated with his Round Table.

As a chronicler, Geoffrey is mainly concerned with glorifying the British past; consequently, the focus of *History* is men and their deeds, with
women more likely to appear in the background. Guinevere's role in *History* is defined in terms of her relationship to Arthur. Since Geoffrey takes
great pains to establish the classical ancestry of Arthur, it is only fitting that
Arthur's wife also be of noble Roman descent: "She was descended from a
noble Roman family and had been brought up in the household of Duke
Cador" (221).[2] Of course, in addition to such an outstanding background,
Guinevere is comely: "She was the most beautiful woman in the entire island" (221). In short, Guinevere's worthiness to be Arthur's wife is based
on ancestry and beauty. Geoffrey's description of the Guinevere-Arthur marriage is consistent with the typical medieval marriage, which was based
chiefly on political and economic considerations, not mutual attraction.[3]
Thus, in *History* Geoffrey devotes little attention to the courtship, and the
marriage of Guinevere and Arthur is never developed. This lack of interac-

---

Reprinted from *Arthurian Interpretations* 3.2 (Spring 1989), 106–18, with permission
of Henry H. Peyton, III, Editor in Chief.

tion between Guinevere and Arthur is also mirrored in Geoffrey's description of knights and ladies at Arthur's court, where the entourages are segregated: Arthur has a following of brave and noble warrior-knights, and Guinevere, of fair and lovely ladies. During a banquet, the knights eat in one hall, the ladies in another; and later, two separate masses are sung to accommodate the knights and ladies (228–29).

In *History*, the only person Guinevere is shown to have any contact with—besides Arthur—is Mordred. Before Arthur departs for the Continent, he names Guinevere and Mordred as co-regents: "He handed over the task of defending Britain to his nephew Mordred and to his Queen, Guinevere" (237). Somewhat later, Geoffrey mentions the betrayal of Guinevere and Mordred: "What is more, this treacherous tyrant was living adulterously and out of wedlock with Queen Guinevere, who had broken the vows of her earlier marriage" (257). Doubtless, the mere mention of this adultery was condemning enough, and Geoffrey quickly turns his attention to the ensuing battles between Arthur and Mordred, a topic more to his liking.[4]

The marriage of Guinevere and Arthur in Chrétien's *Charrette* is similar to that in *History*, since it, too, remains in the background, but for an entirely different reason: it functions as a negative contrast to the affair of Guinevere and Lancelot. From the very beginning of *Charrette*, there is an underlying tension stemming from the uneasy relations of Guinevere with Arthur and his court. Instead of being a respected and participating member of Arthur's court, Guinevere is a vulnerable wife—exhibiting little independence or self-esteem.[5]

When Arthur becomes upset over the impulsive decision of Kay, the steward, to leave the court, he implores Guinevere to do anything in her power to change Kay's mind: "Since he will not consent to stay for my sake, pray him to remain on your account, and, if need be, fall at his feet, for I should never again be happy if I should lose his company" (271).[6] In this scene, Guinevere is the dutiful wife, who prostrates herself before Kay in order to fulfill her husband's wishes. With this request, Arthur displays a callousness about Guinevere's feelings and dignity. Moreover, Arthur shows poor judgment when he unwittingly grants Kay a boon that directly affects Guinevere. Only when being led away by the boastful Kay does Guinevere reveal the extent of her bitterness by alluding to the absent Lancelot, who would have prevented this predicament: "Alas, alas, if you only knew it, I am sure you would never allow me without interference to be led away a step" (272). The reaction of Arthur and his court to Guinevere's departure is disturbing. Although they lament her certain captivity (for no one doubts Kay's impending failure), they do not initially attempt to help her: "But no one was so much concerned as to undertake to follow him" (273). Only after an awkward silence does Gawan, the ever exemplary knight, urge some action.

Even though in the *Charrette* Arthur is already the renowned king and knight of the Arthurian legend, he is a largely passive figure, and therefore, he does not personally rescue his own wife.[7] Nevertheless, Arthur is shown to be ecstatic when he receives news of Guinevere's impending return (337). In view of his previous behavior, however, even Arthur's apparent joy at being reunited with Guinevere is suspect and questionable. His relief has more to do with the recovery of a prized possession than with the return of a trusted and beloved companion: "His heart is so lightened by the pleasure he takes in his Queen's return, that his grief concludes in joy. When he has what he most desires, he cares little for the rest" (337–38). This interpretation gains greater credibility in light of Arthur's subsequent conduct: he immediately grants a second boon that once again directly involves Guinevere. This time, the request comes from the ladies at the court, who ask that Guinevere attend an upcoming tournament (338). Their petition does not stem from any sense of loyalty to or affection for Guinevere, but rather from self-interest: Guinevere is to act as a kind of magnet attracting the most eligible knights and thereby improving the prospects for marriage (346). By making this request immediately after Guinevere's release from captivity, these ladies, too, reveal an insensitivity to Guinevere in that they appear incapable or unwilling to show Guinevere any empathy or support. Having resumed her role as Arthur's wife, Guinevere complies with her husband's wishes and attends the tournament. Guinevere, however, has her revenge: By having the favor of the best knight, Lancelot, she defeats the purpose of the tournament, for the other knights are no match for him, and the ladies do not find husbands (346).

Surprisingly, in *Charrette* Guinevere has little contact with her abductor, Meleagant. This unusual state of affairs is due to the diligence of his honorable father, Bademagu, who protects her from his own son.[8] Bademagu's sincere respect for Guinevere enables her to experience more self-esteem and, equally important, more independence in captivity than at Arthur's court. Their relationship appears to exemplify courtliness: Bademagu treats Guinevere with all the honor and respect befitting her station, and Guinevere repays him by saving the life of his son twice (318 and 323). However, Guinevere seriously compromises their relationship when she uses Bademagu's trust to deceive him and his entire court about her affair with Lancelot.

Critics generally acknowledge that in *Charrette*, Chrétien was the first to depict Guinevere and Lancelot as lovers.[9] In contrast to Geoffrey, who barely mentions Guinevere's adultery, and Hartmann and Wolfram, who ignore it,[10] Chrétien makes this illicit love affair the focus of *Charrette*. Critics have tended to see Guinevere as the vain and demanding *Minne Dame* who exerts incredible power over her lover, Lancelot, who is seen as an Ovidian "slave of love."[11] Thus, because of his love for Guinevere, Lancelot endures continuing reproach and ridicule when he rides in the cart. At a tournament, he first performs poorly and then superbly at Guinevere's command. In these and other instances, Guinevere's attitude seems selfish and self-centered, but her actions confirm her love and fuel Lancelot's greatness. For Lancelot, there is no conflict whatsoever between knightly prowess and love, since his love for Guinevere is shown repeatedly to enable him to overcome his numerous challenges. Moreover, the love which Guinevere and Lancelot share is mutual: "In whose life she found her own" (322), and "It is love that prompts her to treat him so; and if she feels great love for him, he feels a hundred thousand times as much for her" (329). Even if their love is, as some critics have argued, a parody,[12] there can be no doubt that as a result of it Guinevere emerges as a more provocative and engaging figure.

Ironically, Guinevere's captivity in Gorre actually offers her far greater freedom of thought and action than her position in Arthur's court, which, in contrast, is determined more by her status as wife rather than as queen. As has been seen, Guinevere is extremely susceptible to the whims of her husband and those of his court (3–5). In Guinevere's captivity, however, her very role as Arthur's wife and queen permits her greater freedom: She is able to choose Lancelot as her lover. It is noteworthy that in *Charrette* Guinevere's independence is sexual, which is revolutionary because this affair challenges the existing institution of marriage and enhances the role of women. The lovers choose each other, and Guinevere enjoys an equal status in the relationship. However, Guinevere's freedom is still deficient, since her actions and feelings stem from a love relationship.

Whereas Guinevere's relations with Arthur and his court are strained in *Charrette*, they are harmonious in *Erec*, which signifies her altered role as an integrated figure in Arthur's court.[13] This change is immediately evident in Hartmann's depiction of the boon scene (1142–49).[14] Whereas in *Charrette* the two boon episodes reveal and increase the tension between Guinevere and Arthur, in *Erec* the request scene stresses the warm and loving marriage of Guinevere and Arthur. They are no longer merely wife and husband—but also friends. Therefore Guinevere addresses Arthur as "friend" and Arthur, for his part, readily grants Guinevere's petition: He delays choosing the fairest maiden until Erec's return. Their similar thoughts and feelings underscore the closeness and oneness which Guinevere and Arthur have as wife and husband. For Hartmann, the idealization of their marriage is but one of the crowning features of this highly idealized court society where even God becomes a courtly God.[15]

In *Erec* the figure of Guinevere is reshaped to reflect Hartmann's perception of the courtly German heroine: she is loyal and submissive.[16] Therefore, Guinevere is a dutiful and, above all, faithful wife. Hartmann even remedies Guinevere's single failing—her childlessness. With the young Erec and his wife, Enite, as well as the eighty grieving widows (9905–09), Guinevere is able to experience a type of surrogate motherhood.

In the opening lines of *Erec*, Guinevere's genuine concern for the epic's young and inexperienced hero is apparent when she sends a maiden instead of Erec to inquire about the mysterious and potentially dangerous knight (21–22). Later, when Erec declares that he intends to pursue the mysterious knight in order to avenge his injured honor (the knight's dwarf has whipped him), Guinevere is momentarily torn by her maternal feelings for him and the dictates of knighthood:

> Die Königin bekümmerte es,
> dass er, der noch so jung war,
> in so grosse Gefahren reiten wollte,
> und sie bat ihn, auf diese kriegerische Unternehmung
> zu verzichten. (144–147)

In her role as a courtly female figure, Guinevere is expected, of course, to grant Erec's request, so that in typical German courtly fashion he has the necessary adventures to foster his knightly development. Unlike the other mother-adult son relationships in these two German courtly epics (e.g. Herzeloyde and Parzival), which tend to be one-sided (the mother gives, the son receives), the strong bond between Guinevere and Erec is mutual. However, the mutuality of this relationship is dictated by what is generally perceived as acceptable conduct for female and male figures. Therefore, Guinevere's demonstration of her loyalty to Erec is passive and non-threatening. At court she is supportive and approving of Erec's knightly accomplishments.

A warmer and more intimate bond develops between Guinevere and Enite, Erec's wife. As hostess, Guinevere is also responsible for seeing to the needs of the various guests at court. Here, however, Guinevere's primary role is that of the "older" woman, who exhibits a strong maternal concern for the young Enite. Since Enite's clothing is tattered when she arrives at Arthur's court, her status—despite her striking beauty—is dubious; however,

Guinevere immediately perceives Enite's social standing and welcomes her accordingly:

Sie nahm Enite zu sich
und sagte
"Schönes Mädchen,
Ihr sollt andere Kleider bekommen." (1529–31)

As *diu riche* and *diu vrouwe mit der krone*, Guinevere transfers some of her importance and status to Enite by her sincere interest and association. In short, Guinevere gently initiates Enite into courtly society.

A touching and poignant scene between Guinevere and Enite occurs later, after Erec's chance encounter with Arthur's court (Erec and Enite have been traveling aimlessly in search of adventures). Guinevere's reaction to Enite's plight is immediate and decisive: She leads Enite away from her husband, and together in the privacy of her tent, she and Enite talk about the latter's hardships (5100–15). For the frightened and troubled Enite, the "older" caring and compassionate Guinevere is a great consolation. Though very little is actually said about their encounter, one cannot fail to recognize the close and confidential bond existing between Guinevere and Enite.

Although in *Parzival* Wolfram presents many exemplary marriages characterized by sincere *minne* and faithfulness,[17] he does not describe the marriage of Guinevere and Arthur in any great detail. After all, Guinevere and Arthur now embody German courtliness, and therefore their marriage is ideal. Since Guinevere is such an integral figure of this sublimated Arthurian court, Wolfram feels relaxed enough to allow her to be the object of some good-natured humor. For example, the seriousness of Ither's challenge to Arthur is diminished somewhat by his obvious embarrassment over having spilled wine accidentally on the Queen. He tells the young Parzival: "Now tell the Queen, friend, that I spilled wine on her unintentionally" (82).[18] In his haste to fight the mysterious knight (Parzival), Segramors "ran in among the tent ropes, burst through the doorway of the tent, and snatched off the sable cover from the King and Queen as they lay there sleeping sweetly. They were awakened, yet they could not help laughing at his impudence" (154–55). The good-tempered response of Guinevere and Arthur is indicative of the peace and harmony which permeates their marriage as well as Arthur's court. Understandably, in her most idealized portrayal, Guinevere has perfect relations with the court: "The chamberlains vied with each other to clear a wide path for the Queen" (378).

Of Guinevere's relationships with the other figures, none is more puzzling than that with Ither, the Red Knight, who challenges her husband. For, upon news of his death, Guinevere publicly mourns him: "Alas and alas, the renown of Arthur may break in twain at this strange event, that he who had been destined to win the highest fame of the Round Table lies here slain before Nantes" (88). What is at issue here is the unknightly manner of Ither's death (Parzival kills him with a javelin). Whatever his failings, Ither, as a knight, did not deserve such a dishonorable death, and thus Guinevere's lamentations underscore the wrongness of Parzival's act. Here Guinevere is the spokesperson for the courtly ideal. In fact, Wolfram views Guinevere's sorrow so positively that at the end of the sixth book, he includes her with such virtuous heroines as Belacane (the black queen) and Herzeloyde (Parzival's mother) (181).

Like Hartmann's Guinevere, Wolfram's queen also acts as a surrogate mother to a knight, Gawan, but this "mother-son" relationship lacks the warmth of that of Guinevere and Erec. One explanation for this phenomenon is that as a young and inexperienced knight, Erec would be more likely to accept and need mothering than the established and 'older' knight Gawan. Like the Guinevere-Erec relationship in *Erec*, the Guinevere-Gawan relationship in *Parzival* reflects and underscores the acceptable gender roles. Gawan acknowledges Guinevere's role as social hostess when he instructs his messenger to seek the queen's counsel before publicly arriving at Arthur's court (330). The messenger scene permits Guinevere to express her feelings for Gawan in a non-threatening matter: "O blessed the hand that wrote you! I have not been free of care since the day I last saw the hand which wrote this writing" (339). Later, in courtly fashion, Guinevere warmly welcomes Gawan and his companions to Arthur's court (351).

The study of Guinevere in *History, Charrette, Erec,* and *Parzival* reveals two distinct and conflicting traditions concerning her adultery. In the case of Geoffrey's *History*, it can be argued that Guinevere's adultery functions as an indispensable component of the betrayal plot.[19] After having created such an outstanding warrior-king, Arthur, Geoffrey could only bring about his hero's downfall by deception—which is simultaneously marital and political: Guinevere and Mordred enter into a sexual union and usurp power. Chrétien made Guinevere's adultery the centerpiece of *Charrette* and introduced and popularized Guinevere and Lancelot as lovers. This depiction of Guinevere is unique, since in Chrétien's other Arthurian romances, notably *Erec et Enide* and *Perceval*, Guinevere appears as the model wife and queen.

This evidence would tend to support the theory that Chrétien's patroness, the highly intelligent Marie de Champagne, may have provided him with the material for *Charrette:* "The material and the treatment of it are given and furnished to him by the Countess, and he is simply trying to carry out her concern and intention" (270).

Chrétien's *Erec et Enide* and *Perceval* were the sources for Hartmann's *Erec* and Wolfram's *Parzival* in which both writers depict Guinevere as an integrated member of Arthur's court. There is no mention of Guinevere's adultery. Why did these two German poets choose not to treat Guinevere's adultery? Perhaps the reason is too obvious—they simply followed the plot of their French source. (It is unclear whether they were familiar with *Charrette.*) Another explanation can be found in the function of Arthur's court in *Erec* and *Parzival*. Both Hartmann and Wolfram, to a lesser degree, attempted to justify and praise knighthood by creating an extremely idealized courtly society which complemented Christianity. Both Hartmann and Wolfram modified Guinevere, Arthur, and his court to reflect German courtliness, which stressed loyalty and moderation. Therefore Guinevere, as the unfaithful wife of Arthur, was thematically as well as morally objectionable to them. This interpretation raises yet another question: Why did the German faithful Guinevere fail to become a viable alternative to the unfaithful Guinevere? One explanation could be partly linguistic, partly national, and partly thematic. Medieval German literature was not transmitted extensively beyond the German borders, and, as has been pointed out, these two German Arthurian epics reflect a uniquely German-Christian *Weltanschauung.* Finally, thematically speaking, an unfaithful Guinevere has always offered greater possibilities and ideas.

In summation, all four of these depictions of Guinevere represent extremes. In *History* Guinevere remains a peripheral figure whose ultimate importance stems from the adverse effect which her adultery has on Arthur's kingdom (its lamentable fall). Conversely, in *Erec* and *Parzival* Guinevere is the model wife of Arthur and a symbol of courtliness. Upon closer examination of the two German depictions of Guinevere, her personality conforms to the German male concept of womanhood, which was based on female acquiescence: Guinevere is first and foremost a loving and faithful wife. Thus, the German Guinevere is a much more integrated and exemplary figure at Arthur's court: She is sensitive, affectionate, sensible, trustworthy, and passive. As seen above, Hartmann and Wolfram even compensate for Guinevere's one failing—her childlessness—by providing her with younger knights and ladies (Erec, Enite, and Gawan) for whom she can show maternal concern. However, in the mother-adult son relationships, this loyalty must be formal and non-threatening. Chrétien's Guinevere has generated much discussion because of her adulterous affair with Lancelot. Nonetheless, of these four depictions, Chrétien's Guinevere is the most intriguing, since momentarily she emerges as a female figure who fulfills her own needs and desires; away from the confining atmosphere of Arthur's court, Guinevere shows herself to be an intelligent, level-headed, and determined female figure.

NOTES

1. Arthurian scholarship mirrors this ambivalence. Critics such as Barber, Bruce, and Knight have devoted little attention to Guinevere. Without a doubt Goodrich expresses the most radical opinion about Guinevere when she states "Thus did Chrétien lead the French and unquestioning readers all over the world into mere inconsequence, slandering both Lancelot and the queen, accusing them of moral turpitude in the face of their imminent deaths and a national emergency not as it were, but as it was. The allegation is frivolous and absurd."

2. All textual references and quotations are taken from the Penguin edition.

3. Bloch states, "As for marriage, it was often quite frankly a mere combining of interests and, for women, a protective institution" (135).

4. Parry and Cadwell, Bruce, and Knight seem to emulate Geoffrey in that they, too, largely ignore Guinevere in their respective discussions of *History*.

5. I disagree with Noble, who sees Guinevere's relations with the court in a much more positive light: "Similarly, she is greatly admired by both sexes" (532).

6. All textual references and quotations are taken from the Comfort translation.

7. Barber (*King Arthur in Legend*) and Reid have also noted Arthur's changed role in this and subsequent works. In the two German courtly epics, *Erec* and *Parzival,* Arthur also functions as a kind of vortex or "homing ground" for the various hero knights.

8. Father and son are contrast figures: Bademagu embodies courtliness and Meleagant, uncourtliness.

9. See Cross and Nitze, Jones, and Weston.

10. Understandably, they ignore Guinevere's adultery because it has no place whatsoever in their extremely idealized depiction of Arthur's court.

11. For further information see Barber (*The Knight*), Cross, Nitze, and Frappier, Guyer, and Weston.

12. Loomis observes: "It seems most likely that at the command of his patroness he deliberately burlesques the extravagances, the posturing, of certain knightly practitioners of *fin amor*"(54).

13. Here the German *Erec* closely parallels the French *Erec et Enide*. As Noble observes: "Though not a major character in *Erec et Enide* the Queen is presented as more than just a stereotype. She emerges as a mature, active woman, full of sense and ingenuity, whose advice is listened to and respected . . . She is kind and generous, admired by the knights and, together with her husband, provides a stable and glittering background against which one of the younger knight can reveal his true greatness" (528).

14. All textual references and quotations are taken from the Cramer translation.

15. For more information, see my article "The Courtly God in Hartmann's *Erec.*"

16. See Jillings.

17. Within the context of these German courtly epics, *minne* is a strong and pure love which exists in marriage. It is not to be confused with *liebe* which is the love depicted in the Minnesongs.

18. All textual references and quotations are taken from the Mustard translation.

19. See Korrel.

Works Cited

Barber, Richard. *King Arthur: Hero and Legend*. Suffolk: Boydell, 1986.

———. *King Arthur in Legend and History*. Suffolk: Boydell, 1974.

———. *The Knight and Chivalry*. Murlow: Langmon Group Ltd., 1970.

Bloch, Marc. *Feudal Society*. Trans. L.A. Manyon. Chicago: U of Chicago P, 1986.

Bruce, James Douglas. *The Evolution of Arthurian Romance: From the Beginnings Down to the Year 1300*. 2 vols. Göttingen: Vandenhoeck & Ruprecht, 1923.

Chrétien de Troyes. *Arthurian Romances*. Trans. W.W. Comfort. New York: Dutton, 1970.

Cross, Tom Peete, and William Albert Nitze. *Lancelot and Guinevere*. Chicago: U of Chicago P, 1930.

———, and Jean Frappier. "Chrétien de Troyes." *Arthurian Literature in the Middle Ages*. Ed. Roger Sherman Loomis. Oxford: Clarendon, 1959.

Geoffrey of Monmouth. *The History of the Kings of Britain*. Baltimore: Penguin, 1986.

Goodrich, Norma Loore. *King Arthur*. New York: Franklin Watts, 1986.

Guyer, Foster Erwin. *Romance in the Making*. New York: S.F. Vanni, 1954.

Hartmann von Aue. *Erec*. Trans. Thomas Cramer. Frankfurt am Main: Fischer Taschenbuch Verlag, 1972.

Jillings, L.G. "The Ideal of Queenship in Hartmann's *Erec*." *The Legend of Arthur in the Middle Ages*. Ed. P.B. Grout. R.A. Lodge, et al. Cambridge: Brewer, 1983.

Jones, W. Lewis. *King Arthur in History and Legend*. Cambridge: Cambridge UP, 1972.

Knight, Stephen. *Arthurian Literature and Society*. New York: Macmillan, 1983.

Korrel, Peter. *An Arthurian Triangle*. Leiden: E.J. Brill, 1984.

Loomis, Roger Sherman. *The Development of Arthurian Romance*. London: Hutchinson U Library, 1963.

Noble, Peter. "The Characterization of Guinevere in the Arthurian Romances of Chrétien de Troyes." *Modern Language Review* 67 (1972): 524–35.

Parry, John Jay, and Robert A. Cadwell. "Geoffrey of Monmouth." *Arthurian Literature in the Middle Ages*. Ed. Roger Sherman Loomis. Oxford: Clarendon, 1959.

Reid, Margaret J.C. *The Arthurian Legend*. New York: Barnes & Noble, 1958.

Samples, Susann. "The Courtly God in Hartmann's *Erec*." *Proceedings of the Patristic, Medaeval and Renaissance Conference* 11 (1986): 151–58.

Weston, Jessie L. *The Legend of Sir Lancelot du Lac*. London: David Nutt, 1901.

Wolfram von Eschenbach. *Parzival*. Trans. Helen M. Mustard. New York: Vintage, 1961.

12 DESIRE, MEANING, AND THE FEMALE READER

THE PROBLEM IN CHRÉTIEN'S *CHARRETE*

Roberta L. Krueger

I. FRAMING THE PROBLEM: PROLOGUE AND EPILOGUE

The Prologue to Chrétien de Troyes' *Le Chevalier de la Charrete* has probably done as much as any other document of the period to stir up controversy about the role aristocratic women played in the formation of courtly literature. For Gaston Paris and many scholars after him, Chrétien's contention that he undertook the romance according to the wishes of Marie de Champagne and that she furnished both its *matière* and *sens* was proof that Marie and her female contemporaries transmitted a revolutionary concept of love to Northern France in the second half of the twelfth century.[1] This thesis has sparked lively debate about what Marie's *matière* and *sens* might have been, about how Chrétien acquitted himself of the task she imposed—with distaste or pleasure?—and about whether Lancelot exemplifies the perfect lover or a perfect fool.[2] It has also given rise to the notion that the meaning of courtly literature was shaped by powerful women to conform to their desires, despite warnings about the tenuous nature of the evidence.[3]

Most recently, literary critics have sensibly argued against the quest for a single *sens* or authorial message in a romance whose frame and narrative development are so pointedly problematic. They have drawn our attention instead to equivocations, paradoxes, and other inconsistencies in the romance as evidence of Chrétien's self-conscious literary ambiguity.[4] From this perspective, Chrétien's rhetorical display in the Prologue is as inscrutable as his performance throughout the romance; both are unreliable indices of woman's status in courtly society.

Reprinted from *The Passing of Arthur: New Essays in Arthurian Tradition,* ed. Christopher Baswell and William Sharpe (New York: Garland, 1988), 31–51, with permission.

And yet, despite the truth of the ambiguity of truth in this and other Arthurian fictions, the problem of the lady's *sens* and the question of female desire remain central to our reading of the *Charrete*. The narrator inscribes his romance under the sign of Marie's wishes—"Puis que ma dame de Chanpaign / le *vialt*" ["Since my Lady of Champagne wishes"] (2)[5] in a way that has made critics ponder the unanswerable question of *what* it is that she wants.

Immediately after the narrator has announced that he undertakes the romance in the Countess' service, "com cil qui est suens antiers" ["As one who is entirely at her service"] (4), he disclaims other romancers who flatter their ladies with hyperbolic compliments. He then admits, after he disparagingly voices a flattering comparison as an example, that this compliment holds true for her: "s'est il voirs maleoit gré mien" ["Though it be true in spite of me"] (19). After asserting the truth of what he has just denied, he appropriates the feminine authority that he initially acknowledged. Although he insists that her "commandemanz" have been more important than his own "sans ne painne" ["thought or effort"] in the work's creation (21–23), he "signs" his book as he entitles it: "Del CHEVALIER DE LA CHARRETE / comance Crestïens son livre" ["Chrétien begins his book / About the Knight of the Cart"] (24–25). His equivocation about Marie's influence culminates in the baffling assertion that the Countess has given him the "matiere et san" ["The source and the meaning"] and that he scarcely adds anything but his "painne et s'antancïon" ["effort and diligence"] (27–28). Chrétien inscribes his response to Marie's "commandemanz" as the enactment of a kind of *don contraignant*, or a rash boon, where, in exchange for the gift she has given ("matiere et san li *don* et livre," 26, emphasis mine) he must perform in return under obligation.[6]

The narrator's deft manipulation of Prologue conventions effects a *mise en question* of the female privilege and influence he has ostensibly acknowledged. Chrétien undercuts Marie's alleged authority by subtly appropriating as his *own* both the *matière* and the *sens*. Although he credits Marie with the creation of his story and acknowledges her control, his rhetorical agility demonstrates to the discerning reader that he knows who pulls the strings. The effect of this strategy is double-edged: the text displaces Marie by appropriating her "san," but it also flags that displacement. By expressly creating confusion about meaning in his opening lines,[7] Chrétien invites readers to wonder—even as we know that it cannot be known—what Marie's inscrutable *sens* might be.

This problematic is starkly recast in the Epilogue, where the question we ask is not "What did Marie want?" but "Where is she?" In the enigmatic fifteen-line conclusion, the "Chrétien" narrator has been subsumed by the voice of Godefroy de Leigni, who claims to have ended ("parfinee") the romance at Chrétien's behest, "par le boen gré / Crestien" ["with the approval / Of Chrétien"] (7106–07). Amidst considerable controversy about why Chrétien chose to end his story thus and about where Godefroy's authorship begins,[8] the significance of Marie's *absence* has been overlooked. Godefroy's problematic conclusion leaves us an ambiguous ending that erases the woman from the last lines of a romance dedicated to her. The narrative contract so personally defined between a patroness and a clerk in the Prologue has become a narrative contract between a clerk and a clerk. Godefroy promises to undertake the "matire" (7099) given him, as Chrétien has done for the Countess. No mention is made of Marie; the *Charrete*'s final image of service inscribes a male-male bond.[9] More explicitly than the Prologue, the Epilogue appropriates Marie's "san" and writes the woman out of the audience. When Godefroy says, "mes nus *home* blame ne l'an mete" ["Let no one blame him,"] (7104, emphasis mine), he seems to invite the critique of another, female public. Marie's conspicuous absence makes us question the place of the female reader—and the nature of her power and her desires—in the *Charrete*.

Although it is couched in terms that are playful and ironic, Chrétien's problematization of female presence and absence in the frame invites us to scrutinize his representation of women within the ensuing narrative. The implied question "What does Marie want?" foreshadows the question of "What does Guenevere want?," which, as Charles Méla has suggested, is the underlying mystery of Lancelot's quest.[10] In the course of the hero's adventures, a succession of female figures will trouble his path with their elusive presence and their imperious desires.

II. Meaning and the Female Reader

Before we embark on an exploration of female desire in the *Charrete*, some remarks about women as readers of courtly romance are in order. Dedications to historical women appear to give evidence of female patronage; they suggest that women, as well as knights, were an intended audience for the genre.[11] But we must be extremely careful about assuming that courtly literature afforded women social equality or that it reflects their historical power.[12] Recent historical studies suggest that woman's social status under primogeniture and the new marriage system was on the wane.[13] The actual responses of romance's historical women readers are not recorded in letters, journals, or autobiographies. The vast majority of courtly texts are male-authored.[14] The central fact about historical woman in twelfth-century Old

French courtly literature is that her real voice is absent and that her fictional apparitions are filtered through clerical masculine consciousness.[15] Her privilege as a literary figure is less an indication of "real" power than a male mystification of femininity, one that obscures the reality of her historical decline.

In most romances, the lady is neither the principal protagonist—the subject of the narrative's action—nor the narrator, the subject who speaks. Within the adventure, she is typically an object of exchange or an object of desire. She observes the conflicts between knights and valorizes the knights' honor with her approving presence as spectator. In the extra-diegetic sphere of the romance's transmission, the clerk's performance has a double audience: he speaks both to ladies and to knights (as well as to other clerks). If professional differences distance the clerk from the chivalric ideals of male nobles, his gender separates him more acutely from the feminine culture of noblewomen. Like her literary representations, the woman reader or listener is also an observer, sometimes the privileged dedicatee, who valorizes the clerk's performance with her presence. But the meaning of the romance for her may well be different than the meaning of the romance for aristocratic men, for she hears a discourse that casts her not as a subject but as an object.[16]

We cannot hope to reconstruct the actual meanings that romances may have held for their male or female audiences. But to ignore the displacement of woman in the creation and transmission of romance is to overlook one of the central tensions of the genre.[17] Historical findings about the appropriation of female sexuality to the project of primogeniture suggest that we look more closely at the tensions of gender within a genre that paradoxically privileges women as her social status declines.[18]

Reading the *Charrete* from the perspective of the silenced female subject may seem to be reading the romance "as it was not meant to be read"; it "reads against" the dominant structure of Lancelot's love for Guenevere.[19] But Chrétien's equivocation about his implied female patron in the frame and his problematic portrayal of female characters within the romance justify such an alternative reading. As reflections of Marie's inscrutability, the anonymous damsels and the elusive Queen who loom in the landscape of Lancelot's journey invite our reflection on the place of female desire within the hero's quest.

III. The Enigma of Woman

Let us now turn to the romance proper to see how Chrétien recasts the question of woman that he framed in the Prologue. Overshadowed by the dominant mode of Lancelot's quest, by the masterfully ambiguous performance of the clerkly narrator, and by a critical tradition that celebrates the union of *clergie* and *chevalerie* in the affinity between Chrétien and his protagonist, the problem of woman has been subsumed under the dilemma of the hero's identity.

But the enigma of female desire is inscribed at the center of Lancelot's quest in the baffling scene of Guenevere's refusal. After Lancelot has performed a series of difficult and challenging exploits to rescue Arthur's queen from her abductor, Meleagant, and has incurred dishonor by accepting a ride on the shameful Cart in order to learn her whereabouts, Guenevere, the object of his love and the reason he has put his life in peril, refuses to see him or have anything to do with him. By refusing to become the de facto prize of Lancelot's amorous adventures, as Matilda Bruckner has suggested, Guenevere creates another "delay" in romance that is characterized by deferred resolutions.[20] I would add that her refusal not only calls into question the entire code of chivalric and amorous values that have guided Lancelot's actions, but also refigures—maddeningly for the hero and enigmatically for the reader—the problem of female desire.

To put the question in terms suggested by the Prologue, What is the *sens* of Guenevere's *commandemanz*?[21] What motivates her to refuse the knight who has risked death to win her love? What (more) does this woman want? The enigma of Guenevere—the essential mystery of her sexuality—shapes a subtext of feminine desire that is elaborated in a series of puzzling female characters whom Lancelot encounters in his quest.

These secondary characters have been read as "femmes médiatrices" who dramatize the hero's desire for Guenevere,[22] as reflections of his service to the queen,[23] and as "uncanny" projections of an original sexual transgression.[24] Reading them as reflections of the male protagonist's identity—as vehicles for Lancelot's shame and honor, or as figures of his desire for the queen—we encounter an intriguing *conjointure* which, for all its ambiguity, is unified by the thread of the hero's trajectory.

But rereading the *Charrete* "against itself" from the perspective of the displaced female subject rather than from that of the active knight, the reader encounters a troubling *disjointure* that reflects woman's displacement within the narrative of male desire. The romance's female characters form a diffuse, fragmented interlace whose common thread of meaning seems to slip ever out of grasp. These are blank figures who appear suddenly and anonymously.[25] With the notable exception of the "pucele à la mule" who returns as Meleagant's sister, their status and motivations are unexplained and they vanish from the narrative after a brief appearance.[26] Unlike the ladies in *Yvain* who enact a common pattern of helplessness, thereby allowing the hero to prove his mettle as he protects womanhood, these maidens impose a set of contradictory verbal constraints and conditions on the hero.

The first damsel forbids Lancelot to sleep in the Perilous Bed and mocks his shame (471–75/430–590).[27] The "obliging damsel" extracts promises before she will indicate the paths of the Sword Bridge and the Water Bridge, "tant me porriez vos prometre" ["If you are able to promise me enough"] (614/602–709). The damsel at the ford requests the liberty of Lancelot's "prisoner" (888–91/888–927), reluctantly promising a *gueredon* in return. The "immodest damsel" imposes the "covant" that Lancelot sleep with her in return for lodging (940–45/931–2013), and later, she secures his protection under the terms of the custom of Logres (1295–301); her admiration for him throughout the episode is profuse. The "pucele à la mule" demands the "gift" of the *chevalier orgueilleux*'s head, for which she promises a *gueredon* and future help (2797–803/2779–941); when she later appears as Meleagant's sister, she frees Lancelot from his imprisonment and releases him from a constraining situation. Finally, the maidens of Noauz request from Arthur the "don" that Guenevere attend the marriage tournament (5382–96/5358–6056). After mocking his shame when Lancelot fights badly, they all desire him as a husband when he wins (6002–06). Intercalated within this last episode, the seneschal's wife demands the "covant" that Lancelot return to his prison and that he give her his love (5476–81/5436–94).

The contradictory nature of the damsels' demands seems calculated to problematize female desire. If one damsel forbids the hero a pleasurable bed, another seeks to sleep with him. While one maiden demands that Lancelot grant his opponent mercy, another asks for the rival's head. In each case, the narrative emphasizes troublesome or mysterious elements, thereby heightening their uncanny significance and provoking the reader's consternation. As in the Prologue, the narrator's "strange" presentation of woman invites our questions about her place in the narrative of male desire. In the analysis that follows, I can only sketch out Chrétien's exploration of the problems in the most striking instances.[28] Let us look first at two episodes in the first half of the romance that foreshadow the central mystery of Guenevere's reception.

In an episode of the Perilous Bed, Chrétien hints at the dark side of female power, linking it to sexual dangers that threaten male identity. The first damsel whom the hero encounters draws public attention to his shame, wondering why he is led by a dwarf as if "contret" (a crippled or disabled person) (438–39). She then imposes a restriction on the lodging she has offered. She refuses to let Lancelot sleep in the most luxurious bed, which the narrator has said possesses "tot le delit / qu'an seüst deviser an lit" ["all the perfections / One could devise for a bed"] (465–66). The damsel explains that it was not made up so splendidly for a knight who has shamed himself by riding in the Cart. Lancelot, of course, takes the forbidden bed. When a flaming lance thrusts itself down from above, grazes his skin, and nearly pins his flanks to the sheets, he confidently puts out the flame and hurls away the sword. In the readers' eyes, he has vindicated himself against the damsel's emasculating reception and has successfully defied her authority.

Curiously, the damsel's perception of Lancelot does not change because of his victory; she does not witness it. Rather, as she watches him swoon the next morning and nearly fall from the tower on seeing Guenevere in a procession below him, she says he is right to hate his life, since he has ridden on the Cart. Her harsh judgment clearly denigrates the hero's public stature, but her underlying *sens* is inscrutable. So, too, is the conversation she has held with Gauvain at the window. We do not know what she is thinking any more than we can hear what they are saying; "ne sai de quoi / ne sai don les paroles furent" ["I assure you that I / Do not know what was said"] (548–49), insists the narrator.

Just as curiously, Chrétien tells us that after she feels she has mocked Lancelot enough—the verb he uses is "gaber"—she accords him a horse and a lance, tokens of her love and respect "par amor et par accordance" ["As token of her esteem and sympathy"] (590). The conventionalism of their parting jars with the damsel's previous scorn and leaves us wondering whether she is friend or foe. Her uncanny knowledge of the hero's shame and her erratic treatment of him intensify the strangeness of this "marvelous" scene. The perils of the bed are conjoined with the powers of woman.

Lancelot explores that connection more fully in his encounter with the Immodest Damsel. In a bizarre permutation of the hospitality convention, the hero receives a night's lodging from a maiden on the condition that he sleep with her in return for her "gift." When Lancelot reluctantly seeks her after dinner to fulfill his promise, he finds her in the act of being raped by a knight while six sergeants stand guard. Instead of rushing to save her, he ponders the nature of his quest in a lengthy monologue that delays the episode's surprising revelation. Lancelot finally enters the fray against the maiden's assailants. Then, the damsel suddenly calls off her enemies and we learn that she has staged her attack! By lying next to the damsel without removing his chemise or showing any desire for her, Lancelot ultimately remains true both to his promise to her and to his transcendent love for Guenevere.

The damsel's wish to sleep with Lancelot establishes the terms of the *covant* between them, much as Marie de Champagne's *commandemanz* set the terms for Chrétien's performance; the damsel's *don* of lodging entails the *don contraignant* of submitting to *her*. Female desire determines the initial narrative frame. But, as in the Prologue, the controlling power of that desire is subtly subverted. Here Chrétien contains the threatening power of sexuality by presenting it in the form of self-willed victimization. The male fantasy of the woman who wants to be raped takes another perverse form in a lady who exploits her helplessness to obligate a man to protect her and, implicitly, to incite his desire.[29]

As the disappointed damsel requests to accompany him upon his further adventures, she is reinscribed as an object. It is she, in fact, who explains the "custom" of Logres that determines the dependent status of all women in the romance, including Guenevere. A knight cannot dishonor a woman whom he finds alone in the forest without incurring shame or blame. But if she is accompanied by another knight whose protection is contested, the victor may do what he will with her without sanction.[30] As if to exemplify the custom's crude economy, the damsel becomes the disputed object in a potential combat between Lancelot and the presumptuous knight who claims to take her as his God-given possession.

As at the Castle of the Perilous Bed, Lancelot emerges victorious against the forces of a menacing sexuality. Similarly, the female power that initiated the action is quickly contained within the trajectory of the hero's adventures. Once again, though, Chrétien's conspicuously strange presentation of female desire—here in the form of feigned sexual humiliation—raises questions about its nature and effects. Recasting the sexual tensions of the "lit perilleux," the scene foreshadows Lancelot's future reception by Guenevere.[31] Chrétien's portrayal of a damsel who exploits her sexual victimization raises the disturbing possibility that another woman, even the Queen herself, may manipulate our hero with her oppression. The equally troubling idea comes to mind that Guenevere could comply with the terms of her abduction in order to incite her lover's desire. The surprising moment when the damsel calls off her retinue and releases Lancelot presents a paradoxical image of woman, one which seems to reflect male fears and fantasies about female sexuality; even when she appears to be most abjectly subjugated, the woman wields power over men.

IV. RESISTANCE AND SUBVERSION

Guenevere's refusal to speak with Lancelot after he has struggled so long and hard to find her inscribes the romance's most elusive instance of feminine power. When Lancelot comes to see her after his remarkable show of service in the first fight with Meleagant, instead of greeting him with joy, as we might expect, she "fet senblant de correciee, si s'anbruncha et ne dist mot" ["acted as if she were angered. / She lowered her head and said not a word"] (3940–41). She says she has no interest in seeing him and, furthermore, that she will never deny that she is *not* grateful. Lancelot, confused and chagrined, replies: "Dame, certes, ce poise moi / ne je n'os demander por coi" ["My lady, indeed this grieves me; / Yet I dare not ask your reasons"] (3963–64).

Critics troubled by Guenevere's surprising move have attempted to explain it, by suggesting that Guenevere rightly demands the absolute devotion of her lover, that she plays the coquette and deceives herself about her deepest feelings, or that she makes a mistake for which she will atone later with her anguish.[32] Our desire to know just why she has done what she has done is expressly frustrated by the narrator's refusal to provide a single answer. Lancelot, "a meniere de fin amant" ["like a perfect lover"] (3962), is stunned and reticent before his lady's mystery when she sends him away and does not ask for a reason until later. The Queen herself offers two seemingly contradictory explanations: first, that she had only meant her denial "a gas," as a joke (4204), and later, as she tells Lancelot, that it was because he had hesitated "deux pas" before stepping on the Cart (4487).

Interestingly, if we go back to the moment in the narrative when Lancelot mounts the cart, we find that the Guiot manuscript makes no mention of any hesitation and that other manuscripts which do interpolate two lines describing his hesitation may well be the result of scribal emendation, as David Hult has suggested.[33] Critics seeking coherence in the clerk's equivocal performance have seized upon these "deux pas" as the logical explanation for Guenevere's action, because they so neatly encode the absolute devotion demanded of the courtly lover. But this explanation squares neither with her earlier contention that she spoke in jest, nor with the narrator's ambiguous presentation of female authority throughout the romance.

Guenevere's refusal and her contradictory explanations act as powerful counters to the narrative coherence of Lancelot's quest. They throw a wrench into the workings of the chivalric code and make the reader wonder about this exemplar of knighthood. By refusing to become the automatic prize in the Meleagant-Lancelot combat, Guenevere removes herself from the triangle of exchange defined by the custom of Logres. She refuses to be grateful. Her silence and her anger toward the knight who comes forward for her blessing constitute a gesture of feminine resistance to an ideology that circulates women as objects. Like the first damsel's indirection and the immodest damsel's manipulations, and like the depiction of Marie de Champagne in the Prologue, Guenevere's refusal depicts a woman who shapes or opposes chivalric values. As a narrative strategy, it transfers the determinant of the story's outcome from male to female: Lancelot submits himself to *her* will, as Chrétien has done to Marie's: "Or soit a son commandemant" ["Then let it be as she orders"] (4076), Lancelot tells Keu soon afterward, echoing the Prologue's rhetoric.

Even as Guenevere refuses and resists, however, the narrative undermines her powers in significant ways. Chrétien's account that Guenevere feigns her anger and her own admission that she was "only joking," combined with the contradictory nature of her explanations, seem, at the level of characterization, to trivialize her response. More significantly, Guenevere's refusal becomes, in the ensuing events, the condition itself for the masculine plot of desire. She provides the internal obstacle that Lancelot needs to fuel his passions. After she has recognized him (by naming him for the first time in the romance), she refuses him.[34] She then recedes from the narrative as he agonizes over her absence. As Charles Méla has described the *conjointure* of all the women in this and the preceding scenes, they project a fictive woman created by a knight so that he may subject himself to her will: "L'amant courtois a érigé une divinité impénetrable et impitoyable pour être sans fin sujet à sa demande et exposé à ses exigences."[35] Woman's "power" is a fiction of the male subject who needs her to resist so that he can desire her. If we reformulate this from a feminist perspective, woman's "impenetrable divinity" marks her displacement from the position of the desiring subject, a displacement that male desire and the enigma of woman continually enact. Insofar as the *Charrete* powerfully inscribes this displacement, it participates in a cultural mystification of woman whose effects are still with us today in the idea of femininity.

But Chrétien's remarkable narrative, which sets a pattern for future Arthurian fiction, does more than mystify the woman. From another perspective, it also demystifies her by calling attention to that very displacement. Chrétien's inscription of female desire renders it inscrutable, but his narrative presentation problematizes woman's very inscrutability. Looking closely at the romance's subtext of female desire, we come to ask, as Soshana Felman has put it, "What does the question—what is femininity—for men—mean for women?"[36]

V. THE "SENS" OF ABSENCE

In the last third of the story, the narrative's subversion of female desire is even more pronounced. At the tournament of Noauz, Chrétien appears to celebrate woman's power to shape the course of narrative and pay his most brilliant homage to Marie de Champagne. The scene portrays a queen who manipulates the hero into exemplifying the opposing poles of chivalric shame and prowess; she makes him fight "au noauz" or "au mialz" at her behest. It is precisely when the knight humiliates himself to fight at his worst that Chrétien employs the same terms to describe Lancelot's submission before Guenevere as he had to prove his own service to the Countess, "com cil qui est suens antiers" ["As one who seeks only to please the queen"] (5656).

As with the earlier scenes we have examined, a close look at the narrator's presentation reveals that he ultimately subverts female power at Noauz. Guenevere's imperious commands are framed by two female publics who are indispensable components of the episode. One consists of the young ladies of Noauz, who launch the action by calling the tournament and manipulating Arthur to ensure that Guenevere will be present. The other is the seneschal's wife, who releases Lancelot from prison so that he can attend. The women's control of narrative events and their own desires are expressly frustrated in the action that follows. When the wife decides to risk her husband's anger and release her captive if he agrees to comply with a *covant*, she knows that her wishes cannot be fulfilled. She asks Lancelot to come back and give her his love. Although Lancelot promises all the love he has on his return—"tote celi que j'ai / vos doing je voir au revenir" ["I will certainly give you / All that I have upon my return"] (5482–83)—she knows that his heart has already been "bailliee et commandee" ["assigned and given to another"] (5487).

In contrast to the surprising savvy of the seneschal's wife, the ladies of Noauz are extremely naive about the impossibility of their desires. After arranging a marriage tournament to find the best husband, and mocking the unknown knight who fights at his worst, they are frustrated when they cannot marry the knight who turns out to be the "mialz." Some of them vow that if they cannot have Lancelot's love they will not marry! No longer able to control a custom that appears to work to their advantage, the young ladies of Noauz are frustrated observers of a custom that promises them much but delivers nothing. The scene's final couplet underscores the futility of their desires: "L'anhatine ensi departi / c'onques nule n'an prist mari" ["Thus the tournament ended / Without anyone having taken a husband"] (6055–56). The Noauz episode has become a linchpin in the debates about Lancelot's valor or foolishness, about Chrétien's service to Marie, and about the general *sens* of the romance. It is telling that the narrator ends not with a celebration of Lancelot and Guenevere's reciprocal passion but with an image of thwarted feminine desire.

The hero's last feminine encounter is similarly ambivalent. When Meleagant's sister frees Lancelot from the tower where he has been imprisoned by her brother, he promises to be hers ("que je toz jors mes serai vostres" ["To be yours from this day hence"] 6589) and to do as she commands forever more ("ja mes niert jorz que je ne face / quan que vos pleira comander" ["Never will a day come that I will fail to do / All you may be pleased to request"], 6592–93, emphasis mine). Lancelot's grateful submission appears once again to dramatize the narrator's initial gesture before his patroness and to valorize female strength. Furthermore, Meleagant's sister is an active figure who moves autonomously. Her force and ingenuity as she frees him contrast with Lancelot's feebleness; her initiative is indispensable to the hero's survival and the narrative's continuation. Of all the female characters in this romance, the *pucele à la mule* is the only one whose motivations are clear and generous: she tells Lancelot that she has come to repay the *don* that he made her of the *chevalier orgueilleux*'s head (6579–81). She has no hidden agenda, no furtive designs.

But her remarkable strength and the clarity of her motives serve less to restore female power or to "correct" the romance's elusive image of female desire than to further the narrative of the hero. Like Lunete in *Yvain*, she acts as a kind of stand-in for the narrator as she frees the protagonist from constraints and abets his chivalric exploits.[37] Her activity liberates the hero, so that he may conclude the romance unimpeded by feminine demands. Although Lancelot offers her his "cuer," "cors," "servise," and "avoir" (6684–85) (a pledge that would compromise his service to Guenevere were he to fulfill it), the *pucele* expresses no desire of her own. She wishes only for Lancelot's honor and well-being: "que vostre enor et vostre bien / vuel je par tot et ci et la" ["For I seek that which is to your honor / And good, both now and always"] (6698–99). Despite Lancelot's promises to her, he never returns and she never reappears. With Meleagant's sister, female desire has become controlled and deproblematized. It conforms so completely to Lancelot's will for freedom and honor that the two desires have become identical.

By the romance's final scene, even Guenevere's troublesome sexuality has been tamed. In the last combat between Meleagant and Lancelot, the Queen is no longer the resisting reader or commanding force.[38] She appears as a spectator who has fully sublimated her desire to the code of courtly propriety; she makes no public show of her passion. Her "fol cuer" and "fol pansé" are contained by reason: "por ce reisons anferme et lie / son fol cuer et son fol pansé" ["Thus Reason encompassed and bound / Her foolish heart and thoughts"] (6846–47). We hear nothing more about her after Lancelot kills Meleagant.

Within that section of the narrative penned by "Godefroy," woman's desire no longer disturbs the turn of chivalric events. The female participant in the triangle of courtly desires is instead remystified as one whose "rage" (6843) and "folie" (6845)—her threatening female sexuality—are contained by the system that reinscribes her as a forbidden object of desire. Her active voice and her direct influence are conspicuously written out of the text. The woman reader is markedly *absent* in the final lines of a romance that has so often been adduced as proof of her historical presence.

As we try to piece together the disjointed interlace of female characters in the *Charrete*, we encounter a series of disappearing acts. As female desire is subverted and mystified, the female subject vanishes. This negative pattern, if one can call it a pattern, is consonant with the dynamics of the frame, where the Godefroy-Chrétien contract replaces that between Marie and Chrétien. Given what we have seen of the narrator's problematization of female desire and the romance's subversion of female influence, the disappearance of the Countess from the parting lines of a romance dedicated to her seems a calculated move.

What might the female reader—modern or medieval—make of what Marie-Noëlle Lefay-Toury has called the "dégradation du personnage féminin" throughout the *Charrete* and the corpus of Chrétien's romance?[39] At the very least, we might agree with her that Chrétien expressly undermines the "courtly" structure of his material. On the basis of the romance's explicit subversion of the female influence it purports to acknowledge, we must also lay to rest—yet again—the thesis that Marie de Champagne exerted a "feminizing influence" on the ideals of chivalry in the *Charrete* or that, by extension, women shaped courtly literature to their own ends. But must we conclude that the appropriation and mystification of woman within the romance enact the same designs on its female reader?

Chrétien's explicit presentation of woman's influence and desire as a question—his problematization of female reception—resists our hasty judgment. The seams of the romance's ideological surface are not smooth; the narrator calls far too much attention to the uneasy relationship between the hero and his female dependents. Nor is the conclusion a closed case, as critical controversy still attests. Instead, Chrétien and Godefroy conspicuously call attention to the way a clerical exchange ends the romance. The narrative resolution, to adapt Nancy Miller's terminology, is "italicized."[40] The appropriation of Marie's "sens" in the Prologue, the romance's troublesome female agents, and the Epilogue's conspicuous absenting of women are devices that sow the seeds for critical reflection in the discerning reader. They invite our questions about the uneasy relationship of the male cleric to his feminine courtly public, as well as to male aristocratic culture. If the image of female influence, power, and resistance is recuperated *within* the text, female critical reflection on the tensions of gender is pointedly invited *by* the text. *Le Chevalier de la Charrete* provides an object lesson in the dangers romance might hold for women, and, as such, it generates—and engenders—a tradition of critical reflection on sexuality and interpretation that later Arthurian fictions will continue to elaborate.

NOTES

I would like to thank Thomas Bass, Christopher Baswell, Jane Burns, Sheila Fisher, and Nancy Rabinowitz for their thoughtful comments on various drafts of this paper, and Michel-André Bossy, who invited me to present an earlier version for the Committee on Medieval Studies and the Pembroke Center at Brown University.

1. Gaston Paris, "Lancelot du Lac. *Le Conte de la Charrette.*" *Romania* 12 (1883), 459–534, esp. 516–34. For early assertions of the feminine origins of courtly love and literature, see Reto Bezzola, "La transformation des moeurs et le rôle de la femme dans la classe féodale du XI au XIIe siècle," *Les Origines et la formation de la littérature courtoise en Occident* (500–1200), pt. 2, vol. 2 (Paris: Champion, 1960), p. 461, and Myrrha Lot-Borodine, *De L'Amour profane à l'amour sacré: études de psychologie sentimentale au Moyen Age* (Paris: Nizet, 1961), esp. pp. 16–19.

2. For a concise account of the critical controversy surrounding the *Charrete*, see Matilda Tomaryn Bruckner, "An Interpreter's Dilemma: Why Are There So Many Interpretations of Chrétien's *Chevalier de la Charrette?*" *Romance Philology* 40 (1986), 159–80 [reprinted in this volume at pp. 55–78].

3. See John F. Benton, "The Court of Champagne as a Literary Center," *Speculum* 36 (1961), 551–91 and "Clio and Venus: An Historical View of Medieval Love," in F.X. Newman, ed., *The Meaning of Courtly Love* (Albany: State University of New York Press, 1968), pp. 19–42. For arguments supporting the idea of noblewomen's influence on courtly literature, see, for example, Joan Kelly-Gadol, "Did Women Have a Renaissance?" in Renate Bridenthal and Claudia Koonz, eds., *Becoming Visible: Women in European History* (Boston: Houghton Mifflin, 1977), p. 146. Also see June Hall McCash, "Marie de Champagne's 'Cuer d'Ome et Cors de Fame': Aspects of Feminism and Misogyny in the Twelfth Century," in Glyn S. Burgess and Robert A. Taylor, eds. *The Spirit of the Court: Selected Proceedings of the Fourth Congress of the International Courtly Literature Society* (Cambridge, England: D. S. Brewer, 1985), pp. 234–45.

4. Among these studies, see Bruckner, "An Interpreter's Dilemma" and "*Le Chevalier de la Charrete (Lancelot),*" in Douglas Kelly, ed., *The Romances of Chrétien de Troyes: A Symposium* (Lexington: French Forum, 1985), pp. 132–81; Norris J. Lacy, *The Craft of Chrétien de Troyes: An Essay on Narrative Art* (Leiden: Brill, 1980), pp. 54–60 and 88–93; and an unpublished paper by David Hult, "Author/Narrator/Speaker: The Voice of Authority in Chrétien's *Charrete.*"

5. All quotations of the *Charrete* are drawn from *Le Chevalier de la Charrete*, ed. Mario Roques (Paris: Champion, 1972). Translations are taken from *Lancelot, or The Knight of the Cart*, ed. and trans. William W. Kibler (New York: Garland, 1984). Line references, cited in parentheses, are to the edition of Roques.

6. See my "Contracts and Constraints: Courtly Performance in *Yvain* and the *Charrete*," in Edward R. Haymes, ed., *The Medieval Court in Europe* (Munich: Wilhelm Fink, 1986), pp. 92–104.

7. As evidenced by an extensive philological debate begun by Jean Frappier and Jean Rychner. The discussion revolves around whether the "sans" that Marie gives

Chrétien is the romance's "idée maîtresse" (Frappier) or whether it is merely the "inspiration" (Rychner). It hinges on the etymological and semantic difference of "sans," 23 (from the Latin *sensus*) and "sans," 26 (from the Frankish *sin*), a distinction that some have argued is pointedly ambiguous. See Bruckner, *"Le Chevalier de la Charrete,"* 135–38.

8. Godefroy's conclusion has provoked nearly as much discussion as the Prologue. See, for example, David A. Shirt, "Godefroy de Lagny et la composition de la *Charrete,"* *Romania* 96 (1975), 27–52, and Bruckner, *"Le Chevalier de la Charrete,"* 162–65. My inclination is to agree with David Hult that we read "Godefroy" as a fictional clerkly-author figure conceived by the author Chrétien. See Hult, "Author/Narrator/Speaker."

9. For a theoretical discussion of literary texts as a vehicle for male bonding, see Eve Kosofsky Sedgwick, *Between Men: English Literature and Male Homosexual Desire* (New York: Columbia University Press, 1985).

10. Charles Méla, *La Reine et le Graal: La conjointure dans les romans du Graal de Chrétien de Troyes au Livre de Lancelot* (Paris: Seuil, 1984), p. 258.

11. On the female patronage of Old French and Provençal literature, see Rita Lejeune, "La femme dans les littératures française et occitane du XIe au XIIIe siècle," *Cahiers de civilisation médiévale* 20 (1977), 204–08.

12. For a cautionary statement, see Penny Schine Gold, *The Lady and the Virgin: Image, Attitude, and Experience in Twelfth-Century France* (Chicago: University of Chicago Press, 1985), pp. xv–xxi.

13. See Georges Duby, *Le Chevalier, la femme, et le prêtre: le mariage dans la France féodale* (Paris: Hachette, 1981), and Suzanne Wemple and Jo Ann McNamara, "The Power of Women Through the Family in Medieval Europe: 500–1100," *Feminist Studies* 1 (1973), 126–41.

14. This is not to deny the importance of the feminine voices of Marie de France, Héloïse, and the *trobaritz*. But even here, a problematic of absence and displacement obtains, if only in their critical context: the authenticity of the female signature has been, in each case, disputed.

15. This point has been forcefully made by Joan Ferrante in *Woman as Image in Medieval Literature: From the Twelfth Century to Dante* (New York: Columbia University Press, 1975), and in "Male Fantasy and Female Reality in Courtly Literature," *Women's Studies* 11 (1984), 67–97.

16. For a partial discussion of the object status of women, see my "Double Jeopardy: The Appropriation of Woman in Four Old French Romances of the 'Cycle de la Gageure,' " in Janet Halley and Sheila Fisher, eds., *The Lady Vanishes: Feminist Contextual Criticism of Late Medieval and Renaissance Writings*, forthcoming from the University of Tennessee Press.

17. Most studies of the social function of romance have been gender-neutral in their consideration of chivalric ideology. By focusing on class tensions, on the emergence of individuality, on legal structures and kinship, or on self-conscious literary values, scholars have overlooked the genre's troublesome silencing of the female subject and its subversion of female power. Whether willingly or not, they have confirmed the concerns of clerical and chivalric male culture as romance's central problem.

18. A provocative reading of the problematic inscription of female sexuality within one of the first courtly romances, *Le Roman d'Eneas*, has been advanced by Jean-Charles Huchet, *Le Roman médiéval* (Paris: Presses Universitaires de France, 1984).

19. On "reading against" the text as a strategy of the feminist critic, see Patrocinio P. Schweikart, "Toward a Feminist Theory of Reading," in Elizabeth Flynn and Schweikart, eds., *Gender and Reading* (Baltimore: Johns Hopkins University Press, 1986), pp. 49–54.

20. Bruckner, *"Le Chevalier de la Charrete,"* 162–75.

21. Although Chrétien does not refer to her refusal to see Lancelot as a "command" during the scene itself, Lancelot later uses this term to explain to Keu that he must follow the queen's wishes—"Or soit a son comandemant" (4076). The term echoes the Countess's "commandemanz" in the Prologue (22).

22. Moshé Lazar, "Lancelot et la 'mulier mediatrix:' la quête de soi à travers la femme." *Esprit Créateur* 9 (1969), 243–356.

23. Bruckner, "*Le Chevalier de la Charrete*," 148–57.

24. See Charles Méla's brilliant analysis of how the women are used to dramatize the shame and ecstasy of the hero's sexual transgression in his chapter on the *Charrete*, "L'in-Signifiance d'amour," in *La Reine et le Graal*, pp. 257–321.

25. For a very different reading, which views these women as independent and powerful reflections of Marie de Champagne's influence, see McCash, "Marie de Champagne's 'Cuer d'Ome et Cors de Fame,' " pp. 236–38.

26. The longest episode, the sequence of events with the "immodest damsel," comprises over 1000 lines (931–2013), but the other encounters are significantly shorter.

27. The figures in parentheses refer to the utterance of the verbal constraint and to the boundaries of the episode, respectively.

28. This article has been abridged from a longer study on women readers and the representation of woman in the *Charrete* and other twelfth- and thirteenth-century Old French romances.

29. As Kathryn Gravdal has suggested in a paper delivered at the December 1986 MLA, the rape scene is a cynical extension of the "rape is what women really want" argument.

30. Since not all knights are honorable, this means, presumably, that a woman would do well to attach herself to a champion, thereby becoming fair game in the exchange system. See my discussion of this "custom" and its implications in "Love, Honor, and the Exchange of Women in *Yvain:* Some Remarks on the Female Reader," *Romance Notes* 25 (1985), 302–17.

31. Lexical and thematic resonances underscore the parallels between the damsel's staged rape and Guenevere's abduction. As Lancelot wonders where the damsel is after dinner, Lancelot says "Je la querrai tant que je l'ai" ["I'll seek her until I have her"] (1055), as he might for the queen. The hero specifically reflects upon his quest for Guenevere during his delaying monologue at the scene of the "crime" (1097–99).

32. See, for example, Reto Bezzola, *Le sens de l'aventure et de l'amour* (Paris: La Jeune Parque, 1947), p. 44; Eugène Vinaver, *A la recherche d'une poétique médiévale* (Paris, 1970), p. 114; Douglas Kelly, *"Sens" and "Conjointure" in the "Chevalier de la Charrete"* (The Hague: Mouton, 1966), p. 58; Jean Frappier, *Chrétien de Troyes* (Paris: Hatier, 1968), 130–41.

33. David Hult, "Lancelot's Two Steps: A Problem in Textual Criticism," *Speculum* 61 (1986), 836–58.

34. On the role of the "femme bonne" whose recognition and resistance affirm masculine identity in the phallogocentric order, see Hélène Cixous, "Sorties," in Catherine Clément and Hélène Cixous, *La Jeune Née* (Paris: 10/18, 1978), pp. 144–47.

35. Méla, *La Reine et le Graal*, p. 288.

36. Shoshana Felman, "Rereading Feminity," *Yale French Studies* 62 (1981), 21. I am grateful to Mary Jacobus' excellent discussion of reading the representation of women in fiction for bringing the relevance of this essay to my attention. Mary Jacobus, *Reading Woman: Essays in Feminist Criticism* (New York: Columbia University Press, 1986), pp. 13–21.

37. On Lunete's affinity with Yvain and the narrator, see my "Love, Honor and the Exchange of Women." David Hult has remarked, in discussion, that the emergence of narrative interventions in the "Godefroy" section of the poem coincides with

the appearance of Meleagant's sister. Hult emphasizes the centrality of her role, which clearly deserves further attention.

38. Hult has offered another perspective on Guenevere's absence in these final lines in "A Queen is Missing: Guenevere in Chrétien's *Lancelot*," given in a session on "Woman and Old French Romance" at the International Congress on Medieval Studies, Kalamazoo, 1987.

39. Marie Noëlle Lefay-Toury, "Roman bretons et mythes courtois: l'évolution du personnage féminin dans les romans de Chrétien de Troyes." *Cahiers de civilisation médiévale* 15 (1972), 193–204 and 283–93.

40. Nancy K. Miller, "Emphasis Added: Plots and Plausibilities in Women's Fictions," *PMLA* 96 (1981), 44. Miller's comments on "marking" and "italicization" in women's fiction seem applicable to any text that highlights the tensions of gender.

13 WHICH QUEEN?

GUINEVERE'S TRANSVESTISM IN THE FRENCH PROSE *LANCELOT*

E. Jane Burns

"My lady, who are you? If you are the queen, then tell me so" ("Dame, qui estes vous? Si vous estes la roïne, si le me dites").[1]

Thus begins a particularly telling scene of the French Prose *Lancelot*, a thirteenth-century rewriting of the Lancelot and Guinevere story that raises, throughout its many pages, the question of the queen's problematic identity. As King Arthur's wife and Lancelot's adulterous ladylove, Guinevere occupies a central, if vexed position in this protracted account of knightly valor and spiritual questing.[2] Though her role as a sexualized object of desire, ravishment, and exchange between men is first elaborated in Chrétien de Troyes's twelfth-century version of the adulterous tale, Chrétien's earlier romances assign more varied roles to the queen; she appears as a go-between for nascent lovers, a priestly facilitator of marriage, a teacher of love's rules, and a feudal overlord of the young couples in her care.[3] Yet Guinevere's identity proves particularly elusive to the reader of twelfth- and thirteenth-century Arthurian romance, not so much because she slides with ease between varied narrative personae in different works, but because she so often defies definition even when occupying only one of those character slots.

This is the dilemma cogently voiced in the query with which we began. An unnamed knight, galloping through the forest in the company of Lancelot, happens upon one of King Arthur's residences where "a lady," unable to sleep, and having wrapped herself in a dress and cloak, appears at the window (M 7:442). Although the knight thinks that this lady must be "the queen," he asks the question directly. And to the woman's unequivocal reply, "Oïl biax sire, che sui je, mais por coi le dites vous?" ("Yes, I am she, but why do you ask?"), the knight offers a surprisingly befuddled and halting response: "Chertes, dame, fait il, por che que deves bien estre et se vous ne l'esties, sel sembles vous bien" ("Because you probably are the queen, my lady, and if you are not, you certainly seem to be," M 7:442). That

Guinevere *seems* to be the queen, that she *appears* to be exactly like the queen, gives pause to the questing knight and to the inquisitive reader as well. In fact the brief exchange quoted here between Guinevere and Lancelot's traveling companion moves us to wonder how this knight or any knight, indeed how this reader or any other, might best define, delimit, or determine with certainty the identity of the most elusive of Arthurian queens: Guinevere.

WHICH QUEEN?

Lancelot himself asks the question pointedly on more than one occasion. Although Guinevere is typically referred to throughout this prose text by the epithet "ma dame la roïne" (my lady the queen), Lancelot does not always acknowledge the appellation as being uniquely hers. When he hears a squire recount that "Ja est ma dame la roïne en prison en la Dolerouse Garde" ("My lady the queen is in prison at the Dolorous Garde," M 7:413), the concerned Lancelot responds uncertainly, "Laquel roïne?" ("Which queen?"), just as he does a few pages later when yet another squire reports that "ma dame la roïne est chi a Chamaalot" ("My lady the queen is here at Camelot," M 7:438). Again Lancelot reacts with "Which queen?" ("Laquele roïne?"). For Guinevere to be designated typically as "the queen," as opposed to any number of other queens mentioned by name throughout this lengthy tale,[4] indicates the singular distinction of being King Arthur's wife, as both of Lancelot's interlocutors attest: "Laquel roïne?—La feme le roi Artu" (M 7:413, 438).[5]

Yet to be King Arthur's wife, as Guinevere plays that role, is to defy the very definition of the term *feme* with its connotations of female subservience, wifely obedience, and queenly honor. For in addition to being a specific queen, Guinevere is also, as her doubled title suggests, a specific *dame* or lady in this narrative. Readers of Arthurian romance know all too well that "ma dame la roïne" plays simultaneously the contradictory roles of Arthur's queen and Lancelot's courtly *dame* in adultery. Although Lancelot's question "Which queen?" seems initially to ask simply which queen among several possible ones was lodged at the Dolorous Garde or at Camelot, the query also raises the more probing issue of Guinevere's very identity, suggesting that there might be more than one queen Guinevere, or that this lady queen might not always be what she "seems."

It is well known that Lancelot is twice cruelly deceived in later scenes of the Prose *Lancelot* into sleeping with King Pelles's daughter, "believing that she was the queen" ("comme cil qui cuide qui ce soit la roïne," M 4:209) and "taking her for his lady" ("il cuidoit vraiement que ce fust sa dame,"

M 6:174).[6] But the ability of protagonists within the Arthurian world to establish Guinevere's identity with certainty is questioned most fully in the episode of the so-called False Guinevere, a half-sister of the queen, also named Guinevere, who claims to be King Arthur's rightful spouse:

> La roïne Genievre et ele avoit non Genievre autresi: si estoient ansdeus si s'une samblance que la ou eles furent norries connoissoit l'en a paine l'une de l'autre.

> (She was called Guinevere just as Queen Guinevere was; the two women were so much alike that even those who raised them could barely tell them apart. M 1:95)[7]

These two women are identical, we are told.[8] And indeed the Old French text never labels one Guinevere "true" and the other "false." In fact, the narrator's initial distinction between the pretender to the throne as "Genievre, la fille le roi Leodagan de Tarmelide" (M 1:97) and King Arthur's wife as "la roïne" (M 1:97), soon collapses chaotically when the intruder becomes simply "ma dame la roïne" in the speech of the rival Guinevere's messenger, and Arthur refers repeatedly to the legitimate queen as "Genievre":

> 'Sire, fet il, ma dame la roïne enrage de ce que vos voles doner terre a vostre soignant, et sachies que si nus de vos chevaliers li done terre, ele en morra de duel.' De ces noveles est li rois si corocies que tote en mue la color et dist al chevalier: 'Dites li que tote en soit seure que ja ne ferai rien dont ele soit corocie.' Et li rois revient a mon seignor Gauvain, si li dist: 'Bials nies, il est issi que Geneivre ne puet remanoir en ma terre ne en terre que nus de mes homes ait.'

> ("Sir," he said, "my lady the queen is enraged that you intend to give some of your land to your concubine. Be assured that if any of your knights gives her land, she [ma dame la reine] will die of grief." These words so outraged the king that he became red in the face amd told the knight, "Tell her to rest assured that I will never do anything to cause her dismay." Then the king approached Sir Gawain and said, "Guinevere can no longer stay on my land, or on land belonging to my knights." M 1:148)[9]

The reader here experiences the dizzying uncertainty described by the queen's interlocutor in the scene with which we began. Though we think we can discern from one sentence to the next which Guinevere is the true queen and which the impostor, frequent syntactical ambiguities defy any such clear judgment, suggesting instead yet another way in which "ma dame la roïne" may not in fact be Arthur's wife.

Indeed we are thrown off guard from the very moment the rival Guinevere appears at Arthur's court to accuse the queen of treason and disinheritance. She says:

> Diex saut . . . Genievre la fille le roi Leogadan de Tarmelide et Diex confonde tos les enemis et totes les enemies que j'ai saiens!

> ("May God protect Guinevere, the daughter of King Leodagan of Tarmelide and confound all the enemies, male and female, that *I* have here!" M 1:97, my emphasis)

At first, we might readily assume that this second Guinevere is speaking in deference to and in defense of the sitting queen, as if to say: "May God keep her and confound all the enemies she has here." But when the speaker interjects the unexpected "je" at the end of her sentence, clearly equating the Guinevere of her prior utterance with herself, we confront the very difficulty that Arthur's court will soon face in determining which Guinevere is the queen. "Laquele roïne" is in question here? Yet the confusion of pronouns that marks Guinevere's identity in this scene merely outlines a larger question that haunts our ability to read Queen Guinevere throughout the Prose *Lancelot*. This queen's identity is not only conflated with that of other women: other queens, other Guineveres. Her problematic status in the Arthurian world also hinges upon a more complex and more unsettling resemblance to men.

Guinevere's Unmarked Transvestism

Christiane Marchello-Nizia has suggested that the Guinevere of the Prose *Lancelot* may not in fact be a woman. As beauty incarnate, rather than an anatomically beautiful woman, Guinevere represents, in Marchello-Nizia's reading, the royal power that Lancelot seeks to achieve through homosocial bonding with the king.[10] It is ties between men, between Lancelot and Galehot in particular and Lancelot and Arthur more generally, Marchello-Nizia contends, rather than the heterosexual ties of courtly love, that predominate in this prose romance. Guinevere becomes then a mere cipher for femaleness, functioning more accurately as a figure for the male body and the power it represents.

But if we pursue the enigmatic portrayal of Guinevere's potential "maleness" across the many pages of the Prose *Lancelot*, we begin to see how the issue is not so much that Guinevere is absent from the text, rather that the queen is often subtly cross-dressed. Of course Guinevere does not actually wear men's clothing. She differs markedly, in this respect, from the medieval heroines Silence (in *Le Roman de Silence*) and Blanchandine (in *Tristan de Nanteuil*), who dress in men's clothes to compensate for various social limitations imposed upon femaleness.[11] And the Prose *Lancelot* contains none of the grammatical irregularities that often accompany the cross-dressed heroines of these other texts: for example, we find no dyadic femininization and masculinization of Guinevere's name (as in Silentia/Silentius), no gender anomalies in the narrative's syntax (calling a woman "him"), and no misplaced epithets (referring to a seeming male as "la bele," Perret, 332–36). Guinevere's cross-dressing is only metaphorical, but more disruptive in the end than the temporary gender-switching of Silence and Blanchandine, whose eventual reinstatement in pat female or male roles simply underwrites the status quo of gender differentiation.[12] Rather than pretending to be a man who, reassuringly, turns out to be a woman after all, Guinevere seems at times, on the contrary, to occupy both male and female positions at once.

Her metaphorical cross-dressing resembles most closely what Marjorie Garber has called the "transvestite effect," a phenomenon that challenges the very foundations of the binary thinking that distinguishes male from female, whether these categories are considered essential or constructed, biological or cultural.[13] The transvestite effect topples sexual binarism by emphasizing the third term—whether that of the "boy" in Renaissance drama, the "maid" enacted by Joan of Arc, or Maxine Hong Kingston's "warrior"—thereby calling into question the concept of identity itself: identity as oneness, self-sufficiency, and self knowledge (11). Garber derives her definition of the transvestite effect from Lacan's distinction between "having," "being," and "seeming" (121–22, 356). If, as Lacan contends in "The Significance of the Phallus," the sexes are constructed differently, as sexed subjects, only with reference to the phallic signifier, then masculinity and femininity are positions taken up on either side of that crucial linguistic signifier, the phallus. Whereas "to have" the phallus is what men do, in fantasy, according to Lacan, and "to be" the phallus or the object of desire is what women do in fantasy, the intervening term is "to seem" (Garber, 356; Lacan, *Ecrits*, 289). And indeed, this is the crucial and defining term for relations between the sexes in the Lacanian model since "to have" and "to be" are fantasy ideals. As Elizabeth Grosz explains the process:

The phallus functions only intersubjectively, for it is only by means of the other that one's possession of or identity with the phallus can be confirmed. To have or to be the phallus entails having a place within a circuit in which the other's desire plays a crucial part. Ideally, if not in practice, the two sexes complement each other: through a man, a woman can become the phallus (his object of desire); through sexual relations with a woman, a man [can] be affirmed as having a phallus. However, this ideal, like demand itself, is impossible. The demands of each make the satisfaction both seek impossible.[14]

Neither woman nor man ever receives the desired affirmation of subjectivity; they only *seem* to "be" or to "have" the phallus. Hence they only *seem* to be masculine or feminine. In the end, sexual identity or the division of the sexes for Lacan is both essential (a normative ideal) and precarious (a play of semblance), as Jacqueline Rose and Jane Gallop have both explained.[15]

It is that precariousness or the play of semblance that Garber uses to describe the transvestite effect. For transvestism, in her definition, is neither mask nor masquerade,[16] neither male nor female, but a third term, an indeterminate state of "seeming" that significantly calls into question our most basic cultural assumptions about sex and gender (13).[17]

Guinevere, too, I will argue here, provides at key moments the rich potential of the transvestite effect that Garber describes, specifically as it appears in "unmarked transvestism." Different from overt cross-dressers, who are marked transvestites, their unmarked counterparts occupy the space of "thirdness" in more subtle, partial, and suggestive ways. Garber characterizes their transvestism as "latent" rather than overt, often intermittent rather than constant (357–68). Unmarked transvestism issues perhaps the most disturbing challenge to the normative concept of gender differentiation because its practitioners fluctuate unpredictably back and forth across gender lines.

And indeed when the wayward knight in the French Prose *Lancelot* asks Guinevere the key question "qui estes vous?" he comes away only with a vague and unsettling sense of "seeming": she seems to be the queen, but is she really? How can he know? That is, how can he know whether she is a queen, a woman, or even a man? Such crucial questions about gender identity, which dominate contemporary theoretical debate, were already current, I will argue, in the vernacular literature of thirteenth-century France. And they tend to crystallize in the Prose *Lancelot* around the figure of Guinevere. Through a series of cross-gendered performances this heroine seriously calls into question the highly codified conventions of heterosexual courtly love and conduct that her eroticized anatomy also often underwrites. Like

Garber's unmarked transvestite, Guinevere's presence in the courtly world mobilizes anxieties about visibility and difference (Garber, 130) that are not allowed to surface within normative patterns of sexual identity.

Even the most standard definitions of Guinevere—as King Arthur's wife or Lancelot's ladylove—are fraught with surprising gender ambiguities. As an unfailing royal partner who defers to the king's judgment and underwrites his decisions (M 7:351), Guinevere certainly "seems" to function appropriately as King Arthur's queen ("la feme le roi Artu," M 7:413, 438). That she reigns suitably alongside him without preempting his authority, is often clearly marked grammatically by the conjunction "and" ("et"), as when Lancelot pledges to serve his king *and* queen,[18] or when he obeys their joint command, respecting "the will of the king *and* the queen" ("por la volenté le roi *et* la roïne," M 2:108). The king *and* queen together press Galehot to divulge the name of an unknown knight (M 8:93); together "le rois *et* la roïne" listen to Lancelot recount his chivalric adventures (M 2:111). This litany of shared status extends to the power of vassalic overlord that Guinevere holds along with the king, as the Dame de Malehaut attests to Guinevere: "Par la foi que je doi mon signor le roi cui fame je sui lige *ne* vous qui ma dame estes" ("By the faith that I owe to my lord the king whose liegewoman I am *and* to you who are my liegelady," M 8:43).

And yet in her adulterous liaison with Lancelot, Guinevere oversteps this role as Arthur's queen and royal consort to become too thoroughly and independently the lord herself. This is the import, I believe, of the queen's own description of her estrangement from Arthur in the False Guinevere episode, not in terms of the rival woman's fabricated accusations, but as a result of her ostensibly impudent decision to sleep with Lancelot:

> Je sui departie del roi mon seignor par mon meffet, je le conois bien: non pas por ce que je ne soie sa feme esposee et roïne coronee et sacree ausi com il fu, et sui fille al roi Leodagan de Tarmelide, mais li pechiés m'a neü de ce que je me cochai o autre qu'a mon seignor.

> ("I know I have been separated from my lord the king because of my own wrongdoing; not because I am not his wedded wife and queen crowned and sanctified just as he was, nor because I am not the daughter of King Leodagan of Tarmelide. But sin moved me to lie with a man other than my lord." M 1:152)[19]

Guinevere's behavior is deemed unacceptable in this instance because it defies legal statutes and social codes. But her adulterous act is equally threatening to courtly society because it crosses proscribed gender boundaries. "How dare she, a woman, pursue an adulterous passion in defiance of her spouse?" this text seems to ask. Adultery was acceptable for men, not women, in the Middle Ages; the province of lords, not ladies. That Guinevere pursues her adulterous liaison with such resolve smacks inappropriately of male prerogative. This *feme* and *roïne* has taken the liberties of a man.

In her role as Lancelot's *dame*, Guinevere is no more conventionally female. Though she often "seems" to be the perfect object of desire—as the most beautiful and best loved of all women (M 4:205; 8:444); as a woman commodified and traded first between Arthur and Meleagant (M 2:4) and subsequently between Arthur and Lancelot; or as Lancelot's ladylove, "la dame au millor chevalier du monde" (M 8:462)[20]—key moments of subtle gender-crossing mar this lady's courtly portrait. When Guinevere whimsically rejects the supplicant suitor Lancelot who has heroically and humbly performed extraordinary feats of valor on her behalf, she plays again the role of empowered lord, this time in the tradition of the Provençal *domna* who enjoys the social status of a male.[21] In response to Guinevere's surprising assertions that "I owe him nothing" and "I will never love him," King Bademagu points to Lancelot's distinguished service that should, according to the rules of courtly conduct, readily override any mistakes the knight may have previously made (M 2:68). "How dare she as a lady defy courtly conduct in snubbing the deserving knight Lancelot?" the prose romance seems to ask here.[22]

Roberta Krueger has explained convincingly how this enigmatic scene in Chrétien de Troyes's version of the Lancelot story figures the enigma of female desire that pervades a text in which the narrator asks quizzically through a number of scenes, "what do women want?" or "what more than courtly love and courtly life could they want?"[23] But Guinevere here defies the dictates of ladylike conduct by crossing proscribed gender boundaries as well.[24] Rather than "giving" generously to the supplicant knight as Guinevere earlier explains a courtly lady must, "ne il ne me poroit nule chose requerre dont je le puisse escondire belement" ("I cannot honestly refuse him anything he might request," M 8:114), the *dame* here jousts verbally with her lover, relegating him to an embarrassing public defeat (M 2:68). As a woman and a courtly lady, Guinevere cannot physically do battle with Lancelot or any other knight. Yet she does here and elsewhere break the courtly codes of generosity and hospitality by openly sparring with her lover in verbal combat.[25] In so doing she reminds us of knights whose stated duty is to do battle, not to give in to their opponents or to give anything at all.

Lancelot explains the rules of this chivalric game in relation to his brief encounter with a recalcitrant bridge guard when returning from the

Dame de Nohaut's castle: "[Je] dis sans faille qu'il n'en avroit huimais point; si jostai a lui" ("I told him that he would get nothing from me that day; I fought him instead," M 8:106). In detailing the terms of knightly conduct in battle, Lancelot here foreshadows Guinevere's own future reaction to him. "To give nothing but fight instead" is precisely the tactic that Guinevere later deploys, in the form of verbal jousting, against Lancelot in the rejection scene. Though she wears no armor in her dispute with Lancelot, Guinevere has cross-dressed metaphorically as a knight.[26]

GUINEVERE'S GENDER PERFORMANCES

I do not wish to argue here that Guinevere is a man in disguise, nor that she is somehow androgynous. The incidents described earlier are not, to my mind, moments of temporary gender crossing that can be fully corrected by a return to acceptable modes of action. I think, rather, that the figure of Guinevere in the French Prose *Lancelot* functions as a locus of displacement, substitution, and slippage between the categories of male and female, thereby calling into question the presumed natural alignment of sex and gender in courtly romance. In this way the fictional character of Guinevere in thirteenth-century Arthurian romance reveals how the very category of gender might be performative in Judith Butler's sense of the term, that is, "a *corporeal style*, an 'act,' as it were, which is both intentional and performative, where 'performative' suggests a dramatic and contingent construction of meaning."[27] One must, of course, make a distinction here between what historical individuals choose to do and what literary characters are made to do by the authors who create them. Whereas Butler distinguishes three contingent dimensions of significant corporeality—anatomical sex, gender identity, and gender performance (137)—we readers of literary texts have only gender identity and gender performance to consider. But my point is that the literary Queen Guinevere plays out on the stage of Arthurian fiction the role of the drag queen that Butler invokes as a model for denaturalizing sex and gender: "*In imitating gender, drag implicitly reveals the imitative structure of gender itself—as well as its contingency*" (137).[28] When Guinevere engages in the adulterous behavior reserved for men alone in the French Middle Ages, or when she assumes the empowered social status of the Provençal lord, the prose text offers us something more nuanced than the spectacle of a woman "acting like" a man. Rather, Guinevere's disruptive cross-gendered behavior mimics traditional male roles in a way that reveals them to be contingent and constructed. If women can "seem" to be men, even in passing, then how can we be sure they are not in fact men? Or in Lacanian terms, how can we discern the masculine position of "having" the phallus from "seeming to have" it, or the feminine position of "being the phallus" from "seeming" to be it? Butler herself makes the link between her theory of gender performance and psychoanalysis as follows:

> Just as the psychoanalytic notion of gender identification is constituted by a fantasy of a fantasy, the transfiguration of an Other who is always already a "figure" in that double sense, so gender parody reveals that the original identity after which gender fashions itself is an imitation without an origin (138).

In the same vein, the Prose *Lancelot*'s complex portrait of Queen Guinevere shows us much more than a female character imitating male behavior. Incidents of this queen's cross-gendered behavior allow us to glimpse instead the precariousness of the very categories of lord and lady, husband and wife, male and female that the courtly code so staunchly endorses.

KNIGHTS AND LADIES; LADIES AND GENTLE MEN

The courtly categories of gender are perhaps most overtly questioned in the Prose *Lancelot* in a scene that has drawn considerable attention for its homosocial overtones. Yet the scene holds even broader implications for the kind of unmarked transvestism we have been discussing. When Lancelot's close companion Galehot asks Gauvain what he would *give* to have Lancelot liberated from prison and "forever have such a valiant man with him / for himself?" (M 8:94), Gauvain replies:

> Je voldroie orendroit estre la plus bele damoisele del mont saine et haitie, par covent qu'il m'amast sor toute rien toute sa vie et la moie.

> ("I would like to be the most beautiful damsel in the world, in perfect health, provided that he love me more than anyone else for the duration of his life and mine." M 8:94).

Gauvain's imagined scenario of *giving* something in return for Lancelot's affections casts him, not surprisingly, in the role of a beautiful *damoiselle*, a female object of desire loved and adored by Lancelot. What Gauvain has wished for here, at least in some sense, is to switch places with Guinevere, to play the role of Lancelot's ladylove that is traditionally allotted to the queen, that is, "ma dame la roïne." Does this mean, then, that Lancelot's earlier question "which queen?" could now elicit a very different response; instead of "King Arthur's wife," could the reply be "Lancelot's lover?" If so, the queen has switched from female to male. Does this mean then that "the queen" can be of either gender? Or perhaps that she/he can move between genders?

As important as Gauvain's fantasy of cross-dressing in this scene is Guinevere's subsequent response to Galehot's question, for it further erodes pat categories of male and female by setting up another round of verbal sparring. When Galehot asks Guinevere what she would give in order to "have such a knight forever in your service" (M 8:94), the lady—*dame*, as she is called repeatedly in this sequence—reacts more as a knight than a lady, turning the conversation into a contest. Guinevere figures here as a key player, not a prize to be won, as she creates a battle of one-upmanship that she avers she cannot win: "Mesire Gauvain i a mis quanque dame i puet metre, ne dame ne puet plus offrir" ("Sir Gawain has already offered everything a woman could; no woman can do more than that," M 8:94). Rather than standing off as distinctly gendered opponents in the question contest arranged by Galehot, Gauvain and Guinevere merge murkily together, each taking on the sex of the other to a significant degree. Guinevere can say nothing that Gauvain has not already said because he has spoken as she would, as a *dame*. But if Gauvain can perform the role of *dame*, can the lady too become a knight and a man, in some sense?

This fascinating exchange serves pointedly to denaturalize the categories of sex and gender so that attributed gender and gender performance do not necessarily match and male/female binarisms begin to topple. The act of "giving" no longer functions as a stereotypically female trait, nor is "sparring" here typically male. Through these curious scenes the Prose *Lancelot* plays out then the fuller implications of the comment made by Lancelot's fellow knight to the unmarked queen, "you seem to be the queen." It does so not by encouraging us to move from "seeming" to "being," where we might more readily distinguish male from female, subject from object, or knight from lady. Rather, this text pushes us, as it might also have nudged its medieval readers/listeners, to think about just how one determines what constitutes femaleness and maleness in the courtly society of King Arthur's world.

Fe/male Identity: Lancelot as Guinevere?

The issue is complicated by Guinevere's own protracted interrogation regarding Lancelot's identity. Typically, queries voiced to determine Lancelot's social role and status in the prose text meet with a ready and unquestioned response that underwrites the stereotype of the chivalric hero. In reply to rival knights who ask "Qui estes vous?" (M 4:297), Lancelot explains succinctly "qu'il est .I. chevaliers de la meson le roi Artus, et ai non Lancelot del Lac" ("that he is a knight of King Arthur's court named Lancelot of the Lake," M 4:297) or, more generically, "Uns chevaliers sui, fet Lancelos, qui vieng ceste part por ceste demoisele deffendre" (" 'I am a knight,' Lancelot said, 'who has come here to defend this young woman,' " M 2:220). To the queen of Sorestan's "Tell me who you are" ("Dites-moi qui vous estes," M 4:335), Lancelot offers, "Dame, je sui .I. chevaliers erranz de la meson le roi Artus et compainz de la Table Reonde et chevaliers la roïne Genievre ma dame" ("Lady, I am a knight errant from King Arthur's court, member of the Round Table and one of my lady Queen Guinevere's knights," M 4:336).[29]

But when Guinevere tries to ascertain directly from Lancelot "qui vous estes" (M 8:104), the answers to her question produce a curious result.[30] First, Lancelot refuses to say who he is or even to reveal himself as the victor at the preceding day's tournament. Then Guinevere introduces a new line of questioning in order to elicit details of the knight's chivalric background: "Or me dites, fait ele, qui vous fist chevalier?" ("Tell me now, she said, who made you a knight?" M 8:105). The queen's query leads curiously, not to Lancelot's actions but to her own, when the knight replies, "It was you, my lady" ("Dame, fet il, vous"). Rather than help to answer Guinevere's initial and persistent question "qui estes-vous?" Lancelot here provides the answer to his own earlier question, "laquel roïne?" For it was in fact this queen, Guinevere, who made Lancelot a knight. In this instance, inquiring about Lancelot's identity leads us tellingly to Guinevere's identity, and more specifically to Guinevere as a stand-in for King Arthur:

> Dame . . . il est voirs, car la coustume estoit el roialme de Logres que chevaliers ne pooit estre fais sans espee chaindre et chil de qui il tient l'espee le fait chevalier; et de vous le tieng je, que li rois ne m'en douna point: por ce di je que vous me feistes chevalier.

> ("Lady, the custom of Logres dictated, in truth, that one could not become a knight without receiving a sword; the person giving the sword was the one who conferred knighthood. I hold my sword from you; the king did not give it to me. This is why I say that you made me a knight." M 8:106)

It is a commonplace of Arthurian studies that Lancelot's prowess derives from Guinevere: from her look, her inspiring presence, the mere thought of her, and even her words.[31] In this version of the story, Lancelot attributes all his chivalric accomplishments to the single phrase "biax dols amis" ("dear sweet friend") with which he feels Guinevere proclaimed him her knight and lover (M 8:111). But the preceding passage reveals more than the stereotypical influence of the courtly lady behind the heroic man. If Guinevere in fact gave Lancelot the sword with which he now protects and defends her, the sword responsible for Lancelot's incomparable reputation as the world's best knight, does that mean in some sense that, through Lancelot, Guinevere actually defends herself? Is it her sword as much as his, her force as much as his prowess that safeguards her? Does this passage then not reiterate the suggestion made in Guinevere's earlier remarks to Galehot that she too can be a knight, at least metaphorically, much as Gauvain can fantasize becoming a *damoiselle*?

This is the power of "seeming" that the Prose *Lancelot* addresses directly: Guinevere appears to be a woman and a man; that is to say, neither a woman nor a man simply; but not an androgyne nor a transvestite in the traditional sense either. The complex character of "ma dame la roïne" provides the reader, medieval and modern, with the possibility of imagining a locus where such categories do not hold.

In fact when Guinevere "takes pleasure" in further verbal sparring with the befuddled Lancelot ("ele se delitoit," M 8:112), she asks a series of questions that position her impossibly as both the desired feminized object (*aucune dame*) and the speaking masculinized subject (*Dame*) of the sentence, "Et je sai bien que por *aucune dame* aves vous che fait, et dites moi qui ele est" ("I know you did all of this for a lady. Tell me who she is," M 8:110). Lancelot's honest response "*Dame*, che estes vous" ("Lady, it's you") echoes through a series of similar replies to subsequent questions. "Whom did you perform all your feats of heroism for?" "*Dame*, pour vous" (M 8:110); "What's the source of the love you profess to have for me?" "*Dame*, fait il, vous le feistes faire" ("Lady, you yourself are the cause of it," M 8:111). The queen's questions here subtly erode the very basis of male/female relations in the courtly world. Whereas knights typically fight each other for love of (or possession of) the desired and prized ladylove, Lancelot is made to do battle here metaphorically with the queen herself, as he struggles unsuccessfully to define his lady's identity. Every time Lancelot asserts that Guinevere is his *dame*, his inspiration, his love, the queen retreats from those definitions with yet another question that keeps us guessing "which queen?" she might in fact be. She "seems" to be Guinevere, but she is also jousting like a knight.

Elsewhere, visible indications of Lancelot's identity as a knight lead us tellingly to Guinevere. Whereas Guinevere's cross-dressing remains metaphorical, certain articles of Lancelot's chivalric costume come directly from the queen. In keeping with chivalric practice, Guinevere sends Lancelot a pennant decorated with a red ribbon that he is to wear on his helmet when he gathers with other knights at Carduel ("et si port Lancelos sor son hiaume .I. penonchel que ele li envoie a une langete de soie vermeille"; "Lancelot wore a pennant on his helmet with a red silk ribbon that she [Guinevere] had sent him," M 8:408). Guinevere also dictates that Lancelot's shield should bear a diagonal white stripe and she sends him four articles of clothing from her personal wardrobe: the brooch she wears at her neck, the belt from around her waist, her alms purse, and a luxurious comb that holds many strands of her hair (M 8:408). Guinevere gives Lancelot these intimate items ostensibly as love tokens. What he does with the last four we are never told. But the decorative pennant, which Lancelot affixes to his helmet, following Guinevere's directives, becomes a significant element in this knight's wardrobe, a distinguishing feature that later enables the Dame de Malehaut to recognize and identify him: "che fu la premiere connoissance qui onques fust portee au tans le roi Artu sor hiaume" ("this was the first insignia worn on a helmet in King Arthur's time," M 8:437). The very insignia or mark that enables one to distinguish Lancelot from other knights is not then a sign of his family lineage, but a gift from—indeed, like the brooch, belt, comb, and alms purse, a fetishized representation of—the queen. In this scene at least we recongize Lancelot by first recognizing an insignia of Guinevere. His chivalric maleness is signaled by a female garment.

On other occasions, Lancelot is said specifically to have the physical characteristics of a *dame*. As the portrait of the child Lancelot, "li plus biax enfes del monde" (M 7:71), merges into that of the young knight, the narrator says the following:

> De son col ne fait il mie a demander, car s'il fust en une tres bele dame, si fust il asses couvenables et bien seant et bien taillies a la mesure del cors et des espaules, ne trop greles ne trop gros, ne lonc ne cours outre mesure.

> (Need we mention his neck? If it had belonged to a beautiful woman, it would have suited her perfectly, well-proportioned in relation to her/his body and shoulders, neither too thin nor thick, neither too long nor short. M 7:73)

After describing Lancelot's extraordinary shoulders and muscular chest, the narrator speaks of his long, straight arms and then his hands: "les mains furent de dame tout droitement" ("His hands were the hands of a lady," M 7:73). This hero's voice too, as it is described here, reminds us, in retrospect, of that teasing, overconfident voice of his own *dame* in the scenes of rejection and interrogation we discussed above. And this confident tone derives, we are told, not from Lancelot's impressive prowess or his singular accomplishments as Arthur's knight but from "she who was the source of his pleasure" ("ains le disoit par la grant seurte qu'il avoit en che dont toute sa joie venoit"; "He spoke that way because of the confidence he had in the woman who provided all his pleasure," M 7:74).

Like the pennant signaling his unique identity, Lancelot's voice comes to us, we are told, from the queen. His hands and neck, those parts of the body other than the face that are most public and visible in a courtly lady, seem also to be borrowed body parts. Much as he will later receive the tangible tokens of a brooch, alms purse, and comb from his ladylove, Lancelot has already received, metaphorically, her hands and neck. But these features help us little in reading or decoding the ambiguous identity of this curious knight. They contribute instead to the questioning of fixed gender identities that persists throughout the narrative.[32]

The cross-dressed performances of both Lancelot and Guinevere in the Prose *Lancelot* encourage us to ask: how can we tell male from female in courtly society? What are the visible signs that allocate and establish sexual difference in the Arthurian world? To what extent are sexed traits anatomically conditioned or more arbitrarily imposed? Lancelot stages these questions in a scene that both cements and topples the gender categories structuring the Arthurian courtly world. Furious with Morgain the Fay for attacking innocent victims, Lancelot asserts: "Si vos ne fussiez fame, je prisse tel conroi que jamais ne nuisisiez a chevalier errant ne a prodome" ("If you weren't a woman, I would take measures so that you could never harm a knight errant or any valiant man," M 4:337). Morgain remains protected from Lancelot's revenge in this instance because she is in fact a woman within the strictly regulated world of Arthurian chivalry. And yet Morgain breaks starkly with the rules of that world to behave not as a lovely courtly lady but as a fierce and able "seigneur du chateau." When Lancelot asks initially, "Who is the Lord of this castle?" (M 5:63) he is told pointedly, "Il n'i a nul signor, mais il i a une dame cui cist manoirs est" ("There is no lord, but a lady to whom this residence belongs," M 5:63). A lady as lord of the castle, a knight with body parts of a lady. He is not a woman, but what if he were? She, like Guinevere, is no man, but what if these women could be men? What would that mean? In short, what if determining the difference between "having" the phallus and "being" the phallus were not the primary distinction to be made? The Old French Prose *Lancelot* asks these very modern and compelling questions throughout a courtly tale that reminds us constantly, seeming is believing.[33]

NOTES

1. *Lancelot, roman en prose du XIIIe siècle*, ed. Alexandre Micha (Paris: Droz, 1980), vol. 7, p. 442. Subsequent references to Micha's edition will be abbreviated as follows: M 7:442.

2. Jean-Charles Payen explains Guinevere's role in the *Lancelot propre, Queste del Saint Graal and Mort Artu* as that of a sorceress who sucessfully enchants not only Arthur and Lancelot but the reader as well so that her adultery, though unrepented, goes uncondemned. "Plaidoyer pour Guenièvre: La culpabilité de Guenièvre dans le *Lancelot-Graal,*" *Les Lettres romanes* 20 (1966), 103–14; and his "La Charrette avant la charrette: Guenièvre et le roman d'Erec," *Mélanges de langue et de littérature du Moyen Age et de la Renaissance offerts à Jean Frappier* (Geneva: Droz, 1970), vol. 1, 419–32.

3. See Paul Imbs, "Guenièvre et le *Roman de Cligès,*" *Travaux de linguistique et de littérature* 8 (1970), 101–14.

4. For example "la roïne as Grans dolors" (M 7:29), "la roïne de Benoych (M 7:37) or "la roïne Elaine de Benoych" (M 7:86) and her sister "la roïne de Gaunes" (M 7:37); "Reine de la terre Sorestan" (M 4:173) or "roïne de Sorestan" (M 4:332) and "Sedile la roïne" (M 4:173). Though Guinevere is most consistently termed simply "la roïne" or "ma dame la roïne," she is also called by a fuller title on rare occasions: "la roïne Guenievre" (M 2:209) and "la roïne Guenivere ma dame" (M 4:336). Guinevere's highly changeable and phantom identity may derive in part from her Celtic origins: the Welsh name Gwenhwyfar means "white phantom" or "white fairy" (Maurice Delbouille, "Guenièvre fut-elle la seule épouse du roi Arthur?" *Travaux de linguistique et de littérature* 6 [1966], 124). Paul Imbs points out that in Chrétien's *Conte du Graal*, Guinevere is the only major figure who has no ancestors or descendants, adding to the fairy-tale aura of her eternal beauty that makes her seem not of this world. See his "La Reine Guenièvre dans le *Conte du Graal* de Chrétien de Troyes," *Mélanges de langue et de littérature du Moyen Age offerts à Teruo Sato*, 2 vols. (Nagoya, Japan: Centre d'Etudes médiévales et romanes, 1973), I, 59. For an extended discussion of Guinevere's name, see Paul Rémy, "Le Nom de la reine dans 'Jaufré,' " *Recueil de Travaux offert à M. Clovis Brunel*, 2 vols. (Paris: Société de l'école des chartes, 1955), II, 12–19. On the relation between historical queens and their fictive counterparts in courtly romance, see Peggy McCracken, "The Body Politic and the Queen's Adulterous Body in French Romance," in *Feminist Approaches to the Body*, ed. Linda Lomperis and Sarah Stanbury (Philadelphia: University of Pennsylvania Press, 1993), 38–64.

5. This is indeed how Guinevere is designated throughout Chrétien's *Conte du Graal*, where the narrator tells us nothing of her feelings for Arthur, treating her only as the king's official spouse, as Paul Imbs explains. She is "ni l'amie ni la femme," in his words, but only the queen. "La Reine Guenièvre dans le *Conte du Graal*," 47, 57.

6. The seduction succeeds in the first instance because of a potion (M 4:209), in the second, thanks to the astute manipulations of Pelles's daughter's servant, Brisane (M 6:174).

7. At issue is which woman can prove herself to be Arthur's "legitimate spouse." The False Guinevere requests, "que vos me creantés a prendre a feme voiant tot vostre barnage et que vos me tendrois por espuse et por roïne" (M 1:108); and Arthur refers to Queen Guinevere as "ceste que j'ai tenue" (M 1:120) and "cele que j'ai tos jors tenue por ma feme" (M 1:121). Historically, there is further confusion over Guinevere's marital status: Gerald of Wales, Geoffrey of Monmouth, and Wace all hold that Guinevere was Arthur's second wife; see Delbouille, 123–34.

8. Paul Rockwell reads the *semblance* between the two Guineveres as a metaphor used to critique the authority of preceding verse romances by Chrétien de Troyes, in which *semblance* verifies and establishes truth. "The Falsification of Resemblance: Reading the False Guinevere," *The Arthurian Yearbook* 1 (1991), 27–42. I see two warring tendencies within the Prose *Lancelot*, a text that seeks to establish clear distinctions while also cultivating the ambiguity of appearance.

9. Occasional clear-cut demarcations of "the other woman" ("l'autre") in contrast to "the queen herself" ("la roine meesmes"), as in M 1:168, for example—or M 1:153 where "ceste" for the rival Guinevere remains distinct from Arthur's wife as "sa feme"—are not the rule.

10. Christiane Marchello-Nizia, "Amour courtois, société masculine et figures du pouvoir," *Annales E.S.C.* 36 (1981), 969–82.

11. See Michèle Perret, "Travesties et transexuelles: Yde, Silence, Grisandole, Blanchandine," *Romance Notes* 25 (1985), 328–40.

12. Each of these heroines undergoes a transformation by which their anatomical sex is made to match unproblematically their attributed gender, either by means of transsexual miracles that confer a biological penis on the initially cross-dressed woman, or through a return to the female character's given anatomy, often via childbirth. Perret, 337–39.

13. *Vested Interests: Cross-Dressing and Cultural Anxiety* (London: Routledge, 1992), 10.

14. Elizabeth Grosz, *Jacques Lacan: A Feminist Introduction* (London: Routledge, 1990), 133.

15. Jacqueline Rose, *Feminine Sexuality: Jacques Lacan and the Ecole Freudienne*, ed. Juliet Mitchell and Jacqueline Rose (New York: W.W. Norton, 1982), 7; Jane Gallop, *Reading Lacan* (Ithaca, New York: Cornell University Press, 1985), 141–42.

16. Joan Riviere argues that "womanliness" cannot be separated from masquerade because woman is a social, political, and erotic construct dependent for its very existence on the donning of masks, on impersonation. See "Womanliness as a Masquerade" in *Formation of Fantasy*, ed. Victor Burgin, James Donald, and Cora Kaplan (London: Methuen, 1986), 38; and Lacan's rewriting of Riviere's essay in "The Signification of the Phallus," *Ecrits: A Selection*, trans. Alan Sheridan (New York: W.W. Norton, 1977).

17. See also Madeleine Kahn's definition of the transvestite as essentially dependent on being both sexes at once, as someone who dresses up in order to undress, in *Narrative Transvestism: Rhetoric and Gender in the Eighteenth-Century Novel* (Ithaca: Cornell University Press, 1991), 11.

18. Also: "Dame, . . . jou remanrai a mon seignor a son plaisir *et* au vostre" ("Lady, I will stay with my lord as it pleases him *and* you," M 8:487).

19. As Galehot explains to the disconsolate Lancelot, Guinevere has two competing identities as Lancelot's *dame* or Arthur's *roïne*: "je sai bien qu'ele ameroit miels a estre dame avec vos d'un petit roialme que sans vostre compaignie estre roïne de tot le monde" (M 1:33–34).

20. She is said, at times, to suffer undying love for him (M 4:118; 8:115, 464) and she typically inspires his extraordinary feats of prowess (M 8:61).

21. See Sarah Kay's definition of the *domna* as a third gender, morally and socially androgynous, but possessing the social status of a male, in *Subjectivity in Troubadour Poetry* (Cambridge: Cambridge University Press, 1990), 86, 92. Guinevere's behavior in the rejection scene actually constitutes an example of what Kay calls the "feminine" gender, which results when the female character refuses to be sexually passive, or what I have termed the behavior of the sexualized "woman" rather than the sexually neutral "lady." See "The Man Behind the Lady in Troubadour Lyric," *Romance Notes* 25 (1985), 254–70.

22. She later explains her actions in two ways: Lancelot had failed to ask her permission to depart when he left London and moreover he had agreed to wear Morgan's ring thinking it was the queen's (M 2:73–74).

23. Roberta L. Krueger, "Desire, Meaning, and the Female Reader: The Problem in Chrétien's *Charrette*," *The Passing of Arthur: New Essays in Arthurian Tradition*, ed. Christopher Baswell and William Sharpe (New York: Garland, 1988), 31–51, reprinted in this volume at pp. 229–245.

24. If, as Luce Irigaray contends, the enigma of woman lies in her vaginal lips and what she keeps hidden from view, then we are prompted to ask what lies beneath Queen Guinevere's lavish and luxurious gown? "The Gesture in Psychoanalysis," in *Between Feminism and Psychoanalysis*, ed. Teresa Brennan (London: Routledge, 1989), 136.

25. For an extended discussion of the relation between the fictive voices and bodies of Old French heroines, see E. Jane Burns, *Bodytalk: When Women Speak in Old French Literature* (Philadelphia: University of Pennsylvania Press, 1993).

26. For other examples of metaphorical cross-dressing in Old French texts, see E. Jane Burns, "Ladies Don't Wear *Braies*: Underwear and Outerwear in the French Prose *Lancelot*," in *The Lancelot-Grail Cycle: Text and Transformations*, ed. William W. Kibler (Austin: University of Texas Press, 1994), 52–74.

27. *Gender Trouble: Feminism and the Subversion of Identity* (New York: Routledge, 1990), 139.

28. Or, as Marjorie Garber so cogently explains it, "The fashion garment of the drag queen signifies the absent or phantom body. Paradoxically, the body here is no body, and nobody, the clothes without the Emperor" (374).

29. When Arthur asks Guinevere, "Dame . . . savés vous qui li chevaliers est?" ("Lady, do you know who this knight is?" M 8:485), he himself provides the unproblematic response: "Ch'est Lancelos del Lac, cil qui vainqui lez .II. assamblees de moi et de Galahot" ("He's Lancelot of the Lake, the victor in two encounters with me and Galehot," M 8:485). Elsewhere Bademagu answers Guinevere's query about whether a certain knight is Lancelot with an unequivocal, "Yes, lady, without any doubt" ("Dame . . . oïl, sans faille," M 2:65). Knights and ladies within the fictive world of the Prose *Lancelot* inquire constantly about the wayward Lancelot, who is often disguised, lost, or missing in the forest, but this questioning of Lancelot's identity constitutes a requisite part of his character as the quintessential knight-errant, forever in search of adventure as he attempts relentlessly to conquer the Arthurian unknown. Matilda Bruckner has shown how the twelfth-century Lancelot in Chrétien de Troyes's version of the tale must be, at one and the same time, the best and the worst knight in the world: a knight whose very identity resides in the impossible task of reconciling conflicting goods. "Why Are There So Many Interpretations of Chrétien's *Chevalier de la Charrette?*" *Romance Philology* 40 (1986), 159–80, reprinted in this volume at pp. 55–78.

30. One of the first times Guinevere speaks in the Prose *Lancelot*, she asks who Lancelot is: "Qui est. . . chis valles?" ("Who is this young man?" M 7:272). Nearly 200 pages later Guinevere pursues the same line of questioning in a conversation with Galehot, displacing onto the male subject, Lancelot, the issue of gender ambiguity earlier staged in relation to the queen herself. In response to Galehot's "Vees chi li millor chevalier del monde" ("You see here the world's best knight," M 8:104), Guinevere now retorts with a phrase that echoes Lancelot's earlier query, "La roïne, laquel roïne?" She now asks, "Li quex est che?" ("Which one is he?" M 8:104). Offering no definitive response, Galehot reiterates the prior uncertainty of the knight who thought Guinevere "seemed" to be the queen when he asks Guinevere which of two knights "appears" to be Lancelot, "Dame, fet il, li quels le vous samble estre?" ("Lady, which one seems to be him?" M 8:104).

31. Guinevere, like Arthur, is credited with protecting the inhabitants of Gorre via the deeds of Lancelot and other knights of the Round Table. See for example the

knight who sets off to thank the queen for the protection Lancelot has provided him (M 7:377). The queen plays the man in a more general sense when she proposes to trade Lancelot and Galehot as if they were commodities, a role generally reserved in the Arthurian world for men who trade women (M 7:215, 217). And Guinevere's knights are denoted specifically as her possessions ("un chevalier *de* la roïne," M 7:252, 376; 8:429) much as she herself bears the mark of Arthur's possession in marriage, "la femme *du* roi Artu."

32. Because of the limitations of space, this analysis focuses largely on Guinevere's gender identity. But much remains to be said about the complexities of Lancelot's gender.

33. I would like to thank the members of the North Carolina Research Group on Medieval and Early Modern Women for their thoughtful critiques of an earlier version of this essay.

14 Recovering Malory's Guenevere

Sarah J. Hill

It has become critically commonplace to trivialize the role of Guenevere in Malory's work or even to condemn her as the object which prevents Lancelot from achieving the Grail. Critics as diverse as John Walsh, Charles Moorman, and Mary Scott, although perceptive in other areas of Malory studies, are surprisingly eager to distort the characterization of Guenevere, presenting an imperious and clinging temptress in the place of Malory's strong and just queen. Guenevere is not, of course, perfect—none of Malory's characters is except Galahad—and she frequently displays a temper that is less than even, but this is not typical enough a characteristic to be the one upon which to base an analysis. Neither should Guenevere be condemned without pardon for her adultery, although she clearly is so by other characters in the work and by most of her critics; Malory's narrator specifically praises, indeed, rewards her for her constancy to Lancelot. Malory's Guenevere is a complex and pivotal character whose position in the social and political structure of the Arthurian court exposes, to a greater extent than the primary male characters, the brutality and self-destructiveness that lie beneath the veneer of Christian morality and the chivalric code of the knights. This paper will examine, first, the code itself and the power structure of the court; second, the roles available to women within and without the structure; and, third, the development of Guenevere's character as the central female character and the most powerful woman in the court.

Jerome Mandel has described the twin principles which underlie the structure of the Arthurian court as war and love (243–44), which comprise the primary motivations for knights in medieval romance. They are not of detached and equal importance; the desire for success in war is based on the assumption that military success will ensure success in love. Guenevere her-

Reprinted from *Proceedings of the Medieval Association of the Midwest* 1 (1991), 131–48, with permission.

self expresses this to Kay after the war with the five kings: "What lady that ye love and she love you nat agayne, she were gretly to blame" (79). War and love are bound up together into the social construct of honor, a code which appears to be compatible with Christian ethics, but one which, in practice, demands from men that they seek revenge for slights against self or family and from women that they reward force with love. Within this code, David Benson notes, morality becomes irrelevant (270); it is physical strength which determines right. Lancelot's three defenses of the queen make this explicit. In "The Poisoned Apple," Lancelot forces Guenevere's accuser to excuse her under the threat that "I woll nat graunte the thy lyff" (620) after Lancelot has beaten him in battle. Of course, Lancelot *is* on the side of right in this instance, as Nynyve tells the court later. The second accusation, however, finds Guenevere more culpable but Lancelot reacting in the same manner: "I say nay playnly, that thys nyght there lay none of thes ten knyghtes wounded with my lady, quene Gwenyver, and that woll I prove with myne hondys" (659). Lancelot is technically correct, but the defense is morally suspect. Thirdly, he claims to the knights who have trapped him in Guenevere's room, "I cam to the quene for no maner of male engyne, and that woll I preve and make hit good uppon you with my hondys" (677), later repeating the same to Arthur: ". . . my lady, quene Gwenevere, ys as trew a lady unto youre person as ys ony lady lyvynge unto her lorde, and that woll I make good with my hondis" (688). Lancelot's obvious lies in both instances have been noted many times, but, as David Benson points out, Lancelot must defend Guenevere, regardless of the tactics required to do so, because it is through him that she has been accused and condemned (270).

Unfortunately, honor and Christian principles are often at odds, and when Christian principles of truth, sexual fidelity to one's spouse, and forgiveness come into conflict with the Arthurian principles of truth determined by force, sexual reward for physical brutality, and revenge, it is the Christian code which is rejected. Christian morality is openly laid aside; Mandel reminds us that there are restraints placed upon the attainment of desires through the restrictions imposed by Arthur on behavior. The restraints themselves, however, finally ensure the self-destruction of the courtly tradition, because only a Galahad, "who comes late and leaves early," is perfect enough to maintain the code (246). The result is a court split by the divided loyalties of knights among the king, the queen, and their families; of the queen between the king and the knights who expect rewards for their service to her; and of the king between the queen and the knights, either of whom may decide to revolt against his authority.

The queen, then, has a clearly defined position within the court, but she is not the only woman with an important function. Mary Etta Scott has outlined three categories into which most of Malory's women fall: the Good, the Bad, and the Ugly (21). Scott's categorization is useful as a starting point, if her conclusions are not altogether satisfactory. The first group, the Good, consists of those women who lead knights on adventures or who are "maidens in distress who provide an arena for the knights to prove their prowess" (21). Also included in this group are a few women who typify Christian virtue; Percival's sister is Scott's primary example. Scott is perceptive in her grouping of these characters together, but it is not their goodness (nor is it Malory's male chauvinism) which makes them so alike. It is their marginality in the story of the Round Table and the self-destruction of the court which ties them together. These women are good, for the most part, simply because they do not function in the work as fully developed characters; they may start a knight on a quest or be the object of a quest, but they rarely appear after the quest is completed.

Scott's third category, that of the Ugly, is equally both perceptive and limited. Scott includes in this group the temptresses of both Percival and Bors, who change their "fiendish" natural appearances into beautiful forms in order to trap the good knights (26–28). Scott does not, however, include in this category Morgan le Fay, who appears to be the most malevolent "Ugly" of all. If we include Morgan in this third category (and it seems improbable that she would fit anywhere else), then we can easily rename this group. These women are Uglies only to the knights of the court because they have willfully rejected the values of the court. As Scott notes, the Uglies "seem to concentrate their evil wiles on the excellent knights" (26), and, in Morgan's case, on Arthur himself. The Uglies are outside the court, and in this way are like the Good, but they are attempting actively to destroy the knights and their king. They are not just "Uglies"; they are willful malevolents who refuse to adhere to the standards set by the court.

Scott's second category, the Bad, is the most interesting because it contains the central female character, Guenevere. The Bad, according to Scott, are "the ordinary women men deal with every day when they are not on a holy quest" (24). Scott restricts her discussion of this group to a brief outline of Guenevere's role as the temptress who prevents Lancelot from achieving the Grail, but several other female characters could easily be grouped into the Bad, including Igraine, Torre's mother, Elaine, and Isolde. These are the women, Guenevere being the most fully developed among them, whose characters reveal how the objectification of women and their subsequent status as rewards for success in battle leads to unification of males in a power structure (here the Round Table court) for a limited time, but ultimately results in a destruction of that power through rivalry. Each of these women finds herself bound to a male character because he has "won" her by force or finds herself divided in loyalty between a husband who has attained her by social force and a lover who has won her by physical prowess. Scott's Bad women, whose characters she dismisses as another example of Malory's culturally unavoidable male chauvinism (21), are really the constrained women, those who adhere to the values of the court and find themselves caught up in its contradictions.

The first example of a constrained woman is Arthur's mother, Igraine. The near-adultery which results in Arthur's conception is paradigmatic in that Igraine's position illustrates first the manner in which women are passed from man to man (in this case husband to husband), second, the principle of force that governs the morality of the male characters, and, third, the apparent justification of murder and rape, even if only by deception, if the act results in the birth of a son. The queen herself, we are told, "made grete joye whan she knewe who was the fader of her child" (6) and how the conception came about. We are not told, however, why it is that she expresses gladness: does she love her husband despite his battle with her first husband, or is she relieved that the king, who will commit murder in order to gain what he desires, has no reason to be displeased with her?

Along with Igraine, both Torre's mother and Elaine illustrate how the birth of a son mitigates any crime or deviation from Christian morality. Torre's mother leaves no doubt that she has been raped, "half be force he had my maydynhode" (62), but the rape is not only unpunished but even rewarded because Torre is the result. Merlin tells Torre that the rape of his mother "ys more for your worship than hurte, for your fadir ys a good knyght and a kynge, and he may ryght well avaunce you and youre modir both . . ." (62). Apparently rape by a "good knyght" is an event to be hoped for by all young women, because it may lead to social advancement if they should happen to bear sons. Elaine, unlike Torre's mother, is not raped, but her willingness to deceive Lancelot is conditional; she agrees "for well she knew that that same nyght sholde be bygotyn sir Galahad upon her, that shold preve the beste knyght of the worlde" (480). Elaine's loss of virginity, which she does not dismiss lightly, at her father's command—"by hys commaundemente to fullfyll this prophecie I have gyvyn the the grettyst ryches and the fayryst floure that ever I had, and that is my maydynhode that I shall never have agayne" (481)—is compensated for by Lancelot's reputation as a knight and the subsequent birth of Galahad, although Elaine herself suffers Lancelot's unwillingness to marry her and Guenevere's hatred.

In addition, neither of the two occupations open to Elaine, marriage and retirement to a convent, is a viable solution for her; she is left alone in her father's house to raise Galahad.

Of all the women characters, it is Isolde who most closely resembles Guenevere. She is delivered to a husband with no concern for her wishes. She engages in an adulterous relationship which causes a split within the court of which she is queen. Like Guenevere, Isolde has no children, either by her husband or by her lover; there is no son by whose birth her adultery can be forgiven or overlooked. Her lover is the best knight of the court, of whose strength she, as queen, is both rewarder and the reward, the same position in which Guenevere finds herself. In addition, she loves Tristam, as Guenevere does Lancelot, making the temptation to exploit her position in the social structure to maintain the relationship all the more difficult to withstand. Interestingly, however, Malory does not show the deaths of Isolde and Tristam, except as a wistful remembrance, nor does he reveal any hostility toward either of the lovers by the other knights, excepting King Mark, who is described as "that traytoure kynge" who killed Tristam "with treson" (666). Isolde is not a character who exactly parallels Guenevere, but she is close enough to represent the same position which Guenevere has within the Arthurian court, and she is nowhere presented as a "Bad" woman or one who has an evil influence on Tristam, although this charge will be made against Guenevere.

It is clear, then, that most, although not all, of Malory's women fit into one of these three rough categories and that Guenevere is neither marginal to nor politically isolated from the court and so easily fits into the group of ordinary women who accept and adhere to the values of the Arthurian court. Even within this group, however, Guenevere occupies a unique position. She is the only one who is condemned for the adultery and not only for her own immorality but for Lancelot's as well; a gathering of knights tells Bors that "as for quene Gwenyver, we love hir nat, because she ys a destroyer of good knyghtes" (617). We cannot simply dismiss her infidelity to Arthur as inconsequential to her character, but we can examine how Malory has created a social setting, unperceived by the knights with the exception of Bors, in which the adultery is both fateful, that is, a predestined occurrence which Guenevere cannot avoid, and a forgivable, if not inevitable, result of Guenevere's arranged marriage to an unlovable husband and the Round Table code.

It is the king, all characters acknowledge, who is the center of power in the court. As Peter Korrel discusses at length, however, Arthur is not only lacking in the virtues of a king but also in those which are respected in knights. He succeeds in only one test, the pulling of the sword from the stone, and is almost always about evenly matched, if not actually beaten, in tournaments. The king's lechery, before and after his marriage, is one of his least attractive characteristics (although it is clearly de-emphasized by Malory); it is only outweighed by his cruelty in the massacre of the innocents (255–61).

Arthur's cruelty, at least, can be attributed to his dependency upon advice from Merlin; indeed, Malory's "lordys and barownes" hold Merlin responsible: ". . . many putte the wyght on Merlion more than on Arthur" (37). Arthur, however, only follows Merlin's instructions when they happen to coincide with his own desires. Merlin tells Arthur explicitly "that Gwenyver was nat holsom for hym to take to wyff. For he warned hym that Launcelot scholde love hir, and sche hym agayne . . ." (59), but Arthur disregards the prophecy, thus making the affair inevitable. Arthur's knowledge of the prophecy, as Korrel notes, makes him "fully responsible for the future downfall" of the court (269), not just because he acts against Merlin's advice, but because his action is indicative of a character whose behavior reflects a willingness to set aside good moral and practical considerations when he is tempted by physical desire. And this is the king who creates the court, who is the model for action, and the husband to whom Guenevere's father turns her over.

Because Arthur is her husband, Guenevere, like other queens, does wield a certain amount of power, although her power is circumscribed by what Arthur allows to her. To suggest, however, that she uses her position only to control Lancelot is a misrepresentation of her character. Guenevere is not, as John Walsh states, consistently characterized as "difficult" and "changeable" (205); nor is it the case that "Malory highlights the queen's temperamental nature, her insecurity, and her desire to assert authority over Lancelot" (206). Malory includes much more material which vindicates Guenevere than he does that which condemns her. Her primary role in the early books of Malory's work, in fact, is, as Lindsay Holichek phrases it, to "confirm and uphold the same values and standards as the Round Table knights" (114). Guenevere is an active member of the court. Her role is not created by her affair with Lancelot; the affair is a virtually inevitable outcome of her role as queen.

Peter Korrel has outlined the "good" qualities in Guenevere's character. He first explains that she is a good wife who fulfills her duties to Arthur (269), a characterization which is consistent throughout the work. As early as Book IV, she is portrayed as willing to die to avoid bringing public shame to Arthur (78). She expresses "grete sorrow" at the departure of Arthur for

Rome (118) but is willing to undertake at least partial responsibility for governing the country. As late as Book XXI, she refuses to align herself with Mordred against Arthur, again preferring to die than to marry him (708), even though it was Arthur himself who abandoned her to Mordred's care.

Guenevere also functions, according to Korrel, as a moral teacher (269). In "Torre and Pellinor" she chides Pellinor for his unwillingness to interrupt his quest to aid a woman: "A, kynge Pellinor, . . . ye were gretly to blame that ye saved not thys ladyes lyff" (75). He challenges her authority to judge him, but Guenevere is supported by Merlin ("Truly ye ought sore to repente hit"), which lends aid to her role as a judge who rightly reflects Arthurian morality. Guenevere explains the results of envy to a group of knights (466), clearly in the role of a respected teacher, and she praises Kay for appropriate behavior and assures him of eventual reward: "What lady that ye love and she love you nat agayne, she were gretly to blame" (79). Guenevere expresses here her adherence to the Arthurian code and the contradiction which will allow her to carry on an affair and still be within the prescribed code of conduct.

Closely related to her function as moral teacher is Guenevere's role as a punitive judge (Korrel 269). The most striking example occurs in the "Tale of Lancelot" in Guenevere's condemnation of Pedyvere to carry the dead body of his wife to Rome: ". . . ye shall bere this lady with you on horsebak unto the Pope of Rome . . . [a]nd ye shall nevir reste one nyght thereas ye do another, and ye go to ony bedde the dede body shall lye with you" (172). Malory's inclusion of the result of this harsh judgment—"And after thys knyght sir Pedyvere fell to grete goodnesse and was an holy man and an hermyte" (172)—suggests that Guenevere is a righteous judge whose decisions cause improvement in vicious characters.

In addition to public responsibility and good moral judgment, Malory's Guenevere is endowed with a remarkable amount of courage (Korrel 270). We have already examined two instances when she embraces possibility of death when the alternative is shame during the crossing of the "Humbir"—"Yet were me lever to dey in this watir than to falle in youre enemyes handis" (78)—and during Mordred's seige of the Tower of London—". . . she answerd hym . . . that she had levir sle herselff than to be maryed with hym" (708). Guenevere's reaction to Mellygaunt's abduction of her and her knights reveals her courage a third time: "I had levir kut myne owne throte in twayne rather than thou sholde dishonoure me!" (651). If, as Walsh asserts, Malory's intention is to present a queen whose desire is simply "to assert authority over Lancelot" (206), then he has made a serious error in presenting a queen who asserts authority wherever and whenever the courtly code demands that she do so. Guenevere's is not a meek, retiring character, to be sure. We have already seen, however, that in the clash between the Christian and courtly code, it is the latter which predominates. Guenevere asserts her authority in accordance with her position as queen; she does not, in Malory, arbitrarily mete out punishments only to Lancelot.

Walsh contends, however, that Guenevere does single Lancelot out for punishment and that the abduction and Lancelot's attempt at rescue create the perfect setting for highlighting the queen's "temperamental nature" (206). Guenevere's reaction, on the contrary, reveals the same nature she has displayed throughout the work. She acts as judge to Mellygaunt although she is his prisoner: "Traytoure knyght . . . wolt thou shame thyselff? . . . Thou shamest all knyghthode and thyselffe and me" (651). She is prepared to take whatever action the chivalric code demands of her, to the point of suicide (651). Guenevere is conscious of and concerned for the safety of her knights: "Sle nat my noble knyghtes and I woll go with the . . ." (651). This responsible attitude is emphasized by Malory. She demands from Mellygaunt that she be allowed to keep them in her sight with a second threat of suicide and later keeps them in her room for their protection:

> And whan season was they wente into their chambirs, but in no wyse the quene wold suffir her wounded knyghtes to be fro her, but that they were layde inwyth draughtes by h[i]r chambir, uppon beddis and paylattes, that she myght herselff se unto them that they wanted nothynge. (657)

Guenevere is by no means the "difficult" and "changeable" queen that Walsh describes, nor does her character change when Lancelot appears. Guenevere's unwillingness to allow Lancelot to fight Mellygaunt is not an example of her imperiousness; her reason for ending the battle is made clear in her response to her captor's pleading: ". . . bettir ys pees than evermore warre" (655). Certainly Lancelot is irritated by her decision, but Guenevere reprimands him as she has corrected other misguided or overly eager knights throughout the work. Her question, "Do ye forthynke yourselff of youre good dedis?" (655–56), is a reminder that, ideally, knights should act according to their code of honor simply for the sake of the code's moral base, not for the joy of killing or the prospect of material or sexual reward.

An idealistic interpretation of the code is clearly not operative in the Arthurian court, however. Lancelot simply assumes that he will be rewarded for his obedience to Guenevere, "so ye be pleased! As for my parte, ye shall sone please me" (656). That sexual reward for physical prowess is the functional rule is made explicit by Lancelot when he comes to Guenevere's window: "Than shall I prove my myght . . . for your love" (657). It is not, then, that Guenevere is changeable. She is the same character she has been throughout, upholding the same values as the Round Table knights. It is the code itself which is contradictory, demanding of Guenevere that she play the roles both of rewarder and reward.

This is not to suggest that Guenevere does not have flaws in her character; her anger and "impulsive jealousy" (Korrel 272) have been noted often, usually as the key to understanding her. Guenevere's anger or jealousy, however, does not appear at all until Book XI, and when it does appear she is not entirely unjustified. The first two examples of Guenevere's anger occur because of Lancelot's affair with Elaine. In the first instance the anger hardly overwhelms Guenevere's character; she becomes angry, hears Lancelot's explanation, that he "was made to lye by her, 'in the lyknes of you, my lady the quene' " (485), and forgives him entirely within the course of five lines.

The second display of anger by Guenevere is more serious and consequential. It is her banishment of Lancelot because of a second encounter with Elaine which is the immediate cause of his temporary madness. But, as Holichek points out, Guenevere's reaction to discovering Lancelot in bed with Elaine a second time is understandable even if we accept that he simply cannot tell the two apart in the dark (120). After all, Lancelot is aware that Brusen fooled him once into sleeping with Elaine; he even threatens to kill her for it: ". . .and I may fynde her, that same lady dame Brusen shall lose her hede for her wycchecrauftys" (481). He willingly, however, goes with her again to Elaine's bedroom. In addition, notwithstanding the fact that the bedrooms of Guenevere and Elaine are adjacent to one another, it seems unlikely that Lancelot would be unaware, first, that it was not Guenevere's bedroom, and, second, that this was the room assigned to Elaine by the king. Lancelot is guilty, if not of willful infidelity to the queen, then, at the least, of unfaithfulness through gullibility and indiscretion. (One wonders how often he talks in his sleep about Guenevere loudly enough to be heard through a wall.)

Guenevere's outburst at Lancelot after his return from the Grail quest is less justifiable, even by the courtly code of fidelity to one's lady. Lancelot, the narrator states, is only avoiding Guenevere "to eschew the sclawndir and noyse" (611). The unfairness and inaccuracy of her attack is paralleled, we should notice, by Lancelot's reply. He accuses her of being the reason he was unable to achieve the Grail, when, in fact, it is his own inability, as Joan Ferrante phrases it, to "put aside his courtly code for religious teaching"

("Conflict" 171) that caused his failure in the Grail quest. The narrator reinforces this in the opening of "The Poisoned Apple":

> Than, as the booke seyth, sir Launcelot began to resorte unto quene Gwenivere agayne and forgate the promyse and the perfeccion hat he made in the queste; for, as the booke seyth, had not sir Launcelot bene in his prevy thoughtes and in hys myndis so sette inwardly to the quene as he was in semynge outewarde to God, there had no knyght passed hym in the quest of the Sankgreall. (611)

Lancelot is not, with Guenevere, under an enchantment as he was with Elaine; he carries on the affair with her knowingly and willingly. Ferrante's description of medieval biblical exegesis applies as well to Lancelot: ". . . the object of man's temptation becomes the cause of it; in other words, he projects his own weakness onto its object" (*Woman as Image* 21). The two are equally responsible for their conduct, and to condemn Guenevere as the figure who forces Lancelot to forsake his religious vows (Moorman 165) or as "consistently difficult" (Walsh 205) without an equal condemnation of Lancelot is reductive and inaccurate. Indeed, to ignore how uncharacteristic is the pettiness displayed by both Guenevere and Lancelot is to ignore how the divisive social pressures on both of them are reflective of the impending self-destruction of the Arthurian court.

We should not, moreover, discount the assessment by the narrator of Guenevere's character, especially because this judgment is consistent with the dramatic conclusion of her life. The narrator's comment, ". . . whyle she lyved she was a trew lover, and therefor she had a good ende" (649) is borne out by the text. Guenevere does reach the point at which she can embrace a Christian code of conduct instead of a courtly code, and in her penance she is confident of eventual salvation: ". . . and yet I trustse. . . that aftir my deth I may have a syght of the blyss[ed] face of Cryste Jesu, and on Doomesday to sytte on Hys right syde; fo[r] a synfull as ever I was, now ar seyntes in heven" (720). We should note that Guenevere is able to achieve this adherence to Christian morality only within a community of women; that is, she has rejected the inconsistent roles demanded of her by the court, and she prevents the possibility of the creation of another court by refusing to go with Lancelot, although it is perfectly clear that he is eager to take her away: ". . . yf I had fouden you now so dysposed, I had caste me to have had you into myn own royame" (721). Lancelot is still governed by the courtly code, but Guenevere, in rejecting him, rejects an inherently self-destructive political system and regains her position as moral teacher, no longer a "mayteyner of good knyghtes" (617), but a maintainer of a consistent Christian morality.

It is clear, then, that many readers of Malory would benefit from a second look at his Guenevere. She is not the imperious queen whose temptation of Lancelot brings down the noble court of King Arthur. She is a complex character whose position in the court reflects the constraints on all women within the structure and finally reveals its inherent self-destructiveness. Guenevere does not destroy Lancelot and the Round Table court; she is the character who saves Lancelot by her example and restores the ideal of the court in her maintenance of Christian behavior after the actual court, corrupted by its contradictions, has fallen.

WORKS CITED

Benson, C. David. "Gawain's Defense of Lancelot in Malory's 'Death of Arthur.' " *Modern Language Review* 72.2 (1983): 267–72.

Ferrante, Joan M. "The Conflict of Lyric Conventions and Romance Form." In *Pursuit of Perfection: Courtly Love in Medieval Literature*. Ed. Joan M. Ferrante and George D. Economou. Port Washington: Kennikat, 1975. 135–78.

——. *Woman as Image in Medieval Literature*. Durham: Labyrinth, 1985.

Holichek, Lindsay E. "Malory's Guenevere: After Long Silence." *Annuale Mediaevale* 22 (1982): 112–26.

Korrel, Peter. *An Arthurian Triangle: A Study of the Origin, Development and Characterization of Arthur, Guinevere and Mordred*. Leiden: E.J. Brill, 1984.

Malory, Thomas. *Works*. Ed. Eugene Vinaver. 2nd ed. Oxford: Oxford UP, 1971.

Mandel, Jerome. "Constraint and Motivation in Malory's 'Lancelot and Elaine'." *PLL* 20.3 (1984): 243–58.

Moorman, Charles. "Courtly Love in Malory." *ELH* 27.3 (1960): 163–76.

Scott, Mary Etta. "The Good, the Bad, and the Ugly: A Study of Malory's Women." *Mid-Hudson Language Studies* 5 (1982): 21–29.

Walsh, John Michael. "Malory's 'Very Mater of Le Chevalier du Charyot': Characterization and Structure." *Studies in Malory*. Ed. James W. Spisak. Kalamazoo: Medieval Institute Publications, 1985. 199–226.

15 THE FIGURE OF GUENEVERE IN MODERN DRAMA AND FICTION

Elisabeth Brewer

Both in medieval and in modern fiction, the figure of Guenevere personifies the feminine ideal, and in so doing indicates our changing attitudes to women and to sexual morality. In the last hundred years in particular, her character has undergone many changes, some of them startling. In 1895, a dramatic version of the Arthurian story[1] was put on in London by the famous Victorian actor and producer Henry Irving, specially written for him by his friend J. Comyns Carr. With sets and costumes designed by the Pre-Raphaelite artist Burne-Jones, music by the composer Arthur Sullivan, and Ellen Terry starring as Guenevere, the show—it must have been almost a musical, and quite spectacular at that—was an instant success. The play seems to have started a fashion for Arthurian drama: in the next ten to fifteen years, many plays based on the Arthurian legend were put on in little London theatres, and at least three centred specifically on Guenevere.

William Morris once remarked that the best way to deal with old stories was to close the book and retell them as new stories for yourself, and the late nineteenth-century dramatists who took the story of Guenevere as the basis of their plots certainly did that. The "most noble Christian queen" of Malory's *Morte Darthur* now becomes the weak little woman of nineteenth-century convention. Guinevere herself talks of the weakness of women in Comyns Carr's play, and we later see her swoon in Morgan's arms from fear that Lancelot's love for her has been revealed. (She swoons in Malory, too, of course, but from excessive weeping or depth of feeling, as when Lancelot comes to see her for the last time.) Our late Victorian Guinevere, however, begins a love-scene with the confession: "Not brave am I, but blest in my great need, / On thee to lean, and unto thee to yield / My love, my-

Reprinted from *Arturus Rex*, II, ed. W. Van Hoecke, Gilbert Tournoy, and Werner Verbeke (Louvain: Louvain University Press, 1987), 478–90, with permission.

self, and my fond helplessness." She is represented as so clinging that Lancelot has actually to shake her off, saying "Let me go!" when Mordred attacks. "O, for my sake take care!" she quavers; later sending a message to Arthur, "tell him that I cling / To one more noble."[2]

Guenevere as the little woman draws attention to the wish-fulfillment fantasy in these plays. The macho image of the male in his gleaming armour (Henry Irving as Arthur had a striking suit of black plate-armour) contrasts with the yielding helplessness of the Queen, overcome by the emotions that she cannot control. Her relationship with Lancelot is all tenderness and faith: there are no attempts to present her as jealous, spiteful and demanding as she often is in Malory. But where Malory disclaims knowledge of what Lancelot and Guenevere are doing when they are alone together, these playwrights often show delicately explicit love-scenes: "One kiss, the last! O God, the very last," Guinevere murmurs.[3] "Yes, even when I sit here by his side . . . I cannot stop the heaving of my breast." "When you are by my side the darkest place / Is radiant."[4]

The glamorisation of adulterous passion as represented in these Guenevere plays suggests the much more liberal attitude to illicit sexual relationships at the end of the nineteenth century. There are hints, too, that Arthur is perhaps to be regarded as sexually inadequate, and that a wife is entitled to more than he is able to give: "Lips in his creed were only made for prayers / And bodies for anointing," the queen complains. She must "live estranged from love / And yearn in vain for those small tenderings / That, costing nothing, are beyond all worth / In 'complishing a woman's happiness."[5] Arthur—perhaps rather surprisingly—agrees, on being charged by Guenevere with neglect, that their love lacks "full expression."[6] He has been too busy; they must both put England first, he insists. In another play,[7] when Arthur is brought home dying, Guenevere amongst the nuns claims: "I've thought and prayed / For him who did not know / One half the streams that flow / Thro' every woman's dream." And later these nuns, instead of being shocked at the disgraceful moral lapse of their queen, chorus "Oh Knights! This was your Queen / Whose beauty is forgiven," thus displaying a much more lenient attitude than Tennyson had done in his Idyll, *Guinevere*, in 1859. Nothing is said about guilt. The more tolerant light in which Guenevere's infidelity to Arthur is viewed can surely be related to the pioneering work in methods of birth-control and the psychology of sexual relationships being carried on by progressives such as Marie Stopes and Havelock Ellis, work which was contributing in practical ways to a radical change of attitude.

Nevertheless, romance predominates, and the love-death motif so strongly emphasised by Wagner in *Tristan and Isolde* also creeps into the

Lancelot and Guenevere story to heighten its emotional impact. "Oh that we two, we two together now . . . Might put to sea on life's receding tide," says Lancelot as he catches Guenevere to his breast.[8] "Together we go forth into the night . . . In life, / In death, we are together still," Guenevere says to the dying Lancelot at the end of this play when, with Arthur already dead, she clasps her lover in her arms, before falling lifeless upon his body in the last scene.

These plays further draw our attention to the decay of faith, as well as to changes in moral attitudes between the mid-century when Tennyson wrote, and its final decades. Secular attitudes prevail, even though Guenevere often still retreats to a nunnery. In Morley Steynor's Lancelot and Guenevere, Lancelot intercepts her on her way to take refuge in the convent, bursting from some bushes and declaring that their vows are "all the more sacred and binding since / No law save Love's own law had sanctioned them."[9] To such an extent is passion, even in an illicit relationship, regarded as uncontrollable and indeed self-justified, that although Morgan le Fay in Ernest Rhy's Guinevere states that the queen's unfaithfulness had "broken the king," she is, again, never even reproached.

In all these plays, the story of the last days of the Round Table is scaled down and domesticated: the larger perspective of Malory and indeed Tennyson is missing, despite the characters' frequent assertion of the need to put England first. Guenevere's emotions dominate these dramas, and from the dignified but guilty Victorian matron of the *Idylls*, she now, as the feminine ideal changes, gradually becomes a more girlish, even elfin figure, "lonely as a child," roaming "loveless through Arthur's halls."[10] We are called upon to sympathise with her plight, rather than to disapprove. But though the subject of these plays is Guenevere's situation and predicament, there is very little psychological realism, as Bernard Shaw was quick to point out in reviewing Comyns Carr's *King Arthur*.[11] Guenevere has become the white ghost of the character set before us by Malory. Her internal struggle with temptation is presented in the sketchiest terms, and similarly we see nothing of the working of Lancelot's mind.

In Tennyson's Guinevere we see a mature woman, whose faithlessness and deception of Arthur over many years is therefore the more reprehensible. But in Morley Steynor's play Guinevere first appears as a beautiful young girl of seventeen, and she and Lancelot (who is only a year older) still behave like young lovers even when many years are supposed to have passed. Their love has a virginal quality, embodying the romantic dreams of the era. Similarly, Ernest Rhys presents his Guenevere as a wild, simple maiden when she arrives at Camelot riding on a palfrey, accompanied by

Merlin. Indeed, Morgan le Fay is prompted to exclaim on seeing her "This is no queen!" Later Guenevere herself declares "I'm tired of being queen," like a peevish child. The image is still more romanticised in Graham Hill's tragedy, where she is first seen as "A fair white maid with streaming hair of gold . . . / A gleaming amber torrent to her feet. / She seemed like sunlight glinting from a rock / And where she walked the sombre earth was sewn / With a lithemoving skein of gold."[12] The gleaming amber torrent of her hair conjures up a Pre-Raphaelite image, but she is no mere re-incarnation of the temptress whom Dante Gabriel Rossetti was painting some decades before. Rather, she gives expression to that yearning for a return to a pre-industrial pastoral society which had been described in William Morris's *A Dream of John Ball*[13] and *News from Nowhere*,[14] as well as in his last romances. The lovers can thus be seen to be acting in accordance with the precepts of Edward Carpenter, lecturer, writer and Socialist, who was a pioneer of the "free love" movement. In his book *Love's Coming of Age*,[15] he complained that "sexual embraces seldom receive the benison of Dame Nature, in whose presence alone, under the burning sun or the high canopy of the stars and surrounded by the fragrant atmosphere, their meaning can be fully understood: but take place in stuffy dens of dirty upholstery and are associated with all unbeautiful things." In the same year as his book was published, Helen and Edward Thomas (the poet) became lovers in a secret glade on Wimbledon Common, as Helen records in her book *As It Was*.[16] So, not for Lancelot the problem of iron window-bars firmly embedded in castle walls. The sighing wind enhances the wistful melancholy and adds a touch of nature-mysticism to these romantic outdoor encounters.

The shared dream of regaining the unspoilt natural world of course pervades the work of very many other contemporary writers in the early twentieth century. Robert Louis Stevenson expresses this new pastoralism in his once-popular poem, "I will make you brooches and toys for your delight / Of birdsong at morning and starshine at night."[17] In Graham Hill's play, Guinevere claims that she "draws her being from the lowly earth." She is "caught by every breath of life and swayed / As leaves are lift and rustled by the breeze."[18] Elsewhere, in her own words, she is "Not a queen, but a kind of dreamer / Pleased with green leaves" whose association with the natural world is further emphasised as she thinks of the home that she has left to become Arthur's bride. "The green leaves every afternoon / At home will be left wondering / Where I am, who used to sing / Against the blackbird there, and play / The leafy afternoons away."[19] The main function of the natural imagery associated with Guenevere, of course, is to increase the sense of pure, natural, elemental passion.

The mood is continued in the early 1920s, in Chester Keith's *Queen's Knight*. Guenevere is portrayed as a roguish, willful girl, given to wandering in the fields and hunting in the forest, looking like "some embodiment of Spring."[20] Keith updates the forest bower of Gottfried's *Tristam*, as did the earlier twentieth-century writers, in which passion runs riot more energetically than ever. Lancelot first meets Guenevere in a glade of the forest where he crushes her to him, "kissing her again and again until her lips were almost bruised with the adorable roughness that is Passion's crowning glory." Here, she enjoys the free forest life with almost childlike ecstasy, we are told, roaming on foot and crowning herself with flowers.[21]

So the Arthurian legend offered a perfect basis for wish-fulfillment fantasies about romantic love, against a vaguely medieval background enhanced by natural scenery. The image of Camelot with its noble knights of the Round Table still enabled writers to glamorise the battles and the hand-to-hand encounters which were felt to be the very stuff of chivalry. A strong vein of patriotism runs through the plays: Guenevere is England's Queen, and the potential glory and significance of this balances the wild-woodnymph image also projected. But the dream of Camelot was, for many writers, to be shattered by the horrors of the First World War. The vision of chivalry faded, and the image of the Waste Land later came to dominate the imagination.

The twentieth-century writer most deeply interested in the figure of Guenevere is of course T.H. White, in *The Once and Future King*. His famous re-telling of the story is, like Tennyson's, firmly based on Malory's *Le Morte Darthur*. White endeavoured to depict Guenevere with the psychological realism of the modern novel, and indeed, was very successful for the most part in doing so—the portrait is on the whole a well-rounded and convincing one. White explores the complex relationship between the three main characters: Lancelot is at first jealous of Guenever, because he has to share Arthur with her, then attracted to her when he realises that, in a moment of exasperation, he has "hurt a real person."[22] Arthur perceives at once that Lancelot and Guenever are in love: from the beginning White sets out the complexity of the situation, and accounts for everything. Guenever is credited with the virtues of courage, generosity and honesty—and we soon see that she is a much more positive character than most early twentieth-century versions allowed her to be. She is also shown as being unable to comprehend Lancelot's more spiritual nature: "A bold and extroverted queen" is how White elsewhere sums her up, though he does also describe her later as looking like a woman who has grown a soul.[23]

Though in *The Once and Future King*, White allows Guenever to remain "the romantic mistress of a nation," he frequently makes a point of showing her in an unflattering light. For Arthur and Lancelot she is just Jenny, and we see her stripped of dignity, creating ugly scenes when jealousy of Elaine gets the better of her—for example. "Guenever was stiff, as if she were in a rigor, and her face was drained white—except that there was a red spot on either side of her nostrils. She looked as if she had been seasick. She was alone. 'So,' shouted the Queen, moving her hand so that they could see a ball of handkerchief in it, which she had torn to pieces. 'Traitor! Traitor! Get out of my castle with your strumpet.' " Soon, as her anger increases in this scene, we are told that in her trembling, her hair has begun to come down. "She looked hideous."[24] We are allowed no illusions about the decorous homelife of royalty—Guenever, like the rest of us, is made of common clay.

Two years later—White emphasises that she is now forty-two—we see Guenever trying to regain Lancelot as her lover. She is overdressed; she has put on too much make-up, and put it on badly. But "Under the clumsy coquetry, the undignified clothes, there was the human cry for help. The young eyes were puzzled, saying: It is I, inside here—what have they done to me? I will not submit. Some part of her spirit knew that the powder was making a guy of her, and hated it, and tried to hold her lover with her eyes alone. Another part said: I am not old, it is illusion. I am beautifully made-up. See, I will perform the movements of youth. I will defy the enormous army of age."[25] Lancelot's continued rejection of her makes her petulant, cruel, contradictory, miserable. But as White explains, her tragedy is that she was childless; there was nothing for her to do. Unless she felt like a little spinning or embroidery, there was no occupation for her—except Lancelot. Her situation is thus very like that of some middle-aged, well-to-do women in the present century, living empty and frustrated lives. She becomes increasingly more neurotic, "growing madder every day,"[26] increasingly bitter because she has not been able to bear Arthur a son, and White remorselessly shows us how she is ageing. But since White takes realism so far, it is strange that in one respect he makes no attempt to explore the psychology of the Queen. We are never told of her emotions on the three occasions when she is threatened with death at the stake. From Malory, whose interests lie elsewhere than with the personality of the queen, it would be unreasonable to ask more, perhaps, than such terse statements as that "then the queen was led forth without Carlisle, and there she was despoiled into her smock."[27] The anatomy of love is the very stuff of romance, of course; the anatomy of fear would be inappropriate in such a mode, and so we are left to imagine for ourselves what her state of mind would have been.

Of recent decades, since historians have turned their attention to the Dark Ages in their search for the Arthur of history, many writers have preferred a Romano-British setting for their retellings of Arthur's story. However, placing Guenevere in the world of the Dark Ages has not prevented writers from making her a thoroughly modern young woman at the same time, and it is interesting to see the image and the emphases that emerge from these more recent versions. As early as 1944, Edward Frankland's *The Bear of Britain* goes to rather extreme lengths in order to convey a sense of the crudity and barbarism of the period. The romantic reader will be amazed to find that Guenevere, in keeping with more modern attitudes toward sexual morality, is in some of these novels presented not merely as unfaithful, but as promiscuous or even as a former prostitute. It is a measure of the distance that we have come—is it progress or regress?—since Tennyson wrote his *Guinevere*. Many writers, however, do still manage to make her attractive, and it is clear that they mean her to embody a late twentieth-century ideal.

Godfrey Turton, in *The Emperor Arthur*,[28] presents the young Guinevere as beautiful and haughty, in a very down-to-earth manner, in a sixth-century setting. Guinevere deputises for Arthur at official functions like a member of the royal family at the present day; takes to her bed with headaches, and ages noticeably in the course of the novel—we are told that she "hasn't worn well." But Turton, unlike other retellers of the story, does confront Guinevere's predicament when she is brought to judgment, and attempts to give some indication in realistic terms of what her reaction might have been. He shows us the Queen, haggard but stately, dressed with impeccable elegance, and with her hair done in the Roman manner, facing her accusers with dignity. But when she hears her sentence, her screams ring dramatically through the church, and she shrieks, "No, no, you can't do that to me. I appeal to Caesar." Guinevere's accusers are fanatical monks, who are determined to punish her for her adultery, and one of them hoists her onto his back and carries her off to the fire which has already been made ready for her nearby. She is, of course, rescued in the nick of time.[29]

The description of the incident lacks subtlety, as can easily be seen, but it is unusual in so far as it does make an attempt to present the Queen with some psychological realism, even though the dialogue is trite, at a point in the narrative which other writers pass over.

Most recent retellings update the figure of Guenevere in terms of the images created by the modern media. In Catherine Christian's *The Pendragon*,[30] Guenevere is first seen as a spirited horse-woman, a lithe and lively outdoor girl, riding a magnificent chestnut horse. The knights who are escorting her find it hard to keep up, because she rides like an Amazon. She has wonderful hair, of course—the description rather reminds one of the shampoo advertisements—"moon-gold, glinting hair—rippling down to her waist, little, soft curling tendrils blowing all about" her grave, intent face. She naturally also has a perfect figure.

The image of the athletic, healthy young woman, so familiar in the cinema and on the television screen, recurs again and again. In Victor Canning's *The Crimson Chalice*,[31] for example, Gwennifer, whose deep, dark blue eyes, fair hair and poppy-bright lips suggest femininity, is nevertheless dressed like a boy in short leather trews. She is known for her wildness, swears like a trooper, and is able to school a horse and ride as well as a man. More feminine, though also a keen horsewoman, is Mary Stewart's Guinevere in *The Last Enchantment*:[32] she is inclined to outride her escort and plunge about in marshes and forests, to the great anxiety of those who are responsible for her safety. In the same author's most recent Arthurian romance, *The Wicked Day*,[33] Guinevere has matured. Still lovely, she has gained in depth of character and understanding. Here we have the *Vogue* Guenevere, one might almost say the Laura Ashley Guenevere: we see her walking in the garden in a gown of soft dove-grey, with her two silver-white greyhounds, cutting fragrant branches of lilac, or sitting in her pretty rose-bower, doing a little embroidery. It creates a new, improved view of the Dark Ages. She is shown as at the same time the elusive vision of men's desires, the lovely consort of the king, a creature of gaiety and wealth and power and happiness, and as a lonely woman who has to live with fear.

These modern Gueneveres thus show how our images of the heroine and our expectations as to how she will behave have changed in the course of time. The authors are now much more explicit about, and make much more of sexual matters, and in this respect we can see that a new race of liberated young Gueneveres has sprung up in the last few decades. In Victor Canning's novel, Guenevere is so anxious to become pregnant that she takes a succession of lovers, ruthlessly having them killed if she thinks that they are likely to talk. It is all for Arthur's sake, however, and she remains in every aspect a true wife to him. Fortunately, Arthur is understanding.

Recent authors also tend to be less reticent on the subject of Meliagaunt's carrying off of Guenevere when she went a-Maying, and to turn the episode into a case of rape with rather more graphic detail than is to be found in earlier re-tellings. Our modern anxieties about rape, perhaps, find indirect expression through these recent fictions.[34]

Finally, in the nineteen-eighties, Queen Guenevere seems to have become a superwoman, a successful executive and administrator whose role is not merely to attend state functions as a graceful consort, but to rule. In Gillian Bradshaw's *In Winter's Shadow*,[35] for example, Guenevere has to work hard, in partnership with Arthur, to keep the kingdom together. She would rather be a plain man's wife, she claims, than the empress that she is. Through labyrinths of plots and politics she has to grope her way in her struggle to outwit Modred. She has clearly been an efficient organiser; and in addition to tending the sick, has also gone in for fund-raising for Arthur's campaigns.

For the Guenevere of the nineteen-eighties, however, it is not enough to be efficient as an administrator and stateswoman. The Arthurian super-woman must also have experienced pregnancy and childbirth. She cannot, of course, bear a son and heir to the throne without perverting the story, but authors such as Parke Godwin in *Firelord*[36] find ways of liberating her from the charge of sterility. In *Firelord*, she has a stillborn baby daughter early in the course of the novel, so that she has been a mother, at least tech-nically. Her love for Lancelot was, it seems, the result of losing her baby. "I failed," she says pathetically to Arthur. "Failed how? You have never failed in your life" he replies reassuringly.[37] Even the experience of motherhood is seen in terms of a career. Parke Godwin returns repeatedly to the idea that Guenevere is a ruler: competence is everything to her. Arthur rules the north through her; and after his death she is left to rule the kingdom, always im-peccable in public, "the flawless product of her women's maximum efforts."

In the *Idylls of the King*, Tennyson humiliated his Guinevere, as only a Victorian male writer could. Of course he had the good of the nation at heart: as Laureate, he felt it his duty to do what he could to uphold moral standards. Mr. Gladstone, it seems, valued the poem to the extent that he used to read it to the fallen women and prostitutes whom he endeavored to reclaim. One can only speculate as to what he might have said by way of introduction to the reading, and as to what were the reactions of his hear-ers. Through the *Idylls*, Tennyson expressed his anxieties about the future of Britain: "all my realm / reels back into the beast, and is no more," says Arthur despairingly, looking back upon the divisive loves of Lancelot and Guinevere, Tristam and Iseult.[38] His comment represents the very real fear of the late Victorians, that if, as Darwin had shown, there was such a thing as evolution, upward movement towards higher forms might have a coun-terpart in downward movement towards degeneration. It would be ungrate-ful to complain when a poet has striven to communicate a serious message to his society, and Tennyson's Guinevere, humiliated though she is, remains a majestic figure, impressive in her contrition and her sorrow.

When we come to T.H. White's *The Once and Future King*, we meet a vibrant Guenevere who is at times strident, but with whom once again we can sympathise. White, for all the brilliance of his psychological analysis, belittles Guenevere, however, as only a modern realist writer could. No sub-sequent re-teller of the tale can excel Malory: White reinterprets *Le Morte*

Darthur for us, enabling us to see Guenevere as a real woman, to see into her mind and her motives, to understand and to forgive. But do we need so detailed an analysis? Towards the end of the story Malory in fact gives us quite enough clues for us to form for ourselves a very good idea both of Guenevere's charm and of her insensitivity and corroding jealousy.

White knew that he could not reach the high notes as Malory could. "If you want to read about the beginning of the quest for the Grail, about the wonders of Galahad's arrival . . . and of the last supper at court, when the thunder came and the sunbeam and the covered vessel and the sweet smell through the Great Hall—if you want to read about these, you must seek them in Malory. That way of telling the story can only be done once."[39] And when Lancelot and Guenever are together, and Modred and his gang make their attack, we can see how the demands of realism diminish the regal splendour of Malory's Guenevere. Lancelot turns to the Queen and takes her in his arms. "Jenny, I am going to call you my most noble Christian Queen. Will you be strong?"—"My dear"—"My sweet old Jenny. Let us have a kiss."[40] And so on. In fact, the attempt at updating diminishes the realism rather than the reverse. Malory alone is able to perform the astonishing feat of making Guenevere noble, high-minded and majestic amid the disasters at the end of the story, and at the same time her old self still—mean, heartless and totally uncomprehending of Lancelot's genuinely more spiritual nature. The very contradictions in her character, appearing again and again to the very end, make her a "real person," as White would say.

Guenevere, then, has in the course of the last hundred and thirty years been liberated—for better or worse—from the stern demands of Victorian morality. She remains a symbol of changing attitudes to sex, but her liberation has in many cases vulgarised her and often made her a less interesting figure, although of course it gives us White's delightful comedy and the varied portrayals of some more recent fictions. The new views of Guenevere provide some very intriguing reflections, as in a far-distant mirror, of the changing images of woman in the twentieth century, but not entirely without loss. We no longer censure Guenevere—all is understood, all forgiven. She is set free to become a private person, the image of young loveliness, or professional competence, and we do not demand that she should maintain the dignity of "England's Queen." Charles Williams in his *Taliessin* poems[41] presented Guenevere—the queen in the rose-garden—as a symbolic figure rather than as a fully realised individual, and as such she was able to communicate significant meanings about the potential role and influence of women in society. But such moral earnestness no longer seems possible: the latest fictions are straightforward romances more reminiscent of Mills and Boone than of the great retellings of the past.

NOTES

1. *King Arthur: A Drama in a Prologue and Four Acts*, produced by Sir Henry Irving at the Lyceum Theatre, London, on January 12th 1895.

2. Graham Hill, *Guinevere: A Tragedy in Three Acts*, acted at the Court Theatre, London, October 1906.

3. Hill, *Guinevere*, Act II.

4. Morley Steynor, *Lancelot and Guenevere: A Play in a Prologue and Four Acts* (London, 1909), but performed at the Bijou Theatre, London in 1904.

5. Hill, *Guinevere*, Act II.

6. Hill, *Guinevere*, Act III.

7. Ernest Rhys, *Gwinevere*, A Lyric Play (London, 1905).

8. Hill, *Guinevere*, Act III.

9. Steynor, *Lancelot*, Act IV.

10. Francis Coutts, *King Arthur* (London, 1907), p. 154.

11. *The Saturday Review*, Jan. 9th, 1895, p. 93.

12. Hill, *Guinevere*, Act I, Sc. i.

13. (London, 1888).

14. (Boston, 1890; London, 1891).

15. (London, 1896), p. 16.

16. (London, 1926), p. 54.

17. *Collected Poems* (London, 1950), p. 251.

18. Hill, *Guinevere*, Act II, Sc. ii.

19. Rhys, *Gwenevere*, Act I.

20. (London, 1920), p. 113.

21. Ibid., p. 162.

22. *The Once and Future King* (London and New York, 1958). All references are to the Fontana Library edition, 2nd impression (1965), p. 331.

23. White, *The Once and Future King*, p. 560.

24. Ibid., p. 391.

25. Ibid., p. 455.

26. Ibid., p. 483.

27. *Works of Sir Thomas Malory*, ed. Vinaver (London, 1954), Book XX.

28. (London, 1968).

29. Turton, *The Emperor Arthur* (London, 1985), p. 283–86.

30. (London, 1979).

31. (London, 1976).

32. (London, 1978).

33. (London, 1983).

34. See, for example, Marion Bradley, *The Mists of Avalon* (London, 1983).

35. (London, 1982).

36. (New York, 1980; London, 1985). Reference is to the English paperback edition, Futura (London, 1985).

37. Ibid., p. 311.

38. Tennyson, *The Passing of Arthur* (1869).

39. White, *The Once and Future King* , p. 432.

40. Ibid., p. 566.

41. *Taliessin through Logres* (London, 1938) and *The Region of the Summer Stars* (London, 1944).

16 SHARAN NEWMAN'S GUINEVERE TRILOGY

Harold J. Herman

With the publication of *Guinevere* (1981), *The Chessboard Queen* (1984), and *Guinevere Evermore* (1985), Sharan Newman became the first writer to produce an Arthurian trilogy on Guinevere, and her contribution has been duly noted. For example in *The Return of King Arthur*, Taylor and Brewer, who discuss only the first work of the trilogy, point out that *Guinevere*, "though relatively slight" (320), is a novel which sensitively depicts human interactions, treats Arthurian story and characters both naturally and wittily, and combines fantasy with moving, realistic characterizations and descriptions of the effects of war. Raymond Thompson, in *The Return from Avalon*, also discusses only *Guinevere*, but other than faint praise for Newman's use of the faery world to indicate alienation within a character, he considers the work to be "contrived," "sentimental," and "disjointed" (123). There is also an entry on Newman in *The Arthurian Encyclopedia* (407), but if the length of the discussion of each entry is indicative of its importance to the Arthurian legend, then Amelia Rutledge's seventy-six-word critique of Newman's three Arthurian works clearly indicates that the Guinevere trilogy is relatively insignificant. A better understanding and appreciation for Newman's literary contribution proves otherwise. Prior to Newman's *Guinevere*, the first Arthurian work to treat Guinevere's life before her marriage to Arthur, readers were familiar with a few facts of Guinevere's early life: she was the beautiful daughter of Leodegrance, a Roman noble, brought up in the household of Cador of Cornwall and given in marriage to Arthur along with her dowry of Uther Pendragon's Round Table. Using these few facts as a point of departure, Newman creates for Cador, who already had a son (Constantine), a wife (Sidra) and a daughter (Lydia) and then makes Cador a blood relative of Leodegrance. For

Reprinted from *Arthurian Interpretations* 1.2 (Spring 1987), 39–55, with permission of Henry H. Peyton, III, Editor in Chief.

Guinevere, she invents a mother (Guenlian, a second cousin of Merlin), three older brothers (John, Matthew, and Mark), and a household of servants (notably Princerna, the butler, and Flora, Guinevere's nurse and grandmother of Caet, the stableboy), and fosterlings (especially Rhianna, the beloved of Matthew).

These additional figures clearly indicate Newman's emphasis on the family unit, and though most of them are well rounded characters and thus interesting in themselves, they are primarily significant in terms of their relationship to Guinevere, the central character of this trilogy. Because Newman is principally concerned with the development of Guinevere from a teenager to an emotionally mature, self-reliant, altruistic woman, most of the first novel is devoted to a delineation of the character traits of Guinevere as a teenager and especially the effects of her parents and other members of the household upon her.

When Guenlian names her fourth and last child Guinevere after her own mother, she says to the infant, "We will raise you to be a strong, brave woman, just as she was" (G 38), and early in *Guinevere* when the heroine, now twelve years old, wanders into the wood, her parents punish her: for two weeks instead of riding with her father and playing in the fields, Guinevere is to spend her afternoons in the chapel praying for "wisdom and maturity" and reading the Holy Fathers (G 12). Guinevere, Leodegrance adds, must "think about herself and her place in the world" (G 13). Their intentions are good, but, as Merlin acutely observes, the world of Leodegrance and Guenlian and consequently of Guinevere is one of fantasy (G 480). They live in a Roman villa, with mosaic floors, muralled walls, heated rooms, and even a Roman bath, totally unaware that their quiet, ordered, civilized way of life is already an anachronism. For a hundred years no true Roman citizen had lived in Britain, but according to Newman, Leodegrance and especially Guenlian, with their few remaining relatives and friends, behave as if the emperor will return any day, leading fresh legions to reinstate Roman rule. Their fantasy will later be shattered when they learn that their three "Roman warrior" sons were killed while fighting the Saxons. Even her brothers cherish Guinevere as a happy, innocent child, beautiful and untouched by the grief and conflict outside her narrow world. When John notices his sister is developing into a woman, he is shocked and surprised: "I suppose I felt that you must be some sort of faery child who would never change" (G 41). The effect of this insulated world is that Guinevere is emotionally stunted.

Another member of this household is Flora, Guinevere's old nurse, a priestess of Epona who believes that Guinevere, the newly born infant with a divine aura, is destined for the goddess. And then there is Geraldus, frequently a guest at Cameliard, who is accompanied by a sultry faery mistress and a chorus of invisible singers who are mistakenly regarded by everyone who cannot see or hear them as angels. That Guinevere can see them indicates that she is already moving into the otherworld.

Even Merlin unwittingly contributes to Guinevere's insulation from the real world by preventing her from associating with the British soldiers who are to camp at Cameliard. Though able to see the future of Arthur's Britain, he only vaguely knows that Guinevere is somewhere involved in it and that she will cause everyone much pain, especially herself. And determined that Arthur will not meet her, he convinces her parents to send her away from home. Guinevere, who has never been deprived of anything she wants, locks herself in her room, cries and pouts, but goes off with Geraldus, fuming to herself, "I am almost a woman and they treat me as if I were a baby. I will never let anyone do this to me again. I will control where I go and what I do" (G 56)—a declaration of independence, uttered and soon forgotten.

At the hermitage of Gaia and Timon, brother and sister who alienated themselves from the world by vowing chastity, poverty, and unity with God's creatures, Guinevere lives in virtually a garden of Eden, close to nature, but rather than finding God—throughout the trilogy she shows no interest in the spiritual—she is finally united with the only living unicorn. Looking into its blue eyes, she experiences an emotional ecstasy that leaves her, when the unicorn flees from the approaching hunters, bathed in a radiant glow, and coming upon her in the woods, Cei believes her to be the goddess of the woodlands; Caet, Epona, and Arthur, the Virgin Mary, "so beautiful and so remote, and yet I could feel her kindness and wisdom surging through me, just for a glance" (G 94). To them, she represents idealized woman. The unicorn has several meanings. The most obvious one is its association with sexual innocence, for traditionally the unicorn lays its head in the lap of a virgin. More importantly, because the unicorn is a fabulous creature, it represents Guinevere's line with the otherworld and also with Lancelot, who in *The Chessboard Queen* encounters it and learns, "You are the one! At last! I give you my place in her heart . . ." (G 31). It is this otherworldly quality that is emphasized after she returns home, for as her relationship with the unicorn deepens, she lives more and more in the otherworld. Indeed, Newman notes that spending so much time with a creature of fantasy gave Guinevere an "otherworldliness and a serene attitude that half-frightened those around her" (G 119).

Ordinarily, as Thompson has shown (114–39), an Arthurian character who lives in the otherworld has a beneficial learning experience, but for

Newman, Guinevere's relationship with the unicorn is not a beneficial or a learning experience. Granted, when Flora attempts to sacrifice Guinevere to Epona, the unicorn breaks down the chapel door, and with its forefeet pawing the air, it threatens to bludgeon the priestess until she plunges the knife into her own body, showering Guinevere with blood and hissing, "The sacrifice was desecrated. She will not pay, but Britain will. . . . Now all who have her will reap only grief from her. . . ." (G 140). Thus, the unicorn saves Guinevere's life, just as the faery chorus later prevents Geraldus from being slain by Meleagant's warriors. Nonetheless, with this exception, Guinevere's involvement with the unicorn is harmful, for by taking care of her emotional needs, it tends to insulate her from human relationships and, thus, further stunts her mental and emotional growth. "She is drifting away from us," Guenlian remarks to her husband (G 96). In fact, while supposedly learning the routine of maintaining a household, Guinevere, in the company of other females, is present only in body; mentally and emotionally she is united with the unicorn. When her three brothers are reported to be slain by the Saxons, she turns to the unicorn for consolation, not fully comprehending the finality of her brothers' deaths, selfishly weeping for herself, for their absence in her own life, not for the destruction of theirs.

However, at seventeen, after three years as a fosterling at Cador castle, Guinevere is changed because she now lives in the real world with the unwashed, noisy mass of humanity crowded in the great hall of the fortress. True, she still feels the need to return to her childhood home. "You lasted almost a year at this visit," Sidra, her foster mother, remarks to Guinevere. "Perhaps someday you will not need to go home but only wish to" (G 148). This key to Guinevere's maturity is traced throughout the trilogy. Actually, Guinevere has adjusted to life at Cador castle, which in some instances is more exciting than that of Cameliard. And she now has a few companions her own age: Risa, her maid, Gawain, and Alswytha, the Saxon hostage. Moreover, she is exposed to human relationships; for example, she inadvertently comes upon Gawain and Risa engaging in sex, an act that repulses but also attracts her.

Most important is the fact that her relationship with the unicorn has altered. By mental telepathy they still communicate with each other, but their meetings seem to be less frequent, and when they do meet, Guinevere tries to comfort the unicorn, tormented by its failure to find the answers to such questions as: What is the nature of my being? What is the purpose of my life here on earth? Guinevere wishes to help it to find the answers but cannot, for she "had never questioned anything herself" and didn't even comprehend what it is to be "torn by the need to know why" (G 151). On the other hand, if the unicorn represents her later ego note that it refers to Guinevere as "my other self" (G 150)—then she is subconsciously asking herself these questions without, as in the case of the unicorn, finding the answers at this time. The unicorn still represents the otherworld, for it tells Guinevere, "I sense somehow by my presence I am keeping you from being truly human" (G 174). And wishing to die, the unicorn prepares Guinevere for its eventual departure. Significant, however, is the fact that when Guinevere is kidnapped by the Saxons, it is not the unicorn but Arthur who rescues her and her brother Mark, a disfigured slave of Aelle, the Saxon leader.

Actually, Guinevere is the one who rescues Mark, and it is one of the few instances in the novel that she takes the initiative and acts on her own. Sliding from Arthur's horse, she courageously wades through the jungle of riders and frantic Saxons, totally oblivious to the swords and hooves, in search of her brother, whom she finds and drags to Arthur. Later, at the trial of Alswytha, the Saxon hostage whose life was forfeit when her brother kidnapped Guinevere and killed some British soldiers, Guinevere shows genuine concern for her companion, is horrified when the British lords propose that she be maimed and raped, but relieved when Mark claims his beloved as retribution for his suffering. She also aids Mark and Alswytha to flee to Gaia's and Timon's hermitage, both disillusioned by man's inhumanity to man.

Arthur, of course, falls in love with Guinevere. A disarming young man of great ability and personal charm, he is shy and inept in her presence because he feels uncouth in her elegant, aristocratic environment. Guinevere is unaware of Arthur's feelings until Guenlian tells her of his intentions, and though she has not decided to marry him, so many people at Cameliard tell her the matter is settled that she accepts the decision as her own. They are married, and when she loses her virginity the unicorn disappears from her life, along with the memory of its existence. With the loss of the unicorn, Guinevere, who can now participate in a more healthy relationship, turns with new appreciation of Arthur: "There is something very dear about him," she decides at last. "I think I could learn to love him very much" (G 257).

As *The Chessboard Queen* opens, Guinevere, married five years, is the beautiful ornament of Arthur's court at Caerleon. Arthur loves his wife; she is fond of him, and she performs her wifely duty in bed even though she experiences no sexual satisfaction. Because Guinevere's relationship with the women at the court is one of the themes of the trilogy, Newman notes that Guinevere is excluded from the company of women because unlike them she is childless. Nonetheless, she is content at Caerleon with all the Roman comforts of her parents' home and consequently wishes to remain there rather than move for the summer to Camelot, Arthur's new city. In fact, when she goes to Camelot, her distaste and despair are so obvious that Geraldus rebukes her and points out the importance of Camelot to Arthur. Guinevere agrees to try to see the beauty of her new residence and to "encourage Arthur . . . in his dreams" (C 53). But even she does not comprehend his dream of creating an ideal society, symbolized by Camelot, the gleaming city of the arts, with his Round Table knights issuing forth to establish order and dispense justice throughout a unified Britain. Needless to say, Guinevere is immature, but she senses that something is "wrong or missing in her life, something vital" (C 41). This dissatisfaction sets the stage for the entrance of Lancelot.

Influenced by the French *Prose Lancelot*, Newman has Lancelot, as an infant, snatched from his mother's arms by the Lady of the Lake, who rears him in her underwater palace. Thus, like Guinevere, Lancelot lives in the otherworld. According to Newman, Lancelot is a perfectionist. He must master to perfection everything he takes—riding, archery, swordsmanship, etc. "There was a fierce intensity about him that would not allow for his own failure" (C 23). With the same intensity he cares for others. For example, as a youngster he tries to drive a nail through his palm to atone for the sins of the Lady of the Lake and the other hedonistic immortals whom he loves. But, unlike Guinevere, Lancelot is not content in the otherworld. "Burning to enter the world . . . and save it from itself" (C 46), he, with the assistance of the Lady of the Lake, goes to Camelot and becomes Arthur's perfect knight.

Upon meeting Guinevere, Lancelot sees her not as a woman but as a goddess to adore. Guinevere doesn't like him, for he is conspicuously perfect, obviously pious. She even prods Gawain to fight Lancelot, but they are so impressed with each other's prowess that they become friends. Once this relationship between Lancelot and Guinevere is established, Newman can then trace the emotional development of both of them. For example, while escorting Guinevere to Cameliard when he learns that he is the son of King Ban, killed by Claudus, the father of Meleagant, Lancelot experiences hate, longing to avenge his father's death. Tormented because he has vowed never to be tainted by earthly love or hate, he leaves Cameliard to grapple with his own sins and to seek information about his mother.

Guinevere also shows signs of emotional development. For example, when she tells Letitia, her niece, about her father, Matthew, she ends by weeping not, as previously, for what she had lost but for him. And although she is happy in her childhood home, she finds herself thinking more and more of Caerleon. "Could it be that I have two homes now?" she asks Geraldus (C 143). She is eager to return to Caerleon but on the way is abducted by Meleagant as part of his wager to Arthur: if Arthur or his knights can retrieve what he stole of Arthur's, he will recognize Arthur as his overlord and support him against the other kings. When Lancelot crosses the sword bridge, falls on his knees before Guinevere, with his bloody hands clutching her dress for support and his face showing naked, wild passion, she is terrified and lashes out at him: "Why are you here? Arthur didn't send you. . . . Your damned pride! Everyone is laughing at the brave knight of Arthur's who was driven through the country in a cart, like a common thief. . . . You've embarrassed us all and half killed yourself for a game! A stupid wager" (C 170). Lancelot goes mad and flees from Meleagant's castle as Gawain, who crossed the water bridge, arrives. Arthur is furious, and many of the court turn against Guinevere for her harsh treatment of Lancelot until she agrees to spend the summer in religious retreat at Cameliard.

But Guinevere is uneasy; something is missing. Again, Guinevere's dissatisfaction is Newman's prelude to an eventful happening that will effect Guinevere's development. In this instance, a fosterling at Cador castle arrives at Camelot with the news of the Saxon raid and of the death of Geraldus, who incidentally chooses to enter not heaven but the faery otherworld to be with his choir and his faery mistress, later to be joined by Merlin and his beloved Nimue, a servant of the Lady of the Lake. At any rate, thanks to Geraldus, Lydia, Cador's daughter and Cei's love, is safe, but Sidra, Cador's wife and Guinevere's foster mother, who sends the fosterlings to safety, kills herself to avoid being taken hostage. Sidra, like Guenlian, is a strong woman who serves as a foil to Guinevere. But what is significant there is the effect of Sidra's death upon Guinevere, who weeps out her sorrow and her guilt. She now realizes she never thanked Sidra, never apologized for the thoughtless and selfish acts. Newman notes that it was a flash of insight, a moment of humility in the midst of sadness, the first time Guinevere ever doubted her own worth.

This new understanding of herself is reinforced and developed in the next episode. While Arthur assembles his men to attack the Saxons, Guinevere goes to Cameliard, where she recognizes the childlike madman there as Lancelot. Her reaction is far different than that at Meleagant's castle. No longer terrified by the force of his love, she tells him, "Lancelot, I'm sorry. I didn't mean to do this to you. Please forgive me! Come back! I'm not afraid anymore . . . I won't ever deny it again" (C 217). Aware of no understanding on his part, Guinevere sets about to restore his sanity but to no avail. Finally Lancelot is cured by the Lady of the Lake, who intends to take him back to her underwater palace, but Lancelot refuses when he sees Guinevere. Their mistakes with each other are forgiven and forgotten; they will begin anew, and this time they will be, according to the naive Lancelot, friends.

Lancelot leaves to join Arthur and Leodegrance to fight the Saxons, and Guinevere remains at Cameliard with Guenlian. As a result of this giant step in her emotional development, she can now show her appreciation of others. She hugs her mother, who is surprised but delighted, for Guinevere has never been demonstrative. When, after Leodegrance returns with a leg cut, she finds Guenlian asleep, curled up on the floor, with her hand still clasped in her husband's, Guinevere thinks of her relationship with Arthur, and the next day, after being assured of her father's recovery, she tells Gawain, "I want to go home" (C 238). Though Caerleon is her favorite home, Arthur is pleased that she is growing fond of Camelot and is interested in its interior decoration. She now takes an active role in the affairs of the court, during the day sitting beside Arthur, listening to the news and the complaints brought to him, and even offering suggestions to resolve them. At the evening festivities she is Arthur's beautiful and gracious queen. Her influence is impressive. Later Modred remarks that everyone comes to Camelot determined to win concessions from Arthur, but after one evening with Guinevere, they give him anything he wants (GE 82).

Lancelot is tricked into sleeping with Elaine, and Galahad is born. Guinevere believes Lancelot to be completely innocent until he confesses all to her including the fact that he willingly had sex with the girl because he thought she was Guinevere. Several days later, Guinevere suddenly realizes that she loves him and that she wants to have sex with him: "It was like an unexpected brilliant flash of light, showing her all the shapes and corners once decently shadowed. . . . She loved him. She wanted him with her now and forever. She needed him to be with her and to hold him as she had never needed anyone before" (C 271). And the opportunity to fulfill her need is presented by Arthur. Here Newman is like Mary Stewart. Aware of their love for some time, Arthur absents himself from the court to let them have one chance to be together, hoping that it may be enough and then Guinevere will be his again. Taking advantage of this opportunity, Guinevere unbars the door, admits Lancelot to her room, disrobes, and together they consummate their love. As one who always felt somehow apart from everyone who loves her, she is now united with Lancelot in body and soul, and the next day, when Lancelot tells her he must leave her and Caerleon, she wisely remarks to him, "You would have to crack your soul asunder to tear me from you" (C 293). But she agrees to let him go, and when Arthur learns of Lancelot's decision to pilgrimage to Tours, he is relieved, believing that the lovers have given him another chance. That evening in the bedroom, Guinevere, with a stab of guilt, sees Arthur clearly for the first time as a tired and lonely man "who was too good to take what she would not offer first" (C 296), and she decides that although she cannot share with him the love Lancelot gives her, she can at least try to give him comfort and a little understanding and, hence, has sex with him.

The most important effect of her feeling for Lancelot is her love of Galahad. Holding the infant in her arms, she declares, "You are my child, Lancelot's and mine. It was his love for me that conceived you. You have my hair, my skin, and I claim you for my own. . . . You must come to love me, for I am truly your mother" (C 283). And early in *Guinevere Evermore* when he, at the age of five, is brought to court to be fostered, he fills the void created by her childlessness. The fulfillment that she experiences as Galahad's foster mother is different from the frustration that characterizes the childless Guinevere in the Arthurian works of White, Stewart, and Bradley.

Other than the effect of being Galahad's foster mother, Newman shows little further development of Guinevere in the first third of *Guinevere Forevermore*. She mentions that because of Galahad Guinevere now is accepted into the circle of women who talk about their children and the vagaries of their husbands, though she is aware of certain forbidden topics, presumably related to her affair with Lancelot. And Newman notes that when Leodegrance dies, Guinevere returns home, only to realize that Cameliard belongs to the past and that Camelot is now her home. Her relationship with Lancelot and Arthur is essentially the same as that established at the end of the second novel, though now everyone seems to know of her love for Lancelot, but there is no confrontation because no one wants to hurt Arthur; that is until Gareth, and although the situation is awkward, everyone present apparently ignores Gareth's accusation, everyone except Modred and Guinevere, who feels "something is wrong in the world. Everything is coming undone" (GE 116).

The villain, of course, is Modred, who comes to Arthur's court after the drowning of his mother, Morgan, who ends up (or rather down) in the underwater palace of the Lady of the Lake. Determined to be monarch of Britain, he gains Guinevere's and especially Arthur's trust, and then he, with his Aunt Morgause's aid, sets out to destroy his father by spreading rumors that the Queen uses witchcraft to stay youthful, to lure Lancelot to her bed, and to prevent Arthur from attacking his enemies. When Lancelot returns from the Grail quest and is with the Queen in her room, Modred's followers break down the door, seize the Queen—for Lancelot manages to escape—

and take her to Cirencester to be tried for sorcery by the bishops conveniently convening there and for treason by a civil tribunal. When Arthur returns to Camelot and learns what has happened, he is furious and frustrated that he can do nothing, for to rescue her would only confirm the allegations that she has bewitched him, and to dissolve the courts would destroy his system of justice which is based upon the premise that no man, not even kings or bishops, can be above the law. This is reminiscent of T.H. White. Expanding this traditional episode, Newman shows how this experience contributes to Guinevere's personal growth. When Guinevere, during her incarceration, is visited by Geraldus and Merlin, who offer her a chance to join in the faery world, she refuses not only because she will be separated forever from Lancelot and Galahad, but also because, contrary to Merlin's argument, there will always be talk that Arthur or Lancelot rescued her and that she is still alive and still practicing witchcraft. "No, I won't go with you," she declares. "I'll stay here and if the tribunal says I'm guilty, then I'll die" (GE 162). It's a courageous decision. It is also, according to Merlin, the first time in her life that she made up her own mind, and it is the first time she is afraid.

Tricked into admitting during the trial that Merlin came to her, she is found guilty of both charges and condemned to be burned alive. She, of course, is rescued by Lancelot, who accidentally kills Gareth, and they flee to his cousin's castle. Arthur, with his men, goes to Banoit to avenge Gareth's death and to uphold his laws "because that is the only hope of peace we have" (GE 189). And learning that Arthur is willing to take her back if Lancelot proves her innocence in the trial by combat, Guinevere unselfishly decides on her own to return to Arthur if Lancelot defeats his opponent in order to prevent any more bloodshed, not realizing until the next day that the opponent is Gawain, who permits himself to be killed. This unselfish decision is the first of several that are critical to Guinevere's emotional and mental growth. Though she has made slow steps toward selfhood (possibly too slow), her growth will continue more quickly now.

Lancelot is exiled, Guinevere joins Arthur in a poignant scene of reconciliation, and Arthur leads his army off to fight the Franks in Armorica, leaving behind the women and children. Guinevere is now accepted by the women of the court with a friendliness that pleases but puzzles her until Risa, her maid, explains, "It's simple enough. You've lost a child, and you've lost a lover. Now you are one of us" (GE 208). As regent, Modred puts into effect his treacherous plans by falsely reporting the death of Arthur and by filling Camelot with Jute mercenaries, who frighten the women and children. Fearing for their safety and only on the condition that they are permitted to go on to Cameliard, Guinevere agrees to marry Modred—another altruistic act. Once wed, the sadistic Modred repeatedly rapes and physically abuses her. Realizing that the only way to stop Modred is to be stronger than he is, Guinevere calmly refuses to go to bed with him, and threatened with disfigurement, she stares him down, refusing to acknowledge him as her master. And what Modred sees in her eyes convinces him that she has won:

> He looked into her eyes and what he saw there bewildered and frightened him. The Saxon Aelle, and Meleagant, and even Caradoc had seen the same thing, and none of them had understood it. . . . Modred knew that there was nothing he could do to her that could reach what she was, and, after everything, the mysterious essence that was Guinevere would remain. (GE 225)

From this statement it is clear that Newman intended to show that Guinevere always had an inner strength but she never drew upon it until she realized that no one was going to rescue her from Modred but herself.

Learning that Arthur had landed in Britain and realizing that Modred would use her as hostage, Guinevere displays further self-reliance by devising an escape plan, and with the aid of Risa and Father Antonius, they, dressed as monks, leave Camelot and flee to Arthur's camp. When she removes her monk's robe, revealing her cut and bruised body, Arthur shares her hatred of Modred. Evidently, Newman believes that to fully mature, Guinevere must experience the full range of human emotions. On the eve of the battle of Camlann, they declare their love for each other, and each acknowledges the price of his individual pursuits. Thinking of how his enemies used his beloved wife to destroy his dreams for Britain, Arthur tells Guinevere, "I sacrificed you to my dreams," and she, thinking of Lancelot, replies, "And I sacrificed you to my desires. . . . I wonder why we humans are allowed to go blundering through our lives. So many things I should have known but learned too late" (GE 239).

The battle of Camlann occurs; Modred is killed by Arthur, who, mortally wounded, is taken by the Lady of the Lake to a cave in her kingdom to sleep until his spirit is healed. Lancelot, who fought with Arthur, feels he must go on a pilgrimage to Jerusalem: "There must be someone, somewhere, who can explain my life to me" (GE 247), and Guinevere, who needs to find out what she can do on her own, eventually returns to Cameliard, where she discovers her gift of healing, and studying medical books she explains, "I think I've had enough of pettiness for this life" (GE 253). As the plague strikes and thousands die, cutting the British population by one third,

Guinevere risks her life by nursing the sick at Cameliard, and because of the great toll there, Allard, Guinevere's half-Saxon nephew who received his father's share of Leodegrance's estate, convinces Guinevere to invite the Christianized Germanic Alemanni to settle and work the land of Cameliard. This is a different Guinevere, who in *Guinevere* hated the Teutonic invader. Consequently, the melting of cultures that is then taking place in the country as a whole, begins to take place in microcosm on Guinevere's land. Busy and useful, Guinevere is happy, and when Lancelot returns she tells him what she discovered she can do:

> I can help in a sickroom and play with children and, maybe, I can hold people together. I never knew that was a talent before, but I've worked all these years to keep Cameliard, just my own corner of Britain, safe as well. (GE 271)

After a month's stay at Cameliard Lancelot declares that he has found his peace there with Guinevere, but still longing for redemption he enters the monastery at Glastonbury. Nearing her last days, Guinevere is again visited by Geraldus, who offers her one final chance to come to the faery world, praising its beauty and telling her that her unicorn awaits her there. Even with that lure Guinevere rejects this escape, saying "I've grown up. As far as I can in this life. It's time for me to see what else there is. And I promised Lancelot. He can't reach the gates and not find me there" (GE 174). At his monastery, Lancelot receives a similar offer from the Lady of the Lake, and like Guinevere, he rejects it. They die and are buried together at Glastonbury. A generation later a monk reasoned that if the woman buried by the chapel were Guinevere, then the man with her must be Arthur, and since she was not the mother of Modred, Arthur's son, then she must be his second wife; hence, placed on their grave was a lead cross bearing this inscription: HIC JACET INCLITUS REX ARTURIS IN INSULA AVALLONIS SEPULTUS CUM WENNEVERIA UXORE SUA SECUNDA.

Though other Arthurian writers, such as T.H. White and Parke Godwin, have shown the human development of Guinevere, Newman is the first writer to make it her major focus. As the first Arthurian writer to treat Guinevere's life before her marriage to Arthur, she is able to present Guinevere as an innocent, pampered, self-centered teenager, protected by her family from the harsh realities of the outside world and somewhat insulated from human relationships because of her special involvement with the faery world. Once that is established, Newman then concentrates on the various stages of development which enabled Guinevere finally to emerge as an emotionally mature, self-reliant, altruistic woman. Frankly, I know of no other Arthurian work in which Guinevere undergoes so great a change in character. It is a remarkable achievement and an important contribution to the Arthurian legend.

Also remarkable is the fact that Newman has created a refreshingly new Arthurian world, a woman's world in which linen is aired and scented, herbs are gathered and dried for possets and flavorings, and wool is corded, spun, and woven. Written from a female perspective, this trilogy seems to be more highly populated with women than other Arthurian works. Certainly Newman's female characters are much more fully realized, even though their roles are traditional ones. For example, Guenlian and Sidra, both strong women, are outstanding managers of their households, loving wives, and caring mothers. Especially moving is Guenlian's grief over the death of her three sons, and Newman's description of Guenlian's gradual recovery from despair is psychologically sound. Newman's Arthurian world is also one of real infants like Galahad, who yanks Guinevere's hair and heart, and Lancelot, who can't sit up but falls over, shits, lies on the floor, kicking and sucking his thumb, and who later tries to put nutmeats in his nose. Even the youngsters are real; for example, Galahad, as a fosterling at Camelot, is described as a small gold and green whirlwind, shrieking at the top of his lungs to Arthur and Cei, "Save me! She's going to catch me!" (GE 14) as he dives under the Round Table, scattering the loose rolls that Arthur has been reading, only to be caught by Guinevere, who pounces on his foot stretching out from the table, orders him to the baths to be cleaned from head to toe, whether the other boys laugh or not, and then as a special treat, to sit that night at the high table with her, Arthur, and his father. It is also a world in which women are present when the Grail appears at Camelot, and some of them are so spiritually moved that they too want to go on the quest but can't because they are women. In this trilogy, a woman like Risa, after sex with Gawain, can exclaim, "I can't believe it! I never met a man before who lived up to his own boasting" (G 172), and Guinevere can tell Lancelot that honor is something men invented because they can't do the right thing for love's sake, and the wife of Guinevere's jailer can speak out against the clergy who persecute wives who have lovers. Incidentally, Newman's view of religion is a complex but interesting topic which should be discussed at another time.

There is even a touch of the woman in Newman's humor, for many of the witty remarks and humorous incidents involve women and their concerns. For example, when Lancelot goes above the surface of the lake to hunt deer, the Lady of the Lake reasons that if hunting makes Lancelot happy then she must let him hunt, but she declares something must be done soon, for "I am getting extremely weary of venison every night" (GE 28). And when Lancelot decides to go to Camelot and to become Arthur's knight, she insists upon supplying him with the proper gear and clothes, including a sterling silver visor, an ostrich plumed helmet and silk underwear which Lancelot complains, after his joust with Cei, is plastered to his skin. Her visit to Cameliard to cure Lancelot's madness is high comedy, and Nimue's attempt to seduce Lancelot is funny, especially her ploy of requesting a farewell kiss from Lancelot, who bites her lip because she French-kissed him. My favorite character, however, is Gawain, who calls Guinevere "Auntie." Traditionally, Gawain's strength waxes and wanes according to the course of the sun, but Newman adds that from sunset to sunrise, he falls into a deep, undisturbed sleep. It is this tradition that provides humorous incidents like that of the perilous bed. If a man can lie all night with the lord's daughter and not molest her, then he's worthy to be her husband. If he tries anything, then a sword suspended above the bed falls and kills him. Gawain passes the test because after climbing into the bed he immediately falls into a deep sleep, but when he awakes in the morning and finds the naked Alia beside him, he mounts her, so overjoyed with his good fortune that he is unconcerned when his arm is nicked by the falling sword though surprised by the sudden appearance of her parents, who rush them through the marriage ceremony. With her parents weeping good-bye, the mother comments to Alia that they never expected to lose her because the sword seemed invincible. "Mother," Alia exclaims, "Do you know what it was like having men sliced to death on top of me? Some of those stains never came out" (GE 88). And then on the way to Camelot Gawain is jilted by Alia, who runs off with her true love. Unlike the Disneyesque humor of T.H. White and the robust Rabelaisian hilarity of Berger, who is especially fond of ironic twists, Newman's wit is predominantly light and feminine but just as delightful.

That the Guinevere trilogy is written from a female perspective may have prompted Thompson's remark that the Saxons in *Guinevere* are bad because they mistreat women and most of the Britons are good because they do not (124). Actually, the treatment of women is frequently a key to whether a male character in Newman's trilogy is basically good or bad. Aelle, Ecfrith, Uther, Meleagant, and Modred, all of whom mistreat women, are bad. But, one must realize that the treatment of women is only one of the reasons a character is praised or condemned. For example, Aelle mistreats his wife and possibly Guinevere and even willingly forfeits the life of his daughter Alswytha, but he also breaks his oath to Arthur, and as leader of the Saxons, he is responsible for the death of the young Bretons who were accompanying Guinevere to Cameliard. Moreover, long before rescuing Guinevere, Arthur was fighting Aelle and the Saxons, who are Britain's enemy, invaders who are taking more and more British land and killing the British inhabitants. And Modred is condemned not merely because he is sadistic in his treatment of women but primarily because he is a traitor who destroys Arthur and his dreams.

Thompson's remark invariably leads one to the crucial question: is Newman a feminist writer? In her discussion of the Guinevere trilogy, Karen Garthright, who incidentally does not label Newman a feminist, nonetheless pinpoints various concerns of feminists in Newman's development of Guinevere's character; for example, that Guinevere is regarded by others not as a real person but merely as a beautiful idol, a goddess to be adored; that she refuses to be mastered by Modred; that she seeks to find out what she can do on her own; the importance of her being accepted into the circle of the women at the court, etc. And one can add others, such as Guinevere's taking a lover to give and receive love, to be sexually satisfied, to experience passion (Newman calls it joy). Note that it was she who initiated their first sexual encounter by unbarring the door, admitting Lancelot and disrobing. Risa and Morgan select their own lovers; there are strong women like Flora, Guenlian, and Sidra; Aelle's wife should be able to pursue her work as a crafter of gold; Guinevere wills the villa at Cameliard to the church as a house for women who need protection and who "were relieved to know that there was a monastery just for them, where they would be free to study and work without male supervision" (GE 273). For some critics, all of these female concerns may indicate that Newman is indeed a feminist, but she is not one who blames men for the suppression of women. Guinevere's immaturity, for example, is not caused by men but by her family, who keep her a carefree, innocent, self-centered little girl protected from the harsh realities of the outside world and by her own involvement with the faery world that further insulates her from human relationships. Indeed, it is her experiences with males like Arthur, Lancelot, Galahad, and even Modred that enable her to develop into an emotionally mature, self-reliant, altruistic woman. And although there is only one despicable woman (Morgause) in the trilogy, there are only a few men who mistreat women. The roles of Newman's women are, of course, the traditional ones of wife, household manager, mother, and nurse. But with the possible exception of Aelle's wife, the gold crafter, Newman's women are content to fill these roles, and their lives are fulfilled. Unlike Bradshaw's Guinevere, who willingly performs the duties normally assigned to a steward, Newman's Guinevere knows nothing about managing a household. As Arthur's Queen, she is relieved of these duties, and though she occasionally participates in governmental matters, she has no desire to be Arthur's co-ruler or, after Arthur's death, sovereign of Britain, as she is in *Firelord* and *Beloved Exile* by Parke Godwin, who has presented the strongest, most liberated Guinevere in Arthurian literature, perhaps because, as he admits, he was influenced by the feminist movement. In short, if Newman is to be classified as a feminist writer, then her definition of feminism must be explained.

Newman, of course, is only one of a growing number of modern Arthurian writers who have been sympathetic in their portrayal of Guinevere—a difficult task when one considers that traditionally Guinevere was condemned for (1) her adultery, (2) treason, (3) contributing to the downfall of Arthur's realm. Concerning the first charge, Newman does not condemn but glorifies the love affair between Lancelot and Guinevere, without deprecating Arthur, as Chrétien, for example, does in his *Lancelot*. Arthur is aware of the love between Lancelot and Guinevere. Newman notes that sometimes when Arthur sees them together he "hurts more for their misery than for his own" (C 290), and he even gives them a chance to be together. Lancelot is his friend, the only one who truly understands and shares his dreams, and when confronted with their adultery he forgives her because he loves her, even blaming himself rather than her. Lancelot cares for Arthur, doesn't want to hurt him or his dreams, but his love for Guinevere is, as Newman notes, "a profligate whirlwind that cut through the image of Lancelot the savior and left only the man" (C 265). Yet the conflict between lover and saint is always present. Even at the end of the trilogy when he realizes that Guinevere is more a part of him than his soul and he states that he found peace with her at Cameliard, he enters a monastery as a lay brother because "there's a stubborn part of me yet that longs for redemption" (GE 273). Guinevere does not experience this conflict, for she is not concerned with religion. True, before she is to be burned alive, she mentions her love for Lancelot in her confession to Father Antonius, but it is meaningless, for when Lancelot rescues her from the flames, she spends a romantic winter with her lover at Banoit. She declares that he is as much a part of her as her soul, and her reasoning is that just as they are joined in life so shall they be joined in death, be it heaven or hell. That her soul is not damned to hell because of her love for Lancelot is implied by Newman, who states that in death Guinevere's eyes were "wide open as if in delightful surprise" (GE 274).

Guinevere loves Lancelot, and Newman clearly establishes that Guinevere also loves Arthur; even near the end of the trilogy, when Arthur is to fight Modred, she declares to Arthur, "I have always loved you. . . ."

(GE 239). Yet, from the time Guinevere discovers that she loves Lancelot and wants to have sex with him until the night she does, Newman never indicates that Guinevere ever thought of Arthur as her husband, whom she professes to love. Granted, Arthur gives Lancelot and Guinevere a chance to be together, hoping that it may be enough and she will be his again, but there is no evidence that Guinevere knows of her husband's "sanction" of adultery. Consequently, because Guinevere also loves Arthur, Newman should have provided the reader with a conflict within Guinevere or some justification for her decision to commit adultery *before* the sex act rather than during and after it. During sex, in "the last moment before Guinevere forgot herself entirely" (sexual climax), Newman states that Guinevere felt a stab of regret for Arthur and then exclaimed, "This is what we never had. This is the difference—not love, but joy!" (C 291). Unlike Arthur, Lancelot is able sexually to satisfy Guinevere (C 62), but for Guinevere to think of Arthur at such a moment is, from a male's point of view, not only unrealistic but also demeaning to both Lancelot and Arthur. However, Newman maintains that when a woman like Guinevere who has slept with only one man in her life, a man whom she is fond of but feels no great passion for and then discovers how much difference there is in making love with a man she adores completely, she cannot help making a comparison, especially at that moment during the sex act (Letter, April 6, 1987). Obviously, sexual fulfillment is only a part of Guinevere's love for Lancelot, for after sex when she realizes that until then she always felt apart from everyone who loved her, she says to Lancelot, "You are as much a part of me *now* [italics mine] as my soul" (C 292). And the following morning she distinguishes between her love for Lancelot and for Arthur, that it is her duty to love Arthur, her husband and lord, but her destiny to love Lancelot, for they "have been joined in more than flesh" (C 293). Here, then, is Guinevere's justification for her adulterous love for Lancelot, though, as stated before, because it occurs during and after the sex act, it cannot serve as an explanation for her decision to commit adultery.

Concerning the second charge, Guinevere is found guilty of treason, but it is not based upon her adultery as it is in Malory's *Morte Darthur*, which Newman stated is not one of her sources (Letter, February 12, 1987). The setting of her trilogy is from the end of Roman Britain to the beginning of the Saxon era, and although Newman does not explain the civil tribunal's basis for the treason, it seems that Guinevere, as a sorceress, aided Britain's enemies, the Saxons, by urging Arthur to trade with them rather than declare war upon them. Interestingly, there is no discussion of Guinevere's adultery during the trial, though outside the court Gawain and Modred refer to it and after the trial Guinevere states that she was unfaithful to Arthur—a statement that prompts the jailer's wife to attack the clergy, not the landlords and merchants of the civil tribunal. Later Arthur dismisses the civil tribunal's verdict to treason (one must assume that Arthur's law embraces the Roman law of the accused having the right to final judgment before the King), declares that Guinevere will pay the fine for adultery (twenty-five gold coins according to Theodosian Code), and if she is willing to return to him, he will accept her back as it is his right under his laws. Guinevere, of course, is not a sorceress or a traitor, and from the time she is forcibly taken from Camelot until she is rescued from the flames by Lancelot, the reader's sympathies are always with Guinevere. This episode serves a number of purposes, the most important being to show how Arthur's enemies—especially the fanatic St. Caradoc, the vindictive Meleagant, and the treacherous Modred—used Guinevere to try to destroy Arthur. Even Arthur is willing to sacrifice his beloved Guinevere for his dreams and laws.

Because Arthur mentions several times that no one, except Lancelot, understands his dreams and laws, it is necessary to discuss his laws now, for earlier in this paper his dreams were explained. Ideally, his laws, of course, are fair and just. Arthur envisions justice falling evenly upon all in the land, and no man, be he king or bishop, is above the law. When enforced, his laws will bring order and peace by settling family violence and bloodshed. Most important is Arthur's belief that his laws will unite all the Britons. However, in practice, his laws raise a number of questions. For example, note that Arthur never questions the legality of a lay person's being tried in a religious court, and Bishop Dubricius's remark that he will be true to Arthur's laws implies that Arthur's laws apply to religious courts—a remarkable deviation from historical fact. Also it is remarkable that both courts should meet (in a tavern yet) to decide Guinevere's punishment, let alone approve of the revival of the ancient practice of burning alive the guilty person. And because Lancelot, who rescues Guinevere from the flames, is charged by Arthur of thwarting the King's justice, is one to assume that Arthur approves of Guinevere's unjust trial and sentence? Further, when Gawain asks Arthur to invoke his laws by bringing Lancelot back to be tried for the murder of Gareth as proof that "your law is greater than the tribes [sic], that you can punish crimes against them all without the rivers of bloodshed we have known" (GE 188), Arthur agrees but his law turns out to be trial by combat, hardly an enlightened form of justice! Perhaps I should add that although they are flaws, they are minor, for in one sense, they reveal Arthur as a human being who can and does make mistakes. And what really matters is that Newman rightly portrays Arthur as an idealist, a dreamer.

Concerning the final charge against Guinevere, in Newman's work it is clearly not the adulterous love affair of Lancelot and Guinevere that contributes to the downfall of Arthur's realm. The villain is Modred, though others are also at fault. For example, there is Morgan, determined to avenge her mother's rape, though when she steals Arthur's scabbard and replaces it with a nonmagical one, she acts not as an avenging daughter but as a loving mother trying to prevent the certain death of her son, Modred. Far more important is Morgause, who admits later that she never cared about avenging Uther's rape of Igerne but, nonetheless, declares, "You can't ignore the bonds [blood ties]" (GE 210); in reality, her actions against Arthur stem mainly from the fact that she is the witch of darkness, the incestuous paramour of Modred, one obsessed with power. Then there are the rebellious Northern kings, and Bors speaks for those of Banoit when he declares that Arthur "is nothing to us" because "the bonds that hold us to our clans are more important to us than any idea of 'country' some outside ruler may try to impose on us" (GE 124). Meleagant, of course, opposes Arthur for a number of reasons: Arthur's laws which curtail his own power, the death of his oldest son, Mallton, who sat in the Seige Perillous, and the alienation of his heir, Dynfwal, who regards Arthur, his foster father and lord, as his kin. The clergy are disgruntled with Arthur's taxes; St. Caradoc believes his fanatic views should take precedence over Arthur's and even the merchants are discontented because trade is not flourishing as Arthur promised. None of them shares Arthur's dreams, and they all contribute to Modred's destruction of Arthur and his glorious realm. Not only is this explanation more realistic and more convincing, but by clearing Guinevere of this charge, Newman is able to present a sympathetic portrayal of her.

In conclusion, with the publication of her Guinevere trilogy, Sharan Newman has made an important contribution to the Arthurian legend because of her perceptive emotional and mental development of Guinevere from teenager to mature adult, her unique feminine view of Arthur's world, her wit, and her convincing, sympathetic portrayal of Guinevere.

WORKS CITED

Berger, Thomas. *Arthur Rex: A Legendary Novel*. New York: Delacorte, 1978.
Bradley, Marion Zimmer. *The Mists of Avalon*. New York: Knopf, 1982.
Bradshaw, Gillian. *In Winter's Shadow*. New York: Simon, 1982.
Garthright, Karen T. "The Development of the Character of Guinevere in Selected 20th Century British and American Arthurian Works." (M.A. thesis, University of Maryland, 1987).
Godwin, Parke. *Beloved Exile*. Toronto: Bantam, 1984.
———. *Firelord*. Garden City: Doubleday, 1980.

Malory, Sir Thomas. *The Works of Sir Thomas Malory*. Ed. Eugène Vinaver. 2nd ed. 3 vols. Oxford: Clarendon, 1973.

Newman, Sharan. *The Chessboard Queen*. New York: St. Martin's, 1983.

———. *Guinevere*. New York: St. Martin's, 1981.

———. *Guinevere Evermore*. New York: St. Martin's, 1985.

Rutledge, Amelia. "Newman, Sharan." *The Arthurian Encyclopedia*. Ed. Norris J. Lacy. New York: Garland, 1986.

Stewart, Mary. *The Last Enchantment*. New York: Morrow, 1979.

Taylor, Beverly, and Elisabeth Brewer. *The Return of King Arthur: British and American Arthurian Literature since 1900*. Cambridge: Brewer, 1983.

Thompson, Raymond H. *The Return from Avalon: A Study of the Arthurian Legend in Modern Fiction*. Westport: Greenwood, 1985. (Contributions to the Study of Science Fiction and Fantasy, Number 14).

White, T.H. *The Once and Future King*. London: Collins, 1958.